Praise for *Unconquered*

"God, the devil, and everything in between. This book is a great representation of the duality plane on which we exist."

—Leon Russell
Legendary musician and Rock and Roll Hall of Fame member

"*Unconquered* clearly depicts the fascinating story of three great musical artists who were cousins in real life but icons in the world of music. Each man conquered life's roadblocks to achieve his ultimate goals."

—Tom Schedler
Louisiana Secretary of State

"Being from the South and also in the music business, this book gave me a great insight into how these three guys grew up as cousins, as well as what made them choose the paths that eventually turned them all into the hugely successful names that the entire world knows and loves."

—Neal McCoy
Acclaimed country music artist

"The contrast between Jimmy Swaggart and his cousins Jerry Lee Lewis and Mickey Gilley would be rejected as a movie script as too farfetched. But the talents of the three men took them farther from Ferriday, Louisiana, than anyone could have imagined when they were growing up."

—John Camp
Former CNN investigative reporter and
producer of documentaries on Jimmy Swaggart

"The Killer, the Thriller, and the Fulfiller . . . what a great movie this is going to make!"

—George Klein
Memphis radio and TV personality and
one of Elvis Presley's best friends

"*Unconquered* tells the fascinating story of three men growing up in the Mississippi Delta—and how they overcame hardships to become the amazingly talented men we know today."

—Cowboy Jack Clement
Songwriter and recording studio pioneer

"I handled Mickey Gilley's publicity for over thirty years. From time to time, I would visit Ferriday. I have often thought, then and now, how amazing it is that these three cousins came from this town and scaled the very heights of their chosen field.

I think it is safe to say that Jerry Lee Lewis was right up there in popularity with Elvis during the very early days of rock and roll. Jimmy Swaggart was for many years one of the top televangelists and spiritual leaders. And when Paramount Pictures released *Urban Cowboy*, Mickey Gilley emerged as one of country music's biggest acts. Was it something in the water? How could such a small town produce three cousins that would each play a prominent role nationally?"

—Sanford Brokaw
The Brokaw Company

UNCONQUERED

UNCONQUERED

The Saga of Cousins Jerry Lee Lewis, Jimmy Swaggart, and Mickey Gilley

J. D. DAVIS

Brown Books Publishing Group
Dallas, Texas

Unconquered
The Saga of Cousins Jerry Lee Lewis, Jimmy Swaggart, and Mickey Gilley

Brown Books Publishing Group
16250 Knoll Trail Drive, Suite 205
Dallas, Texas 75248
www.BrownBooks.com
(972) 381-0009

A New Era in Publishing™

ISBN 978-1-61254-041-2
Library of Congress Control Number 2012931038

Printing in the United States
10 9 8 7 6 5 4 3 2 1

For more information, please visit: www.UnconqueredTheBook.com

CONTENTS

INTRODUCTION

As a child growing up in small-town East Texas, a town similar in many ways to small towns everywhere, I remember my father watching on television a shouting, singing, finger-pointing bear of a man named Jimmy Swaggart. While Swaggart's preaching didn't mean much to me at that age, his piano playing caught my attention and moved me, as it did millions of others around the world. People were touched and thrilled by his message, and drawn in by his charisma.

As a teenager raised largely in the conservative, fundamentalist Assembly of God world, I struggled with worldly temptations and the discomfiting feelings they aroused, and found that adhering to every edict I had been given in Sunday school was going to be, at the very least, a difficult chore. The words I heard from the pulpit such as "hellfire" and "lost in eternity" and "backsliding" created an increasing sense that I risked slipping into the gates of hell at any inopportune moment. When I heard that the preacher I saw on television had stumbled and made a public and painful mistake of his own, it didn't disappoint me. Instead, it encouraged me. It gave me hope. It taught me that men, who never stop being men, can maintain their spiritual identity even in the face of imperfection. And it provided an early understanding of the need for grace.

Country music dominated my youth. The stereo in the room just off the kitchen played country-and-western and gospel music. Every trip to town from our rural home included songs from the country radio station in Tyler, Texas, forty miles away. Every spring afternoon, the time I spent in the batting cage next to the high school baseball field was punctuated by music that blared through the rolled-down windows of a teammate's pickup truck. Singers such as Merle Haggard, Conway Twitty, Willie Nelson, and dozens of others permeated my very being and are still ingrained in me decades later.

One of the top performers in those days was a crooner who played piano with flair and sang about flowers and honky-tonks. Even today, the lyrics to each of Mickey Gilley's seventeen number one country hits come as naturally to me as if I learned them yesterday. When I hear him sing "Put Your Dreams Away" and "True Love Ways" and "You Don't Know Me," the songs trigger memories that can seem more vivid than anything happening in present time. This is the power of music—that a familiar note or word can instantaneously, magically return us to half-forgotten places, people, and times.

On August 10, 1991, I was a college student in Austin, Texas. That evening, a friend and I headed down to the Aqua Fest music event, just south of downtown. As a devotee of good piano playing, I was already a fan of Jerry Lee Lewis, who was slated to be the main act. The Four Tops opened the show and sang well-known numbers for nearly an hour. As the sun went down, the wind picked up, bringing with it another Texas thunderstorm. Over the fringes of the Texas Hill Country, lightning flickered across the cool night sky. Between the unpredictable weather and the unpredictable nature of the evening's headliner, the continuation of the show was in doubt.

Yet an hour later, Jerry Lee Lewis strode purposefully to the front of the stage. A thin man, then fifty-five years old, he stood looking at the crowd. Then he bowed slightly and made his way to the piano stool behind him. His face looked stern, his eyes piercing as they gazed ahead, somewhere into the middle distance.

The next hour thrilled those who had weathered the elements and the delay to witness the show. This man, who'd become an afterthought in rock 'n' roll history to many, put on an amazing, hypnotizing performance. As occasional lightning flashed in the distance, he pounded both hands on the piano keys and his music became a force, a driving rhythm, oddly similar to the rocking church services I had known as a child.

He laughed with the audience occasionally, growled at them regularly, and chastised his band members when they lost the beat. In a line of a song addressed directly to his evangelist cousin Jimmy Swaggart, he told him to leave him alone while he "got his kicks."

He mixed rock 'n' roll, country, and blues. He rearranged and made up lyrics; he often changed keys.

His music and lyrics took him to another place, somewhere far away. It seemed to me that he was alone with his genius in the midst of hundreds of screaming fans.

He poured everything he had into this performance, until he was exhausted and drenched in sweat. Then he dragged himself off the stool and, after another short bow, exited stage left.

That night, I knew I had witnessed one of the greatest rock 'n' roll performers of all time. I have seen him countless times since, but the power of that first performance has never faded.

The music of Jerry Lee Lewis mesmerized me, as did the music of his first cousins Jimmy Swaggart and Mickey Gilley. As time went by, I became equally captivated by the human story within their music and behind it.

These three, less than a year apart in age, grew up together in the same small town where they were shaped by the music and white-hot theology of the Pentecostal church. The intensity of their music derived from the continuing struggle between themselves and something greater than themselves, between the material and the spiritual, and—in the largest sense—between heaven and earth.

Each of these men has experienced great heights and excruciating lows. Yet, through it all, they survive, still playing, still performing, and still seeking to reconcile their internal contradictions.

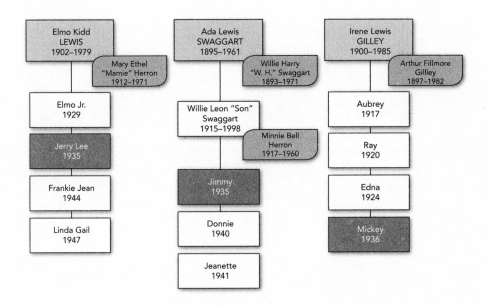

Elmo Kidd
LEWIS
1902–1979

Mary Ethel
"Mamie" Herron
1912–1971

Elmo Jr.
1929

Jerry Lee
1935

Frankie Jean
1944

Linda Gail
1947

Ada Lewis
SWAGGART
1895–1961

Willie Harry
"W. H." Swaggart
1893–1971

Willie Leon "Son"
Swaggart
1915–1998

Minnie Bell
Herron
1917–1960

Jimmy
1935

Donnie
1940

Jeanette
1941

Irene Lewis
GILLEY
1900–1985

Arthur Fillmore
Gilley
1897–1982

Aubrey
1917

Ray
1920

Edna
1924

Mickey
1936

– 1 –

ANTICIPATION

– JERRY –

On a crisp Saturday evening in the Deep South, a black limousine rolls up to the VIP entrance behind a casino hotel. A man and woman step out of the car, checking their watches as event personnel rush to greet them. A moment later, an aging man emerges with difficulty from the backseat, helped to his feet by his two-person entourage. Jerry Lee Lewis has been here many times, in many seasons of his life. Tonight, he's returned to wrest magic from a weary body and slowed yet still nimble fingers.

Inside the casino, a crowd forms in front of the doors leading to the performance hall, their chatter scarcely heard over the constant beckoning of blackjack dealers, the jingle of slot machines, and the shouts of rowdy patrons gathered around a craps table in the vast casino behind them. When the auditorium opens at 8 p.m., an hour before the scheduled performance, these early arrivers—the vanguard of his eclectic audience—flock to their seats.

There's the white-collar professional who rolls in with his twenty-years-younger trophy wife; there's the blue-collar roustabout who spent all week busting his ass and is looking to blow off some steam with his buddies.

"First time I saw him play was back in the early sixties in Birmingham," recalls a middle-aged man whose belly bulges beneath his "Rock 'n' Roll Lives" T-shirt. "I've seen him about twenty

1

times. Man, he can tear that piano up. I've never seen nothin' like it."

Another man comments, "We saw him at the Panther Club over in Fort Worth. He screamed at the guy runnin' the sound and stomped off the stage ten minutes into the show and we all were just standing there lookin' at each other and wonderin', 'What the hell?'"

"He was in Shreveport the year before my husband, Clyde, got sick," says a blue-haired lady. "We drove up to see him. He only played about thirty minutes that night. He didn't appear to be in very good condition."

Most of the young fans attending tonight have never seen Lewis perform. But they've heard his records and know that his music remains as fresh as it was more than half a century ago, when his enduring hits were created.

Many older patrons were introduced to him during his second incarnation when, as a rock 'n' roller shunned by the musical genre he helped birth, he found a haven in country music. These folks don't frequent music venues anymore, and they don't understand the music young people listen to nowadays. Even so, they understand the genius of Jerry Lee Lewis.

– JIMMY –

On a bright Sunday morning, a steady flow of cars cruise along Bluebonnet Road in Baton Rouge, Louisiana. Family Worship Center, the imposing church structure nestled next to this busy thoroughfare, no longer stands out the way it did twenty years ago, when it was one of only a handful of buildings on this long stretch of road. Now the church is nestled between the enormous Mall of Louisiana and a conglomeration of business and retail establishments.

Around 9 a.m., a full hour ahead of the start of the morning service, the church begins to fill with a constant stream of worshippers. Three-fourths are white, the other fourth are black; all appear to interact freely with one another. Walking through the giant glass doors, they enter a stunning facility capable of accommodating 7,500 people. Inside, they are enveloped by the sense of warmth created by the rich, dark-red interior, the open architecture, and the smiling faces of the greeters.

Around the corner from the foyer, the church bookstore is open for business. One wall is dedicated to music CDs, both recent recordings such as "Heaven's Sounding Sweeter All the Time" and gospel classics dating back to the 1960s. There are DVDs of church sermons given in the last several years and of classic crusades from the ministry's glory years in the 1980s, when people in the tens of thousands, in places as disparate as Capetown, South Africa, and Managua, Nicaragua, crowded into vast stadiums to hear messages of hope and deliverance.

Inside the main auditorium at Family Worship Center, women share photographs of their granddaughters' ballet recitals, or discuss summertime plans to visit relatives in Jackson or to camp in the Ozarks. The men discuss off-season activities of the NFL's New Orleans Saints, the impact on their families of current activity on Capitol Hill, and the prospects of the upcoming football campaign of the Louisiana State University Tigers.

This crowd has come to see a man who evokes memories of the little church congregation where they first learned about Jesus and "Do unto others," where they sang in the choir and, following the benediction, went off to Grandma's for Sunday's fried-chicken lunch. Still, the primary memory compelling them is that of the hellfire-and-brimstone country preachers who sounded a whole lot like Jimmy Swaggart, the man who will preach here today and the person they've listened to over the years, through his epic ups and downs.

– Mickey –

On Sunday evening, as the sun begins to slide over the hills west of town, traffic inches along Highway 76, the main drag through Branson, Missouri. Over the last twenty years, this sleepy Ozarks town has become a mecca of theaters, waterslides, miniature golf courses, and other amusements that serve the throngs who come here to escape their daily lives. Today, many of these travelers saunter into the theater that bears the name of Mickey Gilley, the country-music performer they came to hear and see.

In the theater lobby, a store selling music CDs and DVDs prominently displays Mickey's friendly, smiling face. A raft of glossy 8-by-10s include images of him from earlier decades, showing the star sporting giant rings, open collars, and his signature "MG" diamond necklace.

This is a gathering primarily of people fifty and older. Mickey's music has long been part of the backdrop of their lives. He played on the stereo as a family played spades at the kitchen table, as a mother perched on the edge of the bathtub applying alcohol and a Band-Aid to a son's scratches, or as a father stayed up late making sure that questionable young man from across town got his daughter home by curfew.

Now, friendly debate occurs over which is the best of Mickey's thirty-nine top ten country hits, while others remember visiting his storied club in Pasadena, Texas—long closed, but still retaining its distinction of being the world's largest honky-tonk. "Do you remember when we went with Bill and Linda to see him perform?" a pretty, older woman in a flowered dress asks her balding husband. "He was great that night, but then Linda got upset with Bill for getting on that mechanical bull and making a fool of himself."

As Mickey's voice is piped in through the lobby speakers, many softly sing along to "You Don't Know Me," one of his number one country hits from the early 1980s. It's a song that evokes tender memories of first kisses, and of slow dancing at the senior prom. They smile as they sing it. They know every note by heart.

SHOWTIME

– MICKEY –

In the theater, while the audience awaits the main attraction, a video provides a biographical sketch of Mickey's life. Applause rings out at the sight of the face, names, and events from his early years, hard years, barely-getting-by years, and, finally, the years on top. Behind the curtain, band members shuffle back and forth, tuning their instruments while backup singers run through a few last-minute changes to the *Urban Cowboy* medley. Seated in his dressing room, Mickey explains to a cast member the precise intonation he wants him to use when delivering a particular line of dialogue. Though his manner is easygoing and friendly, he knows exactly what he wants and is accustomed to getting it, albeit with honey rather than vinegar.

Just before show time, Gary Myers, the master of ceremonies and Mickey's longtime guitarist, steps onto the stage to welcome the audience. Like everyone associated with this theater, he is friendly, warm, and engaging. He congratulates the five couples in the audience who are celebrating wedding anniversaries, ranging in duration from two years to fifty-seven. As he does before each show, Myers pays tribute to the United States military veterans in the hall.

The lights dim as the curtain slowly opens. The band breaks into a hard-charging rhythm as Mickey walks onto the stage. He wears black jeans, black boots, a black-and-silver striped shirt and two huge diamond rings—one on each hand. The singer moves gingerly, a lingering reminder of the life-threatening accident that left him paralyzed for months and from which he has worked agonizingly to recover. He's determined to walk upright and without assistance, and he does, though visible effort is required. That feat accomplished, one of his band members helps him to his seat and the performance begins.

He breaks into "Number One Rock and Roll C&W Boogie Blues Man," the unofficial theme of the man, the show, and his entourage. While never a chart-topper, the song title, thumping beat, and playful lyrics suggest the depth and diversity of his talent.

Then he sings his first number one country hit, "Room Full of Roses," a slow, moving ballad. He's in perfect sync with his musicians and supporting cast and their easy, relaxed mood is contagious. He welcomes the audience, openly appreciative of the role they've played in his success. As he sings, his eyes scan the faces before him, and he gives each audience member the sense that he's a friend, performing only for him or her.

It took Mickey years to learn that the only way that he could succeed was to be himself. Sometimes, after a show, he'll think back to when the best he could do was come across as a lesser clone of his fabled rock 'n' roll cousin Jerry Lee Lewis—which just about drove him nuts.

Now, Mickey is in his element. As he banters with Joey Riley, steel guitar and fiddle player in the band, the audience feels as if they're sitting around the dinner table with an elderly uncle and a zany cousin.

"You've done so much in your career," Riley says.

"I've been busy," allows the headliner.

"He's had sixteen-and-a-half number one records, ladies and gentlemen."

"Wait. Wait. Wait. What are you talking about?"

"Yeah. That's how many you've had."

"Joey, I think the magic number is seventeen."

"Naw. One of 'em was a duet and you only sang half a song, so you only get half credit."

Neither of his cousins, Lewis or Swaggart, nor most other big-name stars, would allow themselves to be on the receiving end of jokes, or to appear so human in front of an audience. Mickey's humility gives his fans the feeling that he's one of them, an everyday person with everyday triumphs and struggles. It's one of the things about him that they love most.

As he begins to sing Kris Kristofferson's "Why Me," the powerful religious influences of his childhood seep into the music, reflecting experiences in the Pentecostal church that he and his cousins shared. Though each has traveled a varied, sometimes difficult path, their faith in God and their bond with traditional gospel music remains strong. Despite Mickey's numerous country hits, given the audience's connection to his religious upbringing and roots, it is his gospel music that provokes the greatest response in this theater.

He smoothly progresses through more of his signature songs, building toward the closing medley of hits from the *Urban Cowboy* movie soundtrack. Throughout the show, fans approach the stage to take pictures or shake his hand, and he makes eye contact with each person. After so many years spent in the shadows of his two cousins, particularly Jerry, he has found his unique way to shine. His music and its connection to his listeners create the warmth that everyone here hoped to find.

Closing the show with the Ben E. King classic, "Stand By Me," Mickey himself stands on weak legs, arm in arm with his backup singers, displaying the determination and resilience that are his hallmark.

He has had his share, and then some, of bruising adversity and disappointment. Yet, like his cousins, he has battled back and weathered it all.

– JIMMY –

The church music team of singers and musicians prepare for the morning service. Six singers fan across the stage while guitarists and saxophonists take their places behind them. A piano and organ are positioned side by side on the left side of the stage. The piano player guides the timing, but only one man determines how the music should sound. Jimmy Swaggart expects each song to be performed a certain way and his musicians prepare accordingly. He has softened with time but retains his inborn sense of how to stir and inspire. When it comes to what he wants to present to his audience, he is as unbending as ever.

Exactly five minutes before the 10 a.m. service begins, Jimmy emerges through a door at the rear of the stage. Like his two famous cousins, he is in his midseventies. His hair has grayed and thinned and his face is less taut than it used to be, but he remains an imposing, charismatic presence. He looks more at ease than he did in decades past, when the responsibilities of preaching crusades and overseeing a $150-million-per-year ministry often brought him to exhaustion.

Now, he strides to the piano, removes his dark-blue pinstriped jacket, and sits down.

The song he plays is an upbeat, fervent version of the classic hymn "I'll Fly Away." As his hands move across the keys, the distinct sound he produces owes much to the fact that he learned to play sitting alongside Jerry, his rock 'n' roll cousin.

As the church service begins, everyone stands, in the audience and on the stage, as one of the singers leads the congregation in song. Hands clap, toes tap, and arms sway as they raise a collective, joyful noise to the top of the building in this traditional, Pentecostal worship service. Circling behind the singers and musicians onstage, Jimmy makes his way to the front row of "amen corner," where the ministers, special guests, and authorized employees are seated. He plants himself in his regular spot: the second chair from the left. He stands less than he used to, but he is always involved, microphone in hand, and his deep, booming voice carries and captures attention no matter what is happening around him.

"Hallelujah!" he exclaims. "Praise God. Tell Him you love Him. Because He first loved you."

Minutes after the service starts, a sharply dressed woman enters from the back of the stage. She gracefully takes a seat to Jimmy's immediate right. Frances Swaggart, two years younger than her husband, is reserved and stoic. She is always observing, and her purposeful movements and expressions suggest a resilient, controlled woman.

A gifted young pianist who performs with Jimmy's musicians and singers plays a soulful, bluesy solo that segues into his passionate rendition of "I Know My Lord's Gonna Lead Me Out." As the song ends, Jimmy walks slowly to the podium, keeping time with the music. Though the lyrics yield different messages, the music of Jerry Lee Lewis and Jimmy Swaggart are strikingly similar.

Jimmy points to the black organist, who breaks into a rolling instrumental solo as he bounces on his stool and his hands dash feverishly across the keys. Watching him, Jimmy reflects back to an earlier, simpler time when this vibrant young man might have been one of the musicians in his hometown who introduced him to a rhythm and a beat like nothing he'd ever heard.

All the musicians are playing now as Jimmy, eyes closed, keeps the music's beat with rhythmic moves of his right hand, which is extended above his bowed head. When the song ends, he turns to the congregation. "I don't know how you all feel today," he says in a rich booming baritone, "but that kind of music should make you happy! Someone should give the Lord thanks!"

After a few more songs that have the audience rocking, Swaggart gravitates back to the piano. "This song," he says, before taking a long pause, "was one I remember playing for my mother when I was just a boy. Let it bless you as I sing it today."

He plays the old hymn "I've Had a Vision of Jesus." He delivers the verses slowly, almost whispering. His piano solo is riveting; his left hand is deliberate and precise as his right hand performs slow, melodious runs up and down the keys. People watch adoringly, some swaying to the beat while others gaze into the near distance. For many, this music will be the highlight of the morning, taking them to a deeper place spiritually, bringing them closer to God than any sermon ever could.

For Jimmy, who never forgets that he reemerged from universal scorn and personal shame, the congregation that gathers each Sunday to hear him play and preach is a sign of grace.

— Jerry —

As show time nears, the excitement builds in the auditorium and the crowd balloons to more than a thousand. The bandleader, Kenny Lovelace, walks onstage. He has been with Jerry nearly fifty years, and once enjoyed a stint as his brother-in-law. Now, he carefully tests each speaker, well aware that Jerry has been known to explode onstage if the sound isn't perfect.

At precisely 9:13 p.m., the band members take their positions. They play four songs and, as their final number winds to a close, Jerry Lee Lewis makes his way onto the stage. The audience roars. He walks carefully, gingerly, with hesitancy. Slightly stooped and shuffling, he proffers a slight nod to the crowd as he is introduced, though they know—and he knows—that no introduction is necessary.

The wild man of rock 'n' roll is older and slower, and nearly tamed. Still, as his fingers hit the piano keys, a transformation takes place. He's vibrant, focused, and intense as he pounds out "Down the Line," a number from his early days. The lyrics are pronounced less clearly, yet the voice is arresting and rich. His hands no longer fly six inches off the keys when he strikes a note; his motion is limited and concise, but his playing is still masterful and the overall effect is intoxicating.

His playlist is fairly standard now. A few dozen song titles, hand-written on a sheet of paper, are positioned on the piano. Based on his moods and whims, he'll play some, skip others, and occasionally add a tune he learned as a kid listening to the radio with his daddy, or one that he played in some mean-as-hell nightclub in Natchez, Mississippi, when he was young and certain that he was the greatest ever. Now, he's three-quarters-of-a-century old, and just as certain.

As he plays, it's as if his fingers are wiping away all the questionable events in his life—the bizarre episodes, the drunken nights, the fights that didn't need to be started. For the next hour, he will inhabit the one sector of his life in which everything makes sense.

He breaks into "Drinkin' Wine Spo-dee-o-dee," one of the first songs he ever played for an audience. Then, as now, he plays it with a rockin' beat. As the number comes to a close, he says, "Drinkin' wine. Yeah. I never was much of a wine drinker." The mumbled words, and his rueful tone, project a mixture of humor and regret. "I preferred hard liquor myself," he continues. "I was a woolly man. But I don't drink alcohol anymore. My body can't handle it."

The crowd hangs on every syllable, straining to hear this sudden, uncharacteristic, and public confession.

As if snapping out of a reverie, Jerry turns back to his piano. He scorches upbeat rockers, caresses slow country ballads, and moans the blues, in the process resurrecting musical ghosts etched deep within his memory and psyche. For a moment he appears to think back to those days in the 1940s when he was honing his musical genius. It seems so long ago.

"Time waits for no man," he murmurs. The thought propels him into his next song, "No Headstone on My Grave."

At one point, the band loses the beat. Jerry jerks his head up and glares at them. As a younger man, his demand for precision led him to outright belligerence toward any band member who did not perform to his standards. Now the fire in his eyes blazes as hotly and as fiercely as ever, but quickly fades to a barely glowing ember. Age and sobriety have mellowed him, not always in ways he might wish. No longer can he sustain his intensity throughout a performance; these days he teeters between boredom and exhaustion, superseded at frequent intervals by sparks of passion. As he throws himself into Chuck Berry's "Roll Over Beethoven," he is fully engaged, reveling in his ability to summon his magic and transport an audience.

When he fires into "Whole Lotta Shakin' Goin' On," the crowd erupts again. He has played this song tens of thousands of times, but he still infuses it with a vibrating pulse, still gets a kick out of seeing women get up and move to the beat when he exhorts them to "wiggle it around just a little bit." Those wiggling women range in age from twenty to seventy and are a living, breathing testament to the power Jerry Lee Lewis has exacted over thousands of audiences and millions of listeners. When he came on the scene this power was viewed by many as dangerous and threatening; now that he's an old man it seems engaging and harmless.

As he concludes with "Great Balls of Fire," his hands race over the keys and the audience goes wild. Then the music abruptly ends, he nods to the crowd, and rises slowly from his seat. With that, the magician disappears; the illusion of youth extinguished. Having given all that he could for as long as he could, he's weary and spent.

Yet he keeps going, and going strong, even now, when all the men he started out with—Elvis, Carl Perkins, Johnny Cash—are long gone.

There's one thing Jerry knows for sure: none of those guys would have bet a plugged nickel that he'd be the one to outlive them all.

– 3 –

FAMILY TIES

Jerry, Jimmy, and Mickey, cousins united by ties originating in the Lewis clan, were born at a time and place where family trees were apt to resemble tangled vines. The Lewises—Elmo, Ada, and Irene—were three of the eleven children born to Leroy and Arilla Lewis, cousins who married in the 1880s. They lived in an area near Mangham, Louisiana, known as Snake Ridge, a stretch of dusty, unfertile terrain so small that it cannot be found on any map. There they endured a hardscrabble existence, barely surviving on the scant harvests the land would provide. In their rough, unpredictable world, it was music that stoked their spirits and soothed their souls. When they weren't battling to eke out a living, they were playing banjos and fiddles and guitars, and singing hymns and country songs.

Music helped keep them going. It was a balm applied to the scrapes and bruises of their lives. But with the music came whiskey, and with the whiskey came rage, and with the rage came the chaos and violence in which the Lewises lived and rarely flourished.

Elmo and his two sisters would find their life's partners among the hopeful, hard-pressed offspring of three families: the Herrons, Swaggarts, and Gilleys. During the Great Depression, as prospects in Snake Ridge shrank to nothing, they would move some fifty miles south to Ferriday, a town in Concordia Parish, which borders the Mississippi River in eastern Louisiana.

Ferriday is a hundred miles north of Louisiana's state capital, Baton Rouge. Heavily influenced by Napoleon's Civil Code, the state takes pride in its tenacity and autonomy, stubbornly rejecting counties, county commissioners, and common law, and governing its municipalities with a unique brand of parishes, civil law, and police jurors. Through the years the land has drawn the desperate like a magnet, luring them with the promise inherent in plentiful wildlife and fertile soil, and obscuring the inescapable fact that the place offers more trials and hardships than abundance.

As a result of these conditions, Ferriday was known for hardened men and disappointed women, and as a borough for the downtrodden poor consigned to battle the relentless forces conspiring to keep them that way. Ferriday was where God-fearing people prayed for a better life without expecting to find one; where there was punishing labor or no work at all; where plowed fields veered between parched and flooded, and brutal summer heat was interspersed with sudden, violent squalls. It was where men found refuge in liquor and fast women, if only momentarily.

Before it was a town, Ferriday was a cotton plantation gifted to Helena Smith and William Ferriday on the occasion of their marriage in 1827. It was named the Helena Plantation, and life there was destined to be hard. William and Helena would lose nine of their fourteen children in the epidemic-prone lowlands. Still, one of their sons, J. C., would become a local leader and the Helena Plantation would remain in the Ferriday family until J. C. died in 1894.

By 1903, the land was laid out in a grid design of parallel and perpendicular streets. The numbered streets ran north to south, while east-to-west roads were named primarily for Southern states. In 1906, when the new town was christened, it seemed natural to name it for one of its most revered citizens, the Honorable J. C. Ferriday.

Like many a Southern town, Ferriday owed its growth to the railroads: the Texas and Pacific, the Iron Mountain, and the Louisiana and Arkansas all converged in and ran through it. The rhythmic sounds of huge trains passing by formed the pulse of the community, and the cavalcade of railway cars, moving swiftly and purposefully through the days and nights, instilled in Ferriday's citizens a constant reminder that, somewhere far away, a better life existed.

Because of the railroads, Ferriday evolved into a cultural melting pot dominated by blue-collar, hard-living roustabouts for whom the past was something to forget and the future was an unruly kaleidoscope of half-formed dreams. These were people looking to survive by any means necessary, ethical or not, and they imbued Ferriday with a gritty edge and a distinct sense of danger. As back-country fundamentalist conviction vied with the free-and-easy morality of those inhabiting the Mississippi's southernmost shores, Ferriday would earn its reputation as "the alcohol town" comprising saloons, nightclubs, and brothels frequented by bad guys and worse guys.

In the twenties, when Huey Long became Louisiana's governor, slot machines suddenly cropped up all over town. These one-armed bandits could be found in grocery stores, gas stations, and restaurants. They would remain there for years, reinforcing the false and beguiling promise that prosperity could be attained through nothing more strenuous than luck.

By the late 1920s, nearly two-thirds of the town was black, a population who brought to Ferriday savory cuisine, demonstrative religious worship, and most significantly, their music. Racial groups that did not otherwise mingle would harmonize together, discovering a wordless commonality through melody and rhythm. As the region diversified, so did the music. Having begun with African American influences that evolved from the soulful resonance of slave songs, it moved on to incorporate the expressive, improvisational sounds of Delta blues and became inextricably woven into the town's social and cultural fabric.

This, for better and worse, was Ferriday, the place where Elmo, Ada, and Irene Lewis and their respective spouses would migrate to seek a better life.

Elmo Lewis, born in 1902, was the seventh of Leroy and Arilla's children, and the hardest working. Tall and lanky, he was a quiet man until he started sipping moonshine. His low tolerance for alcohol, typical of the Lewises, would land him on the wrong side of the law from time to time. Luck never did come his way and he spent his life toiling as a carpenter and farming meager harvests. He was a loving man who could find something good to say about anyone, but he was not a man to be crossed. "He had a dark side," his daughter Frankie Jean recalled. "He would not take no for an answer. And he could have an uncontrollable temper."

Elmo also had an abundance of the Lewises' talent for music. He played guitar and sang and loved listening to music, especially the songs of Jimmie Rodgers, the "Singing Brakeman." Whenever he could, he'd play Rodgers's songs on his Victor Talking Machine and sing along to numbers like "Blue Yodel No. 9."

Elmo married one of the pretty Herron sisters, Mamie, who caught his eye the moment he saw her. They soon started a family, giving the name Elmo Jr. to their firstborn son. Their second son, born nearly six years later, was named Jerry Lee. Mamie was ten years younger than Elmo and the fifth of seven children in the Herron family. Like the Lewises, the Herrons had always looked to music for entertainment and succor. Elmo loved to hear Mamie sing. She had the light, pure voice of an angel and a love of music equal to his. Music transported her; it bore into her soul and set her dreaming of a life that would offer less hardship and more enjoyment.

Elmo's older sister Ada was fun-loving and affectionate. She married W. H. Swaggart, a sizable, solid-as-a-rock authoritarian who was not averse to bootlegging. He'd get caught every so often and Ada would march their two children in to visit him in the parish jail. In time, W. H. became Ferriday's night marshal, a curious position given his own propensity for skirting the law, but one ideally suited to his stern and commanding demeanor.

In the early years of their marriage, the Swaggart family's income was meager and required their oldest boy, Willie Leon— referred to by all as Son, and born in 1915—to quit school and go to work at an early age. Son longed for a better life and struggled to achieve it. He worked as a fur trapper and trader, pecan harvester, farmer, and part-time gas station employee. All his life, he dreamed of making money. He hated to spend it. A fire burned inside Son, and the hope of doing better was his only antidote to a constant gnawing for success in his gut.

Being a Lewis, Son was also a terrific musician, in high demand to play the fiddle at local dances. He married the youngest of the Herron sisters, Minnie Bell, born in 1917, a beauty with green eyes and wavy brown hair. Minnie Bell played guitar and sang in a clear contralto, which further endeared her to Son Swaggart. From an early age she'd had many suitors, but none more ardent than young Son, who desperately wanted to win her affection and rescue her from the hard life she'd known as a child.

They wed on February 13, 1934, two days before the birthday they shared, his nineteenth and her seventeenth. Their son Jimmy Lee would be born thirteen months later. Minnie Bell was as hardheaded and outspoken as her husband, and constant friction and disagreement came between them. Like her sister Mamie, Minnie Bell dreamt of a better life. Also like Mamie, she had no clear sense of what she was looking for or how to go about attaining it. Yet both had always known how to dream. Dreams were their refuge and, given the severity of their lives, refuge was necessary.

Along with the physical hardships, the Herron sisters had inner torment: Elmo and Son knew well that the women they'd taken for wives came from a dirt-poor family in which the darkness of severe mental illness held sway.

The girls' father, John William Herron, was a sharecropper and a toughened, hard man. While a certain rigor was required for survival in such difficult times, the impact of Herron's stern demeanor on his wife and children had been as bad as it was good.

For one thing, he was incapable of understanding the delicate nature of his wife, Theresa, a lovely, fragile woman admired for her bone-white porcelain skin and long, beautiful red hair. In her youth, she had danced all night at square dances where he played the fiddle.

As she gave birth to their seven children and began to age, everything carefree about Theresa became subsumed by depression. The lack of medical understanding of mental illness, the negative stigma it carried, and the extensive shock treatments she underwent only worsened her condition. In her later years, Theresa became unhinged, throwing rocks at the local school bus as she cursed, ranted, and raved. Ultimately, it fell largely to three of her daughters and a daughter-in-law to provide the constant care she would require for the rest of her life. No one could say for certain how much of her madness was inherited by her offspring, but in later years, some of her descendants would give folks reason to think that their maternal grandmother's debility had been passed on.

In any case, Jerry and Jimmy were double-cousins: their mothers were Herron sisters, and Jerry's father and Jimmy's grandma were Lewis brother and sister. They were, from birth, connected in ways that were deep, abiding, and inescapable.

Irene Lewis fell between the older Ada and younger Elmo in the Lewis sibling birth order. She was determined and tough—traits she'd need to survive her marriage to Arthur Gilley. The youngest of eleven children, Arthur was an infant when his father died at age forty-two. The Lewis family, though poor and in perpetual want, stepped in to help the Gilleys, and the two families drew close as they sought to make ends meet. Ultimately, three Gilley brothers— Arthur, Harvey, and George—would marry three Lewis sisters— Irene, Eva, and Carrie, respectively.

Like many men of the day, Arthur had a taste for womanizing. It was not long before Irene's temper and Arthur's eye for the ladies caused no shortage of trouble. Despite the difficulties in her marriage, Irene came from a line of people who didn't quit on each other.

As a teenager, Irene had been all too aware of the constant difficulties her family had endured at the hands of her father, Leroy Lewis.

"Mama, why should you keep puttin' up with this?" she asked Arilla, her mother, on many occasions. "We work all year, scrapin' by, and Daddy spends most of our money on alcohol before he even gets home."

Arilla Hampton Lewis had seen the disappointed looks on the faces of her children over the years as they witnessed the irresponsible actions of their father. But she had a warm smile on her face as she addressed her daughter's question.

"Irene, darlin', we've made it this far just fine. I expect we will make a way going forward. You know your daddy has a sweet side, a caring side. He's made his fair share of mistakes, I know."

Irene wasn't worried so much about herself. Soon enough, she would be married and away from this. Her mama, to whom she was devoted, was there to stay. Irene hated to see her contend with the irresponsible behavior of her father. She loved her father, she supposed, but she was pretty sure she didn't like him much.

"Mama, it's just not right for Daddy to do that to you—and us. It's just not right. Why don't you get away while you can? You can live with us kids. We'll take care of you."

Arilla smiled again at her dark-haired daughter. She was soft-spoken, but now answered Irene with authority, to make sure her intentions were clearly stated—and fully understood. "No, Irene. I married your daddy—for better or worse. I'm going to stay with him."

Arilla Hampton Lewis stayed with Leroy Milton Lewis. When he died nearly a quarter of a century later, she was still there by his side.

Like her mother, Irene remained in a difficult marriage. She and Arthur would have two sons, Aubrey and Ray, and a daughter,

Edna. When Edna turned ten and the boys were in their teens, Irene was relieved that her children were maturing and past needing constant attention. Then she got pregnant again and, at the age of thirty-five, gave birth to a baby boy she named Mickey.

Mickey Leroy Gilley had much in common with his cousins, Jerry Lee Lewis and Jimmy Lee Swaggart. All three were born into poverty and inherited a mixture of Lewis traits: musical talent, ingenuity, easy charm, stubbornness, and grit. These traits would propel them to beat the odds stacked implacably against them and become Ferriday's most famous sons.

– 4 –

MOONSHINE

In January 1935, the weather was brisk in Concordia Parish, typical for that time of year.

Though the nation was struggling through the Great Depression, the lives of most local folks were only slightly more difficult than usual. If this was a depression, citizens would say to one another, what do you call the rest of the years which have also been pretty damn hard?

In the midst of this grinding poverty, one man was doing just fine and, as a consequence, had become a key figure to many of Ferriday's struggling families. His name was Lee Calhoun, and his wife, Stella, was yet another Herron sister.

Lee was the richest man in Concordia Parish, though you'd never know it from his shabby khaki pants, muddy boots, and worn shirts. Anyone seeing him for the first time would be apt to figure that this rough, bald-headed, weathered man was impoverished and in dire need of assistance.

Lee was a savvy codger, gifted with a knack for making money where seemingly none could be made. He'd bought up so much land—which he'd leased to sharecropping farmers—that folks said he owned a sizable percentage of Ferriday. When Lee was collecting rent from his many tenants, he'd drive up in his rusty old pickup that was missing the door on the driver's side. People would note that he looked downright pitiful, but in fact, Lee had removed the door himself because he made the rounds to so many shacks and houses that it was just too much trouble to keep opening it.

People liked to tell of the time that Lee ran his pickup into the back of an automobile driven by a couple over in Natchez. The furious driver and his wife came storming out of their car, but when they saw Lee's beggarly appearance as he climbed out of his battered truck swearing loudly at himself, their anger turned to empathy. *This poor soul,* they thought, *he couldn't afford to fix his own vehicle, let alone ours.* So they dismissed him and drove away smiling, happy to have been Good Samaritans toward this pilgrim in need—totally unaware that the shabby old man could have bought them an entire parking lot full of brand-new cars.

Lee Calhoun saved a lot of people from a lot of misery. He helped families buy groceries, extended leniency when rent payments could not be made, provided families with enough money to survive until harvesting season, and even paid the college tuition for a local black girl who'd been accepted at Southern University, at a time when a black female from that area going to college was a foreign concept.

When Lee married Stella Herron, who was some twenty years younger, he quickly discovered that her sisters and brothers, along with their husbands, wives, children, nieces, and nephews, were part of the package. He became a benefactor to this extended family and hired them for all sorts of jobs, legal and not so legal.

Prohibition had ended in 1933, but the homegrown production of whiskey remained illegal yet lucrative. So Lee brought his wife's brothers-in-law—Elmo Lewis and Son Swaggart—into a side venture: the illegal production of liquor, in a still that he owned and operated near Turtle Lake, a few miles west of Ferriday.

At the site, Elmo stirred the brew and Son kept the fire going, while Lee shouted instructions and jostled the burning logs occasionally to give the impression that he was an active laborer in this effort. Soon, the brew was boiling and punctuating the air with its sharp, pungent aroma.

"That's cookin' up real nice," Lee told them. Elmo didn't answer. He kept his head down, focused on the task at hand. Lee looked at him sideways.

"You all right?" Lee asked.

"Just got a lot on my mind," said Elmo. "Not much carpentry work within a hundred miles, as best I can tell. It's getting toward planting time and I got no money for seeds. Gonna have a hard time paying you the rent, too." Elmo was embarrassed, though he had gotten accustomed to relying on Calhoun and appreciated that the man was there when times were toughest.

"Don't you worry, Elmo," Lee told him, "Do the best you can and pay the rent when times get better. I've seen bad times before and they always ease up, sooner or later."

A moment later, the bushes rustled. Suddenly three law-enforcement officers emerged from hiding.

"Well, well," one said, "What do we have here? What might you boys be cooking up?" He walked over to the bubbling caldron and looked into it, taking a deep breath as he smacked his lips.

"That's some fine-smellin' brew you got here, Lee Calhoun," he continued. "Too bad you won't be sellin' it to your customers."

Lee looked undaunted, as usual. "I don't suppose any of you boys would be interested in a little discount on what we're selling?"

The question was met with silence.

"Aw, hell, then," Lee said, "Grab that ax out of the back of my truck. If you're gonna bust my still, I want you to bust it with my own ax."

The officers ignored him. Instead, they loaded Elmo and Son—and Lee too—into the back of their truck for a ride back to town as prisoners.

On this chilly day, a young woman in a simple cotton dress was walking down the road. Minnie Bell Swaggart cherished these walks when she could be alone with her dreams, away from the demands of daily existence. She was seventeen years old and seven months pregnant, living a life in which some days seemed full of promise while most offered little more than fighting with her husband and scraping by. Her hopes now rested with the baby growing inside her. Out alone on this dusty road, she allowed herself a few moments to be a carefree teenager.

Looking up, she saw a truckload of law enforcement officers driving by with a raggedy group of detainees. When she saw her husband Son in the back of that truck she screamed and kicked at the dirt on the road, sobbing all the while.

"Who in the hell is that?" an officer asked. "Why is she carrying on?"

Son Swaggart caught Minnie Bell's eye, then quickly looked away. He was mortified and pretty sure that the police truck was the safest place he could be at that moment. "That's my wife, sir," he said.

The officer observed the anguished, unspoken communication between this teenage boy and his teenage wife. He had seen it before, that mixture of anger, disappointment, and mainly fear that comes from the faces of people with no power and few prospects. *Hell*, he thought, *these boys had only been out makin' a little moonshine. I mean, they hadn't killed anybody.*

"Boy," he told Son, "get out of this truck. Take that girl home and calm her down. But if I see you messin' around with this stuff again, I'll drag your ass to jail."

So, on that winter day, Son Swaggart made a narrow escape and Elmo Lewis went to prison, while Lee Calhoun did his usual wheeling and dealing to evade incarceration. The illegal still at Turtle Lake was destroyed, spilling its spirited contents over the hard, red ground.

Son's mother, Ada Lewis Swaggart, could not believe the mess her son had narrowly escaped. That boy was gonna end up just like his daddy, causing trouble, bootlegging, and chasing every get-rich-quick scheme known to man. She felt sorry for Minnie Bell, her daughter-in-law. She liked that girl. Something about her seemed distant, but she had a sweetness that was endearing.

"You know what?" Ada asked her sister Irene. "I'd like to string that boy right up."

Ada's sister, Irene Lewis Gilley, understood what Ada was feeling. When she'd heard that the authorities had caught Lee and Son and her brother Elmo, she was sorry, but she couldn't say she was surprised. Sitting at Ada's kitchen table, she stared out the window, thinking about how their own daddy had gotten into his fair share of trouble.

"Men are just different from women," she told Ada. "Mama is the sweetest woman, but Daddy can be as mean as two rattlesnakes put together."

"You know as well as I do," said Ada, "they all get mean when they drink. These men are going to be in trouble forever. What's the point of even tryin' to straighten them out?"

"What a world," Irene said. She gazed out the window for a long while. Finally she turned back to her sister. "There has to be something better than all this drinkin' and fightin' and womanizin'; doesn't there?" she asked.

– 5 –

BIRTHS

On March 15, 1935, Minnie Bell Swaggart gave birth to her first child. She liked the name Jimmy, and both she and Son wanted to pay tribute to Lee Calhoun, Minnie Bell's brother-in-law who had been so helpful to her family. So the baby was named Jimmy Lee Swaggart and Minnie Bell, barely eighteen, had the son who would be the conduit for her dreams.

Six months later, on September 29, 1935, three weeks to the day after Huey Long was gunned down in Baton Rouge, Mamie Lewis gave birth to her second son. The delivery was a lengthy, difficult one; the boy was delivered prematurely and in breech. They named him Jerry and his middle name, like Jimmy's, would be chosen to honor Lee Calhoun. As an adult, Jerry Lee Lewis would often claim, "I came into this world naked, feet-first, and jumpin'. And I've been jumpin' ever since."

For Mamie, the sun would rise and set on Jerry and Elmo Jr., his five-year-old brother.

Around the time of Jerry's birth, his thirty-five-year-old aunt, Irene Gilley, realized she was pregnant. Six days before Jimmy Swaggart's first birthday, on March 9, 1936, she gave birth to a boy and named him Mickey Leroy. Like Mamie and Minnie Bell, Irene refused to bow to the poverty and hopelessness around her, and harbored nothing less than the highest aspirations for her son.

Jerry's daddy, Elmo Lewis, was a frustrated man. As hard as he worked, he could never get ahead. Fact was, he had trouble breaking even. With two boys at home to feed and a worried wife, drink was his refuge, a substance that both settled him and made him ornery.

Jerry was two years old when his father was arrested again for bootlegging and shuttled off to prison, leaving his young sons and worn-out wife to fend for themselves. Mamie, frustrated and frightened, could hardly contain her anger. On many occasions, she confronted an empty pantry not knowing what the family's next meal would be. Their diet included heavy doses of red beans and rice.

Their persistent poverty, along with that of the Swaggarts and Gilleys, set all three families many rungs down the social ladder from Ferriday's better-off white families, the kind that had chicken regularly on Sunday. Those were the fortunate ones, but fortune didn't seem to favor the Lewises, Swaggarts, and Gilleys.

Elmo and Mamie's circumstances were partially eased by kindly neighbors and shopkeepers who'd give them a twenty-five-pound sack of flour or meal. They were forced to rely on Lee Calhoun, who ignored rental due dates when times were toughest and funneled a little extra money through Stella to her sister Mamie.

Sometimes Mamie, Minnie Bell, and Irene suspected that this earthly life, with its endless trials and heartache, was nothing more than a test and a punishment.

– 6 –

EARLY DEATH

The nine-year-old boy with the brown eyes and already striking good looks sat at the kitchen table, scrawling on a notepad cocked at an angle on the rough wooden surface. His mother, Mamie, stood at the sink, peeling potatoes. His Aunt Stella, standing over the stove and stirring butter beans, wiped her hands on a dish towel, then walked over and leaned out the door, calling to her twelve-year-old daughter, Maudine.

"Come inside and help your cousin with his schoolwork," Stella called.

Maudine loved helping Elmo Jr., her quiet, well-mannered cousin who was also her best friend. Together, they played in the yard, the street, and around town. Even in these hard times, children were able to carry on as if they had not a care in the world.

Elmo Lewis Jr. had been born days after "Black Tuesday" in 1929 and was just shy of six years old when his little brother, Jerry, came along. Junior was a special boy, with a cheerful personality and a sweet, good nature. In a family full of musicians, his singing voice stood out already. To his mother, he seemed like an angel.

Now, he concentrated on the final lines of his school assignment, knowing that his reward for completion would be playing outside before dinnertime. As his handwriting improved and steadied, he had been able to write more letters to his daddy who he'd been told had "gone away," though no one would tell Junior where he'd gone.

"There! Mama, I'm going outside," he said, racing out the door with his cousin Maudine in tow and slamming the door behind them. Maudine was spunky and fun. Elmo always felt safe with her; she looked out for him.

In Ferriday, where everyone knew everyone else, kids played everywhere and anywhere. Junior and Maudine liked to jump in and out of pickups and tractor-pulled wagons, flying up with each dip in the road as they traveled up and down bumpy Louisiana Avenue. As Maudine climbed into the back of a wagon, he followed out to the middle of the road. "C'mon, Junior. Hurry up!" Maudine called.

Suddenly, a truck came barreling by. The driver was too drunk to see the small boy in front of him. Maudine heard a terrible thud that sounded like a fifty-pound sack of flour falling off a shelf. She peered over the back of the wagon and saw Junior lying on the road. He wasn't moving.

Inside the house, Mamie and Stella heard the collision. They rushed outside. Mamie screamed. She knelt beside the lifeless body of her firstborn son. The pain, shock, and grief were overwhelming, unbearable.

Junior was laid out in Irene Gilley's house, dressed in a little white suit, the only one he had, a suit reserved for rare special occasions and happy events. Junior had been excited to have his first grown-up attire. Never did his mother imagine that he would be buried in it.

Elmo Sr. was escorted from prison to attend his son's funeral. He stood by the grave in his gray prison garb and shackles, watching his namesake as the child was lowered into the ground. It was a dark day for Elmo—a day on which the loss of his son was amplified by the grief of his wife, and by the bottomless shame for his own reckless behavior. Immediately following the burial, he was led away and transported back to his cell 140 miles south.

Mamie's grief was deep and wide. Still, she refused to press charges against the drunk driver, insisting that God would straighten out the matter. Years later, the man would write her a letter detailing the anguish and guilt that had plagued him since the accident. He asked her forgiveness. She never replied.

All that Mamie had left in the world was Jerry, her two-year-old son. She grabbed him in her arms, never wanting to let go. He would be a difficult, stubborn child, but in Mamie's eyes, he could do no wrong. Her fierce, unconditional love would make him feel like the most special boy in the world, and set the course for the stunning destiny that awaited him. But for now, Jerry sensed the loss around him and the hope in his mama's eyes as she turned to him, again and again. He stared up at her, wanting to help but not knowing how.

Shortly after Junior's death, Elmo Sr. just up and walked away from his prison work detail and headed back to Ferriday. The authorities never came looking for him. At home, where Mamie controlled everything, Elmo retreated into a shell. When Jerry asked him a question he would say, "Go ask your mama."

With time, Mamie was recognized by her husband, children, family, and friends as leader of the Lewis household. While she would have preferred that Elmo have a stronger presence, his laid-back nature could not combat her strong will.

Mamie needed Jerry, too, for the hopes she had nourished for two sons were now wholly invested in the son who remained. Mamie and Jerry would become bound in a relationship that was unusually dependent and close, even by the standards of Southern mothers and their adoring sons.

– 7 –

MORE HARDSHIP

In December 1940, Minnie Bell Swaggart gave birth to a second child, a son named Donnie. When the infant was only weeks old, Son loaded Minnie Bell, five-year-old Jimmy, and his brother into his pickup and headed for Rio Hondo, Texas, a small town 140 miles south of Corpus Christi. Son's sister, Arilla, and her family had already moved there and Son dreamed of selling produce all over Texas and Louisiana, working on a rig like his brother-in-law, or engaging in any other enterprise that could make his fortune. Jimmy sensed his father's excitement as the family headed out on the 650-mile journey westward from Ferriday.

They had been in Rio Hondo just a few weeks when Minnie Bell got an earache that turned into an infection, and then to pneumonia. Soon baby Donnie was running a high fever and Son was panicked. Both Minnie Bell and Donnie were hospitalized and the bills from that were stripping him of the meager funds he'd mustered to make a new start here in Texas.

Son was worn down and out. The financial strain, the stress of being so far from home, the pressure to succeed burdened him day and night. Angry as he was at life, he was even more disgusted with himself. Now he was sick, too. He mumbled incoherently as he leaned over to pick up the rag he'd dropped beneath the rickety bedside table in the cheap room where he and Jimmy were staying. He flopped back on the hard bed and pressed the cool, damp wash cloth to his forehead, trying to ease his burning fever. He was convinced that he had heard the voice of God telling him that Donnie would die.

As he dragged himself out of bed and stumbled toward the sink, he noticed Jimmy sitting solemnly and silently in a corner of the room. The boy was only five, but the poverty and tension of his daily existence had aged him far beyond his years. He had observed the trip to Texas turn sour as his daddy and mama endlessly argued and bickered. He had seen the fear in his mama's eyes when they visited her at the hospital.

Hours after their visit, Minnie Bell had watched helplessly as her baby died. The infant was given a pauper's burial, and just before he was set into the ground, his tiny casket was opened. Son looked at his child and wept. "I know my baby would be alive if I had lived for God," he whispered. "It's all my fault."

Son vowed that if he could just get back to Ferriday, he would give his life to God. But when he finally got back home, he wasn't able to fulfill that promise. He felt paralyzed and overcome by regret, guilt, and self-loathing.

After Donnie's death, Minnie Bell became more contemplative and serious. She was searching for something that could change her life and ease her pain.

Jimmy saw his parents' heartache in the wake of his brother's death. He saw his daddy's desperate, fruitless efforts to provide; he saw the growing distance between his combative parents. Once again, he was the only hope his mama had.

Jimmy felt the pain of those around him. In the wake of Donnie's death, Minnie Bell and Son fought constantly. Their screaming matches left Jimmy scared and Minnie Bell crying in her room. More than anything, the little boy wanted to ameliorate the pain he saw in his family, especially in his mother. He wanted to do whatever he could to bring some happiness to her life. He became intent on making his parents cheerful, and when he couldn't muster the will or self-discipline to please them, he tried to showcase his attributes for them and hide those aspects of his personality and character that he knew they wouldn't like. He would continue that pattern into his adulthood.

The relationship between Jimmy's grandparents, Pa and Ada Swaggart, was just as rocky, and in some ways worse. Ada had the explosive Lewis temper and Pa was rumored to have taken up, over the years, with several women, including more than one black mistress down in Bucktown. Their battles were often conducted in front of their children and grandchildren.

Following World War II, Ferriday continued to earn its reputation as a rough-and-tumble town. With the beginnings of the post-war boom, crowds increased on Saturday afternoons and evenings. Returning servicemen as well as hard-pressed men from all over the country made their way to the oil fields and energy industries, where jobs were plentiful. A man could stay fully employed if he wasn't afraid of backbreaking work, being constantly covered in oil and grime, and having permanent dirt under his fingernails. The town of Ferriday became a place that could provide a respite from the hard toil and struggle of day-to-day existence. Mixed with the rough codgers who already called Concordia Parish and surrounding areas home, the free-flowing alcohol and spirits found in Ferriday—and some men's general attraction to trouble—created a combustible atmosphere that could, and often did, explode.

On one particular Saturday evening, the sun had been gone half an hour when the streets filled with people. The crowd along Ferriday's main street, Louisiana Avenue, spilled over to Texas Avenue to the north and Mississippi Avenue to the south. Heading down Fourth Street, the crowds waxed and waned all the way to Bucktown, where a huge crowd milled around Carolina Avenue and the famous blues joint, Haney's Big House. Some had been there since the afternoon and the combination of heat and alcohol had already produced loud voices, quick tempers, and increased bravado in men otherwise given to restraint and self-doubt.

The man turning the corner at Louisiana and Fourth was the town marshal. W. H. Swaggart—W. H. to many, Uncle Willie to some, and Pa to his grandson Jimmy and a few others—stood somewhere between six-foot-three and six-five and weighed 240 to 260 pounds depending on whom you asked.

Those who didn't know him by name knew him as the marshal. Not just any town marshal, but the rare lawman in the 1940s who still rode a horse while making his rounds. Rarely did he need to dismount; he was capable, while still in the saddle, of stopping a skirmish or dealing with a drunk disturbing the peace. His deep voice and an authoritative point of his finger prompted many a man to find his way directly to the local jail of his own accord, without ever being touched, or even followed, by Swaggart.

The milling throngs always provided passage to W. H. as he moved purposefully, methodically, peering in the doors and windows of establishments on either side of the street, making sure everything, however rowdy, was still under control. "Evenin', Tom," remarked the marshal, noticing a local man with too much stagger in his walk. "Where you headed in such a hurry?"

"Got some business to take care of. Nothin' to worry about," replied the unsteady subject, a noticeable slur in his voice.

"Then you probably won't be needin' that knife in your pocket, will ya?"

Among those who witnessed W. H. Swaggart cutting a swath through the town of Ferriday, many would be reminded of him years later, when they saw the powerful presence and purposeful stride of his grandson.

At night, Jimmy continued to hear his parents' raised voices. They knew how much their shouting troubled him but they had long since stopped bothering to keep their disagreements hidden. Hearing them carry on, Jimmy would sit quietly, looking straight ahead, flinching at each verbal volley as if he'd been slapped. Why did his mama and daddy fight like this? Was it his fault? Was there something he could do to make them stop? Many nights he lay in bed hearing the battle raging in another room and covering his head, trying to make the noise go away along with the constant tension that accompanied it.

One afternoon when Elmo and Mamie Lewis had come to call, Jimmy sat with them in his family's small living room, listening to his parents in the other room, a knot forming in his stomach. Across from him, Elmo and Mamie made small talk, trying to ignore the yelling. They had their own spirited disagreements, but Elmo, unlike Son, didn't fight back as stubbornly against his strong-willed Herron wife.

Jimmy's mama, Minnie Bell, strode into the room, her face red with anger. She headed through the front door carrying a large metal pot in which she'd been cooking black-eyed peas for that night's dinner. Son followed her, demanding she come back, embarrassed as a man could be that his wife would make a display like this in front of his family. But telling Minnie Bell to do something and having her comply were two different matters altogether.

Jimmy, staring out the window, saw the contents of the pot go flying. Minnie Bell turned and marched back through the front door.

"You want dinner?" she asked Son. "Well, go get it!" Then she stomped back into the kitchen.

There was no other food in the house that evening and so Son, Elmo, and Mamie went into the front yard, empty cook-pot in hand. Bending over, they picked the black-eyed peas out of the dirt, along with a few unintended blades of sun-scorched grass.

Years later, remembering that evening, Jimmy would say, "The black-eyed peas and cornbread had a peculiar taste that night. No one spoke at the table."

The Gilley household was equally tempestuous. Mickey's father, Arthur, was a good man and caring father but he had a weakness: he could not ignore an available woman. Irene Lewis Gilley suspected that her husband philandered and did not regard that transgression lightly.

After Mickey spent one afternoon fixing his bicycle, he joined his parents for a rare family outing. He climbed into the backseat of their 1939 Mercury, a prized possession of his daddy's and a constant source of friction between his parents. Whenever Irene saw the car, she thought of all the rumors she'd heard about how Arthur spent his time. Some married women in town took their husbands' wandering eyes as inevitable and didn't fret. They were more concerned that weekly wages, meager as they were, made it home with their husbands on Fridays before the men headed off to their favorite watering holes.

Irene wasn't that kind of wife.

On this day, Arthur listened to her complaints about the rumored women, the lack of time he spent at home, and his preoccupation with that silly car. He was generally a quiet man, but he spoke right up when Irene said, "You keep this car so nice. I wish you'd keep our house the same way."

"I beautify my car," he said, "to ride my women in it."

As he fixed his eyes on the road in the silence of the car, Arthur felt a strange satisfaction. That had sure quieted her down, hadn't it?

When they reached home, Irene still hadn't said a word. Deliberately, she helped Mickey out of the backseat and told him to head into the house. Inside, he turned and saw her pick up a broken kickstand that lay beside his bicycle. Wide-eyed and incredulous, Mickey watched as his mother used the kickstand to break every piece of glass in his father's car—headlights, tail lights, front windshield, side and back windows. After she had finished, Irene triumphantly tossed the kickstand back in the dirt and marched into the house.

Arthur had proceeded a few feet from the car and turned back with the first shatter of glass. He quietly watched Irene's rampage, feeling a mixture of frustration and resignation. He made no effort to stop his wife. Only after Irene had disappeared into the house, closing the door behind her, did Arthur get inside the car, crank the ignition, and drive away to find someone to make the necessary repairs. He knew that he would face a handful of Ferriday observers who'd be wondering what had happened to the windows and lights in Arthur Gilley's car.

Mamie, Minnie Bell, and Irene felt desperation engulfing them, day after day. They yearned for something that could redeem their lives, give them strength, bring hope to their families, and ease their pain. There had to be something better than what they had. They could feel it.

– 8 –

THAT OLD-TIME RELIGION

Two smiling women cloaked in flowing white dresses arrived in Ferriday in the spring of 1936, resolved to bring godliness to the lost inhabitants of this lawless, godforsaken town. Ignoring the stares and whispers of townsfolk, they rented a lot on the northwest corner of Texas Avenue and Eighth Street and began preparing it for a religious service. Mother Sumrall had indoctrinated her children in the Holiness Church. Her bold-hearted, seventeen-year-old daughter Leona believed that she could hear God's voice and was certain that the Lord had called her to Ferriday.

The two women went door-to-door soliciting people to attend their outdoor services. Mickey's older sister Edna saw them and thought they looked like angels.

The Assemblies of God traces its roots back to the Methodist Church, which held Pentecostal-like revivals when America was fighting for independence from the British in the 1770s. While occurring in every part of the country, these demonstrative, impassioned gatherings became particularly common among rural frontier families in the South and Midwest. By 1870, this Holiness crusade—which was similar to, yet distinct from, the Pentecostal movement—had spread throughout the country.

Over the next thirty years, it would gain acceptance among Christians of all denominations. Not only did it impart something its followers could physically feel and witness, for the poor and struggling it also provided an escape from a frightening and uncertain world. It offered a return to simplicity and childlike faith, with the hope of finding a better world after death. From a religious perspective, its momentum was analogous to the populist political movement of the late nineteenth century.

For generations, the Pentecostal movement had touched the hearts and lives of rural, simple people whose lives of hard toil and narrow survival needed a primal, basic source of inspiration and worship. A defining event would trigger explosive expansion.

On New Year's Eve 1900, a group of students were in prayer with their instructor, Charles Fox Parham, in Topeka, Kansas. Parham had become an early proponent of the belief that the third "blessing"—which followed salvation and the sanctification experience—was evidenced by a power derived from the third member of the Christian Trinity, the Holy Spirit. This power manifested as "glossolalia," or speaking in unknown tongues, and would become a distinguishing feature of the Pentecostal sect. As Parham's group prayed for this "third blessing," one young student, Agnes Ozman, began to speak in an unknown tongue, thought by observers to be a dialect of Chinese. For the next three days she was unable to speak English and could write only in Chinese characters. Parham and thirty-four other students also began speaking in unknown languages.

By the fall of 1905, Parham was teaching at a Bible college in Houston, Texas. A black Baptist minister, William Seymour—unable to enroll because of his race—was auditing Parham's courses. Seymour had migrated to the Holiness movement and accepted Parham's assertion of a third work of grace. He had witnessed many around him receive the ability to speak in tongues, and had tried to experience the phenomenon himself, but without success.

One of Parham's students impressed by Seymour's message invited him to come to Los Angeles to speak. There, he preached in an abandoned church building at 312 Azusa Street. His planned one-month visit was extended and the Azusa Street Revival began on April 14, 1906. It would continue for three-and-a-half years and serve as the seminal event in the modern Pentecostal movement.

The *Los Angeles Times* and other secular media reported on the events on Azusa Street. One story began, "Breathing strange utterances and mouthing a creed which it would seem no sane mortal could understand, the newest religious sect has started in Los Angeles." Crowds swelled as trains brought visitors daily to watch gatherings of men and women who wept and danced, shouted, collapsed on the ground, became lost in trances and, above all, spoke in tongues. The Azusa Street meetings had established speaking in tongues as a clearly defined doctrine, and as the defining trait of Pentecostals for whom speaking in tongues would be a status symbol.

One such group was the General Council of the Assemblies of God, which was established in Hot Springs, Arkansas, in 1914. Over the next decades, it would grow to become the largest Pentecostal denomination in the world, and in 1936—through the work of Leona and Mother Sumrall—it would find a home in Ferriday, Louisiana.

Pentecostals were strict believers in the literal truth of the biblical text. They shared an intense fear of sin and a constant need to repent. What often resulted, particularly in adult men, was a sort of spiritual schizophrenia, in which believers vacillated between genuine attempts to achieve a virtuous life and crippling, demoralizing lapses when their mortal limitations led them to fail. For many, this resulted in a repetitious pattern of sin and repentance, with prayerful Sundays following hell-raising Saturday nights, all of which fed a never-ending frustration with one's own shortcomings, a lack of faith in God's grace, and constant doubts about one's eternal salvation.

Pentecostals also shunned many developments of modern society. In the early years, the women dressed conservatively and wore no make-up, and the group rejected secular entertainments, including radio, movies, party games, secular music, and dancing. Large numbers of the sect turned away from doctors and medical innovations even in the face of possible death, relying instead on God's power and prayer—including the laying on of hands by elders or senior members of the congregation.

Because many Pentecostals rejected society, much of society rejected them. Even other Christians ridiculed and condemned Pentecostals for their puritanical practices, flamboyant displays of worship, and simplistic beliefs. Pentecostal services involved running through the aisles, dancing in the spirit, and rolling on the floor— which led to the coining of the term "Holy Rollers." To many, these practices evoked the pandemonium of a madhouse, and seemed to result from hallucinations or even demonic worship. Further, the Pentecostals' willingness to mix interracially and to allow women to preach made many Pentecostal congregations anathema to more staid denominations.

Yet the Pentecostal movement continued to grow. Music was a key component of their services. Heartfelt singing, musical instrumentation, and passionate rhythms were hallmarks of their meetings. Manipulation of the music from upbeat, praiseful songs to slow, sentimental hymns and spirituals provoked deep emotionalism in the parishioners. The intensity of Assembly of God church music on its family of worshippers would strongly influence a new form of secular music that would emerge in the south, introduced by Carl Perkins, Johnny Cash, and—above all—Elvis Presley.

The Assembly of God Church in Ferriday conducted its services outdoors until it amassed sufficient funds, a few years after its inception, to build the little white church it would call home. (The old codger Lee Calhoun had been one of the primary financial contributors to the effort to erect a proper churchhouse, although he steered clear of the church services held there.) For the Lewises, Herrons, Swaggarts, and Gilleys, the initial draw to the church was the lively music and singing produced by the church's small group of musicians. Elmo soon brought his guitar and joined them. He was a nominal Baptist, without much use for church with its mandates and dark admonishments, but the music profoundly influenced him and his wife and son.

As much as Mamie enjoyed the music, more important to her was the opportunity to give her family a more stable environment than the one she'd endured growing up, in a home where there was no money and two troubled parents. In this small church, she found hope amidst her daily struggles.

Like his Uncle Elmo, Son Swaggart had no use for church. But he, too, was drawn to the music. When Sister Sumrall invited him and Minnie Bell to attend, Son was lured by the chance to play his fiddle with the other musicians. Anyway, the church was just a short walk from their home and so, for a few years in the late thirties, the Swaggarts were uncommitted but regular participants.

Donnie's death changed this. Son, consumed by grief, was also plagued by other wrenching emotions. "I was fighting something all the time," he would say years later. "Couldn't get away from it, couldn't outrun it. If I went yonder, it was over yonder. You see, I knew in my heart that I was the one who had caused God to take my child."

At church, the Swaggarts observed the family of Tom Holcomb. The Holcombs had lost a child too, but instead of being overwhelmed with sorrow and guilt, they seemed filled with a joy that could be explained only by their connection to God. Their example caused Son and Minnie Bell to view the Christian experience in a new way, and in 1942, a year after Donnie died, Son walked down the church aisle, tears in his eyes, and committed his life to the Christian way. His guilt and grief were instantly eased. Minnie Bell soon followed his lead.

Arthur Gilley was having none of this church business and wouldn't attend. The Christian life could only interfere with the things that made his life pleasurable and endurable. The church soon drew his wife Irene, who sought respite from her difficult marriage and financial hardship. Her hope for something better made her an open vessel for the Assembly of God's world of miracles and instantaneous redemption. She had been to other churches, but they had no impact on her. She had needed someone to guide her, but no one had reached out. After she and her daughter, Edna, attended a Baptist revival, where no one prayed with them, Irene had said, "Well, I don't feel any different."

Then Irene visited the Assembly of God church. Sister Sumrall was there, and Irene approached her. "Look," she said, "I don't know if I'm saved or not," she said.

"I'll tell you what," Sister Sumrall said, "let's get down on our knees and pray about it."

That day, with Leona Sumrall kneeling beside her, Irene Gilley found God. She held a long conversation with Him about a variety of topics—her life, her temper, her struggles, her husband, her children, her needs, and her willingness to trust in Him to help her. When she rose from her knees she was changed, and those around her would soon see evidence.

Before, when someone slighted Irene, she wanted retribution. Now she became more prayerful, more forgiving, more spiritual, more patient.

In the early 1940s, as her brother Elmo and her sister Irene became more involved in the church, Ada Swaggart, Jimmy's grandma, attended a revival in Snake Ridge. During that service, Ada believed that she was struck by the power of the Holy Spirit and began to speak in tongues. It was a life-changing experience, and when her daughter-in-law Minnie Bell insisted that there was no such thing as speaking in tongues, Ada ignored her.

One day, well before noon, a glorious noise emanated from the little white church on the northwest corner of Texas Avenue and Eighth Street in Ferriday. Inside, traveling evangelist J. M. Cason was visiting and led the small congregation in singing and worshiping, adding direction with his loud voice and accompaniment with his well-worn accordion. A rough, untrained preacher, Cason had only a small number of sermons from which to choose. What he lacked in sophistication, he more than made up for in enthusiasm. At any moment during a revival service, often unexpectedly, he might launch into a variety of excitable behaviors. He was prone to crying, shouting, and a general habit of "carrying on." It drew in some people and pushed away others.

The small congregation of worshippers had joined for the daily service that was part of the revival Brother J. M. had brought to town. The scene had a free-flowing aura, as some sang and worshipped from their seats, clapping their hands or waving their arms overhead, while others made their way down to pray at the front of the church, kneeling, standing, or sitting on the floor.

Mamie was headed up the aisle, returning to her seat from the altar of the small church. A strange feeling, a strange power, swept over her, and the reserved Mamie ran toward the back of the church. A few steps into her sprint, she fell. When she arose, she was speaking in tongues. At the same time, Irene Gilley was kneeling near the front of the church in the right corner, praying quietly yet fervently. A few moments after Mamie's tongue-talking began, the same power rushed over Irene and she too began speaking in tongues.

Minnie Bell Swaggart had been opposed to the emotionalism and carnival atmosphere she witnessed when boisterous Assembly of God attendees spoke in tongues. Only weeks earlier, she had stated, "This shouting, yelling and hollering is ridiculous. I'll never do it." On this warm, summer morning in 1943 in Ferriday, Louisiana, as her sister Mamie and her husband's Aunt Irene were having their own "experiences," the same atmosphere overwhelmed

Minnie Bell. Within moments, she was dancing, circling the pews, waving her arms, and . . . speaking in tongues.

Jimmy and Jerry and two friends were playing a few streets over when they heard the loud commotion coming from the church. Amid the collection of shouts and hollers emanating from the church, Jimmy could clearly make out the voice of his mother. Immediately, a feeling of embarrassment and alarm enveloped him. While the other kids rushed down the street to see what all the commotion was about, Jimmy Swaggart ran to his home a few blocks away. He was in no hurry to hear how his mother would explain her newfound spiritual experience.

Each day, the women of the church immersed themselves in prayer. In their "prayer circles," they would pray for the sick and anoint them with oil. Many of the anointed would be cured. No one could explain this, and no one tried to. These rituals were no more or less than exercises in the power of faith. They called them miracles.

Soon, Irene Gilley and Ada Swaggart met continually to pray. The two sisters would fall to their knees and beseech God on behalf of a family member or local resident. Mickey would see them heading off to the Assembly of God church on these errands of worship. Much later, he would describe his mother and aunt as "prayer warriors."

When Arthur Gilley opened a saloon, Irene went to battle.

"Arthur Gilley," she would say, "you know it's not pleasin' to the Lord for you to be runnin' that bar."

Her voice was calm but had the authority of a woman who didn't lack for certainty.

Arthur's recently opened saloon had become a popular destination for blacks and whites alike, and Arthur knew that in the South in the 1940s, a businessman who sold to both races had to make accommodations. So he installed a bar in the center of the saloon that functioned as a barrier, running the length of the establishment. His white customers stayed on one side; black customers stayed on the other.

Irene had been pestering Arthur about the saloon ever since he decided to open it. Though he had no use for the rigid tenets of the Assembly of God church, they had forged a détente: he tolerated her sermons and she realized that he had little or no intention of abiding by her wishes. "That bar's not hurtin' anybody, as far as I can tell," he told Irene, "and I don't suspect it will be shuttin' down."

Irene was convinced that the alcohol served to Arthur's patrons was a source of trouble. She saw her husband's customers as feckless men, wasting hard-earned paychecks on momentary escape from their problems. Because of the evils of drink, she told Arthur, poor families had empty cupboards and otherwise docile men became belligerent and aggressive.

Irene also knew that the bar was where Arthur indulged his wandering eyes, and where loose women were more than happy to welcome his advances. Her rage over his transgressions remained uncontainable, so much so that one day, forgetting her newfound penchant for forgiveness, Irene marched down to the bar and fired a gun over the head of a particular woman she knew was involved with her husband. Finally, realizing her temper-driven reactions to her husband's pandering did not produce the changes she desired, she embarked on a different strategy.

"Arthur," she said, "let me tell you somethin'. Just file it away in the back of your mind. I'm not gonna keep on houndin' you about that bar. I'm gonna pray you out of business. It may take a week. It may take a year. It may take ten years. Every day I'm gonna pray and ask the Lord to cripple that business."

Over the next two years, Mickey would hear his mother's fervent requests to her Maker to turn back Arthur's efforts. Faithfully, resiliently, quietly, her prayers continued, unabated.

Within two years, Arthur's business was closed and in its place stood a vacant lot. Mickey was sure he knew why.

His mama had prayed his daddy out of business. When Mickey was grown, every time he returned to Ferriday, he'd look at where the saloon once stood. Sixty years later, the lot was still vacant.

One spiritual event that made a great impression on Jerry, Jimmy, and Mickey was the healing of their aunt Lena's cancer.

Lena Madison lived in a small house behind Mickey's family home on Mississippi Avenue. She had been sick so long that the doctors had given up on her. From time to time Mickey would be sent over to deliver a meal to her. "Aw, Mama," he'd protest, "don't make me go in that house. It smells like death in there."

Each day, Mickey would watch as Ada dropped by his house to collect her sister Irene. "You ready to go to Lena's?" Ada would cheerfully ask, as though she were inviting Irene to a picnic.

The two tall Lewis sisters, in long dresses, would head to Lena's house. Dutifully, faithfully, they would lay hands on her emaciated body, beseeching God to remove the death sentence she faced.

One Sunday, the two women arranged to have several men carry Lena on a stretcher to the Assembly of God church. Lena could no longer stand or sit up, and so they laid her stretcher on the floor and put pillows beneath her. Jerry, Jimmy, and Mickey were seated near the back of the church. They strained to see what was going on. Lena's withered body was so frail and light that she barely dented the pillows.

A healing prayer meeting ensued. Those in the church joined hands, closed their eyes, and prayed. "Delavie Masta," Irene said, again and again. The cousins had heard it so often that they knew that she was saying, "Dear Loving Master." Other church members prayed too, some quietly, others in bold voices.

Within days, Lena was fully recovered, on the way to a long and fruitful life. Years would pass before she died of old age.

For Jerry, Jimmy, and Mickey, the scene was indelible. The images of their mothers praying tirelessly with unshakable belief would always move them, and never leave them.

Still, they knew from the way others stared at them and excluded them from the "in" group of Ferriday that attending Pentecostal church made them laughingstocks to the town's well-dressed citizens who sat quietly in the pristine, "civilized" church down the road. From the day the cousins entered their mamas' church, they would be outsiders.

To a great extent, they would remain outsiders throughout their lives.

On Saturdays, boys in Ferriday headed off to the Arcade Movie Theater owned by Mr. Meltz, where Saturday's matinee provided the highlight of each week. They would pay twenty-five cents each for a ticket and then sit transfixed on thinly veneered wooden seats, absorbed in the adventures of their heroes—like Gene Autry the Singing Cowboy, who rode his faithful horse, Champion, or Hopalong Cassidy who, astride Topper, would ultimately save the day once again.

These larger-than-life images on the movie screen fueled young imaginations and produced a cascade of ideas for another week's worth of escapades through the streets, fields, and railroad beds in and around Ferriday. For boys raised in the strict confines of the Assembly of God church, particularly Jimmy, the theater also became a place of constant struggle between good and evil, self-denial and sin, entertainment and corruption.

One Saturday, Jimmy took his place outside the theater, in the line snaking back from the ticket window and a few yards down Louisiana Avenue. Boys he knew from school were lined up to convert their meager allowances into an afternoon's entertainment.

Normally Jimmy would be with Jerry and Mickey, but Jerry was off somewhere with his mama and Mickey was doing chores.

Anyway, Jimmy didn't mind watching a movie alone; he often spent time by himself. He was excited to be the first of his cousins to see a film, and tomorrow morning at church he would be able to brag and tell them all about it. Inching forward in the line, his right hand nervously toying with the quarter in his pocket, he tried to forget the disappointed look on his mama's face as he left for the theater. As much as she disapproved of him going to the movie, he knew that she would not expressly forbid him. But she had no compunction about manipulating him. Each Saturday as he left the house, he could feel her eyes boring into him, willing him to not walk away.

The two boys directly in front of him grabbed their tickets and headed for the concession stand. Behind the window, the cashier fumbled with the ticket dispenser as she struggled to rescue Jimmy's ticket from its hold. Jimmy watched and waited. Just then, he heard a Voice saying: "Do not go into this place. Give your heart to me. I have chosen you as a vessel to be used in my service."

Startled and unsure of what he was experiencing, Jimmy stood unmoving. The Voice sounded again, "Do not go into this place. Give your heart to me. I have chosen you as a vessel to be used in my service." Jimmy was certain it was the voice of God.

Heeding the Voice's appeal, Jimmy did not enter the theater. Instead he bought a five-cent ice-cream cone from Vogt's Drugstore and walked home, exultant.

"I won't be going to movies anymore," he told his mother. "I gave my heart to the Lord." Minnie Bell gathered him in her arms. She hugged him harder than she ever had.

Jimmy would later write, "Everything seemed different after that day... I felt better inside. Almost like taking a bath continuously, I felt good and clean. A song seemed to bubble in my heart."

Soon, it became known in Ferriday that nine-year-old Jimmy Swaggart had prophetic visions. The first came in the summer of 1944.

Jimmy felt as if he were standing outside his body. Years later he would describe that early image: "I saw a powerful bomb destroying an entire city . . . tall buildings crumbling . . . people screaming. I didn't know it then, but there wasn't a bomb available with the power I described."

Jimmy's daunting prophesies created a stir in Ferriday and beyond. Mickey wondered if they were just further efforts on Jimmy's part to please his parents. To those in the church congregation, Jimmy's visions were proof that he was a chosen vessel for God's message, especially when, a year later, the bombs Little Boy and Fat Man devastated the Japanese cities of Hiroshima and Nagasaki, respectively. Even Son, the father Jimmy continually disappointed and who was so hard on him, began to view his young son with a certain reverence. The words that Jimmy uttered, Son would say years later, "would make cool chills run up and down your spine, because he's speaking in the supernatural. He wasn't speaking like just an ordinary person."

– 9 –

CONQUERED
UNCONQUERED

From the start Jerry, Jimmy, and Mickey had a bond that made them closer than brothers. As youngsters they were together constantly, biking all over the parish, beating paths to each other's houses and meeting places. A favorite destination was Vogt's Drugstore on Louisiana Avenue where they'd eat ice cream cones and stand in the back, chewing gum and reading comic books they could not afford to buy. In the summers, they'd head down to Lake Concordia to go swimming, or over to Vidalia to the swimming pool.

Jerry would argue about anything and would never admit to being wrong. He mouthed off all the time and got his butt kicked regularly by guys who were bigger. Even as a kid, he was known as a smart aleck and was possessed of a wild, free spirit and a curious, fearless nature. Those qualities made him a natural leader, but he did not always use his skills constructively.

The boys often played a game they called Conquered Unconquered, in which one of them would perform a daring stunt and the others would have to follow suit or be "conquered." One early spring day, the cousins took off on the ten-mile ride that brought them to the bridge spanning the Mississippi River, connecting the towns of Vidalia and Natchez.

Arriving at the bridge, Jerry hopped off his bike and bounded toward the slender railing. Wiry and disheveled, ignoring the gusts of wind that ruffled his wavy hair, he laughed and shouted to his two cousins as they rode, at last, onto the bridge.

"Watch this," Jerry called as he climbed on the hand railing and took a few steps, the mighty Mississippi roaring some hundred feet below him. Jimmy and Mickey stared, wide-eyed and wary, their expressions revealing a blend of admiration and disbelief. It was the look that Jerry craved, the look that told him that they were awed by his skill, his daring; the look that affirmed what he already knew— that he was different, special.

Jerry loved being the center of attention. He liked to command, to be seen and heard, to turn bystanders into his audience, to put on a show that would leave spectators in the wide-eyed, openmouthed state to which he had now—once again—rendered his less-daring cousins. Whether they were cavorting by the levee or romping down the alley in Bucktown, Jerry always preferred to lead the way.

"I wouldn't do that in a million years," Mickey whispered to Jimmy as they watched Jerry on the bridge. "It's reckless."

Jerry never bothered to think about the dangers of teetering as if on a tightrope high above the river. He simply knew that the bridge was one of the few places he and his cousins had yet to conquer, and he never doubted that he would be the one to conquer it, although only sure footing and moxie kept him from certain death. As he perched above the thundering current, adrenaline surged through him. He felt invincible, possessed of super powers like the superheroes in his favorite comic books. With confidence and pride, he proceeded down the thin strip of metal.

"You're crazy," Mickey called to him. He knew that Jerry wouldn't stop once he set his mind on doing something.

"C'mon, Jerry," Jimmy called, "Get on down before you get hurt!"

Jerry didn't respond. He was lost in the moment, entranced by the thrill, oblivious to his surroundings. They would never keep him from conquering. He hated to lose. And he didn't lose. Not ever.

Satisfied with his performance, Jerry scrambled down. He surveyed the still-shocked faces of his cousins and smiled. He knew that they'd never venture onto the bridge railing. "Conquered!" he exclaimed.

Jimmy and Mickey looked into his eyes and saw a quality that wasn't just fearlessness, though that was part of it. Beyond that was Jerry's determination to prove that he was the best and to flaunt it, no matter what.

"You bet I'm conquered," said Mickey. "I ain't about to do that. No way, no how."

He would comment on his cousin's courageous act years later, shaking his head. "All you had to do was make the wrong step and you'd a fallen into the Mississippi and it would'a killed you."

One afternoon at the Gilley home, Mickey's sister Edna wrung out the mop in the kitchen sink before picking up where she had left off. Having already moved the chairs into the adjoining room, she slid the wet mop under the small kitchen table as she worked her away methodically across the room. A sweet, helpful girl, Edna had many of the pleasant characteristics of her mother Irene. She helped around the house in any way she could. One of her joys was looking out for her younger brother, Mickey. She loved him intensely. She was like a second mom in addition to being a big sister.

She could only shake her head at times, though, at how spoiled her little brother was. She supposed it was common for the youngest child in the family to command a lot of attention; still, it surprised Edna to see how differently Mickey was treated compared to how she and her two older brothers, Aubrey and Ray, had been handled growing up.

Lost in thought as she carried out her mopping duties, Edna was interrupted by the sound of steps approaching the door. There he was, home from school. The peace and quiet was over, she thought, a smile crossing her face. A violent shaking of the screen door ensued as Mickey tried to come inside. Edna had hooked the screen door to prevent intruders from walking on her wet, freshly mopped floor.

"Mickey, you have to go around. I'm mopping the floor."

"I wanna come in," he said. "Edna, open the door and let me in."

"I said you need to go around the house, Mickey. The floor is wet and I don't want you tracking through here."

Mickey continued shaking the door, harder now.

"I wanna come in! Come open this door and let me in!"

Edna glanced back over her shoulder at the door behind her, watching the flimsy screen door rattling from the other side. The little scoundrel just didn't understand the meaning of the word "No!" Edna walked toward the door.

"I'm going to get you, you brat." As she reached to unlatch the hook and swing the door open, she heard footsteps clicking rapidly away from the door, followed by a mischievous laugh.

"If I get my hands on you, you won't be laughing." Mop still in hand, Edna chased Mickey down the street, but not fast enough to catch her elusive younger brother, whose hollers communicated a mixture of fear and delight.

Years later, Edna remembered the incident with a big smile on her face. "If I'd have caught him, I would have spanked him. But he was too fast for me.

"There were lots of times I wanted to spank him growing up. I loved him so much, but he was so spoiled."

Edna worked at the Arcade Theater for several years and was lovingly referred to around town as the "popcorn girl." She enjoyed the job and the miniscule but precious money she earned from her part-time role. One day, while she was at work, Mickey went through her things and found several dollars in coins, money that she had worked for diligently. He knew his sister would not be happy with his snooping, but he couldn't help it.

As he looked at the shiny coins, he envisioned endless possibilities. Conflicted or not, his hands reached out and grasped the coins, stuffing them into the pockets of his worn pants. Then he rushed away.

When Edna found the money missing that afternoon, she quickly connected the dots to her younger brother as the only viable suspect. She told her mother about the situation and her suspicions. Irene questioned Mickey, a glare emanating from her narrow, dark eyes. Mickey's attempt at adamant denial wilted within seconds. He grudgingly withdrew the coins from his pocket. A few feet away, his sister stood watching him, arms folded across her chest. Moments later, Mickey walked away, head down, embarrassed, dejected, and broke—except for the lone nickel he had held back from the unsuspecting women. A shiny five-cent piece. Jackpot!

He headed toward downtown, knowing the five cents would soon buy him an icy cold grape Nehi. The glass bottle felt so great in his hand, and the grape soda felt magical rolling down his throat on this steamy Southern day. All was right with the world as he strolled back into his front yard, half-consumed bottle of Nehi in his hand.

"Mickey, where did you get the cold drink? How did you pay for it?"

Hearing the voice, Mickey peered up on the porch, where his mother leaned out the front door. She looked solemn and stoic, as she readied herself to deliver a stern lecture on stealing and dishonesty. Mickey turned, his reddening face providing proof of his now-foiled plan. Though Irene didn't show it, her frustration was competing with her overwhelming sense that Mickey was so cute, so sweet, so lovable, even in mischief.

Jerry was courageous, but Jimmy would prove to be tougher, and of the two, he was always the more persuasive. This had been apparent since the end of Jerry's third-grade year, when his teacher flunked him.

"Daddy's gonna kill me," he told Jimmy, "if Mama doesn't kill me first!"

Jimmy had talked to Jerry's teacher. He was only nine years old at the time, but he was earnest, convincing, and well spoken. With his good manners and precocious air of responsibility, he seemed far older than his years.

Jimmy sought to convince the teacher that Jerry really did know the required material. In any case, he argued, with all the turmoil in Jerry's home life, getting a failing grade might even put him in danger. The teacher acquiesced, and a relieved and temporarily grateful Jerry passed third grade.

Supporting and protecting his cousins became routine for Jimmy, who had gained a reputation as a fighter, refusing to back down in the face of conflict. Even as Jerry provoked dozens of schoolyard fights, Jimmy was there to save him, taking pride in defending his cousin's honor. Soon word got around that if you picked a fight with Jerry you had to do something a whole lot harder: you had to whip Jimmy too.

Years later Jerry would tell a friend, "It's a good thing Jimmy became a preacher. He had a mean streak and there's no tellin' what might have happened if he hadn't chosen the direction he did."

As a child and student, Jimmy was quiet and kept largely to himself. Controlled by a domineering father and insulated by the strict tenets of the Pentecostal faith, he often had difficulty reconciling the rules and laws imposed by his natural father with the heavenly Father's message of mercy and grace.

Son Swaggart ruled his household with a stern hand. There was no talking at the dinner table. Jimmy was expected to answer requests and queries by saying "Yes, sir" or "No, sir." If Jimmy challenged or displeased his father, Son could be brutal in his punishment. He was also a notorious tightwad. When the kids were out playing and Minnie Bell called Jimmy to come and eat, the other cousins were not allowed to join in the meal. From an early age, Son expected Jimmy to work and earn money to pay for his personal necessities, including clothes and school supplies. Son's civility and compassion also had to be earned and were dealt sparingly.

Son's expectations of Jimmy were high and he extended the boy little freedom, closely monitoring where he went, what he did, and with whom he spent time. Yet, harsh as Son could be, the Swaggart family, devout in worship, became pillars of the church and were generally respected as "good people" by neighbors and acquaintances. When they came calling on the Gilleys, they'd seem jovial and laugh and talk, but the childhood Jimmy was experiencing was much less happy and easy.

Years later, Jerry's sister, Linda Gail, would recall Jimmy's upbringing. "Uncle Son had the only word in the house, and I think this has made Jimmy very insecure. Everything was so damn tight. Jimmy was not allowed to think, act, or breathe like a normal human being."

While the frugal Swaggarts managed to keep food on the table and meet their basic needs, and the Lewises often were not sure where their next meal was coming from, the Gilleys fell somewhere in between. None of the three families could provide the clothes, toys, or allowances for their children that other children had, and the cousins were aware that most kids in their school were better off than they were.

Compared to the stern rule of Son in the Swaggart family and the chaotic struggles of the poverty-stricken Lewis household, the Gilley home seemed normal by comparison, especially as Irene's violent outbursts were increasingly tempered by her church involvement. Despite Arthur's philandering, the Gilley household was filled with jokes and laughter. Irene Gilley was a generous, good-natured woman who loved to cook and bake.

Mickey would come home from school and say, "Mama, tell me a joke." Irene would make up some small joke and Mickey would laugh and laugh.

Mickey was blessed with a simpler, more stable and fun-loving childhood than his cousins had. He shied away from the trouble the other two were prone to find. Unlike Jerry, he resolutely avoided situations that presented risk of injury or punishment. Mickey seemed to profit from an inborn sense of security that his two cousins did not share. He never had to act out or show off to gain attention or feel accepted. The baby of the family by many years, he could do no wrong in the eyes of his much older siblings.

"He was always sweet," his sister Edna would recall seven decades later. "But he was so spoiled by my mother that he thought he was the king of the roost."

For a while, Arthur Gilley owned a pool hall, which provided a reasonably safe diversion for Mickey and his friends. They would skip study hall, slide down the fire escape of the school building, and race off to the pool hall a block away. Mickey had no use for schoolwork and no patience when it came to book learning. With a cue in his hand, everything changed. He concentrated for hours, honing skills that, as it happened, would come in handy later.

As the church became a growing presence in their lives, it produced a profound effect on each of the young cousins as they sat in the pews, shoulders inching toward their ears as a sense of terror overtook them at the sight of what the so-called grown-ups were doing. They saw people "slain in the spirit," lying prostrate as they shouted words that were unintelligible. From birth, the boys had been inculcated with the fear of God—but the church added the fear of hell and eternal damnation which was far more frightful and dire, especially since they were not at all sure that they could ever be pure enough to qualify for heaven. The rules for that celestial entry were harsh: No movies. No dances. No radios (and later, no televisions).

Though all three cousins were moved by the vibrant, soul-stirring church music, it was Jerry who responded to it most, even though he refused to allow the church to influence his mischievous nature. He was eight years old when he sang his first church solo, "What Will My Answer Be?"

Like the young Elvis Presley in Tupelo, Mississippi, Jerry Lee Lewis discovered that church music brought pure, unfettered inspiration, and he was thrilled by the choir's soaring songs and the wild, rhythmic moves of the singers.

For Mickey, the threats of hellfire and brimstone were real and endlessly daunting. At night, he would lie in bed worrying that he had made some mistake that day that could lead to his damnation. If he committed a heinous act such as going to a movie at the local theater, he would pay an awful price. "I felt like if I died that night," he would say later, "I was going to burn in hell forever and ever and ever."

Jimmy saw the church differently. For him it was, above all, the catalyst that changed his family. After his parents committed their lives to Christianity, there was more tranquility and fewer arguments at home. His mama seemed peaceful and happy; his daddy, freed from guilt, was more confident. For him, the impact of God and the significance of belief had produced a real impact in his life. It made faith's rewards tangible, as Son managed to make a little more money and, now and then, put some meat on the table.

Jimmy was also influenced by his deep relationship with his paternal grandmother, Ada. She was not only the first in the family to receive the Holy Ghost—she was also the most committed to God and religion. Jimmy was drawn repeatedly to sit at her feet, begging her to retell her initial encounter with the Holy Spirit. Each time Ada told the story, she would experience the power again and speak in tongues. Jimmy was captivated by the energy, the emotion. Later he wrote, "The power of the Lord would run all over me, too. Chill bumps would break out on my arms. The roots of my hair tingled. I would begin crying."

He never tired of asking Ada to repeat the account. She always indulged him, and as she did, she spurred his fascination with experiential Christianity, allowing him to sense for the first time the role that presentation played in worship and the importance of setting a mood, a tone, a scene.

– 10 –

MUSIC

Music was in them and all around them.

Jerry's daddy, Elmo, was the best of the family musicians. He loved music and his face became rapt and peaceful as he rhythmically plucked notes on his worn, oft-played guitar. Jimmy's daddy, Son, thrilled local citizens when he played his fiddle at dances and ran the bow over the strings so fast that it became blurred. The boys' mothers were known to sing beautifully, and the boys heard them humming throughout the day as they went about their duties.

Jerry had been listening to music all his life. He and his father would sit in front of the radio and hear the music coming in from *The Grand Ole Opry* and *Louisiana Hayride*. These were many of Jerry's happiest moments, listening to Jimmie Rodgers or strumming his daddy's guitar or hearing his mama sing.

Jerry was the first of the cousins to show a strong attraction to the piano. From an early age, he had shown moments of wonder around the musical instrument. He found it difficult to sit still in church, but would become transfixed listening to Sister Culbreth, the pastor's wife, play the piano positioned in the northwest corner of the small church sanctuary.

When Jerry was six years old, he was walking with his parents down Texas Avenue when he stopped and listened intently. As his parents paused to watch him, they heard the sounds of a piano coming from the home of a Ferriday resident. Jerry gravitated toward the sound. It led him to a neighbor's house, who invited him—and his parents—inside. There, Jerry sat at the piano and picked out the first few notes of a children's lullaby.

Another afternoon, Jerry ambled into the living room of Lee and Stella Calhoun and sat at their piano that they had purchased for their daughter Maudine, who showed little interest in the instrument. He approached it slowly, wide-eyed and reverential. Then he slowly slid down on the stool in front of the shiny, beautiful, mysterious instrument. He stared at the white and black keys. He touched them, gingerly at first, tracing his fingers over the keys, not making a sound. Then he pressed his fingers onto the keys, startled by the resonant notes that emerged from them. He studied his hands for a moment as if trying to comprehend how they had produced such sounds.

Jerry picked out a simple melody. The melodious sounds drew Elmo into the room. He stood in the doorway, watching his son. *The boy was blessed,* he thought to himself, *with the Lewis gift for music.* Elmo was hearing more than a song. He was hearing the potential for magic.

Mamie Lewis came into the room, holding her newborn daughter Frankie Jean, a tiny child with fair skin, deep blue eyes, and pale blonde hair. She felt a chill as she listened to her boy play, who somehow knew exactly which notes to hit.

Jerry also lingered around the piano in the home of his cousin Norma Jean Gilley, which her mother, Eva Lewis Gilley, Jerry's aunt, had bought. It was a piano that all the cousins would spend time playing, and the one that finally led Elmo Lewis to decide it was time for his son to have his own piano, whether they could afford it or not.

Jimmy and Mickey had tremendous musical ability and developed a love for the piano, but it was Jerry who was fascinated by the sounds it produced and the way it worked. He seemed to have a mystical connection to the instrument.

Seeing the talent of his son, Elmo Lewis rejoiced. He was determined to cultivate it in whatever ways he could. To buy a piano for Jerry, he mortgaged the family home and bought a Starck upright for a cost later said to be anywhere from $275 to $900. Even at the highest price, it was the smartest business move Elmo ever made. The piano was placed in the center of the room and provided a gleaming, polished exception to the worn and tattered furnishings in the Lewis home.

"It was," Jerry would say years later, "the greatest sounding piano I ever heard in my life. I loved it. I worshipped it."

He played it constantly, practicing tunes, executing trills and crescendos over and over, his proficiency enhanced by his dogged stubbornness, that same stubbornness that had gotten him into trouble in every other aspect of his life.

Music came easily to him. He could hear a tune and once he played it, he could change keys at will. Music was ingrained in him and making it felt as natural as being a daredevil or a smart aleck. He saw at once that playing piano brought him the attention, praise, and admiration he sought and craved. Soon, he was able to do things that others would be hard-pressed to master, in the process getting irrefutable proof of something he'd always believed: he wasn't only as good as others—he was a whole lot better.

Jerry took a piano lesson from the director of Ferriday's school band. He'd always been bored by anything that smacked of school and studying, and formal music lessons definitely fit this category. His frustration and inattentiveness grew as he followed the director's instructions and plodded through basic scales and chords and exercises. Despite direction to play in a simple manner, he kept changing the tempi and chords to create the bluesy, heavy-beat sound that was the rhythm of his being.

"No, no," the teacher said, "don't play it like that. Play it like this."

Placing his hands on the piano, the teacher offered a generic rendition. Jerry muttered an obscenity under his breath, thinking the director wouldn't hear it. But he did, and he responded by slapping Jerry across the face.

This ended the prospect of further lessons, which made Jerry happy. He didn't want to learn from anybody. He didn't care about reading sheet music. Why should he, when he could take himself down to a local café where they had a jukebox, listen to a song once and come home and play it? Each day he taught himself new songs, new things about music. For the first time in his life, gaining knowledge interested him.

Obsessed with music, he sat happily at the piano, banging away for several hours a day. As he developed, he favored a heavy left-hand pounding out the rhythm while his right hand flew over the keys creating the melody. The more he improved, the quicker the left hand went. Pretty soon, Elmo was saying that his son had perfected the instrument, while Mamie was exclaiming that her boy was a "natural."

As Jimmy watched Jerry play, he was convinced that his cousin had so much talent that no one, nowhere, could out-sing or out-play him. As much as he admired Jerry, Jimmy was drawn to a different type of music, the kind he heard at the Assembly of God church when a visiting preacher named Cecil Janway came to preach and play. Jimmy sat in the pew, looking around, fascinated by the way Janway's music stirred the congregation. If he could be like him, Jimmy thought, he would always be happy. For a child who had had a major spiritual experience, the notion of playing church music on the piano had a spiritual dimension. Sitting in the pew he prayed, "Lord, I want you to give me the gift of playing the piano."

He prayed while Brother Janway preached and he became so lost in his prayers that often he'd get too loud. Son would elbow him sharply. Jimmy kept praying. "If you give me this talent, Lord," he muttered, "I will never use it in the world. I will never play in a nightclub and I will always use the talent for your glory."

Jimmy was certain that the Lord couldn't object to his playing to glorify Him and nightclubs were the worldliest thing he'd ever heard of. Just in case, he added the words, "If I ever go back on this promise, you can paralyze my fingers!"

After that day, Jimmy played in earnest, practicing regularly. He played at the church, at cousin Norma Jean's house, and at various other homes and places around town that had a piano. Soon the Swaggarts also had a piano in their own home.

Jerry taught him many things but Jimmy developed his own unique style. It didn't come as naturally to him as it had to Jerry, but he too had inherited the musical gift common to those in the Lewis and Herron families.

Jimmy was hard-headed as well, a quality that helped him teach himself to play and precluded him from learning from anyone else. When Minnie Bell got a teacher for him, she only had to pay four times. "The teacher was a stickler for playing 'by the book,'" Jimmy would write many years later. "That was a bore. I'd sit and plunk, plunk, plunk on the piano but it didn't have any life."

Mickey might also have played the piano but his mama couldn't afford one, and so she bought him a guitar. Mickey taught himself to play it. As first he was interested only in the guitar, but he grew curious about the piano as he saw his cousins developing their talents. He listened to the music made first by Jerry and then by Jimmy. Finally, Mickey decided to try it. *Anyway*, he thought, *it's a lot easier to see the keys on a piano than to look down at the strings on a guitar.*

What came so naturally to his cousins was an uphill slog for Mickey. He played at Jerry's house and at the home of his cousin Norma Jean, but as the Herron sisters bragged on the piano talents of Jerry and Jimmy, Irene was left to lament that Mickey couldn't play.

"I wasn't very good at it," he would allow years later, "I had to fight for it."

And he did.

Jerry and Jimmy stepped in to help their younger cousin. Jerry in particular would take time to show Mickey how to play certain chords. By allowing Jerry the opportunity to demonstrate and show off his own talents, Mickey benefited from Jerry's good-natured willingness to teach him the basics and a few extra tricks. With the help from his cousins, Mickey played frequently, sitting on the piano bench beside one or the other, learning songs and developing skills.

One day, when visiting her brother Elmo and sister-in-law Mamie, Irene had quite a surprise. She'd been sitting around the table listening to Mamie and Minnie Bell talking about their boys' piano playing and she made the comment, "I wish Mickey could play like Jerry and Jimmy."

Elmo, listening to the women while considering whether he wanted another slice of the half-eaten pumpkin pie sitting on the stove, heard his sister's words and commented, "Irene, Mickey can play a piano pretty good for a beginner."

Irene responded, "He doesn't know how to play the piano."

"He sure can," Elmo retorted, leaning his head out the door and hollering into the yard. "Mickey, come here a minute." As twelve-year-old Mickey entered, Elmo gave a gentle command: "Mickey, play the piano for your mama. Take her in the other room and show her."

Mickey played a few notes that were unmistakably influenced by Jerry's style. Irene stared at him, pleased and proud. "Well," she said finally, "I guess I'll have to get him a piano now."

She went to Eva, who owned a successful little café in downtown Ferriday, and asked for a part-time job as a waitress and cashier. She explained her motive to her sister.

"I should have known you coming down here to work after all these years must have involved getting something for Mickey," Eva said.

As Irene worked, earning $18 each week, her dreams for Mickey crystallized and she would say, to anyone near enough to listen, "He's going to be my little preacher."

One July afternoon, Mickey was playing songs from the little brown church hymnal on the piano his mama had recently bought for him. Irene didn't want him playing "worldly music," and so when she was home, Mickey appeased her by diligently playing hymns like "Amazing Grace" and "The Old Rugged Cross."

Irene could hear the sounds coming from the other room. While he still hit wrong notes, they were fewer and further between. To Irene, the music was perfect. As Mickey pounded out the melody of "Standing on the Promises," she could imagine him at the front of the church someday, playing piano, preaching the gospel, and pursuing the noble calling of ministering to his own church flock.

"Mickey," Irene said, "I'm goin' over to your Aunt Ada's for a little bit. There are cold pork chops in the kitchen if you get hungry."

As soon as his mother was out of earshot, Mickey stopped playing hymns. Within seconds, he was testing out the hand movements of the boogie-woogie music he had heard Jerry playing at Uncle Elmo and Aunt Mamie's house. Smiling, elated, he concentrated on the disparate movements of his left and right hands. The music fascinated him. He figured that he probably had an hour—forty-five minutes just to be safe—until his mama returned and he'd have to play those hymns again.

"But, man," he'd recall many years later, as he smiled his cheek-to-cheek grin, "when she'd leave, the boogie-woogie would roll!"

With Jerry leading the way, the lives of the three cousins revolved largely around music. They spent countless hours together, playing and showing off as Jimmy and Mickey did their best to keep up with Jerry and endure his ever-burgeoning ego.

At school, the three cousins would sit in class, staring up at the ceiling or down at the floor, counting the minutes until recess when they could head over to the gym. There, they'd gather around an old piano that had a key or two missing. Some of the other boys would join them as they played. The boys would alternate playing—

with Jerry usually taking center stage—while the others would circle around. Some would lean against the piano, watching the speed with which Jerry's fingers flew up and down the keys, as other boys would lounge about in chairs splayed haphazardly throughout the room.

The most significant piano influence on Jimmy and Mickey was the way Jerry played. Jerry was influenced by all sorts of music thanks to the radio, which had become a household necessity in the 1940s even for many homes in the impoverished rural South. The music came from places as far away as Baton Rouge and New Orleans and as nearby as Natchez, allowing Jerry to soak up a rich variety of jazz, country, gospel, and blues.

His favorite programs were the ones he'd listened to with his daddy, and included *The Grand Ole Opry*, established by the Nashville-based radio station WSM in 1925. Originated to boost advertising and sales for insurance peddled by the station's owner, *Opry* would become the most-listened-to music program in the country and the primary vehicle for country music artists to gain wide public appeal.

Another special program was *Louisiana Hayride*, patterned after *The Grand Ole Opry* and established by station KWKH of Shreveport, Louisiana, in 1948. These programs filled Jerry's head with the music of country artists Roy Acuff, Eddy Arnold, and Gene Autry, of bluegrass legends the Louvin Brothers, of R&B pianist-singer Fats Domino, and of rockabilly pioneer Merrill Moore. When it came to pure piano influences, one of the most significant was Moon Mullican, a Texas country-and-western performer who incorporated the rhythms of jazz and other musical styles.

Jerry and Jimmy were especially taken by the music of a local black man known to everyone in Ferriday as Old Sam. Whenever he was in the vicinity, the cousins would beg him to play for them. Old Sam affected Jimmy in particular. Although Jimmy was dedicated to his promise to play his music for God, he could not ignore the seductive, hypnotic effect of Old Sam's walking left hand on the piano. "He played with such swinging rhythm," Jimmy wrote years later. "It stirred something deep inside me. How I longed to play like that."

It seemed to Jimmy that Old Sam's left hand danced over the keys. He and Jerry would listen to him play for hours. Though he never taught them, they observed his technique and developed their left hands to play as much like Old Sam as possible.

Three performers affected Jerry most deeply, all of them men who struck him as artists who could stamp their own style and personality on every piece of music they performed. The first was Jimmie Rodgers, the Singing Brakeman, also known as the Father of Country Music. Rodgers was one of the early performers to break through in the 1920s, when his recording of "Blue Yodel"—better known as "T for Texas"—sold a stunning half-million copies.

The second was Al Jolson, a performer largely credited with introducing black music to white audiences during the 1920s. Jolson was exuberant, dynamic, and brash and the first singer to elevate a performance into a major event. He performed in the blackface style of the early twentieth century and revolutionized jazz, blues, and ragtime. Singing songs such as "Swanee" and "My Mammy," Jolson affected scores of performers who came after him.

The most significant impact on Jerry came from Hank Williams, whose voice Jerry first heard in the late 1940s on *Louisiana Hayride*. He knew instantly that Williams was a major talent. But he heard something more: the voice of a man who sang from a haunted place deep within himself, whose music was informed by the struggles and pains of his life. Williams sang for all the hurting people and moved his listeners in ways profound, even spiritual.

Hank Williams lived fast and hard, and it showed on his fragile body and ravaged face. Even in his early twenties he had the face of a man decades older than he was—or would ever live to be. Growing up in the Deep South, Hank's fascination with music was nurtured in all the usual places: at his mother's side singing church music, peeking in the windows of black and white churches, catching the lively music emanating from unruly roadhouses, and listening in on Saturday-night dances while he stole sips of alcohol.

A trying youth followed by an equally trying marriage taught Williams about the many forms of human suffering. The only comfort he found was the kind that came from a bottle.

Williams was a once-in-a-lifetime singer and songwriter, and when he was clean and sober, his potential was limitless. Yet by the age of twenty he was already an alcoholic and causing substantial damage to his career.

"You've got a million-dollar voice, son," he was told by Roy Acuff, one of his idols, "but a ten-cent brain."

Still, no one denied Williams's magical presence, a charisma and confidence born of years of performing on street corners and traveling dark Alabama roads in his Packard to the next fightin' and dancin' hall. Every week, he sang as a featured act on *Louisiana Hayride*. Elmo and Jerry looked forward to Saturday nights when Williams' scratchy, mournful, crooning voice came over the airwaves, a voice that could be sharp as an arrow or gentle as a caress.

Williams died at the age of twenty-nine on a cold, dark New Year's morning. He was discovered by his driver, who had reached back from the front seat to replace the blanket that had fallen from him. He touched a hand that had gone completely cold. The driver sped ahead to the next town for medical help, but all that he got was a death pronouncement. Somewhere in the night, rolling over the hilly roads of West Virginia, Hank Williams's soul had slipped quietly into the night, leaving behind a battered body, a broken heart, and a legacy that decades later still generates by far the most interest from visitors to the Country Music Hall of Fame, and secures his place as the poet laureate of country music.

When Elmo learned of his death, he wondered whether a man would ever again come along who could sing in such a deep, real fashion about the pain and struggle of everyday people.

Haney's Big House stood at the corner of Fourth Street and Carolina Avenue in Bucktown, a few blocks from where Mickey lived. Haney's was where black people went to listen to blues musicians and singers. They performed late into the night, in a dimly-lit room filled with the cigarette smoke of customers downing whiskey after whiskey. During the 1940s and 1950s, Haney's drew crowds from hundreds of miles around, from places like Monroe and Baton Rouge and New Orleans and Shreveport. The mastermind and personality behind the Big House was Will Haney, successful during a time when a black man was hard-pressed to get a step ahead. Raised dirt poor, too embarrassed to attend his own high-school graduation because he didn't have the proper attire, Haney had decided that he was going to be somebody.

Starting with a small food stand where he sold hot dogs and hamburgers from a window, his business interests evolved and expanded. Over the years, Haney engaged in many business pursuits, including selling insurance in Ferriday. But the expansion of his little food business into Haney's Big House would produce his legacy.

Haney's attracted a who's who of musicians: Blues Boy (B. B.) King, Muddy Waters, Ray Charles, Bobby "Blue" Bland, Sunnyland Slim, and many, many more. Their appearances at the Big House resulted from Ferriday's location along the "Chitlin' Circuit," which black musicians played as they moved from Chicago to St. Louis to Memphis to New Orleans. These musicians needed a place to stay and there weren't many hotels in the South that would accommodate black folks. Haney put them up, right behind the club. He also had a venue that seated four to five hundred people, enabling musicians to make a wad of money on their traveling day.

Haney's was a club for blacks, but if a big name was coming in—a B. B. King or an Irma Thomas—Haney would rope off an area for whites who wanted to hear them. Some nights, especially Saturdays, the place got rowdy and trouble brewed. Fights broke out all the time, but Haney kept any violence contained within his four walls. He took special pains to ensure that disagreements did not cross racial lines, which would have devastated his business. White patrons would occasionally hear Haney remind his regular customers, "Don't bother these folks."

Haney's provided a blues education for Jerry, whose disinterest in books and traditional learning was equaled by his curiosity, passion, and sponge-like absorption of all things rhythmic. Though minors were not allowed into Haney's, the venue made a special exception for Jerry, and he was allowed to watch from a little window that looked in on the club. He would listen, wide-eyed and excited as black music, with its distinctive energy and beat, worked its way into his being.

Jimmy was equally drawn to the music at Haney's, finding it intoxicating, but his parents' stern warnings about good and evil made Haney's as much a source of guilt as it was pleasure. Jimmy was seeing the world as his parents saw it: a place in which things were one or the other—and the freewheeling Haney's Big House had too many characteristics of evil. That meant the music was evil too, although Jimmy couldn't dismiss it entirely. Ever since he gave himself to the Lord, he had been subject to an internal tug-of-war that pulled him between right and wrong, between the sacred and the profane. Depending on which part of him was winning, he might sneak down to Haney's with Jerry, or he might avoid it.

Mickey was a different story. He tended not to push the limits or break the rules. "I never did get very involved with Haney's Big House," he said years later. "I stayed away from it. I was too much of a mama's boy."

C'mon, Mickey," Jerry said one day. "Nobody's gonna know about it. We'll slip over to Haney's and be back before Aunt 'Rene notices. Your daddy won't say nothin' in front of your mama, but he probably don't even care."

Mickey could be convinced of many things by his willful, high-spirited, determined cousin. He appeared to ignore Jerry, but his mind buzzed and turned, searching for an easy, believable way out.

"You never go with us," Jerry went on. "Man, with all that bangin' on the piano we do, don't you want to see how they play down in Bucktown?"

Mickey was not going to Haney's. His mother would kill him if he went and she found out. He had already let his cousins talk him into enough things about which he felt uncomfortable—taking too many crazy risks on their bikes, picking on the younger cousins, sneaking off without his mother knowing about it—and he wasn't about to get caught up in the mess down there at Haney's.

Jerry kept pushing him.

"Jimmy used to feel guilty, too, but you don't see him getting all uptight about it, do you?"

Jimmy had his mind on something else, as he usually did. He couldn't keep up with the machine-gun fire of Jerry's talking and had long ago stopped trying. Truth was, he felt sorry for Mickey; Jimmy had his own feelings of guilt about sneaking out of the house and heading the dozen or so blocks southeast to poke his head into Haney's Big House to witness that wild, rollicking scene. The colored folk in Ferriday and from long distances away packed into the place—some spilling out onto Fourth Street. The drinking, dancing, and music had to be of the devil. There was no doubt about it in Jimmy's mind. The place embodied every vice that they had been warned about. How in the world could Jerry ignore those warnings so easily?

That music was something else. The sound and rhythm and beat were so alive, so real. Jerry just couldn't get enough. Jimmy loved the music too, and Jerry knew it. On many nights, he could coax his older, more serious cousin down to the corner of Fourth and Carolina. If not, Jerry was fine going alone. He and Mr. Haney had a deal: Haney wouldn't tell anybody that Jerry had been there, and Jerry would stay out of the way and mind his own business. He would be quiet as he watched that piano man whose fingers looked a million years old, gnarled from the countless tons of cotton he had picked through the years.

"I'll swing by and get Jimmy and we'll head across Mississippi Avenue to your place and we'll tap on the glass for you, Mickey."

"Jerry, I'm not goin'. You two go without me. I don't want to get down there around all that foolishness in the middle of the night. Somebody's liable to start fightin' over some woman and the next thing you know, somebody will start shootin'. I can hear that stuff from my house sometimes. No way I'm goin' down there. Stop buggin' me about it."

Late that evening, Jerry and Jimmy walked quietly through town. As they drew nearer to Haney's, the sounds of blues and boogie-woogie floated along the nighttime breeze. They saw or heard an occasional couple that had gone off to be alone. They heard a fight brewing out front as they eased down Fifth Street and behind Haney's to perch at their usual viewing point. They felt perfectly safe, knowing that Mr. Haney had made it clear that the Lewis boy and his Swaggart cousin who sometimes tagged along were to be left alone.

Jimmy felt a thrill mixed with a sense of fear as he leaned in and watched. He felt like two different people. Once again, he was confronted with the prospect that everything in life was a constant battle between good and evil. Sitting here, watching people sing, dance, gamble, drink, and generally carry on frightened him even as it pulled on him in some strange way. Sometimes the discomfort it produced would lead him to abandon Jerry and run home, seeking safety and protection from that feeling.

As he peered through the open windowsill near the musicians, Jerry felt he was in the only school where he belonged. What he heard exploded in his ears and produced a symphonic kaleidoscope, a limitless range of excitements and emotions. The pull on him to this scene was so great, he knew it had to be part of his destiny. He loved it all: the musicians lost in their sounds, the emotions they evoked in the audience, the cheers, and especially the applause.

Jerry already knew he could play as well as these musicians— no, he could play even better, and every day he was producing a sound that was more and more distinctly his own. Sure, he wanted to play to please God but, more than that, he wanted to play for people and have them adore him—adore his talent, his spirit, his originality.

By now he knew that music was his gift, the only way he would ever receive the adoration he craved.

Another major influence on Jerry and his cousins was the high-octane gospel music of the Pentecostal church, which took sacred music and hymns and gave them a hard beat, a fast rhythm, and an ecstatic, lively worship style. It was music that brought worshippers to a state of heightened praise through the driving beat and sound of the music.

Many denominations devoted ten minutes of an hour-long church service to music. A ninety-minute Pentecostal service often had fifty minutes of music that included congregational singing, choir performances, solos, offertories, and even interruption of the sermon for spontaneous singing. Among the Pentecostals dwelt a conscious desire to emerge from the traditional reverent and earnest hymns and cut loose with music that featured dance instruments such as the banjo and fiddle—music geared to bring the congregants to an ecstatic state.

Those within Pentecostal churches with musical talent were esteemed, encouraged, and given high standing in the church hierarchy. Religious music in the South had an added dimension. It existed largely to help poor, rural Southerners cope with the frustration and desperation of their day-to-day existence. Accordingly, what the cousins found in Pentecostal church music was a connection to their spirituality, a way to break through personal barriers to reach a heightened sense of euphoria.

Growing up in this environment, in this church, the cousins were inculcated with this music, and beyond that, with the extravagant physicality of preachers who responded to the driving rhythms by gyrating, jumping, moving their hips, and stamping their feet. Over at the Assembly of God church in Tupelo, Mississippi—and later in Memphis—the moves of these preachers were making an impression on another young man whose name was Elvis Presley. In fact, church music moved Elvis so much that he considered becoming a gospel singer.

Around the same time in Macon, Georgia, another attentive churchgoer, Richard Penniman, grooved to gospel music and took in the gospel-infused sounds of the jump-blues artist Billy Wright. What he heard from Wright would affect Richard deeply, and would be heard in his music when he began cutting records as Little Richard.

Like Elvis and Little Richard, the more Jerry heard church music, the more he got revved up.

– 11 –

MOTHERS AND SONS

It's said the hand the rocks the cradle rules the world, and that held true when it came to Mamie Lewis, Minnie Bell Swaggart, and Irene Gilley.

Given Mamie's strong personality and Elmo's absences early in Jerry's childhood, there had never been any question about who ruled the Lewis household. Mamie domineered. When she spoke, Jerry listened.

For all that Mamie bossed Jerry, she also worshipped him. Throughout the five years between Elmo Jr.'s death and the birth of Frankie Jean, Jerry was an only child and the focal point of Mamie's existence. He was also the one person over whom she could exert control in a world that struck her as fearfully difficult to manage.

Years later Jerry's third wife, Myra, would write about his relationship with Mamie. "His mother became his sole influence. She was his counselor, coach, teacher, preacher, and best friend. Her preferences became his; her fears were deeply ingrained into his conscience. Mamie drew Jerry closer to her during the absence of her husband. The loss of her firstborn made her remaining son dearer still. If Elmo would not do right by her, she would make sure that he would never disappoint her."

Once Mamie realized that Jerry had rare, abundant musical talent, her preoccupation with him increased and everyone in the family noted her obsession with him. Other mothers might adore their sons—but to Mamie, Jerry was more important to her than anything, or anyone, else.

One day, Mamie's brothers and sisters—and their families—congregated inside the Lewis home while, as usual, the kids were expected to migrate outdoors and entertain themselves. Most were Jerry's cousins, but others were there as well. Jerry led the pack. Two-year-old Frankie Jean, still too young to be turned loose with the older kids, stayed in the house with her mama.

Outside, one of the older boys came up with an idea that must have seemed appealing enough, because moments later they were crowded around Jake Herron, Henry Herron's son, who was several years younger than most of the boys. "Jake, you hide in this box and stay real quiet, OK?"

After some coaxing, Jake sat quietly inside a large box that the other boys dragged into the middle of the gravel road. They thought it was funny and they weren't thinking about consequences. Several minutes later, the box—with Jake in it—was shoved down the road by a truck that luckily had a high front bumper and was traveling at a low rate of speed. As the boys saw the box pushed along by the truck, the idea of having Jake in it seemed much less appealing. Somehow, little Jake escaped with no more than a few scrapes and cuts.

Mamie and her sisters and brothers were enraged at the foolish and dangerous prank, and when Mamie and Elmo demanded that Jerry explain how this could have happened, he ascribed himself a less central role than he'd actually had.

He engaged in a similar stunt trying to rid himself of Frankie Jean, whom he perceived as the constant annoyance that younger siblings so often become. One day when Frankie was five and Jerry was barely in his teens, he convinced his sister to let him push her along for an exciting ride in the baby carriage. She was too big to fit in it, but she could straddle the sides and that was fine with Jerry, who had had enough of his strong-willed sister and decided to rid himself of her—by pushing the carriage right off the side of a hill into a deep ravine.

For Frankie, it was a terrifying ride into the jaws of a yawning, snake-infested pit. "It took me nearly an hour to dig myself out of the vines and brambles," she recalled years later, "but I made it!" Seeing her mother administer a rare act of corporal punishment to the golden child was nearly worth the ordeal.

These events brought attention to Jerry's dangerous, often self-defeating impulsiveness and his recurring tendency to follow through on any idea that popped into his head, without regard for the consequences. For the rest of his life, that tendency that would remain within him—for better and for worse.

As Frankie got older she would, on occasion, ask why her older brother was not required to work, clean, and help with chores, only to be told by an unapologetic Mamie that a different standard applied to Jerry. There's a story that relates to this, which may be apocryphal but is still instructive: When Jerry was a teenager, it's said, Elmo and Mamie were out in the fields picking cotton while Frankie was busy tending to her little sister, Linda Gail. Jerry drove by, saw them, and exclaimed, "Work, you peasants! I am the Great I Am!"

Whether or not this actually happened, there's no doubt that Jerry had an exceptionally high opinion of himself, and that Mamie agreed wholeheartedly with his assessment.

One evening, five-year-old Frankie stood on her trusty stool in the family's small kitchen. From her perch, she could reach the counter and help her mama with a variety of tasks. She could peel potatoes and carrots, set the table, clean up after everyone, or babysit two-year-old Linda Gail. Now she was busy with the rolling pin her mother had given her, spreading out biscuit dough while keeping watch on the baby, whose large dark eyes were focused on her rag doll. As usual, Frankie heard piano music coming from the next room—that constant, incessant, never-ending piano playing.

"Mamie, would you listen to this boy," Frankie heard her father say. "He's a natural, I'm telling you."

Mamie wiped her strong hands on a white dish towel and sauntered from the kitchen into the other room. As Jerry waited for her praise, his face lit up with a grin that was at once sly and sheepish. He never grew tired of his parents' adulation. Both had enough musical ability and taste to recognize talent when they heard it, and in their son they heard great promise. They had instilled in him a confidence about his musical prowess and pretty much everything else.

Mamie walked over to Jerry and placed a hand on his shoulder. For all her hard work and hardship, she was still a pretty woman, her nice figure accentuated by her simple flowered dress. "That was so good, Jerry," she said, "You're somethin' special. You play music second to none. It gets inside me, especially those slow, sad ones."

Mamie took Jerry's hands in hers. "Look at those hands," she said. "Those fingers are so graceful. Perfect. Everything about you is made to play piano and make music, son. You have a gift—a God-given gift. People from all over are going to listen to your music. You will be great. Never forget for what you are meant."

Elmo nodded proudly, serving as the "amen corner" to Mamie's abbreviated sermon. This was so like other passionate soliloquies that had been delivered on many occasions in the years since Jerry had first touched piano keys. Thanks to his parents, Jerry was convinced that everyone who heard him play would recognize that he had found his own gift, his own miracle.

Frankie had heard endless praise cast in her brother's direction. Jerry was the golden child. Years later, she would look back on those years and the way that Mamie and Elmo reaped praise on him. "With all that attention, all that special treatment, Mama and Daddy put something inside of Jerry. In a way—in a nice way—they put hell in him."

Fourteen-year-old Cecil Harrelson was working in Duke's Department Store just across Louisiana Avenue from Pasternack's grocery store. Cecil's mother managed the store and he worked there off and on, among a variety of other jobs. The teenager didn't particularly like working at Duke's, preferring jobs that were outdoors or that he could perform with others his age. Even at this young age, Cecil had grown accustomed to a life full of work. It provided him a means to help his family and earn some spending money.

Short in stature, Cecil was nevertheless unusually strong for his size and age and had gained a reputation among all the kids in Ferriday—even the older ones—as a happy-go-lucky kid who nonetheless didn't mind a good fight and was not to be messed with.

On that uneventful afternoon, Jerry Lee Lewis sauntered down Louisiana, heading west, and happened by Duke's. Standing near the front door of the store, Cecil was pushing a broom when he saw his classmate and friend happening by some twenty-five feet away. "There goes the Killer!" he exclaimed jokingly, loud enough to catch his friend's attention outside.

Several women were milling about the department store, shopping, inspecting goods, or waiting to pay. The unexpected outburst from the young Harrelson boy alarmed them. One scurried behind the counter, ducking for cover. Another clutched her purse tightly. An older, buxom woman crept toward the door to get a hidden peek at the criminal outside. Each spoke excitedly and hurriedly, addressing no one in particular.

"Who's out there?"

"Is he coming this way?"

"Does he have a weapon?"

From his position near the door, Cecil had seen the commotion his words had wrought. Jerry, too, had become aware of the cacophony inside Duke's and as his eyes met Cecil's, their looks of surprise and mild alarm gave way to wide smiles and then bellowing laughs.

The nickname would follow Jerry the rest of his life. He would hear it countless times and respond to it with pride or disdain, depending on his mood. "There goes the Killer!"

As time went by, it became clear that Jerry's job was to play the piano in the hope and expectation that his hands could yield more on a keyboard than in a sweltering Delta cotton field. While Mamie wanted Jerry to use his talents for God, her broad tastes in music extended freedoms to Jerry that his cousin Jimmy would never enjoy, due to the stricter and narrower religious views of Minnie Bell. Though Mamie and Minnie Bell were sisters, their lives and beliefs had diverged. Minnie Bell was dedicated to the church and would proudly tell anyone that she'd given her life to the Lord, while Mamie, though also a churchgoing lady, was less convicted and far more lenient.

"My mother was devout," Jerry would say, "but also broad-minded. She never passed judgment on who was going to hell and who wasn't. The parents of Jimmy and Mickey were much stricter. I could have changed churches if I wanted to. Their parents would have killed them if they went to any church but the Pentecostal church."

Jerry was also close to another of his mother's sisters, his aunt Stella Herron Calhoun, another outspoken woman who offered strong opinions without reservation. In Jerry's world, the women were in charge. In his experience, men were unassertive, drank too much, or had too many women.

As role models go, the men in his life were not the best.

For Minnie Bell Swaggart, coming to the Assembly of God church proved transformative. It transformed her spiritually, and she became less prone to lock horns with Son Swaggart. She became quieter and slower to react to the circumstances around her, demonstrating more restraint and patience in her dealings with family and others. As expected, she became more prayerful and meditative, taking her concerns and worries to a higher power.

Even physically, the changes in Minnie Bell were dramatic. Previously, she had taken pride in her beautiful, wavy brown hair and svelte figure. With her submission to the Lord she gave up her bright red lipstick and fetching hats, as if seeking to make herself as plain as a pretty woman can be. Still, even with her face absent of make-up, a radiance hung about Minnie Bell that manifested in her shining eyes and glowing smile. Yet in church, seated beside Son and wearing unflattering rimless glasses, she looked like nothing more or less than the stereotypical sweet, conservative Pentecostal wife.

For all her sweetness, though, Minnie Bell was a driven woman, determined to spur every member of her immediate family into a life of serving God. From the day Jimmy made his vow to the Lord, she believed that her son was called to be an evangelist. She dressed him in white slacks and shirts and suits, and took ever-greater care over every move he made, every turn he took. She prayed for him unceasingly, especially late at night after he had gone to bed. She encouraged his careful attentiveness in church, celebrated quietly the stories he would relate from Sunday school, and thrilled to hear of his interest in things that happened within the thin white walls of the church house.

Jimmy wanted to please her, yet felt engulfed by her admonitions and wishes. He loved his mama but disliked being manipulated. He soon became rebellious, freighted with anger he wasn't free to express.

Minnie Bell's religious aspirations for her husband were realized when Jimmy was thirteen. That was when she and Son decided that he would give up the store he owned and operated—which had brought the family a modest level of financial security and standing in the community—and enter the ministry as a full-time preacher. Soon Son was preaching at churches in several counties and parishes, spanning all directions. He was adept at unleashing hellfire sermons. He also drew audiences with his musical ability and that of his family: Minnie Bell, Jimmy, and his seven-year-old sister, Jeannette.

Jimmy was concerned that his father's preaching would plunge the family back into the poverty they had so recently escaped. He wanted nothing to do with it. Now that his parents had finally achieved some economic standing in the community, he felt more "normal" than he ever had before. He worried that his parents' entry into full-time ministry would threaten their income and add to the already-heavy expectations they had placed on him. As time went on, he avoided singing and playing at his father's services.

Now that Jimmy and his cousins and friends had reached puberty, their interest in attending church lessened as their appetite for trouble increased. Many of the things that interest teenage boys—girls, hanging out with friends, and getting into occasional trouble—created an internal struggle for Jimmy, who had been taught that desires and interests that emanate from natural human tendencies were sinful and evil, both to the Assembly of God church and to his family.

Still, he spent less time in church. He watched more movies at the Arcade Theater and sneaked off more often to Haney's Big House. His partner in crime was often Jerry, who seemed good at finding trouble. The two cousins trolled about town, breaking into and robbing local stores, even victimizing their uncle and namesake, Lee Calhoun. The unsuspecting Calhoun, an experienced con artist himself, never realized he was buying his own stolen property when he purchased various items from his two nephews.

The boys loved talking to local police officers and town officials, inquiring whether anyone had clues to recent crimes—which they had committed. Finally, Jerry got caught breaking into a store on an evening when Jimmy wasn't with him. Most teenage boys would consider themselves the recipients of good luck. Jimmy Lee Swaggart interpreted this as a sign that God was showing patience with him and warning him to return to the fold of the godly.

Inherent in these scenes of young Swaggart's life was a constant theme of internal struggle. When he was walking the straight and narrow, he was confounded by human desire. When he succumbed to pressure and explored "worldly" interests, he was wracked with guilt.

Often Jimmy was at home alone as his father's preaching schedule increasingly took Son, Minnie Bell, and Jeannette away. Son preached at venues that were sometimes within driving distance from home, and sometimes in places that took them away for days at a time. Despite constant requests from his parents for Jimmy to join them in the services—partly to have him participate with the rest of the family musically, but also to have him stay close to the church influences so important to them—the teenager generally begged off.

When Jimmy knew his parents would be coming in late in the evening, he made sure to be in bed before their arrival. As he rustled in his bed, unable to sleep, he heard the hum of the car and the gravel crunching under the tires out front as Son parked. Jimmy knew his family would be tired after having driven many miles each way to and from the church where his father had preached that evening. Jimmy did not want to face their questions about his evening, or hear them talk about how the service had gone.

From the darkness of his room, Jimmy could hear Son's heavy steps as he carried the sleeping Jeannette in his arms, moving toward her room where he would ease her into her narrow bed and tuck her in. Jimmy could hear Minnie Bell ask in a hushed voice, "Do you want me to fix you something to eat?"

Son replied, "No, let's just go to bed. Mornin' will be here soon enough."

Moments later, Jimmy heard the door to his room opening quietly as Minnie Bell entered. He felt an odd mixture of comfort and dread at these times, which occurred frequently. He heard the familiar sound of his mother moving softly across the floor, her long dress rustling slightly as she drew nearer to his bedside. Jimmy watched her silhouette in the darkness. As he pretended to sleep, he opened his eyes a bit. His eyes having adjusted to the darkness, he could barely make out the soft countenance of Minnie Bell's face.

Quietly, confidently, as if talking to a wise, older relative, Minnie Bell prayed for Jimmy, as she had done so many times before. "God, you know I believe you have called him since he was a child," she began. As she spoke, she seemed to concentrate more with each word that left her lips, softly spoken but clearly audible. "Keep him close to you, Lord. Draw him back to you."

As the words poured forth from his mother, Jimmy felt a familiar feeling, an odd mixture of love and respect for his mother, coupled with a strong sense of discomfort at her words. When she finished and left the room, Jimmy felt hot tears on his cheeks— tears of conviction, tears for disappointing his mother, and tears of anger for being pulled in a direction that he just didn't want to go.

As Son and Minnie Bell kept watchful eyes on Jimmy, he feared doing anything of which they might disapprove, but he was so full of curiosity and so closely tied to his daredevil cousin Jerry, doing "bad" things was inevitable. Jimmy knew that his parents wouldn't approve of his running around town with no accountability, carousing with other kids and getting into mischief, or going to Haney's Big House. Still, he did these things and paid for them with pangs of guilt and the terrible fear of getting caught.

Minnie Bell sought to control him through guilt. She was so intent on what she wanted Jimmy to be that it never occurred to her that pushing him toward that goal was anything but acting in his best interest. The more she pushed, the more guilt he felt, and the more he wanted to do all the things that she deemed bad.

Reinforcing the push exerted by Minnie Bell was Jimmy's paternal grandmother, Ada Lewis Swaggart, who prayed that Jimmy would grow up to be a great preacher. Ada, who had been the first in the family to receive the Holy Spirit, constantly propelled Jimmy toward a life of service to God. Jimmy would remember his grandmother fondly in sermons decades later. "She was my Bible school, my seminary, my everything." Ada mentored the trial-and-error faith of her grandson in whom she sensed a gift, a special calling, placed on him by the Almighty Himself.

When she heard her grandson praying too timidly, she would take him aside, telling him, "Jimmy, don't pray like that, boy. Pray just like this." The lanky, tall woman with the bright smile and penetrating eyes would get down on her knees, showing him how to pray earnestly, with great candor and concentration. When she finished she would turn to Jimmy, and with a perfect blend of boldness and humility, she would tell him, "God is a big God, Jimmy. So you've gotta ask big."

Jimmy learned to pray boldly. On many occasions, Ada would say, "Jimmy, don't just ask God for the possible. Ask Him for the impossible." From her example, he gained the unshakable confidence of his grandmother that God was really there, listening, taking an interest, willing to help.

Most boys want to please their parents and grandparents. Jimmy knew that the only path to pleasing Ada and Son and Minnie Bell ran through God and the Assembly of God church. It was a high calling, and a difficult one to navigate for a boy who sought to be holy even in the wake of the natural appetites that come with youth and burgeoning maturity.

Mickey, the self-admitted mama's boy, was the sweetest of the cousins. His closeness to his mother and dependence on her were so great that he missed a portion of his first year of school. Irene was older than his cousins' mothers and he worried about her all the time. *If anything happens to her,* he'd often think, *there's no telling what will happen to me.*

When Mickey was little, he constantly hung onto his mama's dress, never wanting her out of his sight. He was shy and timid in many ways, but as long as his mama was with him, he felt all right. Even as an adult he would describe her as having been "the only person in my life." They were, he believed, "like a lioness and her cub."

As Mickey grew older, his mother remained the overwhelming presence in his life, and his guiding influence. Arthur, his father, was quiet when he was home and left his son's rearing to Irene. Mickey looked to Arthur for his allowance and turned to his mother for everything else.

The church had made a dramatic impact in Irene's life, and while Mickey adored his mama, he didn't like certain key tenets of the Assembly of God faith. He didn't like that his mama refused to cut her hair or wear lipstick that would make her look pretty. He didn't like that most who attended their church asserted that if he went to the Arcade Theater and saw a Roy Rogers and Gene Autry movie and then died that night, he would burn in hell forever.

Irene and Ada were strong women, but quiet in their strength. They prayed with heart and passion. Other family members noted that if you prayed kneeling in between those two women, you would feel God's presence. Irene's dearest dream was that Mickey would be a minister and use his piano talent in the praise of the Lord. Still, she never pushed him to serve God in the unrelenting way that Minnie Bell and Ada pushed Jimmy.

Southern mothers are encouraged, even expected, to spoil and coddle their sons. They brag endlessly about their boys and nurture the hope that they were meant for greatness. The sons, for their part, worship their mamas as the most significant and powerful force in the universe—with the sole exception of God.

For that reason, Jerry, Jimmy, and Mickey did what they could to please their mothers, yet they knew that they could never be quite as good as their mamas wanted them to be.

– 12 –

EARLY PERFORMANCES

Before long, word got around Ferriday that young Jerry Lee Lewis, local mischief maker, had a way with a piano. Jerry was primed and eager to show off his skills to as many people as possible. His first opportunity came in 1949 when some local auto merchants staged a promotion in front of the Babin-Ford dealership in the center of town and hired a band to play there.

The band quickly drew a crowd and in that crowd were Jerry and Elmo. Seeing them, the owner of the dealership thought it might be nice to give young Jerry Lee Lewis an opportunity to play.

Jerry climbed up onto the back of a pickup bed and sat down at the piano. He gazed out at a sea of familiar faces. Now, he thought, it was his time to show them how a piano is meant to be played. He poised his hands over the keys, and grinned. Then he slammed both hands down on the keys as he beat out the sounds of "Hadacol Boogie" and "Drinkin' Wine Spo-dee-o-dee," a song that Old Sam played frequently. His left hand pounded out the rhythm while his right hand floated all over the keys, adding trills and touches to these familiar tunes all the while stunning the audience and giving a first, tantalizing vision of what could be. The admiring upturned faces were a tonic to him, teaching him in a matter of minutes how his music could capture people. He finished to a burst of applause that he answered with a sly, knowing grin. Then a hat was passed, and as he and Elmo drove away, he counted out thirteen dollars, each nickel and quarter bolstering his nascent sense that playing piano was his calling.

Soon there were more local appearances. He performed at another automobile dealership where, when new model automobiles came out, they'd have hot dogs and balloons and candy and entertainment. Jerry had a bad habit of stealing batteries out of automobiles and agreed to play as penance for being caught by the dealership's owner. His talent as a young maestro offset the punishment he would have otherwise met.

Jerry's style was no-holds-barred, as hard physically on a piano as a boy of slight build could manage. He played with intensity, ferocity, viciousness, like one possessed by the music inside him. Locals marveled at the way he could beat the hell out of a piano, how he could play until the keys literally came off.

Within a year of his debut performance Jerry had worked himself up to having a thirty-minute show every Saturday afternoon on radio station WNAT in Natchez, just across the state line. His family and friends in Concordia Parish, by way of support, sent dozens of postcards to the station each week, raving about his performances.

Jerry and his buddy Cecil Harrelson went down to New Orleans. In the Big Easy, he made his first recording, having paid two dollars for the privilege of squeezing himself into a small booth and making an acetate record of "Please Don't Stay Away Too Long." He had no particular plans for the recording. He simply wanted to hear how his voice sounded on a record and was thrilled with the result, rough though it was. He gave the record to his buddy Cecil who kept it as a prized possession for the next sixty-plus years (losing it for many years in the record jacket of another performer).

Back home he appeared in local talent shows. On many Saturday afternoons, Elmo and Mamie would arrange their family responsibilities and their work—cotton picking and carpentry work when possible—to fit with Jerry's schedule. They made sure that he was dressed and ready to go to talent shows in larger cities like

Monroe and Alexandria and smaller, nearby towns like Natchez and Jonesville.

Even as early as eleven and twelve years old, Jerry was developing into a showman who did things that other talent show contestants wouldn't dream of and wouldn't dare. He'd tear the piano up and kick it and sometimes play it with his bare feet. His hands moved in ways that were machine-gun fast yet always precise. The wilder he became, the wilder the applause, and this wasn't lost on a boy who played piano partly because it was in his blood and partly because it garnered praise and attention.

He won these local contests so often that eventually he was prohibited from entering them. He was transforming from a local attraction to a local phenomenon.

Jerry was getting dressed for a talent show down in Jonesville, sixteen miles west of Ferriday. He took off his worn everyday clothes and put on his one decent pair of slacks and a crisp shirt. This time Jimmy would be coming, too, and Jerry was glad for his company and equally glad to have one more person to impress.

"Come on, Jerry, hurry up!" yelled Elmo as he stood waiting beside his old car. "We're gonna be late and we still need to pick up Jimmy Lee." Mamie was already ensconced in the passenger side of the front seat and Frankie Jean and Linda Gail were seated in the back. Jerry stumbled from the house, licking his fingers and rubbing his hair, trying to make it lay down in accordance with Mamie's wishes. He hopped into the back seat of the car, excited to head out.

They picked up Jimmy outside his little house just a few blocks west and started off on what proved to be a noisy ride. Jimmy, who was quieter than his cousins, listened to them banter while he and Jerry talked about who else might show up that night for the talent competition, who might stand the best chance of winning, and what songs each contestant might play.

Jerry played well that night, as usual, exhibiting once again the skills that already set him apart from other musicians, as his hands found and left the keys with lightning quickness. On this night, he banged and pounded and played with ferocity.

Then it was Jimmy's turn. As the more solemn and serious of the cousins ran his fingers up and down the piano, a strange feeling overtook him and allowed his hands to fly over the keys with increased ease. It was something he had felt before, but this time it was stronger than usual. As he played the notes of "Drinkin' Wine Spo-dee-o-dee," he found himself able to execute runs on the piano that he'd never pulled off before. The crowd was cheering as Jimmy's hands moved across the keys, and he sensed he had been taken over by a force he could not explain.

For Jerry, such a happening would have been exhilarating, but for Jimmy it took on dark and fearsome undertones, for it seemed to him that he was being anointed by the devil. Then he finished and the crowd cheered, standing and clapping and whistling. Jimmy tried to smile in acknowledgement but he was terrified.

This would happen again over the years on the rare occasions when Jimmy played—or even heard—secular music. Though he saw it as the devil's anointing, there were other elements at work: his guilt over using his music for worldly purposes after committing to play only for the glory of God mixed with the grinding self-doubt that kept him from risking defeat or failure.

Because of the family's dire financial situation and Jerry's own unquenchable thirst for the excitements of the night scene, he began working at honky-tonks and bars when he was fourteen. His first gig was at the Hilltop Club in Natchez. He also played in the Under-The-Hill section of Natchez at the Blue Cat Club and across town in Natchez at the Wagon Wheel, dangerous places where men went to get drunk, raise hell, and howl at the moon. Fights broke out constantly and when the authorities showed up to quell them, Jerry would have to hide because he was underage and wasn't supposed to be there at all, much less performing.

In these dark, dirty, hell-raising clubs, Jerry Lee Lewis was exposed to more than music. He observed men searching for temporary respite from their struggling lives. He watched as the liquor they drank manifested in sorrow, sullenness, inhibition, temporary joy, and pure meanness. He watched women ply their wares to get what they wanted, searching for a man to entertain them, if only for an evening.

Jerry was also exposed to something else. His initial experience seemed so harmless at the time, but would lead him down disastrous pathways. In these clubs he had his first taste of drugs.

When long-haul truck drivers and locals saw him tiring in the wee hours of the morning, they offered him a variety of stimulants in the form of tiny capsules of Benzedrine that they called bennies. Jerry quickly felt the effects of the pharmaceuticals. One little pill would wake him up. Two would make him feel real good. When he took the third one, he found euphoria. Hell, with the effects of three of these coursing through his veins, he was convinced he could whip every man's ass in this place if he wanted to. Never mind that he was a scrawny kid in the midst of grown men. Thanks to the pills, Jerry felt bulletproof.

All this was a significant departure from Jimmy's world and even more so from that of Mickey Gilley, who would never go to the Blue Cat Club, much less be employed there.

So while Jerry played and Jimmy agonized, young Mickey went to school, rode his motorbike and spent time with his cousins, all while avoiding the pitfalls of teen trouble. He didn't rob stores or steal hubcaps, and he didn't go to Haney's Big House. More careful and cautious than his cousins, he was also less conflicted.

As Jerry and Jimmy dreamed of getting rich and made plans to form a band that would perform and travel, Mickey rejected their offers to be part of a trio. He was happy to play the piano with them, he said, but he had little interest in playing clubs or in traveling to other towns.

Mickey's sheltered, even mundane life was typical of a cautious mama's boy in small-town, post-World War II America. As a teenager, Mickey held jobs here and there to scrape together extra spending money. He worked as an electrician's apprentice for a time. He also labored for the local power company, responsible primarily for rolling wire and keeping the supply yard clean, all for the princely sum of fifty cents an hour.

He spent his spare time after school at the local pool hall owned and operated for a time by his father. Much of Mickey's teenage fun revolved around getting from place to place on his motorbike and much of his focus was on earning extra money to buy gas and to spend in the places he visited on his bike. Mickey's motorbike could not keep up with the motor scooter Jerry had for a time, but it was more reliable, less likely to be in disrepair, and what hurry was he in anyway?

– 13 –

FIRST WIVES
AND FIRST FORAYS

In late 1951, Jewell Barton came to Ferriday to preach at the Assembly of God church. The reverend's fifteen-year-old daughter, Dorothy, was a church-raised, proper young lady who had little experience with boys, especially wild ones like Jerry Lee Lewis. She was pretty with long, dark hair and Jerry was smitten with her from the moment he saw her. Dorothy was instantly charmed by the brash sixteen-year-old who was maturing into a slender, good-looking kid with blonde, naturally wavy hair that he combed back over his head.

Within a few months they were married and Dorothy's parents were distraught, though according to the Southern customs of the day marrying at such young ages was not unusual. Jerry sought to be a reliable, faithful husband but found it all too easy to forget his marriage vows when tempted in other directions. Performing in clubs meant that he was tempted frequently, and soon he was staying out all night with his pal Cecil Harrelson and letting his eyes wander to other women. This behavior was not at all what Dorothy's conservative Christian upbringing had led her to expect from her husband.

In the summer of 1952, Son Swaggart was preaching at a church in Wisner, Louisiana, about thirty miles north of Ferriday. Jimmy had become a reluctant attendee at church, but he went along occasionally to avoid the ire of his parents.

His sister Jeanette kept telling him about this pretty fourteen-year-old girl she had met in Wisner, but Jimmy had no time for girls. By then, having turned seventeen, he had two main endeavors: playing the piano and throwing dice and playing other games of chance to make money. If gambling was a sin, it didn't seem that way to Jimmy, who had gotten into the habit of gambling all night and sleeping during the day. On this particular Sunday morning he managed to haul himself out of bed and head off to the church in Wisner to take a look at this pretty girl Jeanette kept telling him about.

The girl was Frances Orelia Anderson. Though her family members were not regular churchgoers, she sang in the choir. Frances was an attractive girl with dark, big eyes and thick, full hair.

She had been raised in a tumultuous environment, with a troubled father and a family that was the poorest of the poor. Compared to her own family, the Swaggart family was a huge step up, which was quite a statement considering the low regard in which Holy Roller families like the Swaggarts, Lewises, and Gilleys were often held.

Frances was quiet, observant, and attentive. As Jimmy's mother once had, she longed for a better life, a fairytale far away from the struggle she had endured. Her difficult childhood endowed her with another trait that would eventually be crucial to Jimmy: Frances was tough, gritty as the Louisiana land from which she had come. When a challenge was to be faced she was hard as nails, never backing down. It was a characteristic that would become more ingrained in time.

Jimmy was drawn to her good looks and quiet watchfulness and she was transfixed by him, especially when he sought to impress her by playing a piano solo for the congregation. Their courtship progressed quickly. When it became clear that her parents didn't approve of them dating and certainly didn't want their daughter involved with a Pentecostal—those demonstrative, rollicking, tongue-talking churchgoers down at the Assembly of God church—Jimmy found a good use for his persuasive skills and talked her mother into letting them see each other.

After three months, they were making wedding plans and Jimmy, having lied about both of their ages, bought a marriage license.

On October 10, 1952, seventeen-year-old Jimmy Swaggart married fifteen-year-old Frances Anderson. They were the same ages that Jimmy's parents had been when they married. As Jimmy was frequently to say of Frances over the years, "She was fifteen—and not pregnant."

Early on, finances necessitated that they live with Son and Minnie Bell. After a time, they moved to a small trailer in Irene Gilley's yard.

After months of struggling to be a responsible adult and husband—with mixed success at best—Jerry determined to convince himself and those around him that he could lead a "respectable" life. To demonstrate his intentions, he and Dorothy hopped on a bus to Waxahachie, Texas, thirty miles south of Dallas, where Jerry, who repeatedly claimed that his real ambition was to be a minister, had enrolled in Bible college.

Nothing about the church-supported campus was a natural fit for Jerry. Having recently dropped out of high school in Ferriday, he found the curriculum of present-day Southwestern Assemblies of God College no more interesting or compelling than any other subject forced upon him in school.

Within days, he lost interest in schooling. Within weeks, he had found his way out of the rigidity and self-denial of this small world and was skipping classes, spending time with a female "study buddy" and running off to the night life of Fort Worth and Dallas. In short order, a dejected, embarrassed Dorothy was on a bus back to Ferriday.

Not long after, Jerry managed to book his own passage home. It happened on an evening like many others at the college. In the packed auditorium, the young women in their modest dresses and the young men in their slacks, buttoned-down shirts, and ties sat upright and rigid as they listened to an evening of exhortations, speeches, and sermons that were part of the training they were receiving to become men and women serving God. For many, church attendance was their earliest life memory. Along with eating, sleeping, and staying warm in cold winters and cool in blazing summers, church services were as everyday an occurrence as drawing breath.

Following a familiar message about duty, discipline, and devotion, the seventeen-year-old Jerry Lee Lewis made his way to the piano to accompany a classmate slated to sing. As far as the other students were concerned his three months on campus had been unremarkable by any measure. Many students were not quite sure what to make of this odd teenager from eastern Louisiana with the wavy blond hair, who seemed swallowed up in a suit that was much too big for his slight, skinny frame, and whose countenance always seemed to be just on the verge of a sneer.

As his fingers hit the keys, the riveting sound they produced sent a jolt through the audience, as if he were instilling life into those assembled there. As Jerry launched into the first verse of "My God Is Real," a song he had learned back in the Assembly of God Church, a power emanated from him that seemed quite implausible coming from the lanky kid they had just seen shuffle across the platform.

> *There are some things I may not know*
> *There are some places I can't go*
> *But I am sure of this one thing*
> *My God is real for I can feel him in my soul.*

As he finished up the chorus and headed into the second verse, his hands moved faster on the keys. Any attempt to slow them down would be like pulling hard on the reins of a thoroughbred whose natural, instinctive thrust was to run. The quicker his hands flew the more he could feel the blood coursing through his veins. A thin smile crossed his face, that smile that appeared when he recognized anew the natural fit between his being and this style of music.

Many of the students were visibly appreciative of the beat, the excitement, the feelings of exultation that he evoked from them. Other students, wide-eyed and mildly shocked, didn't understand what they were seeing or hearing, but they knew that whatever it was made them uncomfortable and fearful. Many in the faculty and administration could not find anything redeeming in Brother Lewis's rendition of this song.

Jerry reeled through the chorus a second time, moving at a steady, aggressive pace, both hands playing the boogie woogie that was a natural expression of his hands, his music, and his soul:

My God is real, he's real in my soul
My God is real for he has washed and made me whole
His love for me is like pure gold
My God is real for I can feel him in my soul.

His hands banging away now, part of Jerry knew that this music, the music to which he was called, for which he was destined, would never be the music of respectable church folks, even respectable folks in the disrespected world of Pentecostalism. He knew how this music made him feel. He saw the joy it brought to many in the audience. Then he looked at the stern and disapproving faces around them and thought, *Man, this is happy music, and these people need to get happy.*

Immediately following the performance the dean approached him. Jerry saw the look of displeasure on his face. He was told to come to the dean's office the following day where, before his arrival, the dean and other administrators—after much weeping and gnashing of teeth—had opted for a one-month suspension in favor of the outright expulsion that some supported.

For Jerry, their disapproval was a clear sign that he was in the wrong place and he decided to cut his losses.

As the bus carried him through the piney woods of East Texas and western Louisiana into the familiar lowlands of his upbringing, Jerry contemplated his situation. Clearly, there was a deep, irreconcilable conflict between those who opted for a "traditional" Christian lifestyle and the wild streak that flowed through him and the tempestuous music that flowed from him.

He wasn't old enough or mature enough to have any sense of how to mesh these two powerful forces, but the conflict that arose from them—the age-old conflict between the sacred and the pro-fane—was one that he would struggle with for many years to come.

Mickey faced his own dead end in Ferriday. Like his two cousins, he had dropped out of high school before graduating. His mama wasn't happy about it, though she was aware that formal education had never played much of a role in the development of her family members. Job opportunities were limited and so were his skills to break the cycle of poverty.

Mickey was seventeen when he met and fell in love with Geraldine Garrett. In March 1953, the young couple exchanged wedding vows. After the marriage, he followed her family to Houston, where his father-in-law had pull in the construction industry and landed Mickey a job laying sanitary sewers. It was not quite what Mickey had hoped for. "I was an oiler," he would say later, "a grease monkey, really."

Like any other seventeen-year-old, Mickey's focus was short term. He worked because he had to and his need for work increased when his son Michael was born the year following his marriage.

Shortly after Jerry returned to Ferriday from Bible college and tried to make up with Dorothy, he met the fun-loving, vivacious Jane Mitcham in a Natchez club. He began spending time with her, and the relationship—at least the physical one—moved rapidly. While Dorothy had been the "good" church girl whose lack of adventurous spirit had a difficult time keeping up with Jerry, Jane had no such hesitancy. Soon, Jane was pregnant and her angry brothers were tracking Jerry down, demanding that he do what had to be done for an "honorable" solution. Meanwhile the demoralized, unhappy Dorothy filed for divorce, but before the divorce was finalized, Jerry and Jane were married.

It was a match doomed from the start. Jerry expected a wife to stay home and behave while he was out gallivanting around. Jane was a bit of a free spirit herself and not one to be buttoned down and told to sit around waiting while her husband was out doing who knew what. Though they were living with Elmo and Mamie, they fought loudly, viciously, and often, and Jerry soon figured out that Jane was not to be ruled over as readily as he had hoped. There were breakups and reconciliations, suits and countersuits, confusion about whether the marriage was even legal in the first place. Nonetheless, the marriage produced Jerry's first son and namesake, Jerry Lee Jr., on November 2, 1954.

A year and a half later when Jane gave birth to Ronnie Guy Lewis, the pyrotechnics that characterized their marriage were in full force. Jerry was convinced that Ronnie looked nothing like a Lewis. For all he knew, Jane had been off cheating on him and gotten pregnant. The more he considered this, the more he believed it. He refused to accept Ronnie as his son.

In late 1954, Jerry headed to Shreveport to offer his talents to the *Louisiana Hayride*, the radio show that had recently launched the career of a singer named Elvis Presley. Jerry auditioned for Slim

Whitman, a music icon and driving force behind *Louisiana Hayride,* but felt that he'd been given the runaround. He returned home weary, angry, and unsuccessful.

A month later, he drove to Nashville to find someone—a record producer, a promoter, anyone with influence—who would recognize his talent. In Nashville he squeezed out a meager living playing in clubs while he scurried around town trying to make connections with people who uniformly gave him a cold shoulder. When Jerry Lee managed to meet the great Chet Atkins, he was surprised when Atkins encouraged him to forget about playing piano and take up the guitar. He left Nashville, broke and discouraged, and hitchhiked back to Louisiana.

Jimmy found himself in a world of limited options. Gifted as he was musically, he wasn't willing to play in honky-tonks and nightclubs, despite offers to do so. In 1954, Frances gave birth to a baby boy they named Donnie in memory of Jimmy's brother who had died in infancy.

With little education, few marketable skills, and a family to support, Jimmy became a dragline swamper, a dirty job with limited prospects for advancement. Every day he wondered how he would climb out of the quagmire in which he found himself. His life was so hard and unrewarding that he sometimes wondered if he was being guided to the calling that his mama and grandma fervently prayed for.

Jimmy had had his own prayers. "Lord, please leave me alone," he would say, as he knelt in his room at night, "I don't want to preach."

"God has called you," Ada would counter, "and you're going to follow Him. You can be sure of it."

He did not want to hurt his Nanny. Her unwavering confidence in his fate to become a preacher was, he would say years later, "a powerful drawing force."

Soon his own conscience pulled him in the direction that Ada kept saying he was meant to go. He began preaching on weekends in Ferriday and in neighboring communities.

Back in Ferriday, Jerry was penniless and dejected. The trouble was, aside from playing piano, he had no other skills and no other passions. Elmo had tried to teach him the fundamentals of farming but his efforts proved fruitless. In his status as the family's golden child, he hadn't done anything but play his piano and he had never managed to stick with anything else. He knew he was destined to play the piano. There were no other options.

Still, in need of work, he took a job as a day laborer. One afternoon, while shoveling dirt, he accidentally hurled a shovelful onto the pants of a passer-by.

"Oh, I'm sorry, Mr. Charlie," he said. "I'm Jerry Lee Lewis, Elmo's boy."

"Well, how you doin'?" Mr. Charlie asked.

"Truth be told," said Jerry, "I'm not doing too good." He held out his hands and turned them palms up. "Look-a-here, man. Look at these hands. How can I play piano with hands that look like this?" His hands showed burgeoning calluses and rough skin on the raised edges of his palms.

"Well, son," said Mr. Charlie, "you gotta do what you gotta do."

Jerry nodded solemnly. Then he excused himself.

An hour later, his boss approached Mr. Charlie. "Did you see that damn Lewis boy?" he asked, "One minute he's out there throwing dirt and the next he's packin' up his things and now he's gone."

Jerry next tried selling sewing machines door to door. He'd offer them for a reasonable down payment without explaining that keeping the machine would require additional payments. When company officials and customers discovered what he was up to, his career with the Atlas Sewing Machine Company was over.

After that it seemed that he was always in the middle of some new scheme, flirting with trouble. At one point, he ended up in jail for stealing a .45 revolver and only narrowly avoided a two-year prison sentence.

Upon his release, in what would be one of his many switches between rectitude and sin, he preached in Ferriday and showed some talent for it. Falling back on familiar themes he'd heard repeated endlessly at the Assembly of God church of his youth, he exhorted listeners, telling them that they could recognize a house where the devil visited by the sight of his tail sticking out of the roof. The tail of course, was not really a tail; it was that evil, godless, modern invention: a television antenna.

He could quote lengthy passages of scripture and he drew upon concepts he had picked up on in Bible college on the few occasions when he was listening. Son Swaggart was mightily impressed.

"I've never heard someone move people like you can, boy," he told Jerry. "You could do great work for the Lord."

Preaching could not quench the thirst and fire that burned within him, and soon he gravitated back to the clubs in Natchez where he could make music all night long. At the Wagon Wheel he joined a band in which he played drums at first and then piano. The band was led by a local named Johnny Littlejohn who taught him a wild number called "Whole Lotta Shakin' Going On." Jerry often had trouble remembering the lyrics to the song, but the beat of the music stirred him and evoked deep feelings. He loved the pounding rhythm of the song and loved the way he could make people react when he sang it. As he slowly refined its delivery, he could see the burning embers in women's eyes and he knew something profound was happening to them when they heard it.

Jerry loved playing music. In fact, he *needed* to play. Despite his talent, he wondered if the clubs of Natchez were as far from Ferriday as he'd ever get. Still, when he listened to musicians on the radio he knew that he was their equal, and then some. He had no idea how to break through, but he could envision himself, miles from home, playing on a huge stage to overwhelming applause.

Jimmy slumped in the back pew of the church. He was seventeen years old but he could recall the key events of his childhood as if they had happened yesterday. He could picture his nanny, Ada Swaggart, filled with the Holy Ghost as he sat at her feet, enthralled and silent; he could see himself being saved at the ticket counter of the Meltz Arcade Theater and prophesying while adults and children gathered to witness and marvel at the gift bestowed upon him.

He also remembered the troubles of his early teens—times when he turned his back on the church while he went stealing with Jerry and headed off to ramble through Ferriday at night. He remembered the disappointment in his mother's eyes as she and his father and sister left for a church service or prayer meeting in which he wanted no part. For all of that, he wasn't sure that he was ready to make a change.

Here he was in January 1953, two months shy of his eighteenth birthday, a married high school dropout, working hard, dirty, dead-end jobs and feeling as if he was headed nowhere. All the while he yearned for something better and more meaningful than squeezing out a living doing manual labor.

He thought about the people who had been praying for him, caring about him. He'd heard his nanny and her sister Irene beseeching God to keep His hand on him and guide his life. He'd also heard them and his mother pray to the Good Lord to keep him from playing secular music and to squelch any opportunity that might separate him from the church.

Now his new bride, Frances, was praying a similar prayer, for she had accepted the assertion of his mother, great-aunt, and grandmother that there was a special "call" on the life of her husband. Despite the struggles that call could engender, she embraced it and joined these other women in pursuing its fulfillment.

Frances was quiet but observant, and she was steadfast. Jimmy leaned on her strength, her ability to reassure, her willingness to stay quietly in the background yet support him and push him when necessary. Now it was necessary. Jimmy had seen traveling preachers come through Ferriday. He had seen his own father become an Assembly of God preacher and, in the process, live with diminished prospects both financially and socially.

It was a hard life, particularly for itinerant preachers with no church to pastor. There was the traveling from town to town, uprooting children and families, relying on the goodwill of local churchgoers who were little more than strangers. There was the scraping by through any means possible, with little idea where the money for gas, food, and medical care were coming from. Sometimes it seemed to him that making a living through faith was comparable to glorified panhandling.

Jimmy felt pulled in a direction he wasn't sure he wanted to go. Having drifted away from the Lord, he made a mental list of what he would have to do if he went back to Him:

I have to go to church every time the doors open.
I have to quit shooting pool.
I have to give up movies.
I have to give up some of my ideas for making money.
I might even have to go to the youth rallies.

As Jimmy would write years later, "The last was the worst of all. I hated those meetings. But the pressure of God was greater than my fear of losing my freedom."

He found himself in church, walking to the altar, and on his way he made a promise. "Lord," he prayed, "I'll even go to those dumb rallies if I have to."

Then he fell down at the altar and begged God's forgiveness. He apologized for turning his back on the dedication he had demonstrated as a child. He expressed remorse for feeling shame about the commitment his family had made to full-time ministry. He regretted having run from what he felt God wanted from him, choosing instead to steal, gamble, and stay away from church. Most of all, he repented for rejecting the only direction that offered him relief from a childhood fraught with feelings of guilt and dissatisfaction.

By the time he stood up, he knew his life had changed. "I felt clean again," he said, describing the experience. "The dull ache in my heart was gone."

From that day he moved purposefully toward God and Pentecostalism. He sought to be refilled with the Holy Ghost, which he had experienced many years earlier as a child through speaking in tongues and an elevated state of consecration. It didn't come easily, as he struggled and prayed day after day without success. Finally, one night just before midnight, in a small church in Natchez, as he and Frances and his cousins David Beatty and Mickey were singing "Jesus Is the Sweetest Name I Know," Jimmy felt that strange power flowing through him. He recognized that it was the power of God and that he was on a path that felt natural. At last, he was on the road that would take him where he needed to go.

Jimmy began street preaching on weekends. He could be found in small towns all over the area—Wisner, Clayton, Gilbert, Jonesville, and his hometown of Ferriday—standing on street corners or on the bed of a pickup, passing out gospel tracts or playing the accordion, while sharing the message of the gospel of Jesus Christ to anyone who would listen.

It was an act of courage to implore non-churchgoers, many of whom were doubters or detractors, to listen to the gospel message. Jimmy felt lifted up by something far greater than himself, even in situations where delivering the message left him trembling with trepidation.

He struggled to find the right delivery style and to select topics that would interest his audience. His rawness gave him a bad case of nerves but he didn't allow that to stop him. He preached with his whole heart, mind, and soul. As he stood preaching on a street in Mangham, his knees shaking and his collar wet with sweat, a policeman came up to him and shook his hand.

"Son, you've got the fire," he said. "No question about that."

From that day on, he preached wherever he could. When he wasn't doing odd jobs in the afternoons, he and Frances went house-to-house giving out gospel tracts and telling people about Jesus.

One day, when Jimmy was preaching in Ferriday, his cousins Jerry and Mickey happened by. The two men stood at the edge of the gathering crowd, listening as Jimmy exhorted his listeners, imploring them to repent, take up their crosses, and find the lives to which they were called by God. They were moved by his message, and even more moved by his bold example. Following the service, they approached their evangelist cousin. Mickey put an arm around him, and said, "I wish I had the guts to do that."

Then Jerry chimed in. "Jimmy, I just want you to know, me and Mickey are going out to hit the big time and help support you in the ministry."

Looking at his two cousins, Jimmy felt grateful for having been chosen as the one to follow the true call, yet he constantly wondered if his calling required more of him than he could reasonably give. Growing up under the stern rules of his daddy and the watchful, expectant eyes of his mother and grandmother, Jimmy had yet to find a way to accept and cope with the often messy and unruly feelings that young men encounter as they journey into adulthood. As he made this journey, his every move was met with feelings of guilt and insecurity, a common dynamic among young men of strict religious upbringings. Jimmy's narrow path was about as wide and as comfortable as a razor's edge. Even he could see that he needed room to breathe, that he needed to move ahead without feeling that every decision and every action was so black or white that it could only lead him to eternal salvation or perpetual damnation.

Men, holler at the other guys and bring them all around for a few minutes." The voice of the boss sent everyone scurrying.

Jimmy was an oiler on a dragline, working for the Northeast Soil Conservation Company. He was working long days there, and it was dirty, grimy work that allowed him to eke out no more than a small living.

While many of Jimmy's fellow blue-collar employees spent their breaks and spare time telling jokes, giving each other a hard time, and looking for some modest relief from their trying days, Jimmy would often walk alone by himself in the swampy regions, secluded from the others, praying, much as he had when he was a child.

While he was a likable guy, other workers and even his supervisor, Mr. Whittington, found Jimmy to be different from the rest. Whether they agreed or disagreed with his strong adherence to Christian tenets or thought he seemed a bit self-righteous from time to time, they admired his resolve and boldness in following his faith.

On this particular day, all the men had been called for a meeting with Mr. Whittington. These group discussions were rare and created a natural sense of curiosity and concern. They crowded around the older supervisor, a man who had been in dirty, hard work all his life. As he began to speak in his deep voice they all listened intently.

"I hate to do this, fellas, but I just pass along the orders. Effectively immediately, everyone is taking a twenty-five-cent-an-hour pay cut. It's the only way we can keep everyone on board right now, so we are going to share the pain across the board."

Groans went up from the group, although they were reluctant to be too vocal. Even with the drop in pay they desperately needed their jobs and were careful what they said around Mr. Whittington.

In the back of the group, Jimmy looked dejected. He had a wife and a small child and he was barely getting by as it was. Now, a drop of 25 cents per hour would take his already meager hourly pay of $1.25 down to $1 and make it even harder. He wasn't sure what to think or what to do.

"Jimmy, come here." He looked up and saw Mr. Whittington addressing him. The two men stepped several feet away from the rest of the group, out of earshot from the others. His boss spoke to him quietly.

"You're not getting your pay cut. As a matter of fact, we're increasing your pay by 25 cents, up to $1.50."

Jimmy could hardly believe this was true. The look in Lawrence Whittington's eyes assured him it was.

From the outset, Jimmy saw events like this as proof of God's provision and bounty for his faithfulness. Days and nights of want and struggle still lay ahead, but each time something positive happened, he attributed it to God's faithfulness, recognizing and honoring Jimmy's step in casting his lot with the God of the Bible. It was an event that would be repeated over the years, as Jimmy's belief that his commitment to the narrow path and turning his back on what seemed like an easier way to success was being honored by his Protector.

Jerry wanted to be with the Lord too, yet he knew what his own calling was. He remained committed to it even though he knew that playing the piano at honky-tonks was the polar opposite of performing in front of a church congregation. Yet his move away from the church and toward what would become rock 'n' roll filled him with guilt and confusion. He was getting a lot of mixed messages. His mama spoke of wanting him to use his talent for God but didn't try to dissuade him from playing in "sinful" places where liquor flowed and women rarely said no. He had been taught by preachers to store his riches in heaven, but his only means of easing his family's financial struggle was through the thirty pieces of silver available when he played "under the hill" in Natchez.

Trying to play into the wee hours of the morning at the Wagon Wheel and being expected to attend church the next morning created increasing internal conflict. His music and his church were like oil and water. They didn't mix, no way, no how. Often he'd tell Johnny Littlejohn, the band leader, "I ain't gonna play in no more clubs. I'm gonna live for the Lord."

Littlejohn would beg him to play that night and others. Sometimes he did, though one time he stayed away for two full weeks.

Then, contrite and bowing to necessity, he called Littlejohn and asked to come back to the band, saying, "Well, John, y'know things are gettin' bad and I need the bread."

Jerry did not care half as much about the money as he cared about being recognized for his talent. He saw it, he was proud of it, and he thirsted to have others see it, to have them recognize that this high school dropout from a dirt-poor family was *the* best.

He was confident, arrogant, filled with bravado, ready to put in the hard yards. He practiced every day and honed his skills playing in clubs for hours, coaxing from the piano the brilliant sounds and rhythms that went ceaselessly through his mind.

Mickey didn't grow up in the same crucible as his two older cousins. His parents were positioned at different ends of the churchgoing spectrum—his mother rarely ever missing a service and his father never attending one. This had allowed Mickey to avoid extremes. He was happy to live a quiet, normal childhood. By his late teens, his biggest concern was scoring a big enough paycheck to support his new family.

As these three young men married and embarked on adulthood, their situations were similarly modest and their prospects were similarly limited. Often their dreams appeared headed to the scrap heap, as they focused on taking care of families and settling into jobs to eke out their livings. Each had limited formal education and little interest in book learning. Each could have headed

in a direction taken by the other: any one of them could have become a preacher, by drawing on their intense background in the
Pentecostal church, or tapped into their inborn musical ability. As
they found—or stumbled into—their destinies, they would remain
forever linked.

BIRTH OF ROCK 'N' ROLL

Rock 'n' roll owes much to Sam Phillips, owner and founder of Sun Records and a man as unique, eccentric, and canny as any the South ever produced. Blessed with an amazing gift for spotting musical talent, he would discover and nurture Elvis Presley, Carl Perkins, Johnny Cash, and Roy Orbison, as well as the young man he believed was more talented than any of them: Jerry Lee Lewis.

Sam was born near Florence, Alabama on January 5, 1923. One of eight children, he grew up dirt poor on a tenant farm, his father having lost his money at the start of the Great Depression.

As a boy, Sam saw the ways that people used music. He saw blacks and whites wrestle with sound and rhythm to wring the pain and struggle of hardship from their lives. This moved him and left him seeking the sort of raw emotion that transforms ho-hum musical expression into pure, kinetic energy.

He found an abundance of that energy in black church music, and in the songs blacks sang in the cotton fields.

"I never did see white people singing a lot when they were chopping cotton," he would say years later, "but the odd part about it is, I never heard a black man that couldn't sing good. Even off-key, it had a spontaneity about it that would grab my ear."

Sam worked as a disc jockey and sound engineer. Then in 1950, he opened the Memphis Recording Service—later known as Sun Records—at 706 Union Avenue, less than a mile east of Beale

Street. Over the next years, he recorded the great black musicians of the South. A regular in his studio was Chester Burnett, a soulful singer known as Howlin' Wolf. Sam also recorded Riley King, a dazzling young musician who would take the stage name B. B. King.

In March 1951 at Sun Records, a band led by Ike Turner recorded "Rocket 88," sung by R&B singer and saxophonist Jackie Brenston. While widely debated, many music historians agree that this was the first rock 'n' roll record, though interestingly, its unique sound was largely due to a damaged amplifier that had gotten banged up when Turner was driving from gig to gig.

Sam had the special ability of helping young men dig down deeply into their beings and allow their talent to flow to the surface. He strained to find what noted music writer Peter Guralnick called "perfect imperfection" and brought forth something that moved and inspired listeners the world over.

Sam was searching for something that no one had yet found. He was looking for a singer who could combine the best of white and black music, merging rockabilly—as the early rock music was called—with gospel and country and rhythm and blues. As he put it, he was looking "for a white man who could sing like a black man."

This was a radical prospect, but then Sam was a radical, and stubborn too. He found the singer he was looking for in a nineteen-year-old named Elvis Presley.

Elvis Aaron Presley grew up listening to church music. He was hypnotized by its fervor, its harmonies, its beat, and by the wild, unfettered, hip-churning movements of Southern preachers. He was a shy boy, withdrawn and quiet, and so attached to his mother that when she died years later when he was twenty-three years old, he would be inconsolable, sobbing at her gravesite, "My whole world is gone."

During the summer of 1953, he was driving a truck for Crown Electric when he parked outside of Sun Studio and worked up the nerve to go in. Once inside, he paid two dollars to cut his first record. Sam's assistant, Marion Keisker, asked him, "What kind of singer are you?"

"I sing all kinds," he said.

"Who do you sound like?" she asked.

"I don't sound like nobody."

That day he recorded "My Happiness" backed by "That's When Your Heartache Begins." Keisker suspected that Elvis might be exactly the kind of singer Sam was looking for. Sam thought so too when he talked to Elvis and discovered that he wasn't attached to any single type of music.

Sam was taken with Elvis's unconventional appearance—the sideburns, the long hair glistening with oil—and he was impressed with what he described to Marion as "the innate purity of his voice." The overriding impression that Sam got at his first meeting with Elvis had to do with something less apparent.

"He tried not to show it," Sam told Marion, "but he feels so inferior."

Sam teamed Elvis with guitarist Scotty Moore and bassist Bill Black, but their progress was so slow that Sam, Scotty, and Bill suspected that Elvis didn't have what it took.

Then, during a break on July 5, 1954, Elvis was fooling around in the studio, singing an up-tempo version of "That's All Right Mama," a song written by bluesman Arthur Crudup. Bill Black picked notes on his upright bass and Scotty Moore joined in on guitar. Finally, Sam had heard what he was looking for and he recorded it.

The next night they recorded "Blue Moon of Kentucky," taking Bill Monroe's slow bluegrass waltz and turning it into a bluesy up-tempo tune. Hearing it, Sam grinned and said, "Boy, that's fine, that's fine. That's a pop song now!"

Two weeks later, on July 19, 1954, Sam released the record which he had labeled Sun 209. With that, Elvis was on his way and the world was about to change.

The following year on May 21, 1955, a thin, twenty-eight-year-old musician walked through the doors of 4720 Cottage Grove Avenue in Chicago carrying his guitar. He had been in this place twice previously, once to introduce himself to Leonard Chess, the owner and brains behind the famed Chess Records label, and the second time to drop off recordings of his music that he had made himself. As a follow-up to those earlier meetings, Chess had invited him back for a recording session.

Charles Edward Anderson Berry was born in St. Louis in 1926, the fourth of six children. His father worked at a mill and was a part-time carpenter and handyman while his mother raised the children and managed the finances of a family with many mouths to feed and few dollars to spend. Both parents were firm yet loving.

Berry grew up listening to church music at the local Antioch Baptist Church where his father was the Sunday School superintendent. From his earliest memories, he appreciated the beauty of music. His earliest memories were hearing his mother sing hymns. The family listened to Fats Waller, Bing Crosby, Louis Armstrong, Kitty Wells, and Gene Autry on their Victrola and, later, on a Philco radio.

He began playing the guitar when he was just a kid. His picking and chording abilities developed quicker than his voice. At times, he wondered if he would ever be good enough to become a professional musician.

By the time he entered Chess Records, he was well known in the St. Louis area, where he and Ike Turner were among the key performers. Berry and the band cut four songs that day in Chicago. Leonard Chess particularly liked the sound and rhythm of one of the songs but didn't care for the name. After a few moments of thought, Berry changed the title of the song from "Ida May" to "Maybellene." Within months it reached number one on the charts, and rock 'n' roll had taken another step forward.

Four months after Chuck Berry recorded "Maybellene," a group of men gathered in the tiny J&M recording studio in New Orleans. It was the second day of a failed recording session for a twenty-three-year-old, little-known performer named Richard Wayne Penniman, a man who called himself Little Richard. The producer, Robert "Bumps" Blackwell, felt a sense of doom, for they had invested much in the session in terms of money and hope.

Richard was one of twelve children born to a Seventh Day Adventist preacher. Raised in abject poverty in Macon, Georgia, he was an outcast from an early age. With one leg shorter than the other, he walked with a noticeable limp and was teased about it relentlessly. By his teens, he was displaying a feminine demeanor that subjected him to further scorn from those who pegged him as homosexual.

Music was an enormous part of his youth and most of it came from his church. As he saw it, the poor people of his community "had to sing to feel their connection with God. To sing their trials away, sing their problems away, to make their burdens easier and the load lighter." He drew his own music from theirs. "That's the beginning," he once said. "That's where it started."

Singing songs in church at an early age afforded him the recognition and affirmation he craved. He was exuberant and intensely musical, beating out a constant, unstoppable rhythm with his hands on every flat surface he encountered. As a young performer, he mixed upbeat boogie woogie and rhythm and blues with gospel.

The day he walked into J&M Studio he was a sight to behold, a big, confident man with thin, wavy hair who wore thick make-up, powder, eyeliner, and lipstick. As a live performer he fed off the energy of the crowd, but in the recording studio he seemed to run out of steam. Then—out of nowhere that day—he cut loose with a wild, racy song he had heard and played on the road. Blackwell thought the tune had the makings of a hit and had someone track down a local songwriter who could produce milder lyrics that would keep the song from being censored.

The song, titled "Tutti Frutti," was wildly engaging with an intoxicating beat and lyrics innocuous enough to gain airplay on white pop stations. It swiftly moved up the charts.

What was this new musical form? The rock critic Robert Palmer described its defining characteristics in simple terms: "When rock 'n' roll is really rocking and rolling it combines an irresistible forward motion, a heavy backbeat, and a certain lightness or lilt."

Beyond that, rock 'n' roll was Southern music, born in the South, sung by southerners, and flavored by the cultural influences of poverty, rural life, and—above all—full-on gospel worship.

The recordings of "That's All Right Mama," "Maybellene," and "Tutti Frutti" gave this fledgling music its style and momentum as well as the stars who—along with Jerry Lee Lewis—would make its name.

Elvis Presley, Chuck Berry, and Little Richard all sang the music that Sam Phillips had dreamed of, a music that crossed racial lines and melded aspects of rhythm and blues. These melodies came from blues and country, and were integrated with pop music and a heavy dose of gospel.

Because of this combination, many listeners confused the skin colors of these performers. Chuck Berry had a twang in his voice and leanings to hillbilly music that caused some to mistake him for a white man, while initially many assumed Elvis was black, an assumption that was often made about Jerry as well.

Frankie, why don't you head up with me to see him?"

The teenaged Frankie Jean Lewis was intrigued by the excitement in Jerry's eyes. Her brother, usually slow to show interest in anyone else's music, particularly someone of similar age, was being unusually nice to her by inviting her along to see Elvis Presley.

The two drove three hundred miles from Ferriday to Tupelo to see the burgeoning star perform in his hometown, the place he was reared until his family migrated to Memphis.

Jerry talked frequently about Elvis and his excitement in seeing Elvis was palpable. Even Frankie, otherwise cool to trends followed by most kids, was excited about the show.

Young Elvis was still developing his hip-swiveling, leg-shaking act that thrilled the young people in the crowd who adored this man with the striking good looks and the heavy rock 'n' roll beat. That their parents had little understanding of the appeal of the man or his music only enhanced their admiration of Elvis.

Jerry carefully studied Elvis, noticing his style and evaluating his talent, much as a young, unknown fighter sizes up the talent of a better-established challenger to the throne. He watched the reaction of the teenagers and young adults in the audience. After the show, he chattered to his sister as they returned to their car.

"Frankie, wasn't that somethin'?"

Frankie looked at her brother, amazed that he would like the show they had just seen.

"Are you kiddin' me? Jumpin' around, hollerin', and actin' a fool? That was awful."

Frankie was always looking for an opportunity to needle her older brother, but this time she didn't understand what all the fuss was about. There definitely had been a fuss, no doubt about it. She had seen it with her own eyes.

They argued much of the way home. Somewhere around Fayetteville, Mississippi, Jerry stopped the car and demanded Frankie get out and walk the rest of the way. The combat continued for the rest of the drive, but the two finally made it back to Ferriday.

A couple of days later, Frankie, tired of watching her brother strut around with his Elvis Presley t-shirt on, had enough. With the shirt still on her brother's back, she ripped it off him.

More than fifty years later, Jerry would recall Frankie tearing off his Elvis shirt and both he and Frankie would remember the incident with smiles and chuckles. But on the day it happened, as Jerry chased Frankie out of the house, his newly ripped shirt hanging from his body, it didn't strike him as the least bit funny.

– 15 –

CRAZY ARMS

Jerry was impressed by the music of Elvis Presley and other early stars, but he heard nothing in their music that he felt he couldn't match and even exceed. In 1956, Jerry followed the suggestion made by others—including his cousin Mickey—to drive to Memphis to try out his sound with Sam Phillips. He and Elmo used the proceeds from selling some thirty dozen eggs to finance their journey. They headed north to the southwestern Tennessee town, ready for Jerry's talent to be discovered.

When they arrived at Sun they learned that Sam was out of town. Instead they found Sally Wilburn, Marion Keisker, and twenty-five-year-old engineer and producer Jack Clement, whom Sam had hired earlier that year. Clement, a solid musician in his own right, had been reared by a father who was a choir director and mother who played the piano at little Levi Baptist Church a few miles south of Memphis. Despite his talent and pedigree, he'd been working at a local building supply company before coming to Sun.

Clement was in the back of the studio, fiddling around with the echo they'd begun to use on records by putting thumbtacks in the hammers of a spinet piano, an innovation that would later have a dramatic effect for Jerry.

"There's a young man up front," one of Sam's secretaries said, "who claims he plays piano like Chet Atkins."

"Oh, really?" Clement said. "I gotta hear that. Send him back."

Clement listened intently as Jerry played "Wildwood Flower" and a few other songs of the day. He loved what he was hearing. He recorded Jerry but didn't get around to playing it for Sam. Within days, Jerry and Elmo were in Concordia Parish and Jerry was back playing at the Wagon Wheel in Natchez.

Jerry's first cousin, J. W. Brown, and his family lived in Memphis. J. W. married his wife Lois when they were sixteen and a year later their first child, Myra Gale, was born. J. W. had bounced around in a variety of jobs and ended up in Memphis working for the power company before a near-death accident on the job ended his stint with the Memphis utility.

With a year off work to recuperate, J. W. decided to track down his first cousin in Louisiana to see about getting a band together. He found Jerry playing in Natchez and coaxed him into returning to Memphis. Meanwhile, Jack finally played Jerry's demo for Sam Phillips. Sam listened for a few seconds then turned to Jack and said, "Get that boy back in here."

Jack had written Jerry's phone number on the back of a tape box. He was about to call him when Jerry showed up in the studio. Clement arranged a recording session for a few days later. Jerry played a little spinet piano, the same one in which Jack had put thumbtacks in the hammers. He also brought in Billy Lee Riley and Roland Janes to play guitar and hired a local sixteen-year-old drum player, J. M. Van Eaton, who was skilled enough to follow Jerry's frequent chord changes and fills.

During the session, Jack asked if Jerry was familiar with "Crazy Arms," a song that had been a hit for Ray Price and the Andrews Sisters.

"Yessir," Jerry said, "I know it."

Jerry's rendition of "Crazy Arms" began with a piano intro. When Jack played it for Sam, Sam reached over, stopped the tape before Jerry sang the first word.

"Now, I can sell that," he said.

They made a dub of it right there in the studio and that night Sam took it to the most powerful disc jockey in Memphis, Dewey Phillips, who had a nightly show called *Red, White and Blues.*

On December 1, 1956, "Crazy Arms" was released with a B side of "End of the Road," one of the few original songs that Jerry ever wrote. The record sold 300,000 copies.

The success of "Crazy Arms" was a turning point. Finally, Jerry had found recognition, acclaim, and confirmation of his undying belief that he had a rare talent in his fingers.

Soon after it was released, Jimmy Swaggart was in a little restaurant in Winnsboro, Louisiana, forty miles north of Ferriday. He was still working as a dragline swamper all over eastern Louisiana. He was sitting at a little table, adorned in filthy work clothes and his face covered with grime, when his cousin's voice came over the radio.

He remembered when he and Jerry played piano together, and times when they talked about leaving Ferriday and getting rich and making it big time. Now Jerry's dreams were coming true.

But what about me? Jimmy wondered.

He saw no hope for his future. He was consigned to serve and obey.

"I'll never do anything," he told himself, "but preach in little backwoods churches."

Around the same time, in Houston, Mickey Gilley got himself a copy of "Crazy Arms" and "End of the Road." He was so excited that he went all the way downtown to radio station KNUZ where he talked his way into seeing Paul Berlin, the hottest disk jockey in town.

"My cousin has just made a record," he told him, "and I wonder if you'd play it on your show?"

Mickey was proud to be the one who got Jerry his first airplay in Houston.

A few days after the release of "Crazy Arms," on December 4, 1956, there was a recording session at Sun for Carl Perkins. Jerry was one of the session musicians. The key song they recorded that day was "Matchbox," which would be a big hit. Soon after they'd finished, Johnny Cash happened into the studio. Then, unexpectedly, Elvis, whose Sun contract had been sold to RCA, showed up to visit with his old friends at 706 Union.

As the four sat around talking, they segued into a gospel song, and then another. Jack Clement, sitting in the control room, thought to himself, *I'll be remiss if I don't record this.*

He put a tape on, moved a few microphones around in the studio, and let it roll. For an hour and a half the group sang mostly gospel songs. By the time they were done, Elvis had nothing but praise for Jerry. "That boy can go," he said, "I think he has a great future ahead of him. He has a different style, and the way he plays piano just gets inside me."

When the impromptu session ended, the tape was filed away. Twenty-five years later it was discovered, finally released, and credited to the four remarkable talents who would be known as the Million Dollar Quartet.

– 16 –

MAKING IT

In March 1957, J. W. Brown, Jerry's cousin, came to Jerry's recording session in the little studio at Sun where Jerry, Sam Phillips, and Jack Clement were looking for a follow-up hit to "Crazy Arms." They were cutting a song that Jack wrote called "It'll Be Me," but after a few takes Jack got tired of it and said, "Why don't we do something else for a while, Jerry, and come back to this?"

They were stumped for a song, but then J. W. thought of one that Jerry had loved while playing with Johnny Littlejohn's band in Natchez. The song was written by Roy Hall and Jerry could never remember the words but the beat spoke to him. The tune always gained a rousing response and repeated calls for encores. J. W., who played bass guitar in the band, called that number "the shaking song."

"Hey, Jerry," J. W. said, "why don't you do that number we do on the road that everybody likes so much?"

Jack Clement turned on the recorder and Jerry sang and played "Whole Lotta Shakin' Going On." It was less than three minutes long, and had tremendous energy and bold, suggestive lyrics. They did it in one take.

Sam and Jack didn't pay much attention to the number, convinced that "It'll Be Me," a song Sam preferred, would be the big success. The single was released on April 15, 1957, with an A side of "It'll Be Me" and "Whole Lotta Shakin'" on the B side.

It soon became clear which song would be the smash hit. "Whole Lotta Shakin'" would reach number one on the country and R&B charts and number two on the pop charts. It scored on all three charts because no one knew how to characterize the song. In time it would become the best-selling single in the history of Sun Records.

In the spring of 1957, Jerry joined fellow Sun artists Johnny Cash and Carl Perkins for a month-long tour of Canada and the northern United States. As their caravan rolled over hundreds of miles from one performance stop to another, the demands of their venture weighed upon the young performers, and pretty soon Jerry took up Perkins's taste for heavy drinking and Cash's amphetamine habit.

Jerry revved up his onstage act, expanding its physical aspects and his own showmanship. Perkins and Cash advised and assisted him in discovering how to turn a performance that requires being seated at a piano into a lively, fire-breathing show.

By the end of the tour, an animal had been unleashed inside Jerry. He played piano while his long, blond locks fell over his face. He pounded out songs with his feet, kicked the stool around the stage, stood on the piano, and jumped wildly, all to the delight of screaming fans and the wonderment of other performers.

Like "That's All Right Mama," "Maybellene," and "Tutti Frutti," "Whole Lotta Shakin'" would become one of the cornerstones of rock 'n' roll. The song was banned in many areas of the country due to the widespread impression that it made blatant references to sexual activity. Many disc jockeys refused to play it and many people wouldn't buy it—or even listen to it—because they assumed the performer was a black man.

Sam Phillips's brother, Jud, was a funny, charming guy who was, Sam claimed, the greatest salesman in the world. When Jud saw Jerry perform, he was blown away. He convinced Sam to allow him to take Jerry to New York City for a publicity tour.

Ed Sullivan wasn't interested in booking Jerry, but Steve Allen was. On July 27, 1957, Jerry appeared on his program and gave a riveting, explosive performance. He banged away mercilessly on the keys, his locks flying in the air. He kicked the piano stool backward as he continued to play, inspiring Steve Allen to fling the stool across the stage. It was pandemonium.

Across America, as children leaned in closer to their television sets to watch and listen, parents sat upright, bewildered by this strangeness invading their living rooms. To them, the Presley boy—whom they'd seen on Ed Sullivan's show—had enough soft edges and a sweet smile to make his new music endurable, if not desirable. This Lewis boy was a wild man who looked dangerous and downright scary.

Despite that—and because of it—the show was a huge success. Jerry made a return appearance on August 11, producing some of the best ratings of Allen's career. On his third appearance, on November 3, he introduced a new song, "Great Balls of Fire," which would soon top the country chart, go to number two on the pop chart, reach number five on the R&B side, and sell millions of copies. Meanwhile, his nightly performance fee increased from $100 to $10,000, and Jerry was vaulted into the superstardom he'd always believed he deserved.

But the success had dark emotional undertones. No scene better depicts the conflict Jerry's success introduced than the events that occurred at Sun Studio on the evening of October 6, 1957, when Jerry was set to record "Great Balls of Fire."

H-E-L-L!" hollered Jerry, sitting at the piano, suddenly and totally riled.

Jerry, Sam, and a group of musicians and engineers had gathered in Sun Studios to record "Great Balls of Fire." Everyone anticipated it was the perfect song to be the follow-up to "Whole Lotta Shakin'." Jerry had cut an earlier version of "Great Balls of

Fire" for the soundtrack of the movie *Jamboree* but Sam Phillips wanted a higher-quality recording.

In the studio with Sam and the others, Jerry began to suspect that the song was blasphemous. Suddenly, he slipped into the role of preacher, as he did from time to time, exclaiming, "You're a sinner and unless you be saved and born again and be made as a little child and walk before God and be holy—and, brother, I mean you got to be so pure. No sin shall enter—no sin! For it says no sin. It doesn't say just a little bit; it says no sin shall enter there. Brother, not one little bit."

After several more declarations from Jerry, Sam decided it was time to calm down his piano-playing star. He was not unfamiliar with the mixed feelings these conservative, religious country boy rockers carried around inside. He knew Jerry was an extreme version, but Sam felt inclined to inject some moderation into his views.

"Now look, Jerry, religious conviction doesn't mean anything resembling extremism."

Jerry, having someone with whom to engage, was only bolstered, arguing that rock 'n' roll conflicted with God's mandate for people's lives. The two debated, as the others in the room shook their heads and wondered if they would ever make a record that evening.

Within moments, Jerry's remarks reached a crescendo.

"Man, I got the Devil in me! If I didn't have, I'd be a Christian!"

Sam stubbornly tried again to calm Jerry down, temper his feelings, and move toward getting the song recorded.

Finally, around two in the morning, in a combustible mix of weariness, anticipation, and varying levels of drunkenness and sobriety, "Great Balls of Fire" was recorded.

Jerry's hands pounded out the opening notes. Minutes later, they had the song on tape and Jerry had a crooked smile on his face.

Sam Phillips looked at Jerry through the divider between the studio and the sound booth. He couldn't tell where the wild musical talent stopped and the passionate internal struggle began. He knew where they overlapped—deep inside—where the true magic emanated.

Sam shook his head and smiled. He loved this man's music. He loved the crazy ride with him even more . . . well, most of the time.

Jerry had offers from every direction, big names and small. He was the first performer to appear on Dick Clark's *American Bandstand* and developed a close relationship with Clark. When the show was in trouble with Beechnut Gum, its primary sponsor, Jud Phillips suggested offering copies of Jerry's song "Breathless" for fifty cents and five Beechnut chewing gum wrappers. The gimmick produced an enormous response and tremendous gratitude from Clark.

Jerry made another strong impression on the public through his involvement with Alan Freed, the preeminent rock 'n' roll disc jockey and promoter of the day. Freed organized what he called the Big Beat concerts and tours. In the spring of 1958, Jerry joined him on a tour that lasted approximately forty-five days and covered almost as many cities around the nation.

During those tours everyone understood that Jerry hated being the warm-up act. When he was forced to do so, he'd put extra gusto into his performance and overshadow anyone who came after him, including brilliant performers like Fats Domino and Chuck Berry. Legend has it that when required by Freed to precede Chuck Berry, Jerry doused the piano with gasoline during his own performance and set it on fire. Though the story is apocryphal, it's accurate in spirit, and gives a true picture of how intent Jerry was to have things his way.

Jerry's competitive streak was never more evident than in his interaction with and perspective on Elvis. In November 1955, Sam Phillips had sold the rights to Elvis to RCA for the now infamous sum of $35,000. Sam defended the decision for years, saying that he did it because he needed money to bring along other performers—Jerry among them. Actually, Sam had many moments of regret, as indicated by what he told Jack Clement. "Well, if you're going to make a mistake, make a $12 million mistake."

Jack said nothing, but he thought, *Why don't you call it a billion dollar mistake?*

One thing was for sure: Sam had no intention of letting his new star attraction, Jerry Lee Lewis, get away so easily.

The similarities between Jerry and Elvis were eerie. They were reared some three hundred miles apart; both came from dirt-poor families; both had fathers who spent time incarcerated; and given the death at birth of Elvis's twin, Jesse Garon, both grew up in families that had lost a son.

Both were raised around the music and theology of the Pentecostal world, in the Assembly of God denomination. Both had little education and no background to prepare them for the fame and riches their talents would yield. Each had a close and dependent relationship with his mother that exceeded even the most bonded mother–son alliances in the deep South.

As they grew up, both were dramatically impacted by black music and both were mistaken for black performers in their early years. Both dealt with internal conflict between the music they made and the type of music they felt drawn to by their God.

By the end of 1957, Elvis was in the army and experts predicted Jerry would surpass him as the chief draw of rock 'n' roll. In fact, Jerry's record sales for that year vastly exceeded Elvis's and his recent résumé was more impressive.

"Elvis really liked Jerry Lee," Jack Clement recalled, "and Jerry Lee liked Elvis, but he was jealous of him."

While Jerry's success was intoxicating and satisfying, it was also a case of too much too soon. Money was coming from every direction to a twenty-two year old who had, initially, no idea what to do with it. When Sam cut him a royalty check for $40,000, Jerry had a difficult time verbalizing and even more difficulty comprehending the amount. He carried the check around with him for days, jokingly trying to use it to pay small expenses in order to draw attention to his newfound success.

Soon he began spending the money. He bought his father a farm near Ferriday, his mother a brand-new, light green Cadillac, and a home for his family in the Ridgecrest area on Ferriday's southeastern outskirts. The day they moved in, Jerry laid the cash in his pocket on the bed as his parents told him, "This is more money than we've ever seen in our lives."

"When Jerry Lee made it big," a native of Ferriday recalls, "it was country coming to town. They all had money and they wanted to show it. Elmo on his Harley was one of the things that stuck in my mind."

Jerry signed a five-year extension with Sun Records that would take him through 1963, though he didn't read or understand many of the contract's provisions. It indicated a lack of attention and lack of sophistication that would prove harmful to his career.

For all his ability in finding and developing talent, Sam's business acumen was questionable, largely because of his tightfistedness and unwillingness to fully invest in a business that required a tremendous capital outlay. Some of the people closest to Jerry were convinced that Sam had cheated him out of a lot of money.

Another problem developed when the young star, already stubborn and headstrong, quickly became difficult to manage. In retrospect, the idea that anyone could have controlled him seems almost comical.

He would show up late at performance venues and sit backstage while the audience clamored for him. Onstage, even in the early days, he would ignore audience requests, stop songs in the middle, or glare at the audience. The more he misbehaved, it seemed, the more his fans loved him.

And so, while Elvis fulfilled his patriotic duty by serving in the United States Army, Jerry honed his own persona as Rock 'n' Roll's Number One Bad Boy.

– 17 –

MICKEY GETS INSPIRED

In 1956, while Jerry was in Houston to play at the old City Auditorium, Mickey went to see him. For months, he'd been telling his friends that Jerry was his cousin, but nobody believed that a guy as humble and poor as Mickey could even know a performer whose records were on the radio, much less be related to one.

Sonny James was the headliner. He was riding high with a song called "Young Love" that was a big hit. Jerry and Johnny Cash were the opening acts.

When Mickey hooked up with Jerry before the show, he was amazed that his cousin was driving a year-old Cadillac and staying at the Rice Hotel.

"Now look at you," he said to Jerry, "traveling first-class all the way."

Mickey was proud of Jerry until he saw his show.

"He stood up," Mickey reported to Geraldine later, "and just started tearing the hell out of that piano, and oh, was I embarrassed!"

Most of all he was shocked by the way the crowd responded, the way they screamed and went crazy. Though Mickey was flabbergasted, a small seed was planted in his own mind as he watched his wild cousin take over the crowd.

In the summer of 1957, Jerry, the burgeoning new star on the rock 'n' roll scene, returned to Houston and Mickey was excited. By then he had settled into his life in the Bayou City. His was a blue-collar existence of hard days on the job, returning home each day filthy and dog tired, making $1.25 per hour, and living paycheck to paycheck.

Soon his paycheck would have to extend even further. In January 1954, Geraldine had given birth to Michael, their first son. A few years later, in June 1958, they would welcome twins Kathy and Keith.

The children brought both joy to the marriage and added strain. The most difficult obstacles Mickey faced in forging a successful marriage came from Geraldine, as the couple slowly drifted apart, and from Geraldine's mother, who relentlessly interfered. The mild-mannered Mickey regarded her as "an evil woman" and "a witch from hell."

With these pressures weighing on him, the prospect of seeing Jerry perform again a year following his initial show in Houston gave the beleaguered Mickey something to look forward to. "Whole Lotta Shakin' Going On" had been released and Jerry was no longer the opening act. Mickey had adjusted to the previously unthinkable notion that the Jerry he grew up with was now a full-fledged superstar with a full-fledged smash hit.

Again Jerry put on a wild show. Again the audience went wild, screaming and shouting, blanketing the young star with even more adoration than they had the year before. Teenaged girls huddled together, their hands over their mouths, their legs shaking, hypnotized by the performer onstage. Men and boys alike were drawn to Jerry's total abandon and to the palpable sense of danger in his music.

Mickey went backstage after the performance. There, he was amazed to see a large throng of adoring people around his cousin. *This is just Jerry, for crying out loud,* he thought, *the same kid whose loud mouth has gotten him into trouble since he was old enough to talk. Now he's gawked at and clamored after as if he were royalty.*

Mickey took Jerry to the Houston airport. As Jerry prepared to leave, he reached into his pocket and took out a wad of bills to purchase a plane ticket. Mickey stared at the wad, realizing his cousin was getting rich from standing on that stage and banging the hell out of that piano for all those screaming fans.

"What am I doing?" he said to himself as he drove away in his used, beat-up automobile. "I'm working for a dollar and a quarter an hour doing construction work, and he's making all this money doing a few songs at the piano. If he can do it, I can too."

For the first time, Mickey envisioned the possibility of another life. His cousin had shown him a glimmer of a different path. Mickey had no idea where it might lead, but it looked more promising than his current dismal existence.

Over the next years, Mickey recorded a considerable number of songs for a considerable number of labels, all with limited success. Two early songs, "Tell My Why" and "Oowee Baby," songs Mickey later would refer to disparagingly, were recorded on the Minor label and went nowhere.

"I was terrible," Mickey said, "The first record I ever recorded was just plain embarrassing. I thought it was going to be a smash. I enjoyed doing it, though, and I've never liked to admit defeat. You stay with something long enough, I guess you have to either improve or get out."

Around the same time, he recorded a catchy rockabilly number called "Call Me Shorty" for Dot Records. Mickey and others expected the song to be a hit, with national exposure, but again, it did nothing. He was not deterred—not yet—and continued searching, looking for the right song, the right situation, the right producer to help him catch his own lightning in a bottle.

He went to Memphis. He went to Nashville. He went to New Orleans to record in the famous studio of Cosimo Matassa where, three years earlier, Little Richard had erupted with "Tutti Frutti." These efforts also yielded nothing.

By late 1959, Mickey was still pushing forward, still trying to find that elusive recording success. He recorded a number in the HCA recording studio on Fannin Street in Houston, working with Leland Rogers, a local producer, on a Warner Mack tune from the midfifties, "Is It Wrong (For Loving You)." For the session, Leland brought in his twenty-one-year-old brother, Kenny, to play bass. The world did not yet recognize the name of Kenny Rogers, but someday it would.

"Is It Wrong (For Loving You)" wasn't a smash, but it was a start. For years to come it would be a regular number in the Gilley repertoire.

Mickey's likable personality and persona as the normal guy next door rallied people behind him, particularly friends and family. Back home in Ferriday everybody was pulling for him, keeping up with his ventures, and hoping for his success. To rouse support for Mickey at radio stations, his relatives would send in two-cent postcards on which they'd write, "We want you to play Mickey Gilley's record."

"Every time he released a new record," recalls B. D. Taylor, Mickey's niece, who grew up and lived in New Orleans, "we would all write in. We'd call the radio station. We tried our best to make it happen."

Over and over again Mickey would tell his mother and father, "I think this one's gonna make it."

Recording success remained elusive. Over time Mickey's optimism waned, as recording after recording met with rejection. He ceased telling his family about each one's potential for success, doubtful that any labels would latch on to them or any disc jockeys would play them, aside from a few small guys in the local Houston market. He knew some of the early recordings were junk, but as his talent grew he found some good songs and produced results in the studio that were much better. Industry movers and shakers continued to show little or no interest in his music, which left him increasingly disappointed.

He was too raw as a singer and piano player. He could bang out the boogie woogie of his youth, but unlike his cousin, Jerry, his skills were limited. To get exposure, he played nightclubs and bars all across Interstate 10 from Texas to Alabama, and spent time in cities like Mobile, Lake Charles, and New Orleans.

In 1959, he migrated back to Houston, where he worked at a club called the Ranch House five nights a week. He settled into the life of a regular nightclub singer, squeezing out a living and hoping for a hit.

– 18 –

JIMMY'S WOES

In December 1957, Jimmy Lee Swaggart's and Jerry Lee Lewis's lifestyles were eons apart. Jimmy was still working as a swamper, eking out a meager living and barely supporting a wife and three-year-old son. He spent most of his time on the weekends—and even some evenings after a long day of grinding manual labor—preaching in surrounding towns, in small churches, or even in the streets, passing out gospel tracts to those who showed even a modicum of interest in his message. He was weeks away from becoming a full-time traveling evangelist, an existence that loomed as even shakier financially than his already limited condition.

Meanwhile, Jerry was in and around Ferriday, taking a well-deserved break after his pinnacle year of 1957. "Whole Lotta Shakin' Going On" had been a monster hit and everyone in the music industry knew that "Great Balls of Fire" was destined to be another smash.

On a chilly December Sunday morning at the end of that year, Jimmy was scheduled to preach at his daddy's church in Wisner, thirty miles north of Ferriday, and Jerry was in attendance. Jerry was his usual lighthearted, talkative self that morning prior to church. He peppered Jimmy with questions about Jimmy's preaching efforts and small successes.

"Where have you been preaching? What kind of crowds have

you been having? What books do you pull your best sermons from?"

During his sermon Jimmy held nothing back. Years later, in his autobiography he would recount in detail how he all but pleaded with Jerry in front of the entire congregation to leave the life of fame and glamour, imploring him to repent and devote his talents to God. Jerry clutched the pew in front of him, his mind reeling as he waged his familiar internal struggle between good and evil, God and Mammon.

Jimmy saw Jerry's face turn ashen, his knuckles become white as his grip on the pew tighten. Jerry had been raised to believe that life was a series of decisions between devotion to God and everything else. Now, he was being told that to please God he had to give up his kind of music along with the adoration and acclaim that resulted from his efforts.

Jerry became more and more affected as the sermon continued. Minnie Bell spoke quietly with him, urging him to succumb to his feelings of conviction, come forward, and make things right in his life.

Following the church service, Jerry and Jimmy walked outside. Jerry was calmer by then and ready to counter his cousin's call to return to God. He pointed to his Cadillac. "Do you remember," he asked Jimmy, "when we used to sit on a piano stool and talk about the day we were going to drive one of them?"

Jimmy nodded.

"Well, I've got that one," said Jerry, "plus three more just as nice."

Jerry continued. "Remember when we used to talk about making a thousand dollars a day?" he asked.

"Sure I do," said Jimmy, "We did a lot of dreaming."

"Well, my dream has come true ten times over," Jerry said.

Jerry talked of his numerous fancy automobiles, the new home and all the nice things he had provided for his mama and daddy, and how he commanded $10,000 a day by letting his fingers work their magic at the piano.

Jimmy listened patiently and responded to his cousin's comments caringly, yet succinctly.

"I know. But what if you lose your soul, Jerry?"

Jerry was quiet. He contemplated whether serving God could coexist with his realized dreams for riches and, even more importantly, with the recognition he craved. He couldn't see how God and his dreams could fit together.

After long moments of silence between the twenty-two-year-old cousins, Jimmy put his hand on Jerry's shoulder. "I don't sing or play as well as you do," he told him, "but what little I have is God's. All of it. Just think what would happen if you gave Him all you have, Jerry."

Jerry turned to his double-cousin.

"I can't," he said. The pain he felt was reflected in his eyes and face. "I just can't."

With that, Jerry Lee Lewis turned, walked down the steps of the little church, ambled to his Cadillac in the church parking lot, and climbed in. Jimmy watched him drive away, the shiny car slowly growing smaller in the distance.

Jerry had seen glimpses of what it meant to follow God when he attended Bible college, where he had never fit in. He had struggled to make a living preaching sermons on Sundays and Wednesday nights. He had even tried to bargain with God, pledging to give up secular music after just one more success, one more hurdle crossed, one more thrill of recognition.

However, every accomplishment led to the next possibility, the next feather in his cap. What was wrong with his desire to play music for thousands of people? Yet Jerry understood his rock 'n' roll lifestyle conflicted with the teachings he had received and internalized, and that this conflict would dog him his entire career. Feeling the conviction in Jimmy's words and his own heart, he found himself bargaining with God once again. He'd address the issue again, he promised God, after one more gold record. Or two. Or three.

Like most men, Jerry would not humble himself, not yet, not now. As 1957 turned into 1958, he would soon learn that circumstances have a way of humbling men when they least expect it.

In 1958 Jerry convinced Sam Phillips to offer Jimmy a recording contract that would allow Jimmy to record and perform gospel music. Jimmy wanted to accept the offer but he felt God had better things in store for him. And so Jimmy rejected the offer.

When the Swaggarts passed through Memphis on their evangelical rounds, they would stay with the Lewises. When Jerry was around, he and Jimmy enjoyed their time together. Still, the overnight stays amidst his cousin's newfound life of luxury—the good furniture, the extensive wardrobes, the shiny automobiles—were difficult for Jimmy, who felt that he should be providing similar things for his own family.

Jerry's success did prove beneficial to Jimmy in his early years of preaching, however. His cousin's fame drew crowds. Posters announcing Jimmy's upcoming appearances displayed the name Jerry Lee Lewis more prominently than Jimmy Swaggart.

Jimmy constantly made an example of Jerry in his sermons by relating childhood adventures they had shared as well as stories about Jerry's path to success. He typically cast these stories as part of the universal drama that juxtaposed the holiness of the narrow path to eternity—against the broad and sinful road to destruction that Jerry had taken.

Jerry knew that Jimmy was using his story as a cautionary tale. On the one hand, he didn't mind because he knew it was for a higher purpose. On the other hand, it bothered him because he had a strong, inescapable feeling in his gut that Jimmy had it right.

For Jimmy, self-doubt was a constant companion. Even from his early years, he had never been sure of himself, and it pained him, especially when he contrasted himself with Jerry, who seemed to feel equal to any task. In all likelihood, Jimmy's doubts resulted from his strict upbringing, which can squelch a child's ability to trust his own ideas and feelings and build self-confidence. Jimmy's self-doubt morphed into self-condemnation, which in time led to depression. His exacting standards and the tension that often overtook him could and did trigger unexpected tirades toward Frances or others. He felt guilty about these outbursts but could not always control them. At times, he felt overwhelmed by what he regarded as his own inadequacies and his low spirits affected him physically. He couldn't sleep at night and his nerves were jangled.

"I tried to read my Bible yet all the words were cold," Jimmy would write later. "I tried to pray yet I couldn't reach God."

He had hit an impasse and saw no way out. He was losing hope, and perhaps his faith. His darkening mood was exacerbated by constant financial struggle. As a teenager, he had had many ideas for making money, including less-than-honorable ones. He resented his father's decision to go into full-time ministry, knowing that the family's finances would suffer. Now there were days when Jimmy, driving a beat-up car down some dusty back road of rural Mississippi, would see the irony of the situation in which he now found himself.

When dealing with difficulty in his life, Jimmy often dreamed that a threatening or hideous creature battled with him. This imagery was important, as Jimmy felt the physical challenges and personality weaknesses he faced were closely wedded to forces presented by a spiritual realm beyond the physical one.

Jimmy's internal struggles led to further health problems. After moving into full-time ministry in 1958, he contracted pneumonia. During his hospital stay he listened to Jerry's songs on the radio.

"It seemed as if all the darkened, oppressive forces of hell had been unleashed against me," Jimmy would write later. "I was swamped with depression. Dark, gloomy thoughts roamed through my mind. 'Look at you,' the voices said. 'If your God is so great, why doesn't He heal you? Look at Jerry Lee,' the voices said. 'He used to be a preacher but he's gotten smart.'"

– 19 –

MYRA GALE

Myra Gale Brown, the daughter of J. W. and Lois Brown, was born July 11, 1944, and was twelve years old when she met Jerry Lee Lewis in late 1956. Jerry's father, Elmo, and J. W.'s mother, Jane, were brother and sister, making Jerry and J. W. first cousins. Being J. W.'s daughter, Myra was Jerry's first cousin once removed.

Myra was a beautiful girl, with soft features, big eyes, and beautiful flowing hair. As Jerry's youngest sister, Linda Gail, would write years later, Myra "looked like she was twenty." She was birthed and reared by parents who were still children when she was born and the three of them grew up together.

Jerry met her when he dropped by the Browns' home. He was wearing cowboy boots, blue jeans, and a goatee.

He's so cute, Myra thought.

There was an instant connection between the flirtatious, handsome twenty-one-year-old Jerry and twelve-year-old Myra Gale, though their relationship began innocently. In early 1957, Jerry moved in with the Browns, bringing with him his second wife Jane and Jerry Lee Jr. Jerry and Jane had a rocky relationship and she returned to Ferriday within months.

The interaction between Jerry and Myra soon evolved from simple flirting to something more serious. When Jerry was on the road, homesick and lonely, he called Myra on the phone four or five times a day and again late at night.

When they were together, they exchanged furtive kisses in swimming pools, and he mouthed "I love you" to her while he was performing on stage. In November 1957, Jerry went AWOL in Cleveland hours before a performance. As show time drew nearer, a mad search yielded a phone call to the Brown residence back in Memphis, where Jerry was found. He casually mentioned that he had decided to catch a flight to see Myra. A dash back to the airport got Jerry to Cleveland for a show that, of necessity, started several hours late.

In late November, Jerry and his friend Glenda Burgess went to Mississippi and secured a marriage license, with Glenda pretending to be Myra. Two weeks later, on December 12, 1957, Jerry drove to Hernando, Mississippi, twenty-six miles south of Memphis, which was a popular spot for eloping couples, especially those marrying without parental consent. His now thirteen-year-old cousin accompanied him. They were married by the Reverend M. C. Whitten. The bride wore a brand-new red dress her mother had picked out as part of her daughter's school wardrobe.

While their marriage was ridiculed by many over the years, the reality is that marriage at similarly young ages was not uncommon in that time period, particularly in the South, Appalachia, and other poor and rural areas. Loretta Lynn, the First Lady of country music, married at age thirteen. In the Lewis family, Jerry's sisters, Frankie Jean and Linda Gail, were first married at ages eleven and fourteen, respectively. The taboo on sex out of wedlock contributed to this practice, as did the attempt to escape poverty and the speed in which children in difficult circumstances were forced to grow up.

Marrying within one's family wasn't all that unusual either and Jerry was well aware that his paternal grandparents, Leroy and Arilla Lewis, had been first cousins.

Later, Jerry's sister Linda Gail would write in her humorous, light-hearted manner, "Hell, in Ferriday, I could have married a cousin and not even known it. It was no big deal."

"We were just kids in love," Jerry explained.

Jerry's mother, Mamie, was not pleased. "Boy," she told him, "you're fixin' to ruin your career."

In early 1958, Jerry's fourth single, "Breathless," was released to wide acclaim. Jerry performed all over the country and toured Australia with a group of stars that included Buddy Holly and Paul Anka. In May of that year, Jerry was scheduled to play some gigs in England. He could hardly wait to get there.

Bridge over the Mississippi River between Vidalia, Louisiana,
and Natchez, Mississippi

Sign entering Ferriday, Louisiana

Minnie Bell and Jimmy
(Photo courtesy of Frankie Jean Lewis Terrell)

Mamie, Jerry, and Elmo Jr.
(Photo courtesy of Delta Music Museum)

Irene
(Photo courtesy of Edna Gilley Mequet)

Former Assembly of God church in Ferriday, located at the
corner of Eighth Street and Texas Avenue

Tribute to Will Haney and Haney's Big House

Jerry
(Photo courtesy of Delta Music Museum)

Jimmy
(Photo courtesy of Frankie Jean Lewis Terrell)

The Swaggart family
(Photo courtesy of Sherrie Calhoun Jacobs)

Mickey
(Photo courtesy of Rae Beatty)

Irene and Mickey
(Photo courtesy of Edna Gilley Mequet)

Elmo and Jerry
(Photo courtesy of Delta Music Museum)

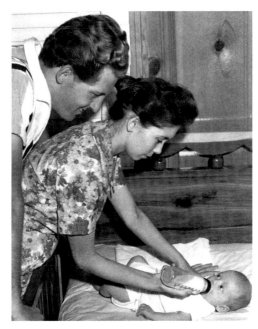

Jerry, Myra, and Steve Allen
(Photo courtesy of Delta Music Museum)

Jimmy as a young traveling evangelist
(Photo courtesy of Frankie Jean Lewis Terrell)

Mickey and Vivian
(Photo courtesy of Edna Gilley Mequet)

– 20 –

THE DEVIL'S MUSIC

The notion that rock 'n' roll was the Devil's music was perhaps nowhere more powerfully symbolized than in a legend about the great Delta bluesman, Robert Johnson. In the early 1930s, Johnson was rumored to have sat alone in the dark Mississippi night; a young man taking in the stillness of the night and the sounds of his guitar as his fingers found the chords he had been struggling to learn. A constant yearning inside him fostered by the hard early years of his life, a need he didn't understand, found its way to his fingertips and the strings of the instrument that rarely left his hands.

He had come to this crossroad, some two hundred miles north of Natchez, Mississippi, and seventy-five miles south of Memphis, because he had been instructed to go there by the older musicians with whom he had sat and to whom he had listened for countless hours. They said this trip to the crossroads was an important step in his journey to become the accomplished guitarist he desperately wanted to be.

Legend claims that on this night, Johnson was visited by the Devil, who took the form of a large black man. The Devil tuned his guitar and an unspoken pact was formed by the two, in which Johnson gained the ability to play guitar with a supernatural ability in exchange for selling his soul to Lucifer.

The story of Robert Johnson's midnight pact with Satan has been passed down through the decades, promulgated by those who knew Johnson during his short, impactful life. All that is known for sure is that Johnson found his unique, haunting voice and playing style through his constant struggle between good and evil, vice and virtue.

From his birth in Hazlehurst, Mississippi on May 8, 1911, to his death twenty-seven years later—just ten days after nine-year-old Elmo Lewis Jr. was killed by a drunk driver—the life of Robert Johnson had been a mysterious one, and stories about him are of necessity laced with fact and fiction, all contributing to the larger-than-life persona of the great blues maker himself.

The loss of his sixteen-year-old wife and child during childbirth in 1929 led Johnson to feel anger toward God. A loner and a wanderer, he roamed from location to location, playing for various lengths of time before mysteriously disappearing—even walking out of a performance in the middle of a song—not to be heard from again for weeks at a time. Musicians who knew him during the 1930s were amazed at the compelling sounds his thin fingers drew from his guitar and the deep, penetrating voice that could stir profound emotion. It was through the legend of Johnson and the Devil that people first referred to the music he made as "the Devil's music."

Best known for songs such as "Terraplane Blues" and "Kind Hearted Woman," Johnson was on the road to widespread recognition outside of the South when he was given poisoned whiskey in 1938, in an incident reportedly motivated by Johnson's involvement with a married woman and a jealous husband. For the three days Johnson suffered before dying, he struggled for the redemption of his soul. Next to his deathbed he had written, "Jesus of Nazareth, King of Jerusalem, I know that my Redeemer liveth and that he will call me from the grave."

As with other music pioneers that blazed trails in the Delta Blues and, later, rock 'n' roll, a great war was waged for the very soul of the performer, as the raw energy emitted from the tireless struggle within produced a sound that would move tens of millions of listeners.

The imagery of performers selling their souls to the Devil in order to play soulful, rocking music had an impact on people everywhere who sensed danger in the music's rhythmic beat and the way it prompted audiences to scream and faint, and sometimes even resort to violence. The rock 'n' roll concert had a message that many detractors felt was negative. It had a pulse, a force that suggested that it was about something more than just music. To many, songs like "Whole Lotta Shakin Going On" and "Great Balls of Fire" openly espoused the joys of sex.

Five decades later, Jerry would tell a writer for the *New York Times* about his music, "I never noticed that it had an effect on anybody that bad. The girls went a little berserk, but that's girls for you."

But in the eyes of many parents who saw this young rocker for the first time on *The Steve Allen Show* in 1957, his music and the way he performed it were anything but harmless. The backlash that rock 'n' roll produced came from people who disliked it or feared it for a variety of reasons. Music purists saw it as devoid of redeeming musical quality. Political conservatives found its message offensive and amoral. White supremacy groups took it as proof that black music had infiltrated what they regarded as proper society. The White Citizens Council in the South declared "the screaming, idiotic words and savage music of these records are undermining the morals of our white youth in America."

Some said rock 'n' roll was a strategy to promote race-mixing. Others murmured it was promoted by Communists to accelerate the self-destruction of American society through a younger generation's depravity.

A bellwether event in the growing repercussions to rock 'n' roll occurred in early 1958 as part of Alan Freed's "Big Beat Tour," in which two of the main attractions were Chuck Berry and Jerry Lee Lewis. As the tour arrived in Boston, chaos erupted. Gang riots spilled out into the streets complete with stabbings, muggings, and vandalism. The Boston shows were cancelled as were those in a few others cities in the Northeast. Naysayers of rock 'n' roll now had powerful ammunition in their fight against this new form of music.

The parties that led the fight against rock 'n' roll had several targets in their sights. Perhaps most notable among them were Alan Freed and Elvis Presley, although Jerry's performances were wilder than Elvis's had ever been. Jerry's persona was more in-your-face and his songs were more overtly sexual and threatening. His bold ego and sneer suggested the desire for a confrontation. He didn't hide his rough edges. They went everywhere with him, especially on the stage, as he proudly pounded his message with abandon.

In March 1958 after Elvis was inducted into the army, he assumed the aura of a good, clean American boy. This left one man to become the poster child for rock 'n' roll. He was the most popular rock 'n' roller of 1957 and early 1958. He was the most dangerous and lascivious performer. He was the most dynamic, out-of-control live performer of the era. He was the least refined, the least manageable, and the scariest threat to parents. His name was Jerry Lee Lewis.

The irony was that Jerry's own mixed emotions about rock 'n' roll echoed the feelings of some of his detractors. In his moments of introspection, he too abhorred the rock n' roll lifestyle, which embraced free-flowing alcohol, hell-raising, and loose women.

In the middle of long road trips he would veer between drinking, drugging, and skirt-chasing and launching into hellfire and brimstone sermons. On one occasion, as he preached so animatedly while being driven to the next gig, he pounded the back seat with sufficient force to sprain his hand, which prevented him from playing the piano the next evening.

Jerry's struggle was an interesting contrast to Little Richard, the other key early rock 'n' roll pioneer who engaged in onstage histrionics and had an obsession with spirituality. Unlike Jerry, Little Richard embraced the mixing of rock 'n' roll and religion almost to the point of what many considered blasphemy.

Late one night on a lonely, two-lane highway, four men rode in a Cadillac. One of the men in the backseat leaned against the door and tried to sleep.

Some miles back, another car followed with members of the same entourage. The travelers had just left a two-show performance to drive six hundred miles to a show scheduled for the next evening.

In the Cadillac the radio played quietly, too softly for anyone to understand the words. The low sound provided a soothing white noise to the journey. In the passenger-side front seat sat a quiet, brooding Jerry Lee Lewis. Some evenings he laughed, joked, and carried on with his traveling counterparts. But not tonight.

His silence determined the mood of everyone in the car. Their small talk became less and less frequent, with each man left to his own thoughts and the sense of what was about to come. It was a scene that had played out before. Days or weeks—or even months—might lapse between episodes, but the episodes always reappeared.

"Did you see how those women in the front row reacted tonight?" Jerry demanded. "Did you see the way they were shakin' uncontrollably? Did you see the looks in their eyes?"

The car's passengers listened to their leader's words.

"We are draggin' these people to hell with us. God is not goin' to tolerate this forever."

From the backseat, a voice of moderation tried to offer some balance to Jerry's extremes.

"Jerry Lee, these people aren't goin' to hell for listenin' to a little rock 'n' roll music."

"The hell they ain't. Listenin' to music is one thing. The way those people were actin' was something entirely different. There's somethin' in that that just ain't right."

He waited several seconds. Hearing no reaction, he continued, his comments morphing into the sermons he preached years earlier.

"God said you better be hot or cold. But don't be lukewarm! The worst thing you can be is lukewarm. He said He's going to spit us out if we are lukewarm. Man, what are we doing?!"

The comments grew increasingly excited over the next minutes before slowly receding back inside the man, where the war continued to be waged.

– 21 –

TROUBLE ALL AROUND

Sam and Jud Phillips tried to dissuade Jerry from taking his young
bride to England. Jerry was convinced that his popularity would
trump any negative publicity, which in his mind seemed unlikely
anyway. He paid no attention to his handlers who begged him once
he'd arrived in London not to draw attention to his child bride.

Jerry didn't see it that way. Sure, Myra was thirteen years old,
but she was a woman in his eyes. As far as he was concerned, that
was that. When he made his mind up about something, he rarely
changed it.

His first shows in London were incredible; the audiences
adored this wild, crazy man from "across the pond" who played
piano and sang like no one else. He made no effort to hide Myra
or the fact they were married, and soon the British press found out
the young girl in his entourage was his wife. Not his fifteen-year-
old wife, as they were originally told, but his thirteen-year-old third
wife—and his cousin.

As this information soon filled the front pages of British
tabloids, attendance at his shows dropped precipitously while
the British population debated whether he should be arrested or
deported. Local officials and members of Parliament added their
own harsh comments. Jerry and his handlers had no way to stem the
onslaught. Within days, the tour was cancelled and Jerry and Myra
flew back to the States.

The seriousness of the situation was lost on Jerry, who assumed America would welcome him with open arms and that the hits would keep rolling. To him the London debacle was a minor blip that would not impair his continuing ascendance.

Instead, he became the subject of one of the swiftest, most dramatic falls from grace in the history of popular entertainment.

Key personalities in the music industry abandoned him. He was simply too hot for individuals like Alan Freed and Dick Clark who, in what Clark would later admit was an act of cowardice, dropped Jerry from a planned appearance. Promoters around the country were scared away from booking him. Disc jockeys everywhere boycotted his records. He could not escape the seriousness of his situation, but as things worsened Jerry became angrier and more obstinate. As far as he was concerned, what he did personally was nobody's business. As he told one reporter, "What's between me and Myra is between us and God."

But Jerry's marriage was a matter in which the public had a major say, as he would learn when "High School Confidential," his fifth record with Sun which came out just prior to his departure for England, stalled at number twenty and quickly fell off the charts. It was the last time that he would appear on any charts for many years. The more Jerry tried to regroup the more the situation worsened. To Sam Phillips, the whole thing was ridiculous. "Jerry's innocence and his trying to be open and friendly and engaging with the press backfired," he said. "They scalped him. It turned out to be a very ghastly and deadly thing. So many people wanted to point a finger of scorn at rockers and say, 'We told you so; rockers are no good.'"

Jerry would later resent that, at the time of his public derision and futile attempts to recover in the early sixties, Elvis was living at Graceland with the still teenaged Priscilla Beaulieu, whom he'd met and romanced during his stint in the army when she was fourteen years old.

"At least I made an honest woman out of Myra," Jerry would say.

The June 9, 1958 issue of *Billboard* magazine carried an open letter from Jerry to his fans. "I confess that my life has been stormy," the letter read. "I confess further that since I have become a public figure, I sincerely wanted to be worthy of the decent admiration of all the people, young and old, that admired or liked what talent (if any) I have. That is, after all, all that I have in a professional way to offer."

Sam Phillips tried releasing a record of Jerry's under a pseudonym. He was optimistic that "The Hawk" would generate healthy sales, but the record failed because Jerry's voice and music were unmistakable.

Yet even as Jerry's career seemed to be over, there were occasional glimmers of hope. His 1961 rendition of Ray Charles's "What I'd Say" cracked the top thirty and suggested that the ice was beginning to thaw. It wasn't. Though he had successful runs on *Shindig!*, a variety music show, and made a return appearance to Dick Clark's *American Bandstand* in 1962, his airplay remained minimal, his record sales were lousy, and a dismal mood continued to permeate the scene. He found increasing solace in drugs and alcohol and, paradoxically, drew enormous strength to keep going from the anger welling up inside him. He was still thrilling those diehard fans who came out to see him perform live but he was quickly becoming an afterthought to radio listeners who rarely heard his music.

On February 27, 1959, Myra gave birth to their first child. They named him Steve Allen Lewis, the loyal and thankful Jerry honoring the man who had given him his big national TV break two years earlier.

Ever protective and controlling, Jerry forced Myra to move to Ferriday during her pregnancy so that she could be close to the Lewis family physician, Dr. Radcliffe, the only man Jerry trusted with the care of his pregnant wife.

One night in Memphis, Elvis was at Graceland talking with his longtime friend George Klein, a well-known Memphis disc jockey, and a mutual friend, Alan Fortas.

Around midnight, the phone rang. Elvis asked George to answer it. After a minute of discussion, George said, "Elvis, Sam Phillips is on the phone. He and Jerry Lee Lewis are out and about and wondered if they could drop by and visit."

A short while later, the men were sitting in Elvis's living room, with Jerry and Elvis on a white couch chatting like old friends—telling stories, spinning yarns, laughing like a couple of country boys in a bar.

Jerry was still clawing his way back from the 1958 scandal. His rendition of "What'd I Say" hadn't climbed the charts as high as it should have, but Jerry still thought it was a start. With little radio airplay or chart success, he was building his base back as a phenomenal live performer at bars and venues all over the country.

After a while Elvis and Jerry ended up at the grand piano in the music room, where George Klein watched an amazing scene unfold as the two men played together. There were four-handed displays as Elvis played the left side of the keyboard and Jerry's hands ran over the higher notes at the other end. Stories were interspersed throughout the performance but it was mainly about music for the two men. Elvis would sing Jerry's songs while Jerry played the piano. Jerry would sing Elvis's songs while Elvis played the piano. A variety of duos were mixed in and Sam would holler out a request at any lull in the action. George noticed the sparkle in Sam's eyes as he watched the two men he had discovered play together.

Later that night, after Jerry and Sam departed, Elvis summarized his feelings about Jerry, the man who remained in the Sun Records depleted stable, struggling to get back to the top.

"You know, George," he said, "that guy's a genius on the piano."

On Easter Sunday in 1962, Jerry and his band were on the road in Minnesota. Myra, who was just seventeen, was at home in Memphis with Stevie and Jerry's father, Elmo, in the house Jerry recently bought with a big yard and swimming pool.

Myra and little Stevie had been to church earlier that day and Myra had found joy in watching her youthful, vibrant son hunt Easter eggs. As the three-year-old ran from egg to egg, he had little idea what he was doing. He picked up the brightly-painted objects and put them in the basket his mother carried beside him. He was especially thrilled as the laughs and cheers of excitement mounted with the addition of each mini-treasure.

In the evening, while Myra cooked dinner and Elmo visited with a Herron brother-in-law, Stevie went into the backyard pool area, typically secured by a fence and latched gate. While playing with a water hose, he fell into the dark water. Moments later, as Myra searched frantically for him she observed the running water hose near the pool. Within minutes, as Myra screamed, a neighbor pulled Stevie's body from the murky pool. Neighbors and a nearby doctor struggled to revive Stevie, to no avail. Shortly thereafter, someone called Jerry. Cecil Harrelson answered the phone and relayed the news to his friend.

Jerry was devastated and mired in mourning, sadness, guilt, blame, and accusations that would not abate for years. Often he blamed Myra. Other times he blamed himself, convinced that God was punishing him for the career he had chosen and the life he was leading. Myra, in her own sorrow and mourning, went through a period of deep religious searching and dedication, devoting her life to God. For a time, she was so crazed with grief that she became convinced that God would bring her dear Stevie back from the grave.

Six days after Stevie's death, Jerry left for a prescheduled trip to England, the first visit since his fiasco four years earlier. He was deep in mourning yet needed to honor his contractual commitments. The warmth of the British fans surprised him. Later Myra joined him on the tour, though she was still dazed by the loss of Stevie. The once-hostile British crowds applauded the shy teenager on the rare occasions she made a public appearance.

His performances were outstanding, but the pain of Stevie's death did not recede. It led Jerry further down the self-destructive path paved with drugs and sleepless nights, and private, unspoken agony.

Two years later, he returned to England. Footage from his concerts showed a heavier, twenty-eight-year-old Jerry, whose struggle and anguish was clearly present in his eyes. As he pounded the keys of the piano, belting out "I'm On Fire," unruly hair fell across his puffy, glassy eyes.

Sixteen months after Stevie's death, Myra gave birth to their second child, Phoebe Allen Lewis. Their newborn daughter made their pain tolerable, but barely. Jerry was slow to accept Phoebe. Maybe it was because Stevie's death made it difficult to connect with another child. Maybe Jerry didn't feel comfortable with the idea of having a daughter. It was weeks later, after holding the little girl in his arms and seeing her smile, that he fell in love.

– 22 –

TRAVELING PREACHER

In January 1958, Jimmy quit his job as a swamper to perform his evangelistic work full-time. He felt it was a logical step in fulfilling God's will for his life, and he accepted the call with enthusiasm and energy.

He knew it was not a lifestyle for the faint of heart. Countless others had struggled to do it, living day-to-day, scratching out meager livings, never sure what was around the next corner, living as Christians would term it "by faith." Anyone who suggested in later years that Jimmy became an evangelist with the goal of obtaining acclaim and riches likely had little or no idea of the situation Jimmy and Frances encountered as they traveled through the southern United States. Seeking to interest local preachers in staging revivals in their churches and relying on the generosity of typically impoverished attendees and hard-pressed local pastors was difficult and often uncomfortable. They stayed in the spare bedrooms of pastors or families, moving from town to town and home to home. Sometimes they stayed in a musty basement or an unused room within the church, or slept at a local camp or even in the car.

Their young son, Donnie, who was born in 1954, shared his parents' nomadic existence, making it impossible for him to develop lasting friendships with children his age. He would later joke about the staggering number of schools he attended in a school year, as his father's preaching itinerary moved them to yet another city for a new series of revival meetings.

His parents felt guilty about the effects of their calling on Donnie. Frances worked diligently to fill in the gaps of Donnie's elementary education, and he benefited from being a close companion to both parents. Still, the absence of a stable home and social environment was another sacrifice that traveling evangelists made.

Later, recalling those years, Jimmy would write, "My battered, blue Plymouth was literally falling apart. Frances had only four cotton dresses. Donnie had so few clothes they could have been carried in a sack. All I had was a twenty-dollar Stein suit and a single pair of shoes. Some nights we went to bed hungry."

Many of Jimmy's prayers and struggles of faith pertained to finances. He made supplications for food, clothes, even for the ability of his beat-up car to make it to the next town. He and Frances covered vast expanses of highway to get from revival to revival driving a worn-out Dodge.

Even as his cousin Jerry struggled to overcome his tumble from grace, his generosity was the answer to Jimmy's prayers. Despite his troubles, Jerry took Jimmy to the Ford and Pontiac dealerships around Ferriday to buy his cousin a vehicle. Secretly, Jimmy harbored his own desire, which he finally introduced to the conversation.

"Jerry, why don't we drive over to Natchez to look at Oldsmobiles?"

Later that day, Jerry bought Jimmy a tan Oldsmobile for $3,000 that would be invaluable to Jimmy's evangelist efforts. It was a gift for which he would always be thankful.

For Jerry, it was a genuine show of his propensity to give to family and to recognize Jimmy's efforts to walk the straight and narrow. He also hoped to buy a little extra rope from God.

By 1959, Jimmy, Frances, and Donnie had been on the road a year and Jimmy decided to go before the District Council of the Assemblies of God in Lake Charles, Louisiana, to seek ordination. He knew from others that the process was pretty much perfunctory, particularly for someone as fully committed as he was.

To his astonishment, Jimmy was passed over for ordination. As he sat before the Council trying to understand why they had rejected him, waves of self-doubt and inferiority engulfed him. He recalled pangs of inadequacy from his childhood, when other families had looked down on him and his relatives as they walked to their Holy Roller church; how he'd endured the snickers of other children as they bought their movie tickets and watched him standing outside, afraid to go in. He felt the embarrassment of living in that tiny trailer behind his Aunt Irene's house with a new wife. He heard his inner voice—sounding distinctly like Son Swaggart—gnawing at him to make something of himself.

As he searched for reasons for the rejection, he decided that his relationship to the controversial Jerry Lee Lewis hindered his ordination efforts, particularly since Jimmy so often invoked the name of his famous cousin and drew attention to their familial status to attract people to his services and youth rallies. Or maybe the problem was the boogie woogie sounds of the music he played on church pianos that sounded a lot like honky-tonk music. Or perhaps the Council had heard that young Swaggart's push-the-envelope, attacking preaching style was too controversial.

Jimmy prayed through the disappointment to find the strength to keep preaching. As he continued on his path, he relied more deeply on his God and his wife.

On June 9, 1960, Jimmy's mama, Minnie Bell, went to a small clinic in Centreville, Mississippi, to have a hysterectomy. Two of her sisters, Stella and Mamie, were there with her and Son. Jimmy and Frances were in Alabama. As they traveled home to visit his mama, Jimmy, anxious for news of the surgery, stopped at a pay phone on the side of the road and called Aunt Stella. She wept as she told him his mother had died. Jimmy wept too.

Minnie Bell's body was laid out in her sister Stella's home for viewing. Family members came to see her in her coffin, stunned that the forty-three-year-old Minnie Bell, the baby Herron sister, was gone.

Minnie Bell's niece and Jerry's sister, Linda Gail, remembered, "Everybody just loved Minnie Bell so much. She was really a favorite with everybody. She was very kind and sweet. I remember my mother and Aunt Stella were just crushed when she died. It was so horrible."

Relatives came from everywhere to her funeral. Jerry cancelled several shows to be there. Mickey was there to lend support and remember the sweet, good-natured woman.

Jimmy was inconsolable, the full impact of losing his precious mother only beginning to dawn. He looked for meaning in everything, yet her loss seemed so pointless.

Son Swaggart was not reserved in his emotions. At Stella's house and later at the funeral, he was unable to stop crying. Minnie Bell had been his strength, the woman he had come to rely on so heavily that his identity could not really be separated from hers. He had a reputation among the family as stern—even unkind at times—but the sympathy for his pain was universal. Even the Herron women, who were angry at Son for taking their sister to a cheap clinic in Mississippi for medical attention, extended temporary compassion to Jimmy's daddy.

Nine months later, Jimmy's grandma Ada had a stroke and died, and with her passing, the two guiding lights of Jimmy's life were gone. Frances would step into the void and become the backbone of his ministry.

– 23 –

NESADEL

In 1960, Mickey moved to the Nesadel, a club on Spencer Highway. He played six nights a week, four sets a night, forty-five minutes per set. His initial salary of $90 a week eventually became $175. He had hoped for something closer to his dreams for success, but the gig was surprisingly satisfying. "I felt successful," he would say years later. "I was making enough to get by on. It was a good, steady job and the people were coming out to hear me play."

He would stay at the Nesadel for ten years, honing his craft and evolving from a man with talent for playing the piano into a consummate professional, singer, and entertainer. The crowd at the Nesadel included many regulars and Mickey developed a loyal, sizable following. He and his band played a variety of music and this diversity added to his appeal, particularly in the absence of chart-topping hits of his own.

"I was doing tunes that people could listen to or dance to," Mickey said later. "We were doing a little Jimmy Reed, 'You got me running, got me hiding.' We were doing what they called 'The Whip' back then. And then we'd do the slow dance music—the belly-rubbing music I called it—and the two-step, anything to keep the people on the dance floor and show them a good time. We'd have people come in and request a song and I'd write it down and I'd go get the record and try to learn that particular tune."

At the Nesadel, Mickey supplemented his income during the fifteen minutes following each set when he headed to the Nesadel's pool tables and demonstrated the formidable abilities that he'd honed in his father's pool hall in Ferriday.

Sometimes his saxophone player, Norman Carlson, would watch him play.

"You couldn't beat Gilley on a pool table. You just flat couldn't beat him. He was very good. Take my word for it."

As proud as Mickey was of Jerry's success, he recognized that Jerry's shadow loomed over him—even when Jerry was struggling. That shadow was both blessing and hindrance, and Mickey turned it to his own advantage, relying on his ability to play Jerry's music. When he'd play "Whole Lotta Shakin'" or "Crazy Arms" or "You Win Again" people would flock to the piano. Mickey understood his success with these songs lay in his ability to copy Jerry's style, a useful tactic for a performer who had not yet developed his own identity.

"People accused me of copying Jerry," Mickey allowed years later. "I wasn't trying to copy him. I was trying to be exactly like him. I could do his music so close to him that it was uncanny."

Often, people came up to him and said, "You play it better than Jerry Lee Lewis."

Mickey knew this was not the case. "You know," he'd say at times, "a copy is different from dreaming something up and doing it yourself."

Mickey mimicked the way Jerry's music sounded on his records, knowing that Jerry was always changing his music so that he never played any song the same way twice. Jerry prided himself on the ability to create these infinite variations of his music and his gift for it set Mickey marveling.

But Mickey's close connection to Jerry proved to be a double-edged sword. "I suffered from Jerry Lee syndrome," he would say years later. "I let it bug me to the point where it just about drove me nuts."

– 24 –

THE EVANGELISTS

Following the end of World War II a great religious and spiritual revival occurred, first in America, and then throughout the world. Its first phase involved those affiliated with or sympathetic to the traditional Pentecostal message, which focused on the power of the Holy Ghost, speaking in tongues, casting out demons, and, preeminently, physical healing and miracle working. This phase of the revival peaked in the mid- to late 1950s.

A second wave would begin in the early to mid-1960s as the message was extended to and embraced by people outside the Pentecostal world, including those from older, more traditional denominations such as Roman Catholics. In this wave of the revival, the message and delivery evolved as it became targeted to a broader, more sophisticated audience.

The first wave of the revival owed its success to a dynamic group of preachers and evangelists who became leaders of the religious world, drawing huge crowds to churches, stadiums, civic arenas, and tents. These men with their extraordinary charisma held thousands spellbound with their messages of hope and deliverance. They were strong and driven individuals, crisscrossing the country, working grueling hours, preaching and praying for the faithful.

Most were born in poverty and raised around deeply seated religious dogma. Some were delivered from some sickness or addiction as children or young adults, and believed they had heard directly from God about the direction for their lives.

The best were also astute businessmen, able to organize large groups of people, drive publicity, establish effective means of communication and marketing, and generate the tremendous revenue necessary to support the big plans they felt called to by God.

They were men like William Branham, who had a soft voice and mild manner yet was was able to capture the rapt attention of his audience. Branham could identify a specific condition or event that hindered the healing of those he sought to help. He would feel God's power to heal moving through him when he felt "vibrations" moving through his left hand. Those who knew him well admired his humility and his ability to avoid the pride that afflicted many preachers once they were acclaimed.

Jack Coe was another well-known name of the era. Unlike the mild-mannered Branham, Coe liked a good fight. He confronted his critics and the leadership of the Assemblies of God, many of whom disliked his methods. He took on the most daunting illnesses in his crusades and prayer lines. His 1956 trial and acquittal for practicing medicine in Florida and his rapid physical decline and death from polio in 1957 were momentous events in the revival's early years.

Other big names—such as A. A. Allen, Gordon Lindsay, T. L. Osborn, and Jack Moore—were among dozens of significant evangelists. Thoughtful leaders like Lindsay and Oral Roberts, who wanted to publicize successful healings and avoid accusations they were make-believe or dishonest, documented their successes in writing. According to supporters, tens of thousands were healed of all varieties of illnesses and physical conditions.

As the 1950s ended, the healing revivals lost much of their attraction, but a second wave would follow.

Thousands of expectant watchers were seated in folding chairs, all packed together under a giant tent erected in an open lot a few blocks from downtown. It was a cool, crisp evening in early fall in 1950. Anxious, blue-collar people, not used to sitting still for long periods of time, slid their worn shoes and work boots back and forth on the sawdust that covered the floor beneath the large canvas structure.

Up on the podium, a line of humanity—people of all shapes and sizes, white and black, young and old, visibly and not-so-visibly afflicted—snaked off the stage and down the side of the makeshift auditorium. Women in wheelchairs, men with limps and crutches, a middle-aged woman with a noticeable, almost-violent nervous tic, and countless others with less visible maladies, waited for their own personal miracle.

At the podium, a husky man lumbered back and forth across the stage, exhorting the crowd. Oral Roberts had been born and bred in Oklahoma and healed of tuberculosis as a teenager. He became the leading evangelist of his day, one who spoke with authority and a confidence in God's power.

"I tell you," he boomed, "God wants to heal these people who have come in faith tonight, and He wants to heal you too! But you must be willing to believe Him, to trust Him, to know your healing is provided in His atonement for you."

As he spoke, each person in line believed God worked through this man, that he was a conduit for God's healing power. Here, tonight, as in similar scenarios across America and the world, scores of healing revivalists brought their unique ministry to tens of thousands.

The lanky minister with penetrating blue eyes and commanding presence strode excitedly back and forth across the stage. Still a young man, he was prone to consuming quantities of butter in hopes that it would help him to fill out his six-foot-three-inch gangly frame.

His voice filled with conviction as he addressed the crowd of six thousand packed under the Canvas Cathedral, a massive circus tent erected for this occasion a short distance southwest of downtown Los Angeles. Now, Billy Graham spoke of the inevitable, damnable verdict that loomed as a result of continued sin and immorality. His rich voice and machine-gun delivery commanded his listeners to attend to his words.

If Oral Roberts was the face of the faith healing movement in the United States, William Franklin Graham Jr. would become the face of the broader Evangelical movement. His Los Angeles revival took place in September 1949—the same year Son Swaggart became a full-time preacher in small-town, eastern Louisiana and two months before Jerry Lee Lewis would dazzle locals at the Ferriday Ford dealership from the back of a pickup.

At thirty years old, Graham was already a successful evangelist, and this revival would vault him to household name status in a country that admired its preachers, especially those who could walk the walk about which they fervently spoke and to which they exhorted others.

Born on November 7, 1918, in Charlotte, North Carolina, Billy Graham was the first child of his stern but loving parents. Frank and Morrow Graham ran a large dairy farm, served as upstanding citizens of the community, and reared their children steadfastly— if unemotionally—in the ways of the local Presbyterian church. Young Billy Frank, as he was called by his parents, was a hyperactive boy. Although his parents cut many a switch from nearby trees and used them on the child, he was a good kid. His adolescent passions were baseball and girls, although he found only limited success with both. As most boys who grew up on a farm in and around the Depression years, he learned early what hard work was all about.

In 1934, a traveling evangelist, Mordecai Ham, conducted a revival in the area. Graham attended. Near the end of a service, as the spirited preacher invited those interested to come down front to give their hearts to Christ—to accept Christian salvation—Graham took those steps. As he would tell biographer William Martin, "I didn't have any tears, I didn't have any emotion, I didn't hear any thunder, there was no lightning. I saw a lady standing next to me and she had tears in her eyes, and I thought there was something wrong with me because I didn't feel all worked up. But right there, I made my decision for Christ. It was as simple as that, and as conclusive."

Following graduation from high school, Graham spent a short time at the strict, fundamentalist Bob Jones University before going on to greater success at the Florida Bible Institute and Wheaton College in Illinois, institutions with similar views of the inerrancy of Scripture and fundamentalist ideals, but which allowed more freedom in their doctrine. At Wheaton, Graham met Ruth Bell, the daughter of American missionaries who served in China, and the couple married in 1943.

While his preaching style was still raw and delivered too rapidly and too loudly and his physical gestures could be visually distracting, Billy Graham nevertheless was always able to attract much greater numbers of his listeners to repentance and salvation than any of the other young, gifted evangelists. Something about his style drew people in and produced conviction in their hearts and he quickly developed a reputation as a dynamic evangelist.

Following frequent debates about the inerrancy of the Bible and fundamentalist principles with another young evangelist of the 1940s, Chuck Templeton, Graham struggled with doubts about his faith. Then, when taking a solitary walk through the woods near the San Bernadino Mountains, he exclaimed, "Oh God, I cannot prove certain things. I cannot answer some of the questions Chuck is raising and some of the other people are raising, but I accept this Book by faith as the Word of God."

With that declaration, he found the undying faith that would support him for the rest of his life.

Shortly after launching his own evangelistic association, Graham showed tremendous awareness and wisdom by calling his tight-knit team together and identifying the potential pitfalls that had befallen other ministers. Following consideration and prayer, the group pinpointed specific strategies of avoidance and account-ability, taking steps to avoid misdeeds—and even perceived mis-deeds—in the areas of handling money, sexual immorality, inflating public perception, and criticizing other pastors. Most importantly, they identified the dangers inherent in garnering power and adora-tion.

His undying care in these matters would differentiate Graham and affect the way the public perceived him. Ultimately, his name would appear at the top of the list of America's "most admired" for decades, more frequently than anyone else.

As he spoke in the unseasonably cold Los Angeles autumn of 1949, he invoked all the sins that beleaguer men—sexual misbehav-ior, crimes of the heart and of the mind. He even inveighed against a new threat in the post–World War II era, Communism. His Los Angeles revival was extended from three weeks to two months, the services increasingly attended by people from all walks of life.

Newspaper baron William Randolph Hearst, a fervent anti-Communist, exhorted his newspaper's editors to feature Graham in their stories, thus catapulting him to new heights of prestige.

As the revival ended, two weeks after Graham's thirty-first birthday, he was well on his way to becoming the preeminent preacher of the second half of the twentieth century. The only individual who would rival him was, at the time, a fourteen-year-old Pentecostal and local thief in Ferriday, Louisiana.

– 25 –

BREAKING THROUGH

After facing rejection from the Assemblies of God, Jimmy headed into the 1960s, a decade in which his life and ministry would be propelled forward. As many within the denomination became familiar with him, he made friends, met influential people, and was able to make regular appearances in large churches with generous crowds.

Many established pastors supported him both financially and emotionally. Individuals he met in this period like Jerald Ogg and Bill Treeby would play key roles in his expanding ministry. He also met older, respected men who spoke with authority and readily shared their experience of how to conduct a ministry.

Through the 1960s, he preached in ever-larger venues with ever-increasing crowds. Many of his engagements ran four to six weeks in length, reducing the question marks about where he, his family, and their U-Haul trailer would head next. He preached and played in numerous camp meetings around the country and he developed a list of churches and groups to "book" regularly.

His success was due primarily to two aspects of his services: his music and his preaching style. His singing voice, his excellent backup singers and musicians, and his own piano playing that he laced with a heavy dose of right-hand runs up and down the keys were the top draw to his services. His preaching was also popular. He often spoke on current topics in the news and how they related to the Christian lives of his listeners. He was bold and unapologetic for his fundamentalist views. Early on he mastered a style where he could speak uninterrupted in long sermons without any notes. His smooth and melodious voice communicated knowledge and confidence that appealed to his followers.

Jimmy had turned down the recording opportunity that Jerry had arranged for him at Sun Records in 1958, and he refused a similar offer two years later. However, with help from Mickey, he arranged a recording session in Houston in 1960. He was dissatisfied with the quality of several recordings he made, including one of the hymn "Some Golden Daybreak." At Frances's insistence he offered it to radio stations for airplay and sold it at the services he ministered. The positive reception it received provided the assurance he needed and afforded him popularity as a musician that he never expected to have.

In 1962, Jerry again arranged a recording opportunity at Sun Records, and this time Jimmy accepted. The session was engineered by Scotty Moore, who had played guitar on Elvis's early records. Jimmy, always his own biggest critic, was not overwhelmed with the result. But the primary recording, "God Took Away My Yesterdays," would become his first hit, which led to increased demand for more records, heightened interest from distributors, and larger crowds when he preached around the country. With this newfound success, Jimmy began recording with increased regularity.

Once again, Jimmy looked back four years and thought about the offer to record at Sun that he had turned down. He was convinced that the path he had followed honored God more faithfully and this gave him special satisfaction.

When his current revival meetings entered their third week with no signs of slowing down, it was clear that Jimmy was succeeding in a way that he never had before. Attendance at the large church had been steadily growing since Jimmy, Frances, and Donnie had been there and it had finally reached full capacity a couple of nights ago. Jimmy wasn't sure how much longer he could continue to hold services in local churches rather than focus on city auditoriums and larger venues.

Many of the faces Jimmy saw in the congregation were now familiar. Large groups of people who had been there every night gave him knowing looks of approval as he preached tirelessly the hard-hitting, old-time gospel messages they longed to hear. Many new people showed up each night as word of this electrifying young preacher with the marvelous voice and dynamic piano talent spread to the churchgoing crowds in neighboring communities. Some who came to hear him had rarely or never found their way inside a church.

Preachers all over America wanted Jimmy to hold revivals at their churches. His presence was good for the morale of those who attended, it was effective in attracting new members, it infused a new excitement and sense of purpose in the congregation, and it was good worship—and entertainment.

For Jimmy—and for many others—it was all about his Christian message, exhorting the unsaved to repentance and the saved to consecration. He was a one-man, singing, playing, performing, preaching, shouting, whispering extravaganza. He had boundless reserves of energy. He was a big man, strong, and able to hold up under the enormous strain of praying, preaching, playing, and moving from one destination to another.

He did everything he could to stay humble, despite the constant pats on the back, the kind words of appreciation, and the onslaught of praise. He prayed continuously to a God that seemed well able to keep him meek and always struggling against the next potential roadblock.

But slowly, over time, memories of the lean, struggling years faded further and further away in his rear-view mirror.

– 26 –

CLUB REGULAR

In the mid- to late 1950s, Mickey decided to enlist in the US Navy to avoid being drafted and to support his young and growing family. On each occasion he failed the medical test, due to a heart defect he had since birth.

As the fifties turned into the sixties, the heart problem posed a more critical risk, and Mickey became increasingly thin and pale. His physician warned him to take his condition seriously. "Mickey, if you don't, you will be in a wheelchair by age forty and probably won't live much longer beyond that."

Then he heard about a doctor named Michael DeBakey, who was doing groundbreaking heart surgery at nearby Methodist Hospital in Houston. In time Dr. DeBakey would become one of the world's most renowned and innovative heart surgeons. DeBakey was a key contributor to the invention of the heart-lung machine, a pioneer in the development of the artificial heart, and one of the first surgeons to successfully perform heart transplants.

In 1961, Mickey was admitted into a program that would allow him to receive heart surgery, though he had no means of paying for the procedure. Doctors readily accepted him given the grave risk to his life posed by his condition. Despite Mickey's concern and a last-minute near-decision to back out of the surgery on the morning it was scheduled, he went through with the dangerous procedure on his heart.

Mickey awoke from his surgery to a room full of relatives who had driven from Ferriday to support him.

Mickey and Geraldine had married when they were both in their teens, two kids who were in love, anxious to get married, and—like countless millions of other kids in similar situations—having little idea how to make a successful marriage and successful life.

Their struggle as a young couple squeezing out a living in Houston, Texas, was made more challenging by the rapid arrival of three children and a life of living paycheck to paycheck. Financial struggle put strain on the marriage. Mickey found Geraldine was not always a good steward in devoting his meager earnings to essential bills.

"I'd bring money home and instead of her paying the bills she would buy things for the house, you know, and we'd get behind and our credit got bad. It was degrading."

Over time Mickey's attempts to achieve success in the music industry further weakened the relationship as the two drifted apart. The time he spent away from her while trying to record and working across Interstate 10 from Houston to New Orleans drove a further wedge between them. As the months passed, Geraldine replaced her earlier attempts to be supportive of her husband with accusations that he had a wandering eye. "Being in the music business isn't conducive to being a family man. I was gone and playing music. I was out at night and drinking and partying and the whole bit. It's not like doing a construction job from eight to five and coming home and being home all night and watching TV, getting up the next morning and going to work. You've got temptations. It happens to others and it happened to us."

One night, Mickey came home to find every light in the house was on. As he stood in his bedroom of the small house he and his family had shared for several years, he suddenly understood what had happened. The dresser drawers were empty, as was the section of the closet where Geraldine's clothes had been. The children's clothes were gone too. Even as he worried about where his wife and children had gone, the inevitability of his situation washed over him. The marriage was over. The two teenagers who had married nearly a decade earlier were now in their midtwenties and headed in different directions.

Mickey's desire to reason with Geraldine and coax her home dissipated as he stood in their bedroom. "I just loaded my stuff up in my car and I moved. When she came back I was gone. I told her I wanted a divorce."

In early 1962, a beautiful young blonde arrived at the Nesadel with her date. Mickey was immediately attracted to her. Her name was Vivian McDonald. Mickey, who was still recovering from heart surgery, didn't make a strong impression on her.

Jeez, she thought, *this guy really looks awful.*

As he recovered, they began a courtship that led to exchanging wedding vows in December of that year. In April 1966, Gregory—Mickey's fourth child and Vivian's first—was born. "We only had the one kid because it's all we could afford," Mickey joked. "It wasn't that I wasn't trying to put the orders in."

The young couple struggled. Mickey played the Nesadel six nights per week while Vivian worked at a mortgage insurance company in Houston. With a modest income, a family to support—including child support payments for Michael, Kathy, and Keith—they counted every dollar. "We were so poor. We used to go to the grocery store with a clicker and try to count so we wouldn't spend too much money. I didn't want to have to put things back."

"Did you get the steaks?" Mickey asked Vivian, as his young wife walked up the aisle toward him.

"Right here. $2.15."

Vivian dropped the package in the cart that Mickey was pushing down the aisle of the grocery store. He stopped to write on his pad, adding the number she had just mentioned to a long row of numbers on the page in front of him. Mickey remembered, "I'd write the prices down and add it up as we went along, because we only had a certain amount of money to spend and we didn't want to be embarrassed when we got to the checkout counter by not having enough to pay."

The young couple, married half a year earlier in December 1962, had now settled into their weekly trip to the grocery store a couple of miles from their small residence at the Glen Echo Apartments in Houston. The Gilleys would have just enough time to shop and get Vivian home before Mickey headed out to Pasadena to play at the Nesadel for ninety dollars per week.

Despite the financial struggle, Mickey felt much better about his position. "I was making enough money to take care of my family. I didn't have hit records but I was successful doing what I did because I had a crowd coming to the club. They'd dance to the music, and I had a band."

Mickey continued to push forward with his efforts at music recording. He even started his own label, Astro, in 1964. In late 1964 and early 1965, Mickey had another regional success, "Lonely Wine." It became a favorite song of one of Houston's top disc jockeys, Paul Berlin. Sometimes he'd play it twice in a row. "That song really boosted me," Mickey recalls. "People wanted to see Mickey Gilley and wanted to hear that song. I'd do it sometimes three times a set because they wanted to dance to it."

During this time Mickey's club act still covered a variety of music, but his recording efforts migrated toward country music. Time after time he would have a recording session and call his mother and father back in Ferriday, his sister Edna in New Orleans, and other friends and family, telling them all that his next release would be a big hit.

Time after time the hit did not materialize. He remembered his repeated difficulties in the recording studio, "Even though I felt like I could perform better now, I still wasn't that experienced in a recording studio. Performing in a recording studio has a different feel than performing to the audience. You're singing to a dead microphone. There's nothing there. What made Elvis and Jerry Lee so great was how they could phrase and get in and out of a song—it was just like they were making love to that microphone. I never had that experience."

By the end of the 1960s, Mickey was questioning whether he'd ever be a recording success. He had tried everything, latched on to every idea, pursued every recording label, and still had not had a hit record.

Still, he dealt with it. "He took it in stride," recalls his sister Edna, "I never saw Mickey get upset too much over anything. He was generally good-natured about it."

In the early sixties, Irene Gilley came to Houston to see her youngest son and attend an evangelical service of the famous A. A. Allen. After some coaxing she convinced Mickey to join her. Having been to large tent services previously with his mother, Mickey was skeptical, yet gave in to the wishes of his mom as usual.

As he sat beside his mother in the large gathering, he watched with raised eyebrows the goings-on, thinking, *This is the biggest bunch of junk I've ever seen. You talk about junk science; this is what I call junk religion.*

Occasionally, he would turn to his mother, noticing how engaged she was in the worship and the words being delivered from the platform. That was her world, where she was most comfortable. She had always been that way. Mickey didn't understand why she was so positive about these sermons but she was consistent in her support and exuberance for these "men of God."

As the two left the tent and walked toward the parking lot, Irene went on and on about how wonderful the service had been until Mickey interjected.

"Mom, you know I believe in God and believe in miracles but that service was the biggest bunch of crap I've ever seen in my life."

His mother stopped walking, whipping her head to her left to peer at her son.

"What?! Son, that's blasphemy!"

Mickey was unfazed, on a roll now with his thoughts.

"I think he's a phony."

"Son, you are talking about God's servant."

"Mom, let me tell you clearly how I feel. If I were on my deathbed dying, I'd have a lot more confidence in you praying for me than I would have in that preacher praying for me."

Despite his suspicions about the revivals, Mickey understood Irene Gilley was for real. He knew she was always praying for him and he never doubted the benefits of her prayers of support.

– 27 –

DOWNTIME

The drop in Jerry's performance fee—widely reported to have gone from $10,000 to $250 per night—was a slap in the face to a man who still believed that he was the most talented performer of his time. Cancellations became common. There were lawsuits, including a nasty dispute in 1964 with his manager. The adversarial relationships Jerry developed with many in the music industry aggravated his situation. He angered numerous promoters and was kicked out of the musicians' union at one point, further limiting his ability to perform. The low point came when the union prohibited him from playing the piano on "When I Get Paid," one of his own recordings. A pattern of sporadic behavior emerged. Pills and booze fueled his bad behavior. At times he was fun-loving and gregarious, performing for hours on stage, and then playing longer still in the bar or restaurant of his hotel for small gatherings. At other times, he was aloof and disengaged from those around him. He was stubborn and argumentative with those responsible for managing his schedule and career.

Another fly in his ointment appeared in late 1963 when a little-known British band released a record called "I Want to Hold Your Hand" for Capitol Records. By 1964, Beatlemania and the British Invasion were in full swing in America. At one time, six of the top ten hits in the United States were Beatles songs. The twenty-eight-year-old Jerry Lee Lewis was regarded as over the hill and was no longer considered a force in current rock 'n' roll music.

Compounding Jerry's lost decade was the lackluster management by Sam Phillips. As good as Sam was at identifying talent and establishing new performers, he found retaining these performers as clients nearly impossible. Having discovered Elvis, Carl Perkins, Johnny Cash, and Roy Orbison, he had seen them all move on to other management.

Jack Clement was sure he knew why Sam lost so much talent. "Because he was a cheapskate. Years earlier, Johnny Cash might have been getting three cents per record and his contract was coming up and he wanted a little more. Sam would have given it to him but he wanted to argue about it and Cash didn't want to argue. Plus, Cash always wanted to cut a gospel album. Sam would have probably done that too but none of us saw the point in it from a business standpoint."

At the time Jerry hit his short-lived zenith in 1957 and early 1958, Sun Records placed a lot of bets on the young star's continued rise. There would be no repeat of the Elvis mishap this time, but the disastrous trip to England and its aftermath strained Sun's finances. When the costs of trying to resurrect Jerry's career did not pay off, everyone at Sun suffered.

After Jerry's downfall in 1958, through the remainder of his contract which ended in 1963, questions arose over the selection of songs that Sam had Jerry record, the lack of promotion of his work, and ultimately the loss of interest in him when nothing they tried proved successful. Other Sun musicians were mad because too much emphasis and attention had been given to Jerry. Jerry was mad because he felt someone else had to be responsible for his lack of success, and Sam was mad because he had spent a lot of money on Jerry with little or nothing to show for it. Jack Clement summed up the mood of many around Sun during those years: "It was dismal. We had a good thing going and Jerry goes over to England and makes a fool out of himself."

Two weeks after Jerry's contract with Sun Records expired, he signed with Smash, a division of Mercury. Everyone was anxious to get to work and the first recording session with the Smash label took place in late September. Optimism abounded but would prove short-lived. In February 1964, Jerry cut another record that should have been a smash hit given its driving beat and terrific pace. But "I'm On Fire" barely cracked the top 100. For the next five years, from 1963 to 1968, Smash struggled mightily trying to determine how to market the still amazing talent of Jerry Lee Lewis and translate the popularity he generated during live performances into commercial success. Producers Shelby Singleton and Jerry Kennedy tried everything they could think of to bring him out of the deep, wide valley in which he had seemingly been left for dead.

Yet for his difficulties and moodiness and irascible behavior, Jerry became the model of resilience. He continued to play $250 or $300 per night at clubs, honky-tonks, high school gymnasiums, and the like, doing the only thing he knew, the thing he was driven to by some internal, unquenchable force: play music.

In the midst of Jerry's troubles, his parents separated. Elmo was prone to womanizing and drinking and when he ran off with a fourteen-year-old, that was the end of the marriage. "It broke her heart that he would do that to her," Frankie Jean recalled. As the years went by, Elmo would further enjoy the fruits of Jerry's labor, including the lifestyle he afforded and the circles in which he traveled.

Jerry always made sure he took proper care of his mother. Mamie never had to ask for money. If she hinted at a need or desire, Jerry was quick to satisfy it, just as he continued to help support his father, sisters, and extended members of his family.

"If you go back through the years," Hyram Copeland, cousin to Jerry and Jimmy, double-cousin to Mickey, and longtime popular mayor of Vidalia, Louisiana, recalled, "he gave money away to many people. If someone in his family walked up to him and said,

'Jerry, I need this or that,' he'd give it to him. Money just never was important. I don't think it ever has been."

Why in the world do we do this?" Linda Gail Lewis asked herself as she pulled the car into the dusty, short, gravel driveway. She looked over at her mother, who sat silently in the passenger seat. Mamie's youngest daughter would never have considered asking the question out loud. Now in her late teens, she had a good sense of what would be deemed acceptable to her mother. Mamie Lewis had a long leash for her spirited children but she did not allow her authority or her requests to be questioned. In any case, Jerry, Frankie, and Linda Gail had too much love and respect for her to risk upsetting her or hurting her feelings.

Linda Gail had driven her mother several miles north out of Ferriday to Clayton, chatting throughout their short drive. Mamie provided an occasional, one- or two-word response as she stared out her passenger window at the open lowlands that rolled by, and as the memories rolled through her mind on these days when this small, familiar cemetery was her destination.

After opening the gate to the cemetery for her mother, Linda followed Mamie into the small family plot, walking several feet behind her, treading the fine line between supporting her mama and giving her space to roam.

The first graves Mamie came to were those of her parents, John William and Theresa Lee Herron, who had passed away a decade earlier in 1955. She still had sharp memories of the father who had never lost his mean streak and the mother who had slowly lost her mind.

Just to their left was the grave of her youngest sister, Minnie Bell Swaggart. The boiling anger toward her brother-in-law Son Swaggart for taking his wife—and her sister—to a cheap clinic to save money had been largely replaced over the years by sadness at the too-early departure of sweet Minnie Bell.

In another part of the little burial plot was the aging headstone of her first-born son, Elmo Jr. When Junior was killed in 1938, he had been buried some fifty miles away in Snake Ridge. In 1963 Mamie, lamenting the long distance away that little Junior's body lay, had the remains of her eldest son brought here to the Calhoun cemetery to join her other loved ones who had departed this world. Jerry's closest friend and road manager, Cecil Harrelson, dutifully, albeit reluctantly, oversaw the exhumation of the child's body and moved him here.

From there she moved to the gravesite of Steve Allen Lewis, a few feet to the right. The loss of her grandson a few years earlier, in April 1962, had been a huge blow to Mamie. Little Stevie had been such a happy child and the pain his loss had caused her son and daughter-in-law was something that always haunted her during her long visits to the cemetery.

Mamie wandered around the small plot, walking gingerly as if to avoid upsetting the ground with too-heavy steps. Lost in thought, she perched herself, as usual, on the ground near one of the headstones. Then her tears would flow as she grieved, sometimes for hours at a time.

Mamie Lewis made her sad pilgrimage to that small cemetery every month or so. And eighteen-year-old Linda Gail Lewis did the only thing that she could do: she sat patiently and watched her mother grieve.

Jerry was back in Ferriday for a breather, off the grueling road, where he had been playing every nightclub, honky-tonk, high school auditorium, and local fairground he could book a show. When he was home, his mama liked him to drop into church. She loved seeing him and beamed, her pride radiating to all who cared to notice. During this visit, the church was having a week-long revival and Jerry accompanied his mother one evening. It was a good chance for him to see several friends and relatives, and to be seen, as even in this small setting Jerry enjoyed the attention that came with being Ferriday's famous son.

During the service Jerry sat a few rows from the back, stoic expression on his face, as his right hand gripped the end of the pew more tightly than he realized. His left hand was at his side, balled into a fist. Everyone in attendance knew he was there, and other congregants, young and old, stole glances at the only superstar they had ever been around.

This was a full-fledged Holy Ghost church service and the evangelist, a woman named L. S. Branham, wasn't holding anything back. Celebrity in the congregation or not, she had a job to do: preach her gospel message and remind the saved and unsaved alike of the need for repentance, consecration, and separation from a sinful world.

As the lively music service gave way to the Pentecostal sermon, Jerry's face became increasingly serious and his body language ever more agitated. It was a scene those who knew him best had seen before. The conflicted feelings that arose from the disparity between his life's direction and the path he felt God expected produced the familiar battle within himself that now, back in church, grew fiercer with each passing minute.

The minister was not blind to the impact of her words on Jerry. She had often seen the impact of the Biblical call to repentance on her listeners. As she gave the invitation for those who desired to come to the front of the church for prayer, she watched Jerry closely. She saw his motionless, uptight body, ready at any moment to give way to the flood of emotion welling up inside. She sensed Jerry's mind working, as he negotiated a compromise with God that would allow him to walk both sides of the aisle, one pleasing to his Maker yet satisfying the burning drive in him to make it back to the top, to feel the adulation, to gain respect from all the people who had counted him out.

The congregation began to sing "Just as I Am" and a handful of souls made their way to the front, followed by elders of the congregation ready to listen to and pray for their individual needs. Branham walked back to Jerry. She could see the tears of the women standing near him. She could feel the power of God, the anointing of the Holy Spirit, in this place. As she approached him, she saw a slight tremor move through his body and she knew he felt the same mysterious power she sensed.

"Jerry, come pray," she said.

He looked up at her. He seemed like a scared child, deep in the throes of judgment, self-doubt, and terror. The tremor became more pronounced and his stoic expression showed signs of breaking. He leaned over to the woman of God, talking softly so that only she would hear. "I can't. If I come now, they'll say I couldn't make it. I've got to get back to the top. Then I'll come back. Then I'll give myself back to the Lord and sing gospel music. But I can't yet. Not yet."

The woman looked closely at him, her eyes piercing his façade of rationalizing, of justifying, of compromising with God. She was kind but she was direct.

"Jerry, you'll never do it. You'll never turn it loose. Come now while God is dealing with you. You sense His power. You know He is real in your life."

As she stood watching him, she could see his inability to move. Tears rolled down his cheeks and became soft sobs. Yet he couldn't move. He couldn't take the step. Not yet. Later, he told himself, trying to find that ever-elusive middle ground. Later. But not now.

– 28 –

THE CLIMB BACK

On August 18, 1936, less than a year after Jerry's birth, a boy was born near Florence, Alabama, 430 miles from Ferriday. The boy, named Kenneth, was a first cousin once removed of Sam Phillips and had inherited natural musical ability from his talented mother.

He remembered his early music aptitude in a dirt-poor family: "I started off at an early age, about five years old, playing a mandolin my mom taught me how to play, just making some chords at first. Then I progressed beyond the mandolin and she taught me some chords on the guitar. Then I kind of wanted to play the fiddle so she played a few little tunes on the fiddle for me. So I had a fiddle and didn't have but two strings on it, the E and the A strings. But I started playing and was doing pretty good. Finally I asked my daddy, 'Do you think there's any way I can get a few more strings on this thing?' and he said, 'Well, if we can get some money, we'll get you a couple more strings.' So when I got two more strings on that thing, I started doing even better. I was going to town on it. I sure was, man."

By the age of eight, Kenny Lovelace was traveling to talent contests and fiddlers conventions, often competing—and winning—against grown men. A pivotal moment in his musical inspiration occurred in 1947, when a notable musician, a fellow Alabaman, performed near Kenny's hometown. He remembered, "Back when I was about eleven years old, at the community center in Sheffield,

Alabama, I was playing fiddle with Eddie McDougal and the Southern Playboys. Hank Williams and the Drifting Cowboys came to town and we opened for them. And of course, I was a fan of Jerry Rivers, who played fiddle with Hank Williams. I was learning some of his licks, you know. So I met Hank and he said, 'I heard you playing fiddle, and son, you sounded good. You just keep it up.' I said, 'I sure will, sir. Thank you very much.' That was an amazing moment to me. That was really a night, when he stepped out there on that stage. He tore that audience up. He was ahead of his time, way ahead of his time."

By May 1967, Kenny had been in a group called the Five Jets for eleven years. Nineteen-year-old Linda Gail Lewis—who had embarked on a musical career that owed much to Jerry's financial aid and encouragement—had been performing in a club in Monroe, Louisiana, and Kenny's band backed her up regularly. On an evening when Jerry was playing in Monroe, he dropped by to see Linda Gail and the talented band she'd mentioned to him. Jerry was immediately impressed with the band, particularly with the musician who played the fiddle, mandolin, and guitar.

"If you get on the piano," Jerry told him, "we're going to have to have a talk."

Jerry wanted to hire the entire band. The other members of the Five Jets were unable to handle the travel demands but encouraged Kenny to join him, which he did. And he would remain there for the entire ride.

Through the 1960s, in the face of derision and—even worse—being ignored by many, Jerry struggled onward. He cut numerous songs that screamed of being hits but nothing found its mark. He recorded fast songs and slow songs and in-between songs, but he was unable to generate any airplay. He did the only thing he could do, the only thing he knew to do: he kept playing that piano and singing his guts out.

He played to some strong crowds, he played to some weak crowds, but he carried his show anywhere and everywhere, rebuilding his base, adding one loyal listener at a time to a significant contingent that had never stopped loving him. He traveled from one venue to another, sometimes two in a day, traveling as many as six hundred miles a day in his black limousine, increasingly bolstered by liquor and pills and determined to go on and prevail no matter what.

At night after the show, Dick West—Jerry's longtime driver and bodyguard—would go get him a hamburger and a bowl of chili and two glasses of milk. The food helped him relax and he'd go to sleep. The next morning he'd get up and watch his favorite soap opera and then he'd get in the limousine and they'd head off to the next venue.

They worked twenty to twenty-five days each month. "On the last day we'd head for home," Kenny Lovelace recalled, "and Jerry and I would get in the back seat. I had my fiddle and he'd get a flat-top acoustic guitar, and we'd play and sing all the way into Memphis."

Despite the exhausting schedule, the long trips, and being on the road for weeks and months at a time, Jerry and his entourage had a lot of fun and mischief.

On one occasion in the early sixties, when leaving Memphis to go on the road, Jerry thought it would be fun to bring along a portion of medication that had been prescribed by a Memphis doctor for Myra, who had been treated for a painful-but-not-serious kidney infection. One side effect of the medication, the production of urine with a reddish tint, struck Jerry as a detail with which he could have some fun.

A few days later, as Jerry and his entourage wove their way in their two-car caravan through rural Iowa toward the next performance, an opportunity for his next prank presented itself.

A young guitarist, Buck Hutcheson, had been playing with Jerry for only a short time. A fun-loving guy himself, he found being on the road perfectly suited at this early stage of his life to his desire for adventure and love of playing music. When he mentioned some minor discomfort from the backseat, Jerry handed him a strange-appearing pill and convinced his guitarist it would help him feel better. Buck trustingly took the pill, chased it with his own saliva, and continued to look out the window in the backseat and listen to the chatter around him.

Later that afternoon, the party pulled over at a small country store surrounded by cornfields for a quick break. Buck casually headed around back of the store to the restroom, accessible from the outside of the building.

When he emerged a few minutes later, he had a look of terror in his eyes. *What in the world is wrong with me? Whatever it is, it must be serious. Am I dying, out here no less, in the middle of nowhere?* As he trudged back to the car, climbed in the backseat, and slumped over, his life slowly flashed before his eyes. *My Lord,* Buck thought, *what in the world am I going to do?*

As the group climbed in the car and resumed their journey rolling along the open two-lane highway toward their next paycheck, everyone returned to their familiar discussions, a few words here, a short sentence there. Jerry listened to banter from the front passenger seat, a barely noticeable smirk on his face. Occasionally, he would steal a quick glance behind him, trying not to laugh as he watched Buck, dead silent, trying to hide the look of concern and fear in his eyes. Finally, Jerry could not hold back any longer.

"Buck, what's wrong with you, boy?!"

"Nothing, Jerry. I just don't feel like talking." His face never left the scene passing his window as he sat slumped over against the door, sitting directly behind Jerry. He awaited the doom that marched toward him; he awaited whatever agony must necessarily accompany orange-red urine. He longed to be back in Memphis, where he could die in comfort and near loved ones.

After fifteen or twenty minutes, Jerry could no longer contain himself. As he confessed his prank to everyone in the car, howls of laughter erupted and color began to ebb back into Buck's face.

In the midsixties, in the midst of another grueling year, Jerry made an appearance at the Coliseum in Louisville, Kentucky. That same night Janis Joplin was appearing across town at the local fairgrounds. Following her appearance, she crossed town to see one of the performers she most admired both for his musical talent and for his reputation—which was so like hers—as a devil-may-care rock 'n' roll wild child.

Only in her early twenties, Joplin had already forged a reputation as a talented singer, crowd-stunning live performer, and tortured soul. From her conservative upbringing in Port Arthur, deep in the southeast corner of Texas, Joplin had been an outsider from her youth; characterized as physically unattractive and odd, she was regularly taunted by her classmates. Her family's conservative Church of Christ ideas and Janis's contrary opinions on a variety of matters produced a conflict within her that plagued her all of her life. Following a short stint at the University of Texas at Austin, she migrated to San Francisco where her views fell much more in step with the burgeoning hippie movement of the sixties.

Her conflicted life was exacerbated by consistent problems with drugs. Around short stints of trying to achieve a clean and sober existence, she battled drugs and became known as much for her wild lifestyle as for her music. Long-standing struggles with amphetamines, heroin, and alcohol—among other addictive substances—drew Joplin into an ever-increasing downward spiral over time.

Joplin invited herself backstage after Jerry's performance and burst into the room where he and others lingered. Her hair was unkempt, her eyes bloodshot.

Jerry and his entourage were headed to an after-show gathering destined to turn into another all-night party, with plenty of drinking, generally rowdiness, and Jerry's impromptu piano performances.

Joplin approached Jerry and starting talking about all the musicians and entertainers to whom she had made love. She promptly declared that a logical next step was for her to bed one Jerry Lee Lewis, a consummation that she declared should happen on that evening.

She invited herself along with the others to the after-hours gathering, but her forthrightness—aggression, even—took Jerry aback. What kind of woman conducted herself this way? He had plenty of experience in seeing the distinctions between the saintly women which he held in high regard and the more forward women who had provided many evenings of companionship and physical exploration. But Janis Joplin was a different animal, a woman who represented the antithesis of what Jerry held women to be, in any acceptable manifestation.

Twenty minutes later, with Joplin following Jerry's car, the caravan was within minutes of reaching their intended destination. Jerry turned to the driver and matter-of-factly uttered two words: "Lose her."

A few zigzagged left and right turns through a nearby residential section later, the group resumed their drive to their destination and Janis Joplin was left in the night.

Years later, in 1970, Joplin died, victim of an apparent heroin overdose. Jerry Lee Lewis would go on, outlasting a slew of entertainers whose self-destructive tendencies were similar in many ways to his.

Jerry rebuilt his reputation on the strength of his talent as a live performer. Everything else in his life moved to the background when he sat down at the piano and hammered out songs for crowds that sometimes numbered in the dozens and sometimes in the thousands. Through the keys, he could express anger, frustration, aggression, sadness, or longing.

In 1964, near the low point of his lost decade, Jerry arrived in Hamburg, Germany, to play at the storied Star-Club. When he hit the stage that evening, he played with enormous intensity and aggression to a raucous, largely German audience.

His performance that evening was recorded and released as *Live at the Star-Club*. It would be generally regarded as one of the best live rock 'n' roll performances of all time.

A few months later in July 1964, Jerry brought his show to Birmingham, Alabama. A fixture of clubs and venues all across the Deep South for decades, Jerry had special appeal to the largely blue-collar demographic of his home region. People there were strongly connected to the land. They exhibited raw emotion and felt the music deeply. From the moment he came onstage, diving first into his then-current release "High Heel Sneakers"—another worthy effort that could only barely crack the top 100 list—he put on an electrifying performance that was also recorded and released in October as the *Greatest Live Show On Earth*. In an era when live albums were rare and risky, Jerry's dynamism as a live performer produced rare success for him by capturing the scene enjoyed by legions of adoring fans who traveled long distances to hear him play.

In October 1964, Jerry returned as a guest on Dick Clark's *American Bandstand*. It was a big step, and potentially an important one. Still, his trips to the recording studio produced hope followed by frustration.

After ten years of banging his head against the wall, the high-flying days of his early success seemed like a different lifetime.

As 1967 gave way to 1968, there was no reason to believe things would improve in the new year. On January 5, Jerry and his Smash–Mercury handlers descended upon a Nashville studio for yet another recording session. They cut several songs, including Ernest Tubb's "Walking the Floor over You." Toward the end of the session, Jerry listened to an original from Jerry Chestnut. The song was "Another Place, Another Time," a country balled that he played back beautifully, with his own country style and charm. With so many other potential hits from previous sessions having fallen well short of projections, the expectations for the new tune were, at best, modest.

Less than a month later, the record was released and it roared up the country charts, topping at number two, an amazing rush considering what little identification he had as a country artist. While his previous records had sold considerably fewer than 100,000 copies, "Another Place, Another Time" sold well over 200,000. It was the elusive turnaround hit for Jerry and returned him to mainstream relevance.

With "Another Place, Another Time" Jerry captured the country music fan base, many of whom had loved early rock 'n' roll but had migrated to other music.

Jerry's love for country music had never diminished. The music and feeling of "Another Place, Another Time" evinced the same passion he had brought to Hank Williams's "You Win Again" in 1957, when he recorded it as the B side to "Great Balls of Fire."

When Jerry was asked about his transition to country he said, "Man, I've been doin' country music from the word go. What was I doin' ten years ago? 'You Win Again' is what I was singin'. You think that ain't country? Oh, sure, they called it rock 'n' roll. Now I do it again and they say I'm going country. I'm doin' the same kind of music I always did. I'm doin' Jerry Lee Lewis."

Like machine gun fire, the hits popped out. "What Made Milwaukee Famous (Made A Loser Out of Me)," recorded in April 1968 and released in June, zoomed up the country chart and topped out at number two as well. The song, another country ballad about regret, disappointment, and too much time spent in a barroom, was perfectly suited to Jerry's rich voice and personal experiences.

Then came "She Still Comes Around to Love What's Left of Me," which peaked at number two, and "To Make Love Sweeter for You," which became his first number one hit since "Great Balls of

Fire" over ten years earlier.

In 1969 he continued his run of big hits with "She Even Woke Me Up to Say Good-Bye" and the Kris Kristofferson song "Once More with Feeling." That year *Billboard* magazine recognized him as their Country Music Artist of the Year.

Jerry had always felt close to Jud Phillips and had stayed in regular contact with him. That relationship paid off again when Jud made it possible for Jerry to record the song that would be his biggest country seller. In 1972, Jerry recorded "Chantilly Lace," the song initially made famous by J. P. Richardson—better known to music fans as the Big Bopper. Not only did the song go to number one on the country charts, it cracked the top fifty on the pop charts and garnered Jerry his first Grammy nomination.

Around the time of Jerry's successful crossover into country, another development catapulted him back into the spotlight of success. In 1969, Shelby Singleton had purchased the entire catalog of unreleased Sun Records recordings. With Jerry's rise, Singleton released many of his Sun recordings over the next four years, producing several chart hits including "Invitation To Your Party," "One Minute Past Eternity," and other Sun recordings from five to ten years earlier that fit the song pattern of Jerry's recent country emergence.

Yet despite his country music success, Jerry was always an outsider to the country music establishment. Folks there disapproved of his roots in rock 'n' roll, his connection to the Memphis area (which had a strained relationship with Nashville), his unwillingness to devote himself to or label himself under the country genre exclusively, and his overall lifestyle. He relished banging out heavy-duty rock 'n' roll when he was playing country venues. Similarly, he would launch into slow, country ballads for rowdy rock 'n' roll crowds and become obstinate if the audience expressed any displeasure with his music selections.

For all his country success, Jerry was never honored with any CMA Awards. "None of them cats could've followed me onstage," Jerry insisted. "They could all go out there on stage nekkid and I could still take 'em beatin' on the piano with m' damn foot! Hell, man, I think I shoulda won Entertainer of the Year."

People might love him or hate him but no one ever denied his talent. A cousin of Jerry and Jimmy, David Beatty, provided insight from the family's perspective: "Jerry was the king. I mean, he was the originator and Jimmy followed him."

One night, when Jerry was performing in Baton Rouge, Jimmy accompanied David to see their cousin.

"Jerry was sober that night and putting on a good show," David recalled, "and he just really got down on the piano. And Jimmy looked at me and said, 'As bad as I hate to admit it, I believe he's got me there, David.'"

No one sang the praises of Jerry's piano playing more than Mickey. "You had to be in awe when you saw him perform. We all were. I was mesmerized by what he could do. I was on a show with him in Nashville once, and when he got on that piano, I said, 'My God. I can't believe he can do that.'"

As an accomplished piano player himself, Mickey spoke of a key aspect of Jerry's talent. "There's technique in music. Whether it's playing drums or any instrument, technique is what gives the instrument the sound that it makes. Jerry could get the piano to sound better than other people because he was so quick with his hands that it gave him the particular sound on the piano that nobody else had. Even as a kid, when he started playing piano, he was just unbelievable.

"Jerry plays a sharp piano. And when I say sharp, I don't mean if he hits a C note, it's sharp. What I'm saying is if he hits a C note, he's on and off of it so fast that it gives you a different tone."

Along with his rare musical talent, Jerry had the ability to exert control and power over his audience. Jimmy noted this. "His full, strong voice had an almost magnetic effect on people," he wrote. "They were drawn to him as if by some supernatural power."

His performances were sparked by a palpable sense of the life-and-death tug-of-war that raged inside him, as his wild, impulsive nature battled his strong sense of moral code and Old Testament judgment.

"Jerry Lee Lewis did not so much push the envelope," wrote Ellis Iain, "as rip it up and scatter the pieces to any who would listen."

Part of Jerry's magic was the way he worked in a recording studio. Spontaneous and unpredictable, he might pick up on a particular song for which he found a momentary passion. The tape better be rolling when the mood struck him, because often his best take was the first or second.

The producer Bones Howell declared, "With Jerry you get one, two, three takes maximum, and he's given you the most he's gonna give you and wants something else."

"You could take him in a room that had a piano and two or three people," Jack Clement recalls, "and he'd sit down there and give you the whole show, you know. That's one of the things I liked about him. The studio didn't intimidate him. He'd just go in there and go nuts."

Linda Gail was awed by the way Jerry adapted to unfamiliar music in his recording sessions. "'What Made Milwaukee Famous' and many of those hits were handed to him on the spot and he just sat down and sang and played them immediately. That's incredible. How in the heck did he do that?"

As part of Jerry's stylistic genius and spontaneous creativity, he prided himself on never playing any song the same way twice. His band members constantly watched for tempo changes, key changes, and unpredictable nuances Jerry might add, lest they miss the cue and draw the ire of their leader.

But perhaps his greatest talent was his ability to take any song and put an indelible imprint of his own on it. As a self-proclaimed and confirmed stylist, he prided himself on the ability to transform every song based on his interpretation, imagination, and personal feeling. "He's got a God-given talent in the way he sings a song, the way he phrases a song," Kenny Lovelace said. "I don't care what it is, country or rock 'n' roll or whatever, he just puts his stamp on it. He does it Jerry Lee style. If he does somebody else's song, he changes it to the way he wants to do it and he makes it better."

Some of his most compelling songs through the years were previously popularized by others, but given new life in his hands— "Crazy Arms," "What I'd Say," "Chantilly Lace," and the list goes on.

He never stopped admiring the three key voices of his youth: Jimmie Rodgers, Hank Williams, and Al Jolson. In time he would add a fourth name to that pantheon of greatness: Jerry Lee Lewis.

– 29 –

SATISFACTION

On January 1, 1969, the radio ministry of the Jimmy Swaggart Evangelistic Association was inaugurated with a fifteen-minute program called *The Camp Meeting Hour*. It aired initially in Atlanta, Houston, and Minneapolis–St. Paul and included a hymn, short message, and closing prayer.

The program's potential to reach thousands of unseen folks who needed to hear his message excited Jimmy. However, the program drew little response from its audience, if indeed there was an audience at all.

The financial strain of paying for the radio production, while limited, was still substantial for Jimmy's limited financial resources. Even though he believed that he was following the direction God had given to him and had strong encouragement from the managers of the three stations that carried his program, his situation seemed hopeless. Without continued financial support for the program, it would be a losing proposition. The longer it continued, the greater the losses.

Jimmy spent every free second, while on the road preaching revivals, agonizing over the radio situation. Finally a frustrated, exhausted Jimmy wrote three letters—one to each of the stations—asking that the programs be canceled. All three station managers begged him to keep doing the program.

The manager in Atlanta went on the air to ask listeners to support the program. Previously, Jimmy had been reluctant to ask for financial assistance but the station manager leveled with the listening audience, letting them know that the program was near cancellation.

When the need of the ministry was made clear to radio listeners, the response was significant. Hundreds of letters arrived in Baton Rouge, many with financial assistance, more than enough to keep the program on the air. This support was a staggering surprise to Jimmy, who began to understand the need to ask for help and the benefits which come when one willingly accepts the help that arrives.

Ten stations were added in 1969, and by 1971 Jimmy's singing and preaching were airing on over fifty radio stations. In 1973, he purchased the WLUX radio station in Baton Rouge. The costs of maintaining a significant radio presence were daunting but would pale in comparison to the challenges of his next massive venture.

In 1969 Jimmy Swaggart became the youngest keynote preacher in history at the annual General Council of the Assemblies of God meeting, held that year in Dallas.

Jimmy wrote of that special night, "Many times I had experienced the anointing of the Holy Spirit on my preaching but never before as that night. Words, expressions, and thoughts all blended together as I exhorted the story of the woman who had faith enough to declare 'if I may touch but his clothes, I shall be made whole [from the fifth chapter of Mark].'

"Not once but several times, the crowd of ten thousand came to its feet shouting and praising God. At times I thought the situation was going to get out of control. Hundreds of people in the balcony were singing, dancing, and praising the Lord until I thought someone might accidentally dance over the retaining wall and fall to the floor below. The presence of God swept the entire coliseum from floor to ceiling.

"Hundreds of people later told me it was the greatest service they had ever attended. One man expressed a fear that the compliments might cause me to share God's glory. But that would not happen now, not after all the years of struggle, disappointment, fear, and frustration. After all the times of rejection, even being refused ordination, it would not happen. After some of my early attempts at preaching brought derision and ridicule I could not be so deceived."

As he delivered his memorable message that night, he remembered ten years earlier, when he was seeking ordination and had faced a group of men who determined he didn't yet measure up. Now that time seemed so far away.

By the early seventies Jimmy had left all but the largest churches and expanded to weekly crusades in metropolitan areas around the country. The Swaggarts built and moved into their first home in Baton Rouge and bought extra property to expand their office space for their quickly expanding ministry. By 1973, the Jimmy Swaggart Evangelistic Association would be grossing $3 million per year and the needs for space, staff, and other resources would continue to grow.

As time went by, Jimmy's music became more and more popular until he was one of the leading gospel recording artists in America. The revenue generated increased accordingly. This growing income helped Jimmy and Frances achieve financial stability at last.

Jimmy struggled to determine what portion of profits from his music should be kept for himself and how much should be diverted to ministry efforts. One day as he was sitting in front of a historic state building, readying for a photo shoot for an upcoming album cover, Jimmy felt pushed by God to give up all of his royalties to the ministry. As he would later write, Jimmy thought a little negotiation might be warranted.

"God, I will give 90 percent to your work if you will let me keep 10 percent."

God's quick response, according to Jimmy, followed.

"You can keep all of it if you want. But if you want my will, you will give 100 percent to me."

Later that day, back at the ministry's Goya headquarters, Jimmy agreed to give the recording profit to the ministry—all of it.

Michael Gilley sat between his daddy, Mickey, and grandmother, Irene, taking in the unfamiliar scene around him at a religious service in western Louisiana where Jimmy was about to sing and preach. He could sense the enthusiasm of his grandmother by the wide smile on her face. He also picked up on the cautious mood of his dad who seemed somewhat disengaged.

Michael had not grown up in Pentecostal church services, and so he sat wide-eyed and watched the service even as he felt some concern about the people surrounding him. Hands clapping, arms waving, and dancing in the aisles were not what young Michael thought happened in a church service.

As the music stopped and the crowd took their seats, Jimmy spoke to the audience about the expenses associated with the use of the facility. Local supporters and organizers of the event passed collection baskets up and down the aisles. Michael noticed his dad dutifully dropping in a couple of dollars and his grandmother making a contribution as well. Over the next forty-five minutes prior to Jimmy's sermon, the collection baskets were passed twice more. With the second passing, Mickey's eyebrows raised. As the baskets were passed a third time, Mickey said, "That's it. I'm done."

He nudged Michael and the two left their seats, made their way down the crowded aisle, and headed outside where they waited through the remainder of the service.

Finally, a radiant, smiling Irene filed out with the other congregants. Among the praying women in the family, Jimmy was the golden child. Irene's love for Mickey was unsurpassed but the path Jimmy had chosen had a special importance to her. On some level, Mickey admired and respected the direction Jimmy chose; however, he never approved of the monetary and financial requests made by his Bible-preaching cousin. They rubbed him the wrong way.

– 30 –

RAGE AND PARTYING

Jerry's off-hours activity on the road became wilder. Women were readily available in every city, at each performance, backstage or in the audience. While these women were diametrically at odds with the idealized woman in Jerry's mind, he still was drawn to them.

Often he'd tell his cousin, Cecil Beatty, "Get me a woman."

"Cecil knew just what kind of woman Jerry liked," Cecil's wife, Rae, recalled. "He would scan the whole place and he'd come back with a girl for Jerry. Jerry said Cecil had a special talent for that."

The partying on the road elevated to more dramatic levels. Jerry could stay up for days, riding whatever high he was on at a particular time, pushing his body to its physical and emotional limits. Myra was disturbed and alarmed by the party atmosphere. "I always wanted Jerry to make it a business and not make it a party, but it was always a party."

She'd tell him, "You drink and you take drugs and all these kinds of things and then you go onstage. It can't have a good ending. It just can't."

He paid no attention.

Coming off the road didn't mean the party ended. On many occasions, Jerry would exert pressure on band members and others in the entourage to delay going home to see their families, urging them to head to another club or party. "I want to go out," he would say, "I don't feel like going home. Let's go see what's going on at the Choctaw Lounge."

No one could keep up with Jerry. He pushed everyone to their physical limits and tried to drag them into the same crazed existence in which he found himself. Over time, Jerry's behavior on the road became more extreme and the parties got even crazier. His performances at concerts became more unpredictable and fans knew they were rolling the dice each time they saw him live. They might see the dynamic, devoted artist who belted out a variety of songs, putting his heart and soul into the music, or they might see an angry drunk, taking his frustration and paranoia out on his audiences, becoming belligerent, simply refusing to play, or walking off the stage after only a few short minutes of performing.

When he was scheduled to play Miami, Conway Twitty told the club owner a few stories about what Jerry had done to pianos. "The guy went out and got an old beat-up piano with boards across it," Twitty commented. "Jerry showed up at the club the afternoon before he was gonna open, took one look at the piano, and kicked it all the way out of the building, across the parking lot, and into the water. Then he came back in, blew cigar smoke in the club owner's face and said, 'Now get me a goddamn piano.'"

The sporadic behavior grew more pronounced, financial chaos abounded, and Jerry became even more self-destructive. In 1973, Cecil Harrelson and Eddie Kilroy, frustrated and tired of watching an unfolding train wreck, left Jerry's camp. Without Cecil's steadying influence and loyal friendship close at hand, the situation worsened.

Jerry was jealous by nature. He was suspicious of Myra and quick to accuse her of wrongdoing. He tried to control every aspect of her life and make her into what he considered a "virtuous wife": conservative appearance and hairstyle, no makeup, and plain clothes. He placed dramatic limitations on television viewing and her choice of reading material. Jerry was cruel at times and Myra would later write about the abusive treatment she received from him. He would call late at night and question where she had been and what she had done. He accused her of adultery and pelted her with blame over Stevie's death. He was violent and overpowered her sexually. His anger, resentment, and frustration with his life boiled over and she was often the recipient of his brutal emotions.

By 1970, Jerry's comeback had taken hold but the relationship between him and Myra was increasingly strained.

Over time she had become isolated from his life while he was ingesting chemical substances and enjoying the company of adoring women. When Myra and Jerry quarreled, Mamie often came to her daughter-in-law's defense. Frankie Jean commented, "Mother was so outspoken and she didn't have the education to place her words correctly. But she would take up for Myra behind closed doors and she would get onto Jerry. He would bitch about Myra, her wearing makeup, her dress not being long enough. And she felt so sorry for Myra, and told him, 'You've ruined Myra's life and you know it. You had no business marrying that child.'"

Finally Myra hired a private detective who confirmed her suspicions about Jerry and other women. She filed for divorce and moved with Phoebe to Atlanta. Jerry was touring in Australia when Myra arranged for the divorce papers to be drawn up. He was served with the petition a few days later.

After his initial shock and indignation, Jerry tried earnestly to win Myra back. He acknowledged his errors, offered to give her everything he earned if she returned, even pledged to give up rock 'n' roll. But the thirteen years of cruelty and mistreatment she had endured made it impossible for Myra to accept, or to believe, that things would ever really change. She had heard these apologies before, the claims to make amends and fly straight, and they rang hollow in her ears. Six months later, on May 12, 1971, the divorce became final.

After her divorce from Elmo, Mamie had settled into a new life in Ferriday, where she vacillated between the life of the church she had known and her affinity for socializing. At night, Linda Gail recalled, "Mama would relax and have a Tom Collins. That was the drink she liked and Uncle Lee used to tease her and call her Sister Collins. Even though she was really a spiritual person and loved the church, Mama would have a drink and enjoy her life."

Over time, Mamie grew to love designer clothes and high-quality home furnishings, and her devoted son was always quick to provide whatever she desired. She was also quick to keep others in mind. Many times she would drive up to the pastor at a local church.

"Brother Nolan," she would say, "Jerry sent you some money. Here's $500 to help you."

In 1970, Mamie was diagnosed with cancer and the prognosis was bleak. She made a trip to the renowned MD Anderson Hospital in Houston, where little could be done for her. The cancer spread from her lungs to her heart and esophagus. She returned to Ferriday to live the remaining months of life. Jerry could not face her impending death and did not visit her. *Maybe,* he thought, *if I stay away and don't set my eyes upon her, it won't be real and she'll be better.* But in April 1971, a month before Jerry's divorce from Myra was final, Mary Ethel Herron Lewis drew her last breath.

The impact on Jerry was dramatic. The woman that Kenny Lovelace called Jerry's "heart and soul" was gone. Later, Myra would write, "If ever Jerry suffered a deeper hurt than this, no one knows it; he could not speak it. His soul was bound up with his mother's soul, his heart with her heart; all the good was gone."

Facing the loss of his marriage and his mother, Jerry listened to his conscience, whose voice sounded much like those preachers who had delivered their sermons from behind the pulpit in the little white Pentecostal church of his youth. The voice urged him to give up this rock 'n' roll music and head back to gospel and the church.

A few weeks after divorce papers had been served, he gave his heart back to Christ and purposed not to set foot in any more nightclubs. It was a big enough story that, in December 1970, Walter Cronkite of *The CBS Nightly News* reported Jerry was giving up rock 'n' roll for gospel music. Jerry proclaimed to the world, "I've made a stand for God. I'm just letting the people know openly that I went back to the church and I got myself saved, and the Lord forgave me of my sins and wiped 'em away."

David Beatty, his cousin and Church of God preacher, went to visit him in Memphis at that time.

"I'm going to play country and gospel," Jerry told him.

"That's wonderful, Jerry," David said.

David wanted to encourage him but sitting around Jerry were six or seven guys who were smoking, drinking, and carrying on.

"He can't hold on in that environment," David told his wife when he got home. "You've got to get out of that. You've got to just let it go."

Jerry couldn't. Soon he was back in the nightclubs, a bottle perched on the piano, having returned to a life from which he could not seem to escape.

A few months after Mamie's death, Jerry was still reeling from his divorce from Myra and grieving for his mother. Never good at being alone, Jerry married Jaren Gunn Pate, a Memphis divorcee who worked in the sheriff's office. By then Myra had married the private detective she had hired to follow Jerry.

Jaren was an attractive woman, with long, thick brown hair and a pretty, girlish face. Having become self-conscious about showing her smile due to a capped tooth that had been replaced on multiple occasions, she developed a lasting habit of holding her hand in front of her mouth when she laughed.

She was materialistic and liked nice things, although she didn't pay much attention to caring for them. She had dreamed of marrying a celebrity but had little idea what she was getting into with this one.

Jaren exposed Jerry to all manner of harmful substances, supplying him regularly with a variety of drugs. Now, in addition to swallowing them, he was injecting others and his dependency on the drugs rapidly escalated.

After a few weeks of marriage, Jerry insisted that he and Jaren move to separate residences. They would never live together again. Many people had begged him not to marry Jaren, convinced that he was attracted to her solely because she had the drugs he wanted. She would visit him, they would have sex, and then he'd send her home.

"That was a very difficult time for Jerry," his sister Linda Gail recalls, "and Jaren, bless her heart, was trying to have a marriage with a rock 'n' roll celebrity like you would have with an accountant or someone more 'normal.' She had unrealistic expectations of what she could have with Jerry at that time in his life."

– 31 –

THINGS ARE LOOKING UP

While Mickey Gilley was spending the late 1960s settling into his role as the nightly singer, piano player, and entertainer at the Nesadel, another man was busy with his various interests up and down Spencer Highway, around Pasadena, and throughout the greater Houston area.

Born in September 1926 in the town of Diboll deep in the heart of East Texas, Sherwood Cryer had faced his own rough upbringing, not unlike one he might have found in Ferriday, Louisiana. In an area where poverty was rampant, the Cryer family stood out. "Even in Diboll, we were considered hicks," Sherwood recalled, "That's because my father bought me those old high-top work shoes for me to farm in when I got out of school every day. The kids at school called 'em 'clodhoppers' and I was a 'country hick' for wearin' 'em, and, yeah . . . I had a few really good fights over that shit."

Sherwood also experienced the strong pull between sin and guilt in early childhood. His mother would haul him off to the conservative Apostolic Church every Sunday for a dose of good old-fashioned religion. His grandfather had been a moonshiner, selling his potent concoctions and homemade syrup on the rounds he made to customers on a regular basis. His father regularly consumed alcoholic beverages, generally to excess. His mother sent Sherwood out late at night to bootleggers in the area to find his drunken father and bring him home. As a result, for all the questionable practices and habits that Sherwood would develop over the years, he never touched a drop of alcohol.

As a young man, Sherwood ended up in Houston working as a welder at Shell Chemical. In addition to being a no-nonsense kind of guy, his coworkers understood early that no one got an upper hand on him. When a fellow employee stole the Oreo cookies that Sherwood brought each day to eat during his afternoon break, Sherwood quietly replaced the white filling with chicken manure.

Perhaps the best-known episode of Sherwood's Shell days signifying him as a man not to be trifled with involved a strike at the local plant at which he worked, a story he related to writer and friend Bob Claypool. "We were picketing in front of the plant, walking the line with our signs, and I was the picket captain for that shift. Our orders were to keep a tight line and not let anything or anybody in or out, so we were walking back and forth tightly. I was right in front of the gate when this big truck, this goddamn Red Ball tried to come out. How he'd ever got in I don't know, through the line. Well . . . we'd been told to keep it tight, so I did . . . and the motherfucker ran right over me! Knocked my ass down good! I had a Corvette at the time, and I picked myself up, jumped in it and took out after the bastard. I chased him clean over into Pasadena, and finally I got ahead of the fucker and stopped right in front of him. We . . . uh, exchanged a few words about what he'd done, and I told him if he ever pulled any shit like that again, I'd kill him!"

Sherwood was blue collar all the way and his understanding of the basic needs and wants of a man who busted his ass all day doing hard, dirty, hourly paid work led him into other ventures, including stakes in several clubs and joints on Spencer Highway. The best known and most popular was Shelly's, a rough place with a tin roof and corrugated iron walls that could be rolled up on steamy nights.

Sherwood was a shrewd businessman. "He was dumb like a fox," recalls Sandy Brokaw, Mickey's publicist for many years and a man who encountered Sherwood regularly. "He didn't say much, but he was one of the smartest people I ever knew, a welder by day who put that club together at night. He was a marketing genius."

He was also known for meting out his own brand of justice and stories of his antics became local legends. He would use any means necessary—fists, teeth, pool cues, furniture, and weapons—to protect what was damn well his. He personally broke up attempted robberies and chased would-be thieves of his establishments up and down Spencer Highway. He resorted to firearms on many occasions.

"I have never shot a man who didn't deserve to be shot," he said. "Of course, there's some needed to be shot I never got around to."

Mickey's first impression of Sherwood was telling. He saw him as "a guy that would kill you if you didn't do exactly what he wanted you to do. I was scared of him. Over time, he had a lot of people in his pocket. He was almost like the Godfather and he got away with things that a normal person could not get away with."

In 1970, after nearly ten years at the Nesadel, Mickey teamed up with another guy and went into business at the Bellaire Ballroom on the other side of Houston. "He pulled me away from the Nesadel to be the talent," Mickey recalls. "I went in at a promise of $400 a week. But he took all the money. For the first three weeks, I never got a dime. If it hadn't been for Vivian working another job we'd have gone under because we didn't have any money saved."

To keep the club going, Mickey and Vivian mopped and swept and cleaned it. Then one Saturday, Hat Robinson, a wealthy gentleman who owned the building, came in and saw them mopping floors and cleaning toilets.

"He just couldn't believe it," Vivian recalls. "He took his jacket off, rolled his shirt sleeves up, and started helping."

A few weeks later Hat called Mickey and told him, "I'm coming to close that club down."

"Wait a minute, wait a minute," Mickey said. "just do me a favor. Let me go in there and work it through the weekend because we're going to have a big crowd. You can keep all the money. Just give me enough money to pay the band. I don't have the money to pay them if you shut the club down today."

The club stayed open and on Monday Mickey piled all the money that he'd taken in on the table for Hat.

"What do you owe your band?" Hat said,

Mickey responded, "$200 apiece, $600 total."

"Well, what are you supposed to get?"

"I was promised $400 a week but I'm not worried about me," said Mickey. "I just want to make sure we get the band paid."

Hat counted the $600 out for the band and then counted $400 for Mickey, who figured that now he'd need to go look for a job.

But Hat said, "You can run this club." So for the next year, Mickey did.

Sherwood Cryer was vaguely familiar with Mickey, having seen him perform once or twice at the Nesadel when Sherwood had been there peddling the vending machines and jukeboxes he leased to many clubs in the area. He had seen how well Mickey worked the crowd. Sherwood also noted Mickey's stage presence and the high quality of the band backing him. He filed the information away.

When Sherwood came peddling his wares at the Bellaire Ballroom, the two men struck up a conversation.

Sherwood asked Mickey, "What are you doing over here?"

"Trying to make a living," said Mickey.

Sherwood wanted Mickey to play at Shelly's and took him out to look at it. "You need to take a dozer," Mickey said, "and just tear this thing completely down."

"I can fix it," said Sherwood.

Mickey figured the club would never be presentable, much less draw decent crowds. But he was not yet familiar with Sherwood Cryer.

Mickey gave Sherwood a list of demands: he wanted an acoustic ceiling, a better sound system, a good piano, and new chairs and tables. Sherwood did these things though he didn't tile the floor as Mickey wanted, painting it instead. They agreed to split the proceeds fifty-fifty with Sherwood running the club and Mickey performing as the headline act and handling promotions.

"What do you want to call the club?" Sherwood asked.

"I don't care," Mickey said. "You can call it the Sin Den."

"How about Gilley's?"

Mickey replied, "That has a nice ring to it."

Mickey never forgot the thrill he felt the first time he drove down Spencer Highway and, near the intersection of Spencer and Watters Road, saw his name on a big sign in bright lights.

On March 8, 1971, Gilley's officially opened for business.

"After that first week," Mickey would recall a year later, "Sherwood brought me my share of the profits and God! I couldn't believe it! I don't even remember now how much it was but it was a lot more than I'd ever gotten for playing. I just sat there staring at the money, amazed and tickled to death." As the featured performer at Gilley's, Mickey's regular pay immediately doubled. In the early days of Gilley's the crowd was not hardcore country and Mickey's performance still contained musical variety. There was plenty of country to be sure but he still mixed in rock 'n' roll numbers— showing he hadn't lost the boogie woogie of his roots—as well as a variety of pop tunes. He brought a faithful audience from his years in the area, but Gilley's was a different club than the Nesadel and the potential upside was dramatic.

Gilley's was a success from the outset. Mickey and Sherwood were a great team. They bought radio spots, sold bumper stickers, and put billboard signs up and down Spencer Highway reminding the romancing couples and petrochemical cowboys driving by, "We doze, but we never close." The promotional efforts continued, venturing into local television as Furniture Outlet sponsored a 30-minute show, *Gilley's Place*, during which Mickey performed for free in exchange for promoting Gilley's and receiving free advertising. The club attracted big stars. Over the years the list of acts became a who's who of popular performers: Willie Nelson, Waylon Jennings, Merle Haggard, George Jones, Loretta Lynn, and Conway Twitty, as well as Fats Domino and Little Richard. Not surprisingly, the list of featured acts included Jerry Lee Lewis.

The club held 750 people when it opened in 1971, increasing in capacity to 1,000, then 3,000, and ultimately to 6,000. Over time, it would add an adjoining rodeo arena, where frequent live rodeos took place, and a recording studio. Gilley's in Pasadena, Texas, eventually made the Guinness Book of World Records as the world's largest honky-tonk.

If you turned into the parking lot of Gilley's in the 1970s—as the place became increasingly well established—the generations-long battle between Ford and General Motors was clearly evident, as the pickup trucks made by each auto maker were represented evenly throughout the enormous lot. Young men, largely of Hispanic descent, scurried around the parking lot slapping red-and-white Gilley's bumper stickers on vehicles not yet christened with the decals. On a dry evening, there would be no mud to contend with on the trek from your vehicle to the club's entrance where there was the famous sign over the awning that read "Welcome To Gilley's." Closer to the door, a smaller sign read, "Check guns, knives, chains, knucks, all weapons at the front door."

Upon entry into Gilley's a separate universe opened up. Activity abounded in every direction, even early in the evening when the place was not yet at maximum occupancy.

Near the front was Minnie Elerick, a regular fixture at the club and Sherwood's girlfriend. A large crowd nestled up to the large wraparound bar, chatting and socializing, while a handful were already settled in for a night of serious drinking.

Beyond the bar a large area was devoted to all manner of games designed to superficially measure a variety of skills. The primary test of one's "manliness" was the KO punching bag, where the ferocity and power with which the contestant punched a suspended bag was measured and a rating was returned. A popular game for men settling bets, the game was also installed to help cut down on aggression and disagreements that might otherwise end up in the parking lot.

As at any good nightclub, Gilley's was lined with row upon row of pool tables, forty at the pinnacle of the club's existence. One of Gilley's signature elements was the famous mechanical bull, El Toro, or "Old Ohmaballs" to those who knew it more intimately. Unlike a regular bull, it had no legs, hooves, or head, just a big torso meant to both emulate the four-legged creature and buck like hell. Underneath the bull read an aptly themed message, "Ride the bull at your own risk." If the KO punching bag was a test of manliness, El Toro was the final exam. With adjustable speeds and movements, the operation of the bull could be modified based on skill level, which ensured that everyone remained humble. When Aaron Latham was writing an article on the club for *Esquire* magazine in 1978, he jumped on the bull and was given the following advice: "Put your left nut in your right hand and hold on."

The mechanical bull was the result of Sherwood's inspiration. When he decided he was going to put a mechanical bull in the club, Mickey said, "What side of the bed did you get up on this morning? That's the most ridiculous thing I've ever heard. Sherwood, no one is going to ride that thing. That's a rodeo training device."

"I know it," said Sherwood. "But just think of all the people who like to go to rodeos and things. We'll get them in here."

And they did. Soon there was a line of people wanting to get in to ride the bull.

Fights were a constant feature of Gilley's thanks to what Sherwood described to Claypool as "hard work, sad feelings, and too much liquor.

"But it's the liquor that does it every time," Sherwood continued, "it makes tigers and bad asses out of the goddamnest people you ever saw. Makes 'em think they can whip everybody in the place.

That's what honky-tonks are, I guess, places where people can forget their troubles for a while, but sometimes they—and we—have to pay a price for it. What we're doing, sir, is taking advantage of those people, in a way. We sell 'em instant happiness—that's what they come here to buy. If it wasn't us, they'd be buying it somewhere else. But sometimes it can be a sad thing to watch, and sometimes, it's not the groups, like the cowboys and the shit-kickers, that cause the most trouble, but certain individuals. It only takes one, you know, to put the whole place in an uproar."

Over the years, a myriad of techniques and weapons were employed to quell the violence. Pool sticks, chairs, clubs, and finally, Mace were used regularly by Sherwood and other employees to stop altercations before they extended beyond two people at odds to a broader group looking for a reason to start swinging. Over time, increasing numbers of security and police were onsite or nearby and short leashes were extended to rowdy patrons before they were arrested and dragged off to jail.

In the midst of the club there was a large, open dance floor surrounded by dozens and dozens of tables. In front of the dance floor was the stage where Mickey Gilley and the Bayou City Beats performed. From here, Mickey was able to ply his trade, further refine his talents, and get inside the heads and hearts of his listeners. He learned to read their thoughts by their facial expressions and the looks in their eyes that showed jubilation, sadness, hope, and sometimes depression. He knew just when to play the love song, the lonely ballad, the upbeat rockabilly tune. Like his rocking cousin in Memphis and his preaching cousin in Baton Rouge, Mickey was becoming adept at touching his audience, using his piano, soul, and charisma to make connections and help people validate their own feelings through his music. From the opening number to his closing each night with "Goodnight, Irene," Mickey figuratively put his arm around the shoulders of his fans and led them through the evening.

Beyond the bandstand, there was little question of who was in charge, and Sherwood Cryer was not averse to getting personally involved when necessary. In a particular episode recounted in *Saturday Night At Gilley's,* Sherwood described a battle that occurred one night, coincidentally when the headliner for the evening was Jerry Lee Lewis.

"One night, these two odd girls came in and really caused some trouble. They were very close, sir, if you know what I mean. Well, some old boy tried to put the make on one of the girls and it made her girlfriend mad and they got into a big struggle. The old boy was out the side door, waiting by the fence and that girl went out there and hit him with a bottle of VO she had—and I mean hit him, busted that bottle on his head and knocked him colder'n a wedge! Actually gave him a brain concussion.

"Well, I went out there to his rescue and she cut me with the broken bottle, stabbed me in the back of the neck with it. I was wearing a white shirt and that sumbitch turned all red immediately. That's when I reached out and got her by the hair of the head. But I found out it wasn't her hair and I pulled her damn wig off right in my hand! So I grabbed her by her real hair and started strummin' her head with my fist, and goddamn! The biggest brawl broke out—there must have been twenty or thirty people out there fightin' by the fence. A lot of people went to jail that night. But that's the way it was then, back before we discovered Mace—just one little thing would set it off and that sumbitch would spread like wildfire. Everybody would want to pitch in and help, you know, and pretty soon they'd be fighting among themselves. That was a big damn brawl, and all the time Jerry Lee Lewis, who was playing that night, stood there in the doorway with his hands in his pockets and a grin on his face and said, 'Hey, buddy, can I help ya?'"

These episodes and others contributed to the legend of Sherwood Cryer.

Mickey and Sherwood grew close to one another. "After I got to know him," Mickey commented, "he became like a father to me. I really cared for the guy and I wasn't scared of him anymore."

During that period, Mickey described his interaction with Sherwood to music writer Peter Guralnick, "He just loves for me to call him and shoot the breeze. I'll tell you the reason Sherwood admires me. Because I'm the first person that he's met in this business, when I say I'm going to do something, I actually sit down and figure things out in my head and do it. I direct the TV show, I write the ads, and I really study it, I watch it religiously to learn from my mistakes. That's the reason why everything I tell him, he listens; he takes it serious because he knows I'm serious about it."

The two men had formed a union, a partnership in which the total was greater than the sum of the parts. The two men from impoverished upbringings watched together as their extraordinary success unfolded around them.

Yet in time, Mickey became aware of other aspects of Sherwood's character. "I knew that as long as I was making him money, we were OK. The bottom line was he was a friend to anybody that could make him money. He was a user, and I hate to say that, but that's the bottom line. He wasn't a nice person when it came to taking care of the people that really worked for him and worked hard for him."

A few years into his time at Gilley's, Mickey had settled comfortably into the life of an established nightclub performer, part owner, and local celebrity. He was satisfied, having made a long journey from the days of construction and small clubs he had played. No longer did he feel compelled to hassle with the struggle and rejection of a recording career. The fickle record producers from Nashville and Los Angeles and all around the country could find some other whipping boy, some other guy whose sound and style to tinker with and modify endlessly, some other guy whose hopes to build up and then dash, time and time again. He had come a long way with his talent and perseverance, but he had also been in the right place at the right time and found great success with Gilley's. He was thrilled. He didn't care if he never recorded again.

– 32 –

USING HIS
TALENT FOR GOD

In 1973, Jimmy moved toward television, a medium tailor-made for him. After initial experiments taping a program in Baton Rouge and New Orleans, he ended up in the *Hee Haw* studios in Nashville where he would tape two dozen thirty-minute programs at a time, comprised of roughly fifteen minutes of music, ten minutes of preaching, and the balance devoted to announcements and tying up loose ends.

Radio had tripled or quadrupled the size of his ministry. Television would expand it even further.

His dynamic performance style was the key to his success. He told his audiences that music was the highest form of worship, and he lived what he preached. While Jerry's style was hard-charging and frenetic and Mickey's was playful and frolicking, Jimmy's musical style specialized in slow, moving gospel tunes. Each piano solo was complete with melodious right-hand runs up and down the keys, stunning arpeggios, and tremolo flourishes. The second verse was often spoken rather than sung while Jimmy looked into the camera as if speaking personally to each viewer. He became a sensation.

From his earliest days on street corners and in small churches, Jimmy had worked tirelessly to hone his craft and improve the dramatic delivery style that enhanced his reputation. His ability to reach an audience was especially appreciated by others asked to do the same thing.

Ted Koppel of ABC called him "a master of communication" and "a man of enormous telegenuity." Dan Rather of CBS described him as "the most effective speaker in the country."

Kenneth Woodward, *Newsweek*'s religion editor described him this way: "Singer and preacher, shaman and showman, Swaggart is simply the most talented—and histrionic—of TV's celebrity evangelists. He can speak for hours without notes—shouting, crying, whispering into the microphone as if it was the ear of Lazarus. At times his knees sag, his torso goes rigid, and his voice grows husky in a paroxysm of choked passion. For his TV audience and especially for the enraptured folks in the auditorium, it's like watching a well-dressed soul pass through the gates on Judgment Day."

Another hallmark of Jimmy's career was his work ethic. He bore the exhausting effects of traveling the country, preaching, performing, writing, dealing with the myriad of issues involved in staying on top of a large ministry, and addressing the constant needs and requests of those around him with patience and fortitude. While the pace would take an enormous toll on him emotionally and even spiritually, his ability to handle the physical toll of his existence became legendary.

With little formal education, the high-school dropout took his self-education seriously. The time Jimmy spent alone with the Bible was a testimony to the seriousness with which he took his role as an evangelist and was seen as clear evidence by his supporters that he was sincere in his dedication to God.

Over the years, Jimmy incorporated current events into his sermons. Spending large amounts of time on the road, always listening to the radio, he was interested in and knowledgeable about current events—political, social, economic—and found that it was effective to include these issues in his sermons to illustrate his points and maintain the interest of his audience. Topics such as increasing tolerance of lifestyle decisions, governmental spending habits, or United States relations with Israel were hot buttons for conservative, churchgoing crowds and useful for exhorting individuals and society as a whole to repent and shift back toward God and Biblical standards of living.

Given that the second phase of the charismatic revival, which began in the 1960s, appealed largely to non-Pentecostal crowds, Jimmy was a throwback, but with style. He described himself countless times over the years as an "old-fashioned, Holy Ghost-filled, shouting, weeping, soul-winning, gospel-preaching preacher." Older crowds loved his demonstrative style of traditional preaching and delivery of messages.

Yet his world-class musical style and current-event-laden preaching also appealed to an audience that didn't measure a preacher's ability by how loudly he shouted or by the height of his vertical jump.

Jimmy's services offered something for everyone: in addition to the musical performances delivered by Jimmy and skilled musicians and singers, there were sermons espousing genuine belief in Biblical infallibility and extensive knowledge of scriptural content. There was the ability of this charismatic man to stalk a stage or dominate a podium with the presence and ferocity of a lion, talking for an hour or more with no notes, weaving his message around engrossing stories.

As his momentum grew, so did his confidence. Over time, he learned to connect better with his audience, how to reach them, and how to stir them. Just as the healing revivalists of yesteryear had exhorted their crowds to believe the unexplainable could happen, so was Jimmy able to stir his audiences to hope, believe, and accept his message.

In addition to his talent as a musician and a speaker, Jimmy was a master producer. He was precise in what he wanted and able to create an environment perfectly suited to his listening and viewing audience. He was a master organizer and natural leader who commanded immediate respect and undying loyalty among his supporters, who were awed by him.

David Beatty was with him when he started his television ministry. "I was playing rhythm guitar for him," Beatty recalls, "and we were in an open-air television station, where there were no sound acoustics, nothing much. He had everything organized and placed like he wanted. He'd say, 'This is what we're going to do and how we're going to do it.'

"He would tell the guy handling the lights and everyone else exactly what he wanted, putting it all in place. But when they turned that camera on, Jimmy Swaggart was in church, ready to go. Beat anything I ever saw. In an instant he went from all the particulars of what he wanted and how he wanted it to captivating you right then."

In the 1960s and early 1970s, Jimmy became less engaged with his family members and relatives beyond Frances and Donnie. With the increasing demands of the ministry, his ties to others in the family lessened. He angered the family when Lee Calhoun died in December 1969. In preaching about his uncle, Jimmy spoke of his heavily cursing Uncle Lee, suggesting the man had rejected God and gone to hell. According to Jimmy, as Lee lay in bed, near death, he could feel the flames of hell around his feet. These comments infuriated many of his relatives, especially those Herron relatives who held Lee in high esteem and who claimed Jimmy had distorted the facts, twisting a comment made by Lee in the hospital that his feet were too hot because of the heavy socks and thick blankets with which they had covered him.

In 1971, his grandfather, W. H. Swaggart, the man he referred to as "Pa," was on his deathbed. Jimmy was gravely concerned about his salvation

At his bedside, he prayed. "Lord," he whispered, "I love this old man. Heaven won't be the same if he's not there. I don't know if he's conscious or not, but if he isn't, would you let him regain his mental capacities long enough for me to talk with him?"

He held his grandfather's hand. "Pa, this is Jimmy," he said. "I don't know if you can understand me but I've asked the Lord that you might. The doctors have said you won't make it through the night. Nannie has already gone. So have Mama and a lot of others. One day I will follow along. When I get there, you're going to be one of the first ones I look for, but I'm not sure all is well. I want to know."

Jimmy watched as tears ran down his grandfather's wrinkled cheeks. Then he felt him squeeze his hand. Later, recalling that moment he would write, "Peace flooded my heart. I knew he was telling me everything was all right. He had made things right with God. I laid his hand down, wiped the tears from his face . . . later that night, Pa joined Nannie and Mama."

The more beloved people he lost, the more he relied on Frances for support and strength. Frances had become a master—typically behind the scenes—of knowing when to push certain causes and steer her husband in directions she thought he should go. While Jimmy was never a pushover, Frances had a way of garnering his support and acquiescence. For all his talents, Jimmy needed help in overcoming his shortcomings, most notably the self-doubt acquired in his difficult youth. Frances, with her undying belief in the special call on her husband, was able to shore up his confidence when this help was needed.

By 1975, even Jimmy could see that his message was resonating. According to his own figures, *The Camp Meeting Hour* was being broadcast on 550 radio stations, the telecast was carried on 200 television stations and 2,000 cable outlets. The ministry employed roughly 150 employees and operated on a budget of approximately two million dollars per month.

Only seventeen years had passed since this young man with a tenth-grade education set out to preach the gospel.

– 33 –

ALL THIS HEARTBREAK

On January 20, 1973, Jerry Lee Lewis made a long overdue first appearance on *The Grand Ole Opry* in Nashville. He performed to an appreciative audience that didn't want him to stop. *Opry* management allowed him a rare honor: to run long, preempting other programming. He performed a wide collection of country and rock 'n' roll chart-topping hits and clearly savored the event. He was warm and engaging. He invited a woman named Del Wood to perform with him on stage. She was one of the few who had shown him kindness during his unsuccessful trip to Nashville twenty years earlier. He had a long and good memory for those who had supported him (and those who hadn't).

Jerry Lee Jr. had been born in 1954 and lived in Ferriday with his mother, Jerry's second wife, Jane. He was a sweet, nice, good-looking kid, and by 1970 he was in his teens and spending more time with his daddy. Jerry asked his drummer, Morris "Tarp" Tarrant, to teach the kid the ropes. Junior developed into a good drummer and played regularly with Jerry's band. He also became involved with drugs—including LSD and PCP, among others.

Jerry had taken Junior on the road to spend time with him but the drugs to which Junior was exposed caused him to spiral downward. Sadly, he had spent considerable time in psychiatric wards and rehabilitation facilities by the time he turned eighteen.

Jerry took him to one of Jimmy's crusades and Junior was

moved by the service. Shortly after that, he had another deeply felt spiritual experience at a Mississippi tent revival and those around him began to feel some optimism for his future.

Less than two weeks after his nineteenth birthday, he was towing a car behind the brand-new Jeep his father just bought him. Rounding a corner, the towed car swerved and hit the abutment of a bridge. The impact flipped Junior's Jeep, broke his neck, and killed him instantly.

Jerry was devastated. Linda Gail would call this dreadful event the "death that changed him most."

As Jerry sat at the funeral in Ferriday watching his second son being buried while his wife, Jaren, and a longtime girlfriend fought over who would sit next to him, he was obsessed with the thought that he had brought all this tragedy on himself. He no longer believed he had the strength to repent and leave his current life, and so he would go to the depths of that life to find relief—or just numbness—for the pain he felt was too profound to bear.

There is a stark contrast in descriptions of Jerry by those who have encountered him in the public domain and those who have spent time in or near his inner circle. Though he has been a wild man, a party animal, and, on more than a few occasions, dangerous, most of his outrageous behavior occurred when he was under the influence of one chemical substance or another.

"I'd be out on the road with the band," Jerry once said, "and we'd take some biphetamines and be way up. Then we'd decide we'd try placidyls and go way down."

By now he'd moved on to drugs like Demerol and harder stuff. This led to multiple arrests for driving under the influence, continued outrageous behavior, and, most damaging from Jerry's perspective, the diminishing of his musical genius.

When he was married to Myra years earlier, she would be amazed and infuriated at Jerry's fans when one of them gave him pills. *You damn fool,* she'd think, *why are you doing that? Do you want to kill him?*

Things worsened when he married Jaren. Jerry's road manager, J. W. Whitten, was among those who were alarmed and dismayed when she introduced him to new drugs. "He just couldn't handle it," J. W. recalled, "and it made him different—and mean."

In 1972, Jerry went to Houston to perform his fiery brand of rock 'n' roll and mellow country hits that had taken him back to the top. Mickey was becoming well known locally as the featured talent at Gilley's but was still awed by the crowds and excitement that surrounded his cousin.

As he often did when Jerry came to town, Mickey dropped by to see his show and head backstage afterward to visit and hang out. On this occasion, he brought along a friend of his who also happened to be a lifelong fan of Jerry's.

"Mickey, I can't thank you enough for this," Gilley's companion remarked excitedly as the two walked down a narrow hallway to a dressing room backstage.

When they entered the dressing room, a small crowd had already gathered and they were ushered over to a group of chairs where Jerry was holding court and coming down from the usual performer's high, beer in hand.

Mickey joined in the ensuing discussion but his friend was silent, stunned to be in the presence of the rock 'n' roll icon whose music he had listened to for years. He watched Jerry's every move and utterance. This didn't surprise Mickey: *the guy was a huge fan*, he thought, *what do you expect?* He certainly wasn't the first star-struck fan to hang around Jerry. Then suddenly Jerry turned and faced Mickey's friend.

"What the hell are you lookin' at?" he said.

The man was too shocked to reply.

Then Jerry shouted, "Git 'im outta here!"

"Jerry, he's a friend of mine," said Mickey. "He's a huge fan of yours. He didn't mean anything by it."

Jerry turned his icy stare from the stranger to his cousin.

"I don't give a damn who he is or why he's here! Git 'im outta here right now!"

After a moment of uncomfortable silence, Jerry added, "And you can go with 'im too, Mickey."

So Mickey and his friend walked out of the dressing room. Mickey knew Jerry always had a temper, but no one ever knew when he was going to go off on someone for no good reason.

Jerry came by his temper naturally. It was a Lewis trait, one that could also be readily seen in Frankie Jean, the oldest of Jerry's two sisters and the one he'd pushed off the cliff many years before.

One day, after flying into Natchez to perform in the Ferriday area, Frankie picked up Jerry and several of his entourage at the small local airport. On the drive into Concordia Parish, Frankie and Jerry argued over some trivial matter, just as they had done all their lives. As the fight continued, their voices got louder and the situation took on a serious tone. All conversation ceased as everyone observed the harsh interplay between the Lewis siblings.

Within minutes, Frankie pulled the car to the side of the road and dug under the seat in the vehicle. No one knew what she was doing except for Jerry, who understood Frankie's volatility. As hotheaded as he was, he knew his explosiveness was no match for Frankie's.

"I'm gettin' out of here," he told his men, "And if you boys have any sense, you'll do the same."

Jerry opened the passenger door and the others made quick exits of their own. They all hurried down the road away from the car. The remaining soul, a large bodyguard of Jerry's named Dagwood, made a slow exit and moved deliberately to the driver's side where he met Frankie as she stepped from the car. Sure enough, she held a small pistol in her right hand and her face glowered, bright red.

Dagwood stepped close to her, ready to calm her down. Recognized by those who knew him as a genial but dangerous man who had experienced his own fair share of violence, he was not easily unnerved.

"Come on now, little lady, you're not going to do anything with that pistol. Why don't you just calm down and give ol' Dagwood that gun."

Jerry and the others watched the scene from a distance, too far away to easily hear or see events unfold. Within a minute or two they saw Dagwood walking purposefully toward them. His face had a pale, grim look they had not seen before.

"I went to calm her down," Dagwood said, "and take the pistol from her. She reached up and pointed that gun right between my eyes. As I looked in her eyes, I didn't have the slightest doubt in my mind that she would pull that trigger in a heartbeat if provoked. I ain't scared of nobody, but my whole life flashed right before my eyes."

As Linda Gail and others in the family would laughingly—but with a strong touch of seriousness—point out, "Frankie's probably the only one of us who would really kill you, but she would only do it if she felt she needed to."

– 34 –

MICKEY RETURNS
TO THE STUDIO

You want me to what?" Mickey couldn't believe what he was hearing. The last thing he wanted to do was return to the recording studio. That part of his life was over. He didn't need the headache. He didn't need to relive all the prior trips to recording sessions when he'd be full of hope and enthusiasm, only to be told once again that he wasn't good enough.

Mickey Leroy Gilley was in a rhythm. He was the featured performer at Gilley's, already the preeminent honky-tonk nightclub in south Texas and quickly gaining national and international prominence. As the club packed thousands night after night into its ever-expanding facilities, Mickey was increasingly recognized, appreciated, and satisfied in his role on the stage. He was a fifty-fifty owner in the enterprise, had a big, bright sign outside that bore his name, and was thrilled to be playing and singing every night.

"Yes, Mickey, I was hoping you would record 'She Called Me Baby' for me," replied Minnie Elerick, Sherwood's longtime girl-friend. Minnie was aware of Mickey's aversion to recording but she loved that song which Mickey played at Gilley's and on his local Houston television show. Minnie was involved with Sherwood's lucrative jukebox business which placed boxes in clubs from Beaumont to Huntsville to Galveston.

"Minnie, I'm not recording anymore. Harlan Howard had a release of that song. Why don't you just get his version of it?"

"You can't find that record anymore, Mickey," she said.

Mickey sighed. Minnie was always sweet and friendly, and she lived with Sherwood, which was enough to make Mickey admire the tough, determined little woman. As he looked down at her, dressed in her men's plaid, button-up shirt and Gilley's suspenders, with that warm, pretty smile on her face, he relented.

Three months later, in October 1973, Mickey was in the studio handling some matters related to the production of his television show. The show was sponsored by a furniture company with extensive operations in and around the Houston area, and had developed into a popular local program. Furthermore, it provided valuable advertising for and awareness of Gilley's.

That day, his earlier conversation with Minnie popped into his head. It shouldn't take but a few minutes to fulfill her wish, and she would appreciate his thoughtfulness.

"Hey guys," he called to his band, "come in here for a few minutes and let's lay down a track Minnie's been asking for."

Everyone headed over and picked up their instruments.

"Let's record it real quick," he added, "and get out of here."

Within a few minutes they had an acceptable take. Pinpoint technical and musical precision was not a requirement. "What are you playing for the flip side?" one of the sound guys asked.

Mickey hadn't given thought to the need for a B side on the record. He considered for a moment. A song from his childhood popped into his head. It was called "Room Full of Roses."

As he launched into the initial piano arpeggio and began the song, he suddenly stopped. The other band members looked at him. Mickey seemed to be lost in thought.

"What's wrong?" one of the musicians asked. "Why did you stop?"

"I can't play this song," said Mickey. "It'll sound too much like my cousin Jerry."

As he sat at the piano, the years of disappointment in the recording studio, the struggles to forge a life in the music business playing piano five and six nights per week, and the constant comparisons to his famous cousin flooded back. Why in the hell did he even come in here? On the stage at Gilley's, in front of thousands, he forgot the the rejections, the critical comparisons to Jerry, and the long search for his own identify. The troubling memories lingered.

"Oh, just play it, Mickey. No one's ever gonna hear it anyway."

Nothing like friends to keep you humble, Mickey thought, as he grinned and launched back into the song.

Two minutes and fifty seconds later, the recording was complete. Mickey wanted to hear the songs played back. "She Called Me Baby" sounded great but "Room Full of Roses" sounded terrible to him. "All I could hear was the steel guitar," Mickey recalls. "The echo was bouncing everywhere. I asked the engineer, 'Why's it so loud?' He said, 'I mixed it the way I felt it.'

"I thought it was so bad I needed to remix it. I actually cued the tape up and then thought, 'I don't want to mess with this. It's just a local record. It's only going to be played on local jukeboxes.'"

Shockingly to everyone, the record became a big hit in Houston, but the song everyone latched on to wasn't "She Called Me Baby." Instead, it was "Room Full of Roses."

Trying to gird himself against more disappointment, Mickey shopped the record to major labels with no early success.

"Some of the people didn't like the record at all," he recalled. "Others said it was OK, but they eased me on out the door, too. They didn't want to take a chance on it. I just couldn't figure it out—it was a number one record in Houston and none of these major labels wanted it. I felt like I was so close but still a million miles away."

Finally, Mickey made a deal with Eddie Kilroy, a friend from earlier days and the man who had been an integral part of Jerry's comeback with Mercury–Smash. When Kilroy released the record on the newly established Playboy Records, Mickey achieved his first national hit. It had taken nearly two decades of struggle and failed attempts, but "Room Full of Roses" would go all the way to number one on the national country charts. It was a remarkable turn of events, a life-changer, and a complete thrill for Gilley. He was thirty-eight years old.

"I just had to get the idea of getting away from the style of Jerry Lee out of the back of my mind and starting thinking about Mickey Gilley," he would say later. "You know, when I sang those two songs, I knew there wasn't nothing that was going to happen. I almost wasn't even trying, and they came out better than anything else I ever recorded."

"I have fun with it now, you know," he recently told a friend. "I tell people I grew up singing that song with Jimmy and Jerry. Jerry missed it. He didn't record it. I say, 'Don't you think I'd have recorded that sooner if I'd have known it would be a hit?'"

In the late spring of 1974, Jerry slid into the back seat of a limousine as his friend and soon-to-be agent, Al Embry, circled around, hopped in the other side, and motioned to the driver they were ready for the drive through Manhattan and out to John F. Kennedy Airport.

While Jerry and Al chatted in the backseat, the driver absentmindedly flipped through radio stations, unaware that the man in the backseat typically didn't like to listen to any music other than his own.

Al, worried about Jerry's potential annoyance, asked the driver, "Can you flip the radio off?"

As the driver reached down to fulfill the request from the backseat, Jerry shouted, "Wait!"

"What's wrong, Jerry?"

Jerry leaned his wiry frame forward, straining to hear the song being played, concentrating on the right-hand piano run and words. His first reaction was delivered with a quizzical expression on his face.

"Is that me?" he asked.

If I sent a rose to you
Every time you made me blue
You'd have a room full of roses . . .

Jerry knew the song; he had played it as a child. He didn't remember playing it recently and he damn sure didn't remember recording it. It didn't sound like his voice or his piano-playing, exactly, even though it seemed familiar.

Al chuckled, watching the comical scene unfold. "Jerry, that's not you. That's Mickey. He cut this and it's turning into a hit."

Jerry looked out the window as the buildings and the people rolled by in his line of sight. Mickey? Mickey Gilley? Turning a song he had learned from Jerry decades ago into a hit? After a moment, he chuckled.

"Well, I guess he pulled a fast one on me."

In 1974, building on his newly successful theme of flowers, Mickey recorded "I Overlooked an Orchid," which also raced up the charts to number one. In late 1974 his third single was released. "City Lights" had been recorded in the late fifties by Ray Price—the same performer who had success with "Crazy Arms" prior to Jerry recording it and making it his first hit. Any suspicions of music industry executives that Mickey's earlier successes were mere luck were quelled when "City Lights" reached number one. Those close to Jerry and Mickey, and the men themselves, were aware that Jerry had never scored three number one hits in a single year.

After three more top ten songs in 1975, including "Window Up Above," originally written and recorded by George Jones, Mickey was on a roll. Soon after, he stumbled across another song that he immediately loved and wanted to record. His friend and superstar entertainer, Conway Twitty, had advised Mickey not to cut the song because it might alienate his heavily female fan base. But Mickey felt it was a song just begging to be sung. He found his fifth number one hit with "The Girls All Get Prettier at Closing Time." As part owner of the world-famous honky-tonk that bore his name, no one was more appropriate to sing that song.

"It's a true story," Mickey liked to explain. "You go in a nightclub and as the evening passes, the guys look better to the girls and the girls look better to the guys."

As the hits kept rolling along, awards accumulated as well. In 1974, he was recognized as the "Most Promising Male Artist," an unusual honor for an entertainer just two years shy of his fortieth birthday.

Two years later, he garnered six awards at the annual Academy of Country Music awards, including Best Male Vocalist and the highest honor given to country music performers, Entertainer of the Year. In early 1977 the state of Texas designated March 10— one day after his birthday—Mickey Gilley Day. It was a swift and remarkable journey for a man who, three years earlier, had just happened to cut "She Called Me Baby" for his friend at Gilley's.

Mickey began touring, marking a new phase in his career. He joined a touring group opening for Conway Twitty and Loretta Lynn.

"We were in Denver," Mickey recalled, "and the man introducing me gave me a big build-up: 'Here he is, ladies and gentleman, all the way from Houston, Texas. He records for Playboy Records and he's a cousin to Jerry Lee Lewis,' and on and on and on. When I walk out about five people applauded. I thought, 'Gee, they don't know who in the hell I am.' So I did 'Sweet Honky-Tonk Wine,' some up-tempo tunes, and maybe I did one or two of Jerry's songs, but the crowd was just waiting for Conway. But when I got to 'Room Full of Roses,' 'If I sent a rose to you,' the crowd woke up and started nodding their heads because they recognized it."

Sometimes Mickey had the misfortune of coming on after Conway Twitty had sung his numbers and received multiple ovations. One night as Twitty was coming off the stage, Mickey was going on. Twitty turned to Mickey and said, "I wouldn't give that spot to a dry cleaner."

On another occasion, the two were interacting with fans. Twitty was signing autographs and after he signed for one woman she looked at it and asked, "What does it say?"

"You're not supposed to read it," said Twitty, "you're supposed to recognize it."

Mickey loved touring. He loved the audiences, he loved to see them having fun, he loved to perform, and he loved seeing the whole country. One of the things he loved most of all was walking into a truck stop in Chicago or Sioux City and hearing his songs playing on the jukeboxes. After years of claiming to his parents that the next recording would be the breakthrough hit, Mickey was thrilled to share his success with them.

As part of that success, Mickey attained the true symbol of success of a country act in the 1970s—a touring bus. After negotiating the purchase, he and his driver flew to Nashville to pick up the bus Conway Twitty and his troupe had used for many years. Upon taking possession of the famed Twitty Bird, Mickey and Terry Rhinehart headed toward Texas. One key stop was essential along the way. The bus went west to Memphis, south toward Jackson, Mississippi, and stopped in tiny Ferriday, Louisiana, 550 miles from Nashville.

When the large coach was finally parked on Mississippi Avenue across the street from his parents' tiny home, Mickey crossed the street like an excited kid and bounded into the house where he had spent the majority of his youth. The grin on his face was like one he would have had thirty years earlier when he'd had something exciting to tell his mom. Inside, he found his dad in the living room sitting in his favorite chair and his mom standing over the sink in the kitchen, just like old times.

"Hey, Mom, you've got to come look at this."

As they walked outside, Mickey thought back to the long-distance phone calls he'd made to his daddy assuring him that the next recording would be that elusive hit. He thought of the supportive smiles of his mama when he'd talked about his continuing struggles to taste the big time. Now there was a huge bus out front, tangible evidence that he had finally crossed the threshold of true success as a music artist.

"It was exciting, you know," says Mickey. "I mean, here I was, a hillbilly with a bus."

Mickey's popularity continued to increase. One night his bus drove to a big fair in Kansas. About an hour before show time, his guitar player looked out at the audience.

"You're really drawing good tonight, Gilley," he told him.

Mickey looked out. Only a handful of people were in the stands.

"Oh, my God," he said, "this is terrible."

Fifteen minutes before they went on, the place was packed.

"How they got them all in there that quickly, I have no idea," Mickey told his guitar player. "There must be 8,000 to 10,000 people."

Mickey now made regular television appearances on shows like *Hee Haw* and *Pop! Goes the Country,* as well on the talk shows of Dinah Shore, Merv Griffin, and Mike Douglas. He appeared on *The Grand Ole Opry* in Nashville and was a featured guest on *The Today Show on NBC* with Tom Brokaw. He had arrived.

During the endless nights on stage, sitting at the piano, watching his audience, Mickey eased into a mellow crooning style that appealed to dance crowds and country-western fans. The more he relaxed, the more he found himself and discovered how to make his own distinctive style of music. "I was just being myself more than anything else," he says, "not trying to copy Jerry, not trying to be anything close to anybody else. That's when success happened."

Jerry had been a stylistic master from the start, putting his imprint on every song. Now Mickey was able to do the same, applying his own unique talents to a song rather than just copying the way others played it.

In the early eighties, Mickey met and worked extensively with Jim Ed Norman in the recording studio. Norman sensed the unique potential of Mickey's voice and was able to take Mickey's performance style and voice to the next level. He told Mickey, "You don't have to play the keyboard to be successful. I'm interested in your voice."

Mickey spent more time concentrating on phrasing, though every once in a while he'd go back in the studio and with his right hand on the piano, add something distinctively his own to a song.

Ultimately, Mickey perfected a softer, flowing style of music. Compared to Jerry's hard-charging, aggressive domination of the piano and powerful ownership of a song with his voice, Mickey's playing and singing were more relaxed, easygoing. Jerry was forceful, taking charge and commanding compliance from his music as he aggressively twisted and turned it in his hands. Often, he was lost in his own world on stage, as he and his piano conversed with each other, oblivious to the world around them. Mickey was laid back, always smiling, engaging, as though he was sitting at the family piano at a Sunday afternoon sing-along. His style had a resonating soft touch, perfect for songs about country-western themes of unrequited love and lots of flowers.

As a standing club act for many years, Mickey developed a penchant for diversity in his music as well. His fans noted his wide range of honky-tonk country tunes, hard-charging boogie woogie and rock 'n' roll, and the slow love ballads that made him famous. His band leader for many decades and a gifted musician in his own right, Norman Carlson, developed his own ideas about Mickey's success.

Carlson says, "I think his style was unbeatable. He could do anything from a good old-fashioned rockabilly song to a way-out, whining, old-fashioned country song to ballads that just knock you over. He could make them all sound good . . . I loved his rockabilly songs. And his piano playing just blew me away. His left hand was amazing, and the stuff he did with his right hand, I'd never seen anybody do that before."

Mickey's oldest son, Michael, remembered many nights he spent at the Nesadel and Gilley's with his dad working, shooting pool, and listening to his dad's music.

"He and the band played everything. They didn't play just one kind of music. So you'd go and you'd hear pop music and you'd hear soul music and you'd hear them do the country music. They really mixed it up. You enjoyed listening to it because you didn't have to sit there and listen to the same thing all the time."

Another key to Mickey's distinct style of playing and entertaining was his keen ability to read and react to his audiences. A down-to-earth person, his fans loved how he interacted with them during his performances. Writer Bob Claypool summed it up nicely in *Saturday Night At Gilley's*, his tribute to the Gilley's honky-tonk: "From the stage, Mickey Gilley watches over them all—the flashy young cowboys and cowgirls, the solitary hardcore drinkers, all of the desperate and lonely along with the braying, flush-faced large groups who whoop like conventioneers—watches them as he has done from the stage of various 'tonks' for more than twenty years now. In that time, Gilley has learned to detect and gauge every mood, every slight emotional nuance and oh-so-quiet change in 'his' crowd. It is fascinating to watch, to really study the way he orchestrates this entire, seemingly uncoordinated mob. He drives the dancers to a sweat-drenched, gut-busting level with a pair of rockabilly-based tunes, then, just as many of the couples are about to drift off the floor at song's end, he snaps them back in their places with a sweet, soft ballad."

With an ever-evolving talent, a sharp mind for recognizing opportunity, and a praying mother back in Ferriday, Louisiana, looking out for him every day, Mickey's successes were not over. As the seventies closed, the next step in his career would elevate him to superstardom. Like his two famous cousins, Jerry and Jimmy, Mickey Gilley would also have to deal with the pitfalls success produced.

– 35 –

PLAYING WITH GUNS

W hat is wrong with him?" The murmurs began early as the situation in the concert hall seemed ominous.

Jerry was up onstage. He'd only been playing a few minutes. But he seemed lethargic and lost. He was slurring words, forgetting lyrics, and had stopped the first two songs not even halfway through them. He mumbled to himself, mumbled to the band, and mumbled to the audience.

Within a short time the boos began. They started as a random offering from a few corners of the audience and quickly spread into broader symphonies from large sections of the crowd. Hundreds of unhappy, paying customers were more than willing to express their frustration.

Jerry had waited too late to take the drugs that would stimulate him, pick him up from his perpetual exhaustion, and give him the energy to perform. By the time he hit the stage, he typically would be ready to go, spurred on by the medication coursing through his veins. But not tonight. He sat at the piano stool, looking over the crowd, not really caring whether they were happy or not, simply trying to get through the moment.

His departure from the stage was rapid as Jerry was rescued from the dissatisfied crowd. He was rushed from the venue in North Carolina and flown back to Memphis.

A few hours later, at a small hole-in-the-wall club in Memphis, a few random patrons were treated to the unexpected appearance of Jerry Lee Lewis. He was active, energized, and engaging, much different from the man who had appeared hours before. While the throng of paying customers several hundred miles to the east had received nothing from Jerry that evening, this small, unsuspecting group in Memphis was given the free concert of a lifetime. He played for more than two hours, with fire, with passion, simply because he was now ready. His drugs had kicked in.

Jerry loved guns. He regularly brandished firearms during interactions with people and while under the influence of mind-altering substances. Gunfire and flying bullets were regularities at his business office in suburban Memphis. Visitors to his home noticed an abundance of guns lying around and he often kept a weapon on his person.

On September 29, 1976, Jerry's forty-first birthday, he was at Jaren's home in Collierville. That evening he shot Butch Owens, a bass player in his band, in the chest with a .357 magnum. By some miracle—considering the weapon used, the point of entry, and close proximity of the shot being fired—Owens survived. Jerry claimed the shooting was an accident and was never charged with a crime. Several months later Jerry fired Butch from the band and a few years later Butch Owens filed a lawsuit against Jerry for $400,000 in damages. This action resulted in a judgment against Jerry for $125,000.

Two months after shooting Owens, Jerry decided that Elvis Presley was suffering from being isolated—even detained—at Graceland. In November 1976, he rolled up to the Graceland gate in his Lincoln Continental on a mission to save him. Agitated, drugged, and wielding a gun, he demanded to see Elvis. After considerable screaming, cursing, and yelling threats at the guards in front of Graceland, Jerry was arrested by the Memphis police and hauled away.

Elvis and Jerry were actually friends, although the limits of that friendship would always be constrained by how guarded and secluded Elvis was, and by Jerry's jealousy and unpredictability. Yet Elvis was always forthcoming about his admiration for Jerry's talent. When Elvis first opened in Las Vegas in 1969, seeking to re-establish himself as a serious artist after years of making movies, one of the first people he invited to see him perform was Jerry Lee Lewis, who gladly accepted. On that occasion, they spent time together talking, playing, and singing.

On August 16, 1977, less than a year after Jerry's would-be rescue of Elvis from Graceland, Elvis Presley died at the age of forty-two, and the world went into mourning.

While both men had enormous ability, most experts agreed that Jerry was more talented—dramatically more talented according to many—as a pure musician. Certainly, Jerry believed that.

"Oh, sure I liked him," he told a reporter, "Who wouldn't have liked him? He was a nice man, and I considered him a close friend. Of course his talent was never as great as mine."

Though Jerry refused to acknowledge it, Elvis was the bigger star, in part because superstardom is heightened by a sense of mystique and the lack of availability to the public. Fans become less connected with the person and more connected to the persona which is often a press agent's concoction. Throughout the seventies, as Elvis became less accessible, the perception of him became distant from the real man and his many troubles, whereas Jerry was out in front of the public, warts and all. Elvis's sexy message was wrapped in soft, tender terms that made him a romantic figure. Jerry's message embodied more aggression, both threatening and primal.

By the time Elvis died, Jerry's wild decade had eroded his ability to perform onstage or in the recording studio with his former consistency. His last hit with Mercury–Smash was "Middle Age Crazy" in 1977, which went to number four on the charts. In 1978, he left Mercury to join Elektra Records and created some short-term momentum with compelling songs like "Rockin' My Life Away" and "Over the Rainbow."

But he could not stop the tumble. In early 1981, he would achieve the last top ten hit of his career, "Thirty-Nine and Holding."

Through the 1970s, Jerry's daddy, Elmo, was burnishing his own reputation as a hell-raiser and a favorite guy among everyone in Jerry's camp. They called him "Papa Lewis."

On the early morning that Jerry was hauled away from the gates of Graceland, Elmo was released from jail after one of many trips there for a variety of offenses. Elmo was never a man who benefited from idle hands. With Jerry's success and his own departure from the hard life of farming and carpentry, Elmo was constantly involved in a variety of shenanigans.

Jerry had a white stretch Lincoln limousine that Elmo often drove. On one occasion, while Jerry was at the studio recording, Elmo was speeding in the limo. The police went after him, resulting in a chase. At an opportune moment, Elmo drove out of sight of the law, emerged from the car, and jumped in the back seat. When the police approached, he said, "Man, I'm glad y'all came, the guy driving this was scaring the hell out of me. I'm glad you ran him off."

They let him go.

Elmo never lost his love of music. He always loved to sing and would often tell Jerry that he wanted to sing "Mexicali Rose" at Jerry's shows.

"Now, son, you've got to call me up onstage," he'd tell Jerry, "I'm going to sing tonight."

At some point during the show, Jerry would call Elmo up and his daddy would proudly come onstage and sing.

Elmo died in Memphis on July 21, 1979 of stomach cancer. Jerry went back to Ferriday for his funeral, back to the little Calhoun family cemetery in Indian Village, several miles north of Ferriday, and watched his father's coffin lowered into the ground beside the grave of his mother. Jerry had experienced more death, disappointment, run-ins with the law, and recklessness in one decade than most people experience in a lifetime. But the run of trouble was not over.

– 36 –

SQUEAKY CLEAN

Through the late 1970s and into the decade that followed, the evangelical movement in America picked up steam. It garnered special attention when President Jimmy Carter acknowledged that he was a born-again Christian. Through the country and around the world, the fundamentalist movement progressed with significant momentum.

By 1980 the Christian right, the self-proclaimed Moral Majority, was gaining ground inside the religious world and beyond. Within church walls, the growth in this body was driven largely by increased interest in the charismatic movement, including Pentecostalism. While traditional, non-fundamentalist churches experienced little or no growth, the evangelicals expanded rapidly. Ronald Reagan relied heavily on the Christian right in achieving a landslide election victory in 1980, and he counted on their strong support for his reelection four years later.

As part of this growth pattern, the Assemblies of God denomination enjoyed a tremendous increase as well. Pentecostal denominations, of which the Assemblies of God was the largest, were the fastest growing churches in America.

The Assemblies of God had spent the majority of its existence as an outsider in the Christian world, looked down on by other churches as a home for the unsophisticated, the mystical, and the social and spiritual misfits of society. Pentecostals were accustomed to the dismissive comments of Methodists and Presbyterians, but second-class treatment was thrust upon them even by the more conservative Baptist and Church of Christ denominations.

The Assemblies of God's early days were played out on street corners, in open-air congregations, under tents, and in small, poor churches with dusty floors and makeshift furnishings. Its congregants were largely drawn from the down and out, the impoverished, a rough, even criminal element, and social outcasts.

But by the 1980s it was acceptable, even trendy, to be part of an Assemblies of God congregation. In 1988 their adherents numbered over two million.

Paralleling the increased interest and support for conservative Christianity was the growth of its popularity on television. Early preachers enjoyed a significant presence in radio and many of the more successful ones took the next step into television. Men like Oral Roberts, Rex Humbard, and Pat Robertson, seizing an opportunity, adapted their ministries and deliveries to a television audience and blossomed. Over time, others would follow, many of whose faces would be beamed around the world to millions upon millions of supporters and sympathizers. Among them was a husky, wide-shouldered man broadcasting from Baton Rouge, Louisiana— Jimmy Swaggart.

By the mid-1980s televangelism enjoyed a massive following and was a big-time business. *US News and World Report* reported that television ministers and ministries drove two billion dollars each year. Ted Koppel reported on ABC's *Nightline* that thirty-four million US households had access to television evangelism. Pat Robertson's Christian Broadcasting Network (CBN) and flagship *The 700 Club* program generated $230 million each year, and Jim Bakker's *PTL (Praise The Lord)* ministry brought in approximately $130 million annually and included a 2,300-acre retreat and theme park. When Robertson declared his candidacy for President in 1988 and fared exceedingly well in the early Iowa caucus, many who previously had little awareness of evangelical Christians took notice.

The trajectory of the Jimmy Swaggart Evangelical Association (and, later, Jimmy Swaggart Ministries) was headed upward during the mid- to late seventies and throughout the eighties. The rate of growth was steady and impressive. By 1979, he was on 600 radio stations, 250 television stations, and thousands of cable outlets. Career record and tape album sales crossed the eight million mark.

At the core of the ministry's success stood one man who drew the crowds, the attention, and the adoration. Having come from nothing, he had reached this point through tireless efforts to hone his style and his message, to move supplicants with his music, his resonant speaking voice, his faith, his conviction. People enjoyed his directness and willingness to take on all challengers, with a populist-type message that promulgated simple ideals and attacked high-minded members and ideas of society. His sermons were often harsh and confrontational, the conscious choice of a man who had specific ideas about his obligations as an evangelist.

"It's my business to make you squirm," he told the crowd at one of his crusades. "It's my business to make you kind of hot where you're sitting. It's my business to keep you up at night, to make you toss and tumble, unable to sleep."

Beyond his connection with the traditional Assemblies of God enthusiasts, Jimmy's charisma and plain speaking won him large audiences in unexpected places like Los Angeles and New York. In 1982, he was forced to turn away thousands from a crusade at Madison Square Garden. He effectively steered the Pentecostal message away from the appearance and impressions left by the faith healers who had preceded him in the Pentecostal movement. Yet he was able to do so without losing the down-home, traditional message that conservative Christians accepted and admired.

Jimmy's personal popularity was evident everywhere. By 1986, when the audiences for Oral Roberts and Jerry Falwell were declining, Jimmy's increased to three million and he attracted huge crowds wherever he conducted a crusade. When he chastised mighty Wal-Mart from the pulpit for selling rock-oriented publications in their stores, they were removed from the shelves within days (although a Wal-Mart spokesman denied any connection between the two events). Jimmy was even nominated in 1985 for a Dove Award in contemporary Christian music. His nomination for gospel artist of the year pitted him against Christian music superstars Amy Grant and Sandi Patti.

Jimmy's squeaky clean, humble image was a major component of his popularity. He was quick to deflect attention from himself, telling a reporter from the Associated Press, "I just want to please God and that's the whole thing."

The few who gained close access to him came away impressed. One man who met Jimmy for lunch in a Baton Rouge Mexican restaurant recalled the occasion this way: "Right after we were introduced, Brother Swaggart said, 'Let's pray.' He prayed over the food. He prayed for the lost people in the restaurant, and the lost people in the city. He prayed for the politicians. Then I look up, and I see he's crying. Now I thought you're only supposed to do that on TV—you know, a ploy when you're trying to raise money. God told me he was genuine right there."

One morning Jimmy awakened feeling agitated. He paced around the house, full of nervous energy, unable to shake certain images in his mind.

Jimmy was prone to dreaming, to having visions in his mind's eye that often yielded great substance and significance. He would struggle to find the meaning of an unusual or difficult-to-explain dream, and he sought to understand what the dream might be telling him.

The dream last night had required no special interpretation. The images were clear, the characters discernible, the meaning quite obvious. In this troubling dream, Jimmy had seen the dead body of his great-uncle, Arthur Gilley, Mickey's father. He had seen that unwashed, unsaved Uncle Arthur had not made it to heaven, but was actually in hell. Jimmy awakened from the dream greatly unsettled, unable to erase the night's images from his mind.

As the morning continued, the dream troubled Jimmy. He had always been close to Arthur and Irene, especially his Aunt Rene (pronounced Ree-nee), the woman who reminded him most of his grandmother, Ada. He knew that the power of Irene's prayers had lifted him up for decades. He might not always trust the power of others' prayers, but Irene exhibited a confidence to those around her that convinced them of her legitimacy as a prayer warrior.

Finally, Jimmy decided to meet the matter head-on, if only to give himself some peace about the whole situation. There was no point in pacing around, his mind unnerved by the unsettling dream.

"Well, I wonder who would be at the door in the middle of the day," Irene said to Arthur.

As Irene crossed the living room to open the door, Arthur Gilley looked up from his chair. The door opened and Jimmy Swaggart entered the home. He leaned forward to return the warm embrace of this woman he so admired.

Arthur, obviously surprised, roused himself slowly from his chair, ignoring the stiffness in his joints as he crossed the room to greet the man his relatives rarely saw in person. Something was on Jimmy's mind. After a brief conversation about how everyone in both families was, Jimmy cut to the chase.

"Uncle Arthur, I had a dream about you last night. You died and you didn't make it to heaven." Jimmy looked at Arthur.

"I want you to pray with me right now."

Irene Lewis Gilley was not sure what to expect next. Here, her favorite great-nephew, whom she loved only a little less than her own children, had boldly addressed her husband, a man who had shown little interest in church for the six decades of their marriage, and for whom she had prayed endlessly. She was Jimmy's biggest supporter but she had witnessed the determination with which Arthur had rejected the goings-on of church folks, including his own devout wife. He wasn't a vocal critic or naysayer. He simply kept his mouth shut and stayed a safe distance from organized religion.

To her surprise, Arthur looked calmly at Jimmy with little emotion or surprise in his eyes. His moment had come. He recognized the moment and embraced it.

Jimmy told Arthur that God loved him, that Arthur was a sinner, and that Jesus had died on the cross to save Arthur's soul. He led Arthur in the sinner's prayer that fundamentalist Christians believe is the prayer of salvation. Irene watched the scene with joy.

"After Daddy prayed the sinner's prayer with Jimmy," said Mickey's older sister, Edna, "he started going to church all the time."

Jimmy was accountable on financial matters and open to questions about ministry revenue and expenses—early on, at least. Jimmy's musical success had been parlayed to the ministry and helped it enormously, as he continued to give 100 percent of the royalties from his millions of albums sold to the coffers of the Jimmy Swaggart Ministries.

"We could be millionaires [from the sale of records]," Frances told the *Washington Post.* "That is fact . . . but we're not . . . I could be dripping in luxury. I don't have to work here every day . . . I do that because I love God and I want to do it."

Friends and family members were also convinced that Jimmy was beyond reproach when it came to sexual misconduct or misbehavior. Even those watching him closely, suspicious of financial misdeeds or other wrongdoings, were convinced of his clean reputation when it came to women despite the throngs of females that found him attractive. He had been careful to guard against any request for "counseling" or "therapy," for he had seen fellow preachers and evangelists who had been negatively affected, even destroyed, by a variety of mistakes and the intoxication of power.

– 37 –

DEEPER AND DEEPER

As the decade of the seventies closed and the eighties emerged, every warning light that Jerry could see was flashing ominous signs of danger. Yet he kept his foot fully extended on the pedal, speeding headlong into the next curve without caution or reserve, unable to impose any reasonable limits on his life.

For his entire career, Jerry had taken a cavalier approach to finances. In the early days he carried large wads of cash in his pockets, caring little for financial accounting or keeping track of dollars and cents as long as he had access to enough currency to meet his immediate needs.

"I don't want anything to do with the business," he said. "Show me the piano. Let me play and sing. Let somebody else handle that part of it."

Jerry measured his success in adoration and recognition for his musical talent. Linda Gail wrote of the clear difference between Jerry and his two cousins: "Money was always more important to Mickey and Jimmy than it was to Jerry. Whenever Jerry had it, he just gave it away to his family and the people with him."

With the departure of Cecil Harrelson and others he trusted and who looked out for him financially through the seventies, his situation had grown dire. Beginning in 1979, his Nesbit ranch was visited by the Internal Revenue Service. They routinely seized personal belongings which they auctioned off to the public to reduce the staggering amounts he owed for unpaid federal income taxes. In early 1984, the IRS accused Jerry of owing just under a million dollars in back taxes and in October of that year he went on trial for the amount to which it had grown, roughly $1.1 million. A Federal judge acquitted him of the charge of income tax evasion but found that he nevertheless still owed approximately $650,000. The battles with the IRS continued into the next decade and there would be continuous charges, court appearances, negotiations, and cat-and-mouse episodes in which Jerry would find his performance fee at a given show seized by the IRS.

In June 1981, Jerry was rushed to Methodist Hospital in Memphis, where he underwent nearly five hours of surgery to address a two-inch tear in his stomach, a procedure from which he almost died. Less than two weeks later, he faced another surgical marathon due to infection, and that time he was given only a 50 percent chance for survival. As many feared the end was near for Jerry, there was an enormous outpouring of support from friends, family, fans, and other stars. But his recuperative power, his tough-as-leather ability to survive that would become part of his legend, was taking hold. In a few weeks and against the advice of doctors, he was back in his wild lifestyle, mistreating his body and searching for more cheap thrills.

Not long after his recovery, he and Mickey were sitting at a table with several men at the Bullpen in Nashville, all of them laughing, talking, and vying to see who could tell the best story.

Watching his cousin, Mickey thought to himself, *Jerry is still wound up tighter than an eight-day clock. I guess some things will never change.*

Also seated at the table was Kris Kristofferson. Mickey had admired the songwriting talents of the Rhodes scholar, who had written such hits as "Me and Bobby McGee," "Sunday Morning Coming Down," and "Why Me."

Kristofferson could almost rival Jerry in the realm of hard living. Janis Joplin had once said the only two men she couldn't outdrink were Jerry Lee Lewis and Kris Kristofferson. That night, from Mickey's perspective, both men were in strong form.

Mickey knew Jerry's reputation and had seen a lot of his cousin's antics with his own eyes. Knowing Jerry's recent nearly fatal health struggles and the emphatic claims of his doctors that continued heavy drinking would kill him, Mickey was shocked to see Jerry chase shot after shot of whiskey with Coca-Cola all night long. No one in Jerry's entourage seemed even slightly surprised. Mickey finally felt he had to say something about his cousin's behavior.

"Jerry, I don't think you should be drinking like that. Man, you haven't been out of the hospital that long."

Jerry, in a good mood with the whiskey flowing, looked across the table and grinned devilishly. The strain of his recent health struggles still showed in the lines on his face, but the look in his eyes suggested the same old stubbornness and the attitude of the invincibility he tended to project.

"Oh, man, I'm fine," Jerry responded. "Ain't nothin' gonna happen to me. We're just havin' a good time."

The man is lucky to be alive and here he is guzzling hard liquor. Is he completely crazy?! Still, Mickey knew if he pushed the matter he'd be met with stubbornness that could easily turn into belligerence. Once Jerry's mind was made up—right or wrong—nothing was going to change it.

He watched Jerry laughing, carrying on, and drinking with his usual abandon.

Man, Mickey thought, *Jerry is trying to kill himself.*

On multiple occasions in 1985 Jerry was treated for bleeding ulcers that nearly took his life. After a particular crisis Jerry would fly right for a short time and then fall back into doing as he damn well pleased. He was twice damned: dogged by the Lewises' low tolerance for alcohol and incapable of quitting drinking.

He was nothing if not stubborn and he was still the man his daddy had described many years earlier as "hard-headed as a rock."

The writer Colin Escott would note, "When musicians sit around and trade their stories of wildness, onstage and off, the conversation almost inevitably turns to Jerry Lee Lewis. In a profession founded on excess, Lewis has made his name as one of the most excessive." As talented and dynamic as he still was, by the mideighties the events of the prior two decades had taken an enormous toll. At times he seemed uncontrollably angry and at other times he could seem unhinged.

Working on an album with Jerry in 1984, Carl Perkins stated to Elizabeth Kaye, a writer for *Rolling Stone*, "I don't know much about medicine or brain damage, and I'm not saying he's got it, but there's a switch in there that violently flies off. It's frightening and it's pitiful. Growing older strengthens you in some areas of your life, weakens you in others, definitely changes you. And it looks like it's not changing him for the good."

The Herron bluntness and the Lewis temper had created a combustible mix and Jerry could show a mean temper. With the mind-altering impact of drugs, the result could be explosive.

"Just don't get too close to Jerry Lee," Waylon Jennings once said, "and you won't get hurt."

Psychologist Jim Dolan noted Jerry's frequent claims in interviews.

"He'd say 'I'm a mean-ass son of a bitch. I'll kill you. I'll mess you up. I'll hurt you. Get out of my way and leave me alone.' I think it should be taken as true and honest. The mistake people made when they got into a personal relationship with him is they said, 'Oh, no, he's not really like that,' right after he told them that he was and then behaved in such a way that proved it."

Each night that he performed, the crowd waited to see which Jerry would show up to perform. Through the course of a performance, a smiling, engaging Jerry could become dark if something in the band's performance or audience's attitude didn't suit him. His mood backstage was mercurial and his reactions to circumstances were difficult to predict. Nowhere were the contradiction and unpredictability of his moods more evident than in the relationship with his fans. There were countless stories of a personable, engaging, and charming Jerry hanging out with fans in the lobbies of hotels or of him playing for hours in a dark hotel lounge for a handful of fans who found themselves in the right place at the right time. On other occasions, he could be dismissive, curt, even abusive toward his fans. It was as if he viewed them as representatives of the broad public that had turned on him after his marriage to Myra.

"I think that he really cared very deeply," says Jim Dolan, "and he wanted their love and approbation. But like unruly children do a lot of times when they want attention, they act out and behave badly and I think that's what Jerry Lee was doing. In other words, he was showing his pain."

At a concert in the eighties he sang one verse of a song, stopped, and said, "Y'all want to hear some more of my songs?"

The crowd yelled, "Yeah."

"Then go home and play my records," Jerry said and he walked off the stage.

Jerry's ego was as big as his talent—and everyone noticed it. As Mickey observed, "I tell everyone in my show, 'You know, if you don't believe he's the best, ask him. He'll tell you.'"

Displays of grandiosity can often be matched by contradictory signs of insecurity. Jerry was generally uncomfortable alone. He jumped into relationships quickly, and surrounded himself regularly with a large number of hangers-on and a sizable entourage. He didn't like anything that remotely suggested anyone was equal to him.

You want me to open for someone else?!?" Jerry said to his agent and longtime friend, Al Embry. "Forget it."

Al was not surprised by Jerry's reaction given his feelings about always being the star attraction and the last to perform in any show. But Al was adept at positioning matters in ways that would most likely gain acceptability with his difficult client.

Jerry was living in his own world. He didn't stay closely tuned to the rest of the entertainment industry. He wasn't aware of new performers and he didn't listen to anyone's music other than his own (with the possible exception of a few old favorites like Jimmie Rodgers and Hank Williams.)

"Jerry, there will be a huge crowd." Al told him, "They've made us a generous offer to open for Eric Clapton."

"Who?"

Al looked at his star client. "Jerry, Eric Clapton. The phenomenal guitarist? 'Lay Down Sally?' It's at the top of the charts right now."

Jerry hiked his left foot up on the coffee table in front of him and looked up, a solemn look on his face.

"Never heard of 'im. You think I'm gonna open for someone I've never heard of?!"

"Jerry, this is gonna be a big show and a chance for a lot of people who've never seen you perform."

Jerry just chuckled, mostly to himself. Al had seen that look before and shook his head in exasperation. Weeks later, Eric Clapton thrilled an adoring rock 'n' roll audience, gaining further acclaim as one of the world's foremost guitarists and a reliable hit maker. Jerry Lee Lewis was nowhere to be found, still adamant about not opening for a massively talented superstar of whom he had never heard.

In the few frank, honest moments when he allowed himself to open up, Jerry always returned to a familiar theme. He was still wracked with tremendous guilt about the life he led and the violation of the ideals established in his conservative, religious background. Speaking of this, he would drop his head and look as if he were about to cry.

"My one aim and goal," he would say, "was to preach and to play gospel music."

J. W. Whitten was one of the people in whom he confided. "He used to wonder sometimes, with all the tragedies, if he was living under a curse, if God was punishing him for his lifestyle. He'd get on a guilt kick, play a gospel song, look me in the eye and say, 'J. W., maybe I'm wrong to play rock 'n' roll. What do you think?' And I'd say, 'No, Killer, you make a lot of people happy. Maybe it's God's way for you to minister.'"

Compounding the struggle was the constant reminder of the life of his double-cousin, Jimmy Swaggart. The path Jimmy had taken—a path that Jerry had considered for himself—was a constant reminder of what he saw as his own failure and weakness.

"The way we were raised," Jerry's sister Frankie Jean said, "you really got brainwashed. You'd go to hell for the least little thing. It took me years of nervous breakdowns to get over. Poor Jerry, he let it sink in. His mother and father pushed him to play music, and then he'd go to church and hear that he was going to hell for it. Play, pray, play, pray—Jerry'll never be normal."

Yet even in the most difficult years of his life and career, Jerry never lost his knowledge of Bible-based theology. "I've tried. Tried and tried and tried. I tried once for three long years. Just couldn't do it. Had to back off. It's just not in me an' I can't live a lie. . . See, it's like, Satan, he's got power next to God. Anyway, it seems like the two o' them are always playing some damn game against each other, using me as their pawn. That's what it feels like anyways."

As a result of Jerry's inability to reconcile the desires of his life, he established a pattern of repenting and falling back. Each time he fell off the wagon, he believed a little less in his ability to right himself and instead swam deeper into the waters of self-loathing and guilt.

Myra had observed the constant conflict in Jerry's heart and mind during their marriage. "It wasn't what you would see. It was what he would say. He would play religious songs at home or he would listen to one on the radio, and he would say, 'One of these days, I'm going to quit this business and go back to preaching.'"

Jerry bargained with God, trying to convince his Maker—and himself—that the next success would bring the satisfaction and fulfillment necessary to turn his back on the secular world for good. Myra remembered these conversations. "Jerry kept saying he was going to quit and go back to preaching and farming. This was something he talked about continuously. I think he felt like if he talked about it, it would keep God happy for a while, as his intentions were being spoken of and that this was what he was going to do someday."

As tragedy unfolded in his life, Jerry's feelings of being punished for his lack obedience compounded his guilt, and his running from that guilt resulted in more drugs and hell-raising. Mickey offered his perspective on this syndrome: "He promised the Lord that if He let his mom live he was going to give his heart to God and quit rock 'n' rolling. But he went right back to the same old thing and his mama up and died. I believe in my heart he blamed himself for his mama's death. Whether it's true or not, I can't be sure, but I believe it."

Throughout these dark times of his life, Jerry would acknowledge a fear of his own damnation as he did when telling author Lawrence Wright, "A man can't serve two masters . . . I'm a sinner. I know it. Soon I'm gonna have to reckon with the chillin' hands of death."

Jerry sat backstage, sweat still pouring from his exhausted body. His jacket had long since come off, up there on the stage, as the lights bore down on him during his performance. Now the white button-up shirt, crisp and clean two hours earlier when he had left the confines of this guarded area, was drenched, as he once again had given the people what they had come for. They had shown their appreciation for his big country hits of the sixties and seventies. They had ooh'ed and aah'ed for "You Win Again" and "Cold, Cold Heart" played in homage to ol' Hank. They had stood up and gone crazy for "Whole Lotta Shakin'" and "Great Balls of Fire," as they always did. He hadn't felt particularly well all night long but he sang and played from deep within.

He clutched the whiskey bottle waiting for him backstage—not the one he had left sitting on the piano out front. He had seemed so dynamic up on stage but here he looked small and frail.

A journalist—prearranged earlier to have a few minutes with Jerry—was ushered into the room. Noticeably deferential and admiring of the star, he was invited to sit in a chair as Jerry sank further into a bulky couch. Jerry's handlers eased in and out of the room, attentive to any requests he might have but keeping to themselves. Tonight Jerry seemed quieter and more reflective than usual, and those close to him were sensitive to his mood swings.

"Nice show, Mr. Lewis," said the writer.

"Thanks, Killer," Jerry said. He was polite but disconnected. He didn't like giving interviews, and though he understood they were a necessity, he typically gave little more than the minimum effort. Hell, he had been asked these questions millions of times. Why every reporter felt the need to ask questions he had already answered countless times was beyond him. But he was in a tolerating mood and would play the game—tonight, anyway.

After a few standard questions the interview took a different turn.

"Mr. Lewis, do you think you are going to hell for playing rock 'n' roll music and living the life you live?"

In an instant, Jerry's razor-sharp, piercing eyes looked directly in those of his inquisitor, looking for a clue as to where this was going. A few seconds later Jerry averted his gaze, looking off in the distance. The color drained from his face and his voice grew soft, quiet, reflective.

"I don't really see how what I'm doing can line up with what I was taught and believe. It's hard for me to imagine God being OK with "Whole Lotta Shakin'." No, sir, that doesn't sound much like the God of the Bible that I learned about." He shook his head as if trying to ward off the thoughts that had taken hold of him at this moment.

"If a man is going to be saved and sanctified," he went on, "God demands righteousness, purity. Sometimes it seems like an impossible way to live, but I've seen men and women do it."

As he peered off he saw a reel of mental images flow before him, all in vivid colors in his mind's eye. He saw several caskets pass before him—little Steve Allen, his mother, Junior. He saw the image of Myra as she was leaving him, tired of his harsh treatment. He saw a collage of all the female strangers who had provided temporary company but no real respite from his pain. He thought about all the nights of partying, booze, and drugs. Somehow, some way, he knew he had brought all his difficulties upon himself. He had turned his back on what God expected. He had selfishly chosen fame and rock 'n' roll. He had capitulated again and again to that powerful force within him that couldn't stop speeding up the beat whenever his hands touched the piano keys.

He continued, speaking more to himself than to the reporter, "I have felt the power of God. I know the Way. I just can't seem to stay on course. Too weak, I guess. Constantly caught off guard by temptation, the ways of man, the path to destruction."

He took another swallow from the bottle cradled in his lap, a wistful look on his haggard face.

"Mr. Lewis, how do you think your life would have turned out if you would have chosen a different path?"

Jerry sat solemnly, not answering. He had asked himself the same question countless times.

"A lot of people have criticized me, Killer," he said, "But what I do remains to be judged in the eyes of God. Nobody else is qualified to judge me. And God might have a different view of things than most people."

A few seconds later, he sprung from his seat, took another swig from his bottle, excused himself from the interview, and eased out the door, resigned to let God render the final verdict, believing that it might not be rendered in his favor.

Yet he was a man of many facets, and it was not unusual for those who found him in a less conflicted mood to walk away impressed with his generosity and kindness. Among these people, he fostered loyalty, admiration, and respect. It may be that his sister, the outspoken Frankie Jean, summed him up best. "Jerry's a charitable person. He's mean as hell at times, but he's charitable. He's a good man."

Jimmy's pursuit for Jerry's soul never stopped. The two rarely saw each other but Jimmy read in the newspaper or heard from friends or relatives about Jerry's life. He still felt a burden for his double-cousin.

On many occasions, Jimmy, when asked about Jerry, responded, "I will not be satisfied until I know Jerry Lee has entered the kingdom of God."

In December 1976, Jimmy made a televised plea for the salvation of Jerry's soul. Jerry rarely seemed bothered by Jimmy's efforts. He understood why Jimmy was doing what he did, appreciated it, and even felt it was something he should have been doing himself.

In 1979, Jerry was performing in Baton Rouge, heavily under the influence and struggling to make it through his show. Jimmy arrived there unexpectedly, helped him off the stage in the middle of the show, and took him home. He offered him sanctuary in his home while he recuperated. Soon, however, the appreciative Jerry was gone and had returned to his wild ways.

By 1982, Jaren was so frightened by Jerry's health, behavior, and drug problems that she contacted Jimmy, who was in Ohio for a crusade, and begged him to intervene for the benefit of his cousin. After his crusade service that evening, Jimmy ventured to the nearby venue where Jerry was performing to find his cousin struggling at the piano.

Jerry, shocked to see him, put up no resistance to his physically imposing relative.

Jimmy walked up to him and took the microphone away. "I'm Jimmy Swaggart," he told the audience, "and Jerry Lee is my cousin. I love him, and I think you know that I love him, and I've come to take him home.'"

He paid off the promoter, took his cousin out the door, and flew him back to Baton Rouge on his private plane.

For the second time in three years, Jimmy's plan was for Jerry to dry out at his home. Jerry was willing, for the Swaggart home was comfortable and he felt well cared for there. He also understood that he was not safe on his own.

Jerry had been there a few days when his agent received a phone call at his home in Nashville. Al Embry was surprised to hear Jerry's voice as Frances had told him that Jerry was recuperating and not allowed to take calls. Now on the phone, Jerry's voice was muffled and Al realized he was making this call unbeknownst to his hosts.

"Al," he said in an urgent whisper, "you gotta send somebody to get me outta here!"

As soon as Jerry was on his feet he went back to drinking. Within a year, he would again wear a hole in the lining of his stomach and end up back in the hospital.

Jimmy was disappointed but not deterred. Jerry was, he thought sadly, his own worst enemy. When pressed on the matter of whether he thought Jerry was going to hell, Jimmy invoked his consistent message of repentance and salvation for the lost.

"Jerry Lee will not go to hell because of being involved in rock 'n' roll music," he said. "No one goes to hell because he's a sinner, or because he's an alcoholic, or because he's a doper. He goes to hell because he rejects Jesus Christ as his personal savior."

As Jerry sunk deeper into his own destructive habits, Jimmy rose to the top of the world of televangelism and Christian ministry.

Having witnessed the free fall of Jerry, Jimmy would have been hard-pressed to imagine the trouble that he would face on the next leg of his own journey.

URBAN COWBOY

By the late seventies the hits were still coming for Mickey but they weren't coming nearly as rapidly or finding their way as far up the charts. It would turn out to be a temporary lull.

In 1978 a Texas-born writer living in New York, Aaron Latham, headed back to Texas to explore the honky-tonk craze for *Esquire* magazine. What resulted was a lengthy article in the September issue entitled "The Ballad of the Urban Cowboy." It detailed the world of Gilley's and the relationship of two individuals that frequented it, Dew Westbrook and Betty Jo Helmer. At Gilley's they experienced the initial spark of romance, competitiveness on the mechanical bull, a reception following their wedding, and the soap opera that developed when another woman entered the picture, creating a strained love triangle.

The article depicted the lifestyle of blue-collar types in the Houston area whose social life revolved heavily around regular trips to the world's largest honky-tonk. While illustrating the life of the urban cowboy, Latham couldn't resist interjecting some mockery when depicting the stereotypes of the oil-and-gas industry workers who donned their cowboy hats and cowboy boots and escaped to Gilley's several nights each week. The cavalier treatment angered many of the "Gilleyrats" who frequented the establishment, and it also angered Mickey who felt that Latham was putting down country music and its fans.

Sherwood didn't care what anyone thought because he saw the bigger opportunity the article presented. "I know you didn't like the article," Sherwood told Mickey. "Don't say anything bad about it because we could get a film out of it."

"Are you crazy?" Mickey asked.

"No. They're talking to John Travolta."

Mickey didn't believe it.

Despite all the talk about screenplays, film stars, and movies, it felt to Mickey like wishful thinking, nothing more. He remembered, "Even after we had been to Los Angeles and signed the paperwork for them to use the club for filming, I still didn't believe they were going to do it."

If there was any doubt about the movie being made, reality dawned when John Travolta did agree to star in it. Fresh off the recent success of *Saturday Night Fever*, his star was shining brightly and his presence on a set gave the project immediate credibility and commercial potential. It had taken some persuasion—and two million dollars, reportedly—to garner his commitment. It was, after all, a risky proposition for a trendy, disco-dancing star to become a country boot-scooter.

After an initial visit to Gilley's to survey the world within its walls, Travolta immersed himself in the role and persona of the main character, built around Latham's portrayal of Dew Westbrook. Debra Winger was chosen to play the lead female role and shooting started.

On a typical summer day in 1979, large trucks and throngs of people came rolling into the parking lot at Gilley's. "I was sitting right there in the recording facility when all of a sudden I heard this commotion," Mickey recalls, "and I ran to the door and looked. Here were all these Paramount trucks coming in, and I'm thinking, they're going to actually do this film right here at Gilley's."

In the following months Gilley's became a madhouse, with filming at any and all hours of the day. The actors and film crew operated under a grueling schedule. Movie extras and personalities from Gilley's—never having been part of anything remotely as exciting as a movie—scurried about, some with irrational dreams of fame and movie stardom. Throngs of fans were everywhere, many waiting expectantly for a chance of seeing Travolta emerge from his trailer on his way to shooting a scene.

The filming schedule did not conflict with the operation of the club in the evenings, but the chaotic environment of running a huge nightclub was impacted by the excitement and buzz of a major motion picture being filmed. Norman Carlson, Mickey's bandleader, remembered the craze: "We thought it was great. When it first started, we couldn't imagine that anything better could ever happen. As the filming went on, by the time we got done with it, we were burnt out. But we enjoyed every bit of it."

Sherwood Cryer, in his typical contemplative fashion, sat back and watched the scene unfold, studying these strangers from another world, thinking that he could learn things that could help his own business ventures.

Mickey was on the road touring during much of the filming but he enjoyed playing and singing in the movie, serving as the ringmaster in a rodeo scene, and heading up a Dolly Parton look-alike contest in another scene. He also developed a friendship with John Travolta with whom he shared a love of flying airplanes. "He was flying a 414 Cessna, working on his pilot's license," Mickey recalls. "I already had mine."

The movie *Urban Cowboy* was released by Paramount Pictures in mid-1980, and for Mickey and those close to him it was an exciting time.

Mickey told his older sister Edna, "Sister, if this movie does well, I'm going to buy you a brand-new car." And he did.

"And he's bought me three more since then," Edna remarked later.

The movie changed Mickey's fortunes, literally and figuratively. He had recorded "Stand by Me" for the soundtrack and it became a number one song. In the wake of the movie's critical and commercial success a country music craze swept the nation. Everything that had anything to do with Gilley's became a hot item and the club, always wildly popular, got even busier. Sherwood didn't miss the marketing opportunities presented by the craze. Almost everything that could have the Gilley's logo emblazoned across it was for sale: glasses, mugs, baseball caps, beach towels, posters, jewelry, and all manner of western wear—from cowboy hats to boots. Sherwood even had Gilley's beer produced and sold it to faithful, alcohol-guzzling fans.

Another unlikely star of the *Urban Cowboy* phenomenon was the instantly recognizable, ornery El Toro, the mechanical bull. As the bull became an iconic part of pop culture, Sherwood purchased the rights to it from its creator in New Mexico, Joe Turner, for an amount reported to be somewhere between $100,000 and $150,000. Sherwood's bull-manufacturing enterprise would operate for the next twenty years producing the lifeless, bucking creatures and shipping them all over the world in numbers that eventually reached the thousands.

Urban Cowboy introduced country music to a wide swath of people who would otherwise have never given it the time of day. Much of the notable crossover success of country music stars in the 1980s was due to *Urban Cowboy*. In the middle of it all was a man from Ferriday, Louisiana, who had at last emerged from behind the shadow of his rock 'n' roll cousin.

For the third time in his career, Mickey had taken another monumental step forward. His new album, with the title song "Stand by Me," would become his first album to exceed one million copies in sales. He had again found his stride and was bigger and more popular than ever.

In 1980 he pulled off the rare feat of having two songs—"True Love Ways" and "Stand by Me"—head up the charts simultaneously, both going to number one. Several more of Mickey's best songs were recorded during this period of time, including one at which Mickey initially balked.

"When they brought it in for me to record," Mickey recalls, "I said, 'Wait a minute, I don't want to do that song because too many people have recorded it.' Eddie Arnold wrote it and he had a version of it. Elvis Presley recorded it and my favorite version of it was by Ray Charles. I said, 'I can't follow those guys.'"

His producer, Jim Ed Norman, insisted, "You're going to have a good recording with this song. We're putting it on an LP album."

"You Don't Know Me" ended up being released as a single and going to number one.

Looking back on his string of seventeen number one hits, Mickey saw that the three receiving the most recognition were, as expected, "Room Full of Roses," "The Girls All Get Prettier at Closing Time," and "Stand by Me." When asked about his favorite, he said, "The tune that I feel was one of my best—if not the best—was "That's All That Matters to Me." It was written by Hank Cochran and it was a great song that I felt very strongly about, even though it wasn't a monster number one song for me like some of the others."

One of the songs that most surprised him was "Bring It On Home to Me." "I didn't think it would go to number one," he said, "and I thought 'Put Your Dreams Away' was a good song but I didn't run out of the studio saying that'll be a number one song."

His initial reaction to "Paradise Tonight," the number one duet he sang with Charly McClain, was eye-opening. "I thought it was the biggest piece of junk I'd ever recorded. When I walked out of the studio my pilot said, 'Man, that's a fun song,' and I said, 'That was the biggest bunch of crap I've ever heard in my life.' When he told me he thought it could be a number one song, I told him he was full of BS. Then that son-of-a-gun shot right to the top of the charts."

His success brought monetary rewards that were far from the $200 to $225 per week he was making at the Nesadel only slightly more than a decade earlier. In the wake of *Urban Cowboy* his fees rocketed from $6,000 and $8,000 a night to $25,000 to $35,000 per night. In 1984, Mickey and Vivian built a two-million-dollar home on fifteen acres in the heart of Pasadena, Texas. It was a beautiful place on a well-tended, scenic property. Mickey had come a long way from the days when he and Vivian had counted pennies at the grocery store so they wouldn't exceed the woefully limited budget on which they operated from week to week.

Mickey also ventured into television, which was unusual for a country music star. Through his close association with the Brokaw Company headed by his friend Sandy Brokaw, Mickey appeared on highly rated television programs of the eighties like *Murder She Wrote, The Dukes of Hazzard, Fall Guy, Fantasy Island,* and even *Chips*.

In 1984, he garnered a coveted star on the Hollywood Walk of Fame. Through all the success, Mickey never lost sight of who he was and never forgot the path he had taken to reach this pinnacle.

"Had I become a star when I made my first record," he says, "I'd have been a cocky, no-good jerk. But since I had to fight to end up where I did, I learned to appreciate it when I got there."

It was a thrill for him to share his success with his family, who had been there through it all: the hopes, the predictions of looming success, the disappointments. "It was so important to me that my mother and dad lived long enough to see me have success.

"Every time that I'd get a chance to stop in Ferriday, I would. I had the King Air and I could carry the whole band on that plane. I had two buses and the eighteen-wheeler, but nobody in the band wanted to ride the bus. So we're flying everybody around the country in this King Air, and every time we'd get a chance we'd stop in Ferriday and Mama would fix a big meal for us. She was famous for biscuits. The others would ask her, 'How do you fix those pork chops?' And she'd say, 'Well, I just take a big thing of lard and put it in there and I melt it and put those pork chops in it and they fry.' That's what we would eat. And they were so good. You'd think our arteries would have been clogged up like crazy, huh?"

One of the highlights of success came in 1984 when Mickey appeared with Irene on *Hour Magazine* with Gary Collins.

"You're famous for your cornbread, I understand," the mild-mannered Gary Collins commented as he shook the hand of the aging guest.

Irene, black hair up in a bun, wore her thick-lensed glasses behind which her dark eyes shone. She wore a long, modest pink dress with a white flowered apron as she stood between the talk show host and her youngest son. Mickey was wearing a yellow shirt, a fashionable tan sports jacket, and blue jeans accentuated with a large rectangular belt buckle. He looked very relaxed even as he displayed the attentiveness of a grown child helping an aging parent through unfamiliar circumstances.

As Irene prepared to make the cornbread she had made thousands of times through her eighty-plus years, Collins asked Mickey about his mom's cooking. "Her pork chops and biscuits are my favorite," he said, "but her cornbread is just superb."

Irene measured out the ingredients—"one cup of cornmeal, half a cup of flour, half teaspoon . . ."—while Mickey clarified for the audience the need for self-rising flour. The sassy Irene interrupted her youngest son, "I know what I'm doin'."

A few minutes later, as Collins removed a pan of baked cornbread from the oven, he said, "I don't know what to do."

Irene reached out and took the potholder from him.

"Well, I know what to do!" she exclaimed as she grabbed the large pan of cornbread and flipped it over so that it fell onto a plate.

The audience erupted in laughter.

"Let me tell you how this is good. It's good with buttermilk," Irene said. "It's good with sweet milk. It's good with whole milk." She giggled like a schoolgirl.

Mickey reached over and hugged her, his love for her visible on his face and in his eyes. Irene laughed. The sound was infectious and a sign of her feisty, lovable nature.

Later Mickey would laugh as he recounted the behind-the-scenes details of Irene's television debut. "To get my mom to the show I spent several thousand dollars to fly her and my sister first class all the way from New Orleans to Los Angeles. *Hour Magazine* sent my mom a check for a thousand dollars for doing the show. So when my mom got the check, she called me up and she said, 'Son, if you've got any more shows you want me to do, call me.'

"I guess I spent about eight grand for her to make a thousand."

By the mid-1980s a dramatic reversal of fortune had occurred for the three cousins. Having always been in the shadow of the larger-than-life personality and sword-swallowing self-confidence of Jerry, Mickey and Jimmy had now surpassed him in public popularity. While Jerry's hardcore fans would scoff at the notion that any Lewis relative would ever command higher regard than the Killer, the results spoke for themselves. Public awareness, television appearances, award nominations—by any measure, Mickey had become a more recognizable music figure to the casual music fan. Jimmy, with his tremendous worldwide outreach, high television profile, and $150 million flowing into his ministry, was better known and more highly regarded than his wild double-cousin.

For Jerry, who had been the ringleader of the three and recognized by the other two as the preeminent musical talent, his cousins' success must have been difficult to acknowledge. But he could not deny that self-destruction and bad decision making had compromised his rare musical genius. He had spent his adult life proving the public wrong and clawing his way back out of the ashes—and he knew he could do it again. It was hard to see the cousins he had always overshadowed take off and soar beyond him.

Jimmy never stopped praying for his wayward cousin and Mickey consistently showed Jerry the utmost appreciation. Even at the height of his fame, Mickey, easy-going and comfortable in his own skin, was quick to defer and take a backseat to Jerry.

Mickey remembered a particular occasion in 1982 when the two played a show together in Shreveport, Louisiana. "I flew into

Shreveport after just completing work on a television show. It was either *Fantasy Island* or *The Fall Guy* with Lee Majors. When I got to the venue the promoter was pacing back and forth, almost in a dead sweat. My pilot went to see how things were going, came back out, and said, 'We've got a problem.' My first reaction was 'Jerry Lee's not here.' He said, 'No, he's here.' I responded, 'So what's the problem?'

"'He wants to close the show.'

"At that time I was at the top of my game because the *Urban Cowboy* had been so hot. They had booked me to be the star but Jerry's ego wouldn't allow him to say, 'Hey Gilley, you've had a lot of success. Maybe you ought to close the show.'

"I said, 'That's not a problem. I don't want to follow Jerry anyway.'

"So, he went in and he told the promoter, 'Hey, Gilley doesn't care if Jerry Lee closes the show.' The promoter was surprised, 'Really?'

"My pilot said, 'In fact, Gilley told me if Jerry Lee wants him to bring him out, he'll sing some songs with him.' The promoter calmed down, 'He'll do that?'

"So they put two pianos out there on the stage. I went in and talked to Jerry. 'Jerry, look, I'll come out and do my half and if you want me to come out and close the show with you, I'll be more than happy to.'

"So he called me out onstage later and said, 'What should we do?' I told him, 'Any of your songs you want to do.' I knew all his material. We did 'Great Balls of Fire,' 'High School Confidential,' and I don't remember what else. We got a standing ovation and the people were going crazy because they wanted to see us together. They wanted to see Jerry Lee and me, the two cousins from Ferriday, Louisiana."

That event showed Mickey the compelling power of the two cousins appearing and playing piano together. He told his agent, "Look, why don't you book me and Jerry Lee on some shows together? We can both play and then close the show together. It'll be dynamite.

"So they booked several shows for the two of us together. But it didn't work because Jerry went out there and he wasn't interested in having me out there on the stage with him. On one particular occasion he tried to make a fool out of me. He went out there and he started singing religious tunes and he tried to make me feel lower than low, saying "You know these songs. We grew up singing them in church." And I told him, "I didn't come out here to sing religious tunes. I came out here to do a show for the folks.

"I got up and walked off. And the next night in Lake Charles, Louisiana, when we had the show, I left after I was finished. He tried to call me out on the stage and I was gone. I wasn't into it. I was into entertaining the people, not to be berated. But he was probably on something, I guess."

– 39 –

NOT ONE TO WALLOW

In June 1982, Jerry's estranged wife Jaren was found dead in a friend's swimming pool. It was a sad ending to a sad marriage and a sad life.

By then Jerry was already smitten with a twenty-three-year-old cocktail waitress named Shawn Michelle Stephens, and the young, beautiful Shawn was taken with the life of a celebrity. Their romance quickly evolved into a tumultuous relationship, made worse by Jerry's unpredictable mood swings and drug habits. They broke up, then reunited after Jerry vigorously pursued a reconciliation.

They were married at Jerry's Nesbit residence in June 1983. The relationship continued to be strained. "She was in over her head," recalls Kay Martin, Jerry's friend since the fifties and long-time head of his fan club. "She didn't have the slightest idea who Jerry Lee Lewis was really and she should not have married him. He was more complicated than she thought."

Shawn was fun, vivacious, and drop-dead gorgeous. She had an amazing body, full of curves in all the right places, and could turn the head of every man in a room, which led to troubles since Jerry was prone to fits of jealousy.

Having seen the troubles that had led to the ruination of Jerry's numerous marriages, his close friend Gary Skala offered a suggestion to the couple.

"If you enjoy each other's company and love each other, why get married? Jerry, I'm not sure marriage suits you."

Jerry's conservative upbringing and stubborn nature took over. When he was stirred up, he had a habit of jutting his head forward, giving a menacing look, and shaking his head from side to side as he spoke.

"If I want to get married, son, I'll get married," he said.

A few months later, Gary was tapped on the shoulder. As he turned to see who was seeking his attention, he looked down to see Shawn's beautiful face looking up at him.

"Gary, I understand what you were trying to say now."

Gary could see that she felt overwhelmed, strained by the discord of her new marriage. She knew Jerry loved her, but he was hell to live with.

On August 24, 1983, less than three months after their wedding, Shawn was found dead in a guest bedroom at their Nesbit home. Accusations were fired at Jerry. Shawn's family believed foul play was involved and Jerry's bizarre behavior around the time of the death—his unpredictable outbursts, intense jealousy surrounding Shawn's coming and going, his raging temper, all driven by his heavy drug use—contributed to suspicions. *Rolling Stone* magazine and the ABC News program *20/20* wrote and presented indictments about Jerry's purported misdeeds and the possibility of a cover-up.

After an autopsy, a formal ruling was made that Shawn died from a methadone overdose. Jerry was never formally accused of wrongdoing. In an interview over two decades later, Jerry was asked to identify the worst night of his life. He sat silently for a long time, thinking, and finally replied, "The worst night of my life . . . well, when my wife killed herself . . . we was arguing about something, and she went into the restroom, to the medicine cabinet—and took out a whole bottle of methadone pills. Now you don't do that—methadone pills, there's no antidote for 'em. And it killed her. That was about the worst experience I went through."

A few days after Shawn's death, against the wishes of her family, Jerry made another trip to Ferriday with another dead body. The procession made its way toward the Calhoun family cemetery. Jerry looked out the window of his limousine and saw the roads and fields he had traversed as a child. As he sat in the little cemetery watching her casket being lowered into the ground, he looked down the line of headstones just to the right of Shawn's freshly dug grave. He saw the headstone over Junior's grave, followed by Mamie's and Elmo Jr.'s, whose little casket had been moved here from Snake Ridge many years earlier. He saw the graves of Elmo Sr. and of little Steve Allen.

Jerry felt sad, lonely, and hopeless. The burden of it was more than he could handle. Somewhere there was a bottle of booze or a vial of pills that would alleviate the pain.

Upon his return from Shawn's funeral, Jerry was disoriented and vulnerable. He spent his nights at Hernando's Hideaway—drinking, playing, and raising hell. Kerrie McCarver, with whom Jerry was already familiar, sang and performed at the club and lavished attention on Jerry. Kerrie's being there, waiting on Jerry in these dark hours, had been, according to many, choreographed by the McCarver family in hopes of forwarding the prospects of a relationship between their daughter and Jerry.

Ten months after Shawn's death, Jerry and Kerrie were married. The happiest man at their wedding was Kerrie's father, Bob McCarver. He would tell anyone who would listen about his pride on this day. He had always hoped that his daughter would marry Elvis Presley or Jerry Lee Lewis, and now he could not contain his happiness at his family's good fortune. But it would be a marriage of continuous struggle and difficulty.

Have a seat, Jerry," commanded the middle-aged counselor with an authoritative tone in her voice. He glared at her but she seemed unimpressed and unfazed by his fame or his anger. The year was 1987. Kerrie McCarver Lewis had recently given birth to Jerry Lee Lewis III and was back in Memphis, on the western side of the state. Reluctantly but with an undeniable sense that he needed help, Jerry had agreed to enter the rehabilitation clinic at Vanderbilt University. He had been urged to go there by Kerrie and by his agent, Al Embry, who lived near Nashville and this facility.

Valerie, the woman with whom Jerry now sat face-to-face, looked up and saw the tell-tale signs of an addict. Jerry was thin, frail, skin drawn tight over his face, deep pockets around his eyes. How he kept going night after night in the face of the abuse to which he subjected himself was not a mystery to her. As a former addict herself, she knew the superhuman ways in which those under the influence could push themselves, always looking for the next high as they did their best to cope with the struggles of day-to-day existence. Jerry had been doing this for many years and it was a life he now accepted—even embraced—because he could barely remember anything else, even though he could not honestly convince himself he was a happy man these days.

With her face showing the effects of her own years of struggle and hard living, Valerie spoke to him in her heavy northern accent, softened only slightly by her few years in the South.

"Jerry, I'm a straight shooter. I've been to hell and back myself. I'm from New York City, and Jerry, I've taken every kind of dope there is. I've taken it through every vein and every part of my body. I mean everywhere. But I was able to get clean."

Jerry sat there listening, hearing the words, knowing that the gist of them was a message he'd heard before from professionals and those close to him. He could tell this woman meant business. He knew he needed this even as he dreaded what lay before him.

Valerie continued, "Jerry, you have to get off drugs or they will kill you. You will be stone cold dead. You cannot survive this way forever. You need to stay in here and let us help you get clean."

For a few days Jerry bit his lip and willed himself to suffer the pain, the physical sickness, the denial of the substances which had been his refuge. He endured all the shit that Valerie and others in the facility gave him. Every complaint about his discomfort was met by his tough counselor with a seeming lack of compassion or empathy. He knew a hundred people on the outside who would get him what he wanted. Hell, he had encountered hundreds of strangers at shows and performances who were happy to give the great Jerry Lee Lewis drugs. Here he was controlled by one woman, who told him he wasn't getting what his body craved.

After three days he was fed up. He knew he needed to quit, but he couldn't. He didn't want to, at least not badly enough.

Valerie called Al Embry. She was providing daily updates to Al and Kerrie.

"Jerry's sitting out on the sidewalk," she said, "and he's refusing to come back inside."

Sitting there now, in the same jeans, shirt, and cheap sandals in which he had arrived, Jerry waited as the hours went by for someone—anyone—to come get him and take him away from this place where they required him to do things that were too hard and for which he had not reached the level of desperation necessary to comply.

The justification rolling around in his head was that he didn't like being told what to do and he wasn't going to put up with it. Deep down inside, on some level, he realized that he just didn't want to quit badly enough to suffer what was required to get clean, to beat this.

After a few hours Al Embry rolled up beside Jerry.

"I begged him to go back," says Al, "but it was not going to happen. When Jerry made up his mind about something it was impossible to convince him otherwise. That day I could look at Jerry and tell there was no point in continuing to try and convince him."

On another occasion, Jerry was performing at the Westbury Music Fair in New York state. One of Jerry's handlers was backstage with him before the show, worried.

"Jerry, you cannot go onstage like this. You are in no condition for it."

The opening act had finished. Jerry's band was already on the stage opening his performance. Jerry was in bad shape, as the dangerous substances he had ingested were producing another revolt by his frail, weakened body. He was having convulsions, throwing up, and spitting up blood. Those around him felt a mixture of numbness from familiarity, sympathy for his situation, and marvel at how one man could heap so much agony on himself.

Those with him decided he couldn't perform, finally convincing Jerry that it was pointless to try. The last-minute cancellation displeased the show's promoters but Jerry was whisked away by his handlers in a limousine headed to the airport. He was encouraged several times to stop at hospitals along the route but he wanted to get home as quickly as possible.

As the entourage reached the plane awaiting him for his return to Memphis, Jerry continued to be violently sick and intermittently coherent. Kerrie, unsure who to reach out to, called a man who had been a last-gasp solution on prior occasions. The man was Reverend Jimmy Swaggart.

Once on the phone, Jimmy asked to speak with Gary Skala, good friend and super fan of Jerry. He told him, "Young man, you send that plane here. When it lands, I don't want to see any drugs, alcohol, prostitutes, or anything of the sort. Give me your word now."

When Jerry was told he was heading to Baton Rouge and Jimmy's, a look of resignation came over the face of this stubborn, obstinate man who took orders from no one.

"OK," he said, "Let's go see Jimmy then, I guess."

– 40 –

STRUGGLE AMID SUCCESS

Mickey understood the perils of success but wasn't immune to them. As his performance fee soared to $50,000 a night in the wake of the tremendous success of *Urban Cowboy*, the cousin who'd always had his feet on the ground lived the high life.

Along with success came the challenge of being the same, approachable guy he'd always been. He fought assertions that he was less accessible. "Like I told a lot of people, when *Urban Cowboy* hit, I didn't change. The people around me changed. They wanted to be closer. They wanted to talk more. You can't talk to everybody. So they said, 'Well, he's got the big head.' I couldn't get out and do some of the things I wanted to do at that particular point in time because I had to be careful where I went.

"We had season tickets to the Houston Astros' games. I was a big baseball fan and liked to watch the Astros play. But I quit going to the ballgames. People would recognize me and they'd come down and stand in front of other people wanting me to sign autographs. I didn't want to say, 'No, I can't sign it.' I didn't want to be rude. But I didn't want people coming up and standing up in front of other people that were baseball fans while I was signing autographs."

Looking back, Mickey also recognized that he'd gotten caught up in the rush to capitalize on his success at every turn.

"Back then it was money, money, money. I was playing every concert they threw in front of me. I wish I had cut what I did in half. I wanted to make as much money as quickly as I could. It was like a dragon: you feed it to keep it. I had a lifestyle of airplanes and buses and trucks. I did stupid things. I prostituted myself for the money."

Though Mickey never strayed into the world of drugs, he liked to drink socially and was prone, from time to time, to drink too much. Like his father, Arthur, he developed a wandering eye. Women became the ultimate intoxicant, to whom it became difficult to say no.

His penchant for other women began in the early years before his marriage to Vivian. When they met and married, he had been overwhelmed by her and had found her beautiful and awe-inspiring. After a few tough years together when both were working long hours and spending too much time apart, the marriage changed. As his popularity grew, so did his access to attractive women. Three years after they married, Mickey was looking elsewhere. He developed a relationship with Cathy, a beautiful, vivacious woman who lived in Pasadena. A key complication was that they were both married. The four-year, on-again-off-again relationship led to a period of several months in the late sixties when they separated from their respective spouses and lived together. While the physical aspects of the relationship were compelling, Mickey and his mistress had a volatile relationship mostly because she was not willing to limit her physical interaction to Mickey. Ultimately they parted and over time Mickey and Vivian were able to reconcile.

With the heavy touring of the seventies after Mickey's chart-topping success and the explosion of popularity following the release of *Urban Cowboy*, the temptations rose dramatically. One night when Mickey was playing in the Midwest, he met a couple in a club. After a short visit Mickey danced with the wife and, later that evening, ended up with her in his hotel bedroom while the husband slept in the same hotel downstairs. When the husband called looking for his wife the next morning, Mickey whisked her away, wondering at what point this would get him in serious trouble.

Women constantly made overt sexual advances toward him in clubs or out in public. Other women—beautiful women—waited patiently for him after shows or passed notes to him, anxious for an opportunity to spend the evening with a successful country performer.

In 1980, Mickey began a seven-year torrid romance with Connie Moore, a stunning woman with beautiful brown hair and a fantastic figure. He met her when he and Vivian visited the Opryland Hotel in Nashville, where Connie worked. Mickey would later say, "I have loved a few women in my life but Connie was my fantasy."

Despite the difficulty the pair had during their regular encounters over the next years, the relationship never suffered in the bedroom. Ultimately, however, they grew apart. Mickey didn't flaunt his relationships with other women in Vivian's face but, like his father, he was attracted to pretty women and he was often cavalier about their marriage and not always discreet. Over time Vivian became aware of Mickey's habits and it created a complicated dynamic. Understandably, she would give him hell when she heard the rumors or found evidence of his affairs. They would fight and she threatened to leave him on many occasions.

But that departure never occurred. As time went on, Mickey's continuing success and the lifestyle it afforded made it increasingly difficult for Vivian to leave. She had fought with him through the hard years and now enjoyed a way of life for which she too had worked diligently.

A more interesting dynamic was at play, in a world where black and white often gives way to gray: Mickey was a playboy. Mickey was a womanizer. Still, Vivian loved him. While it angered and humiliated her that he strayed, she managed to accept his weakness.

As for Mickey, it was obvious that he loved Vivian. They were always close friends and even years later when he spent time away from her for long stretches of time, he would call her at least twice each day. He seemed able to love two women at the same time, walking the difficult line of maintaining functioning—albeit very different—relationships with both women without alienating either.

In rearing Mickey, Arthur Gilley provided a balance to the church-loving Irene. While Irene was a praying woman, Arthur was not. He did as he pleased. He was a man who enjoyed the pleasures he was able to scratch up from his world, whether they pleased his wife or not.

As Arthur aged, however, he mellowed. He dealt with medical problems that limited his mobility and opportunities. Around Ferriday, he was remembered for years as the driver of a taxi, happily shuttling people to and fro, generally within the confines of Concordia Parish, neighboring parishes, and Natchez, just beyond the eastern boundary of Louisiana. Mickey's oldest son, Michael, spent time as a youngster with Arthur with some regularity.

"I used to ride with him in the taxi all the time. It was fun for me because I never knew where we were going to go. I can remember we'd get into the car in the mornings and we'd park next to a big brick wall that had a single phone hanging on the wall. We'd sit there in the car until the phone rang. He'd answer it, come back to the car, and say, 'All right, we're going to go pick up Ms. So-and-So at her house and take her to the grocery store.' You could go anywhere in Ferriday, Louisiana, you wanted to for fifty cents.

"He used to chew those old cigars that were very big around. He didn't really smoke them all that much but he chewed on them all day long. He and I, we were pretty good pals, doing the taxi thing together and spending time just talking."

Arthur Gilley died in 1982. All four of his children and Irene were at his bedside when he passed away. Two days later friends and family gathered to bury him.

As Mickey mourned the death of his father, Jerry sat next to him, frail and gaunt. Jimmy delivered the eulogy and the message became evangelical, as it typically did when he was around.

"Jimmy was preaching hard," Mickey recalls. "By the time he was done there wasn't a dry eye in the church."

Near the end of his message, Jimmy said to the congregation, "If any of you believe you wouldn't go to heaven with Uncle Arthur if you died today, please come forward."

One man stood. Jerry Lee Lewis once again acknowledged the fierce internal struggle he faced.

Later Mickey asked Jerry, "Why did you do that?"

"Because Jimmy expected me to," Jerry said.

It was almost as if Jerry looked at Jimmy and saw what he would have been had he taken a different fork in the road. Accordingly, he was compelled to prove to himself that he had not strayed so far from that straighter, narrower path that he had reached the point of no return.

How are you feeling, Mama?" Mickey's sister, Edna, sat near her mother, opposite the window through which Irene was looking as morning light came shining into the hospital room. Irene's health was failing and the family had brought her to the New Orleans medical facility to ensure she received top-notch treatment and so she would be near Edna, who lived in the area. Mickey made sure his mama got the best attention possible.

Irene turned to look at her daughter. Her eyes showed the discomfort she felt but also the undying spark that remained within. Her spirit soared, as always.

"I'm doing just fine, Edna. Now don't you worry about me."

A nurse entered the room to attend to another patient in a bed only a few feet away, separated by a thin curtain pulled together to provide a modicum of privacy. Edna turned back from the sounds emanating from the other half of the room as the nurse awakened the patient gently. As she looked at her mom, she smiled. She knew that Mickey, who was at the pinnacle of his career, would have gladly reserved an entire wing of the hospital for the most special woman in his life, his mama. But Irene would have no talk of a private room. She insisted on taking a shared room so she could be around other people and have someone with whom to talk.

"Mama, I brought you some slippers. I noticed you walking around here a few days ago in bare feet. We don't need you catching pneumonia." Edna reached into the bag of items she had brought along for her mom and pulled out a pair of colorful house shoes.

Irene motioned her daughter. She had been in bed for days and sitting up, putting her feet on the floor for a few minutes, would be a welcome change of position. Edna helped her eighty-three-year-old mother put her feet on the floor. Then she helped Irene put on her fuzzy, new slippers.

Two days later, Edna was back at the hospital to visit Irene.

"Mother, your feet are gonna get cold. Where are your slippers?"

Irene laughed. It was a laugh recognized by everyone who knew her, deep and full of life. "I don't have them anymore," she said with a twinkle in her eye.

A few seconds later a hospital staff member entered the room, pushing Irene's roommate in a wheelchair. The patient's discomfort was visible as she slumped over in the chair. She didn't acknowledge anyone else in the room. The elderly lady was not having a good day.

As the attendant carefully helped the woman back into her bed Edna saw the woman's feet. There were the slippers she had given to Irene only two days prior. She turned back to look at her mother, and saw the sly grin she recognized. Just as she had seen her mom do countless times over the last sixty years, Irene winked at her.

"She needed the shoes more than I did, dear."

Jimmy lost his mother, Minnie Bell, in 1960. Jerry said good-bye to Mamie for the final time in 1971. Mickey was able to enjoy the relationship with his mother for another fourteen years. She had never been more than a phone call away and he thought of her daily. Though he rejected much of the religious influence of his youth, he had never doubted the real impact of his mother's faith and the benefits of her prayerful lifestyle on his existence. "I saw what my mom did praying for the lady that was eaten up with cancer, who was healed. I saw her pray my dad out of business when he ran a bar. When I got into the music business and I started playing clubs, I told my mom one time, 'Mom, please don't pray against me. You can pray for me or not pray for me, but please don't pray against me.'"

No man raised under the loving, guiding hand of Irene Gilley could fully turn away from the strong, permanent influences impressed upon him. Mickey remembered a discussion he'd once had with a minister: "A preacher came to Vivian's mom's house and wanted us all to come over to his church. And I said, 'Well, really, I'm Assembly of God.' He asked me, 'Have you ever been baptized?' and I told him, 'As a matter of fact, I have. When I was a kid, I was baptized.' When he asked how I was baptized, I told him, 'I was baptized in the name of the Father, the Son, and the Holy Ghost. That's the way the Assembly of God does it. They put you under water, bring you back up, and you're baptized.' He looked at me and said, 'You can't make it to heaven like that because you've got to be baptized in the name of Jesus Christ only.' I said, 'Well, let me tell you something. If my mom didn't make it to heaven, you can forget it, there won't be one.'"

In 1985, Mickey rushed from Reno to New Orleans to see Irene, thinking her situation was dire, but when he got there she was doing much better. Mickey left after a short visit, reassured that her situation had stabilized. A few days later Irene passed away. The woman that had been his life, around whom his world had turned for the majority of his youth, was gone and her departure was difficult for him to bear.

Irene Gilley was laid to rest next to Arthur near her birthplace of Mangham, where she had spent the early years of her life.

Mickey felt lost, unsure of his next steps. Irene had been his protector, his compass, the standard by which he measured goodness and unconditional love. Often suspicious of the motives and intentions of others, he never questioned his mother—her convictions, her beliefs, and her faith. When difficult times came—as they did for everyone—he never doubted that his mother was in his corner, encouraging him, wanting the best for him, and lifting him up prayerfully.

Now she was gone. He couldn't help feeling alone. He had been—and always would be—a mama's boy. At her funeral, Mickey's tears flowed unashamedly down his face.

Irene's favorite great-nephew performed the ceremony. Jimmy Swaggart, never shy about addressing issues from the pulpit or podium, spoke to the gathering. "Here's the lady who used to pray for you and hold you up to the eyes of God. I just want to let all of you know that she's not gonna be here sending up prayers for you anymore. And don't you think that wasn't directed toward you, Mickey Gilley."

At the graveside, Mickey pulled David Beatty aside.

"With Mama gone," he said, "I don't know who I'm going to have praying for me."

"Well, I'm going to be praying for you," said David, "but it'll be a different experience with her gone."

Years later, David would point out, "He's never had a hit record since his mama died."

By the mideighties Mickey's momentum in the music industry slowed. Country music executives were looking for new twists and new angles and an era of flashy, glitzy stars with designer hats and cowboy boots were coming into vogue. Some of the marquee stars of the seventies and early eighties still had strong, faithful followings, but decision makers were interested in performers with crossover appeal whose albums could sell in the millions rather than the hundreds of thousands. As a fifty-year-old singer and entertainer, Mickey's down-to-earth and guy-next-door style didn't fit their new mold.

The longstanding relationship between Mickey and Sherwood Cryer was also souring. The two had been successful together but the years, personality conflicts, charges of financial misdealing, and key differences over how Gilley's should be run were reaching a critical level. Efforts at compromise were fruitless and Mickey's attempts to steer Sherwood in a direction he did not want to go were going nowhere. These factors would lead to a contentious culmination of their partnership.

In late 1986, Ferriday's three famous cousins descended on Jimmy's sprawling ministry empire in Baton Rouge. Mickey flew in with two friends on his own plane from Houston. He loved flying around the country and a flight from Houston to Baton Rouge was a fairly quick trip. He looked forward to seeing his two cousins, as the three were rarely together in the same place. On the drive over in a chauffeured limousine from the airport to Bluebonnet Road, Mickey relegated his diamond rings and pendant to his pocket. No need to be showy for Jimmy or the reporter from *People* who was meeting them there to do a story.

Jerry came in a while later on a chartered jet with Al Embry. Jerry and his band had been in New Orleans working on an HBO special with Fats Domino. The drive would have been a little more than an hour but appearances needed to be maintained, so the jet barely had time to level off before turning its nose down toward the Baton Rouge airport seventy miles away.

Modesty—and understatement—had never been strong suits of Jerry's. Unlike his younger cousin, he arrived adorned in bling, including a showy piano-shaped ring. Upon seeing Jerry's attire, Mickey fished his own jewelry out of his pockets, including the familiar diamond pendant flashing the trademark "MG" letters.

Along with Frances and the small group who had gathered, the three cousins spent a few hours touring the ministry grounds and answering questions, but mainly visiting with each other, catching up, and rehashing shared memories.

"Remember when your daddy and Brother Culbreth used to get on us in church for cuttin' up, Jimmy?" Jerry joked.

"Do you two remember the time when we carved our initials in the back pew of the church?" Mickey remembered.

Jimmy made no pretense of liking Jerry or Mickey's music, but he took a minute to tell Mickey of his fondness of the number one hit "True Love Ways," particularly the piano introduction.

Jimmy needled the other two about tithing—giving 10 percent of their earnings to the church—but mainly in jest. Jerry, never one to let anyone else get the upper hand, popped back at his older cousin.

"Jimmy, quit bugging us. You've made more money than both me and Mickey put together."

Jerry was constantly fidgeting and jittery. But he was friendly and engaged, and everyone seemed to be enjoying their time together.

In the recording studio on the ministry grounds, the three crowded around and sat at the piano just as they might have done in the school music room forty years earlier. Their common denominator was always gospel music. They played and sang with Jerry taking center stage, which didn't surprise anyone. Later they headed over to Ruth's Chris Steakhouse for dinner.

Jimmy sang the praises of the filet mignon. After some discussion, Mickey decided on the ribeye. Jerry settled for a glass of iced tea, declaring he wasn't hungry and whispering to Al that he would get something later.

After a while, the easily bored Jerry started stacking drinking glasses. Within moments, Jimmy decided to join his rock 'n' roll cousin. Jerry went three glasses high and Jimmy surpassed him to four, although he had to hold the glasses to help balance them and keep them from falling.

Mickey just shook his head while he watched the two, entertained yet puzzled as to why Jerry and Jimmy had chosen to undertake a glass-stacking competition in a nice steak house. After a few minutes of watching the events with a strained smile, Frances reached over like a mother who had tolerated enough silliness and restored the glasses to their previous positions on the table.

"You two stop that," she said, "before someone makes a mess."

Jerry, the wild child and the maestro
(Photo courtesy of Sherrie Calhoun Jacobs)

Early Mickey as a performer
(Photo courtesy of Mickey Gilley)

Jerry and Mamie
(Photo courtesy of Delta Music Museum)

Sherwood Cryer and Mickey
(Photo courtesy of Troy Payne)

Jimmy, the solemn preacher
(Photo courtesy of Edna Gilley Mequet)

Jerry and Mickey at Billy Bob's
(Photo courtesy of Michael Gilley)

Mickey and John Travolta
(Photo courtesy of Delta Music Museum)

Mickey in the recording studio
(Photo courtesy of Troy Payne)

Jimmy singing the house down
(Photo courtesy of Mickey Gilley)

Jimmy preaching to the masses
(Photo courtesy of Mickey Gilley)

303

Jimmy, Jerry, and Mickey
(Photo courtesy of Michael Gilley)

Jimmy and Mickey at their induction to the Delta Music Museum in 2002
(Photo courtesy of Tim Vance)

Mickey and oldest son Michael

Mickey performing in Arlington, Texas
(Photo by Irene Formillo)

Jimmy at the piano at Family Worship Center in Baton Rouge
(Photo by Don Kadair)

Jerry performing in Richardson, Texas
(Photo by Kevin Baldes)

– 41 –

BUILDING PRESSURE

The growth of Jimmy's ministry was trending upward. In 1983, Arbitron figures pegged the viewership of the weekly Jimmy Swaggart telecast at 1.88 million households. By then his career record sales had exceeded twelve million, the ministry publication *The Evangelist* was reaching a monthly readership of 800,000, and the ministry's intake of annual revenue had increased to sixty million dollars. The ministry was in the midst of huge growth plans and the numbers of employees were growing dramatically.

After outgrowing offices established on Goya Avenue, the ministry developed a plan for its physical assets to keep up with its overall growth and outreach. In 1981, Jimmy Swaggart Ministries embarked on a massive campaign to develop 257 acres of land it had purchased on Bluebonnet Road, just south of Interstate 10 and on the southeastern edge of Baton Rouge. Within a few years several plush, impressive buildings, including administrative offices and a home church used as the base for the ministry, were erected. There was a state-of-the-art television production center, a full-color printing operation, a twelve-grade Family Christian Academy, and Jimmy Swaggart Bible College, which served 1,000 students and had plans for 4,000 more.

The crown jewel of the ministry's physical facilities was Family Worship Center, built and dedicated in 1983. According to the *Baton Rouge Morning-Advocate*, the congregation had moved around for years, meeting in a Holiday Inn in 1979, progressing to a local performing arts theater and another site before moving into its permanent location on Bluebonnet. With capacity to seat 7,500 people and at a cost of nine million dollars to build, it was constructed with state-of-the-art acoustics and production amenities, allowing services conducted there to be beamed all over the world. Jimmy took an active role in the layout of the church as he had even envisioned the specific octagonal design.

Author Barbara Nauer, one of Jimmy's strong supporters and a later editor at *The Evangelist* magazine, attributed the growth and success of the Assemblies of God denomination largely to the popularity of Jimmy and his ministry, stating, "the denomination's Great Leap forward in enrollments related very directly to the spectacular energy and charismatic preaching power of Louisiana's Jimmy Swaggart."

In 1987, annual revenue for the organization was roughly $150 million. According to *US News and World Report*, 3.6 million people were watching Jimmy each week, second only to Pat Robertson's daily program, *The 700 Club*, which was at just over four million. The ministry was still distributing *The Evangelist* to 800,000 addressees each month and there were large numbers of books, teaching series, sermons, music albums, and other materials for consumption and purchase, creating a direct-mail order blitzkrieg handled by the burgeoning group assigned to the mountain of mail and correspondence that rolled into the ministry each day, an avalanche that comprised Louisiana's largest mail-order business. Different sources placed the mail volume handled by the ministry at between 50,000 and 100,000 letters . . . per *week*.

The ministry's headquarters had flourished into a full-fledged empire employing approximately 1,500 people, making it the largest employer in the Baton Rouge area and one of the largest in the entire state of Louisiana. The ministry also had its own zip code, the only operation in the State of Louisiana to hold that distinction.

Jimmy Swaggart Ministries made its presence felt internationally in a big way. By 1987, Jimmy's telecast was aired around the world, numbering 143 countries at the height of its operation. The shows were dubbed into sixteen languages, including Icelandic, Arabic, and Japanese. Almost every non-Communist country in the world aired at least some of the broadcasts.

The ministry—and the preacher himself—had an especially significant presence in Latin America. Pentecostalism was exploding in Central and South America and the growth was in no small part attributable to the personality of the Bible-waving preacher from Ferriday, Louisiana. Jimmy was a celebrity in countries like Nicaragua, where a reception in his honor was hosted by President Daniel Ortega. When other preachers were looked upon with suspicion or disdain by political leaders in the region, Jimmy was beloved. The three-day crusades, a staple of the ministry's outreach, became increasingly focused on the international realm. Places like Johannesburg, South Africa, and Managua, Nicaragua, became international destinations where huge public stadiums were filled by those coming to hear Jimmy deliver his message of hope and deliverance for their often bleak lives. With a stage perched in the middle of the huge, open-air venues, the singers belted out moving gospel songs as tens of thousands sang in unison. Jimmy strutted back and forth across the stage, pausing every sentence or two as a man walking behind him translated his words into the language of the local citizenry. When the crowd was invited forward to pray and receive Christian salvation, thousands flooded across the field: some running, some crying, all creating a human experience that was stunning and moving to behold.

The ministry's commitment to international missions outreach was monumental. By the mid- to late eighties, a quarter of the Assemblies of God's outreach to international missions was funded by the ministry, accounting for twelve million of the forty-eight million dollars invested annually. Claims varied, but by most accounts the ministry operated 200 schools around the world and fed over 20,000 impoverished children each day in all corners of the world.

In the name of Jesus, stop it!"

It was a Saturday evening service in Monrovia, Liberia. Inside the largest stadium in that city, 80,000 people sat, listening to the evangelist from Louisiana tell of Jesus and His crucifixion on a cross nearly 2,000 years ago.

When the stadium had opened at 5:30 p.m. in the still-blazing sun, people had poured forth into the facility like ants stirred up with the toe of an intrusive boot. Many had woken early that morning and walked many miles to attend the service, all for a chance to hear the burly preacher whose coming had generated much anticipation.

This international crusade, like others before it, had been a daunting undertaking. Two 747 cargo planes had hauled all of the equipment necessary for the crusade team. Dozens of local pastors and ministers helped with the support and assistance that people would need. Off to the side of the huge platform constructed in the middle of the stadium was a sizable white tent. When Donnie asked a local preacher helping with the event why the tent was there, it was explained that Liberia had a problem with demon-possessed citizens and the tent was there so that local clergy could deal with those so afflicted.

That evening, as the sun set on Liberia and the stadium, following the singing and introductory worship, Jimmy began to preach. In his typical fashion, he paced back and forth along the length of the large platform, holding a large microphone in his right hand as he spoke emphatically and used his left hand demonstratively, pointing his finger, waving it overhead, and balling up his fist, depending on the point he was making.

All of a sudden, to the right of those on the large stage, a large noise erupted. Hundreds of voices began barking in unison, generating an eerie, unnerving feeling throughout the entire crowd. The air seemed stifling, as though a firm grip had been placed over the throats of everyone in attendance.

Jimmy looked at the crowd, sweat glistening on his forehead. A knowing look came into his eyes as he heard the throaty, guttural sound which he believed to be emanating from those possessed by demons. Within a few seconds, he growled loudly into the microphone, in the direction of the noise.

"In the name of Jesus Christ, stop it!"

The noise immediately ceased. Those singers and staff near him, unfamiliar with this type of spiritual warfare, felt the hair stand up on their neck and arms. A weird mixture of fear and peace flowed through them. Jimmy continued to preach. Within a few moments, the barks erupted again from the same section, even louder, attempting to drown out Jimmy's voice.

Walking down the platform he repeated his words, even louder and more forceful this time.

"I said, in the name of Jesus Christ, shut up!"

The barking sounds silenced, not to return. At the end of the service that evening, an estimated 10,000 people flooded the area around the platform to pray the sinner's prayer. People jumped, others threw their arms in the air, and hundreds shed tears of hope for their seemingly hopeless lives. The white tent housing the possessed was bursting beyond capacity as dozens of ministers prayed with hundreds of Liberians, freeing them from the demons that had oppressed them for years.

Donnie stared in amazement, numb from the experience. People could say what they wanted about his dad. They could call him a fake if they felt so compelled. The last two hours—and the role Jimmy had played—had been just another event in a long list of amazing occurrences that confirmed his own belief in his father's legitimacy as a genuine man of God.

Jimmy Lee Swaggart was on top of the religious and church world. But with the success and high profile came a multitude of responsibilities. The pressure mounted and by late 1986 and into 1987 it only continued its upward climb. Jimmy was involved in weekly church services in Baton Rouge, conducting a dozen or more crusades each year, traveling domestically and internationally to meet with a variety of dignitaries, including heads of state. He wrote extensively, producing books and making regular contributions to *The Evangelist*. Along with Frances, Donnie, and a small inner circle, he drove operational and administrative decision making for a $150-million-per-year business. He prepared sermons, fought off the attacks of those who despised his views and governmental entities that challenged his tax-free status, and somewhere in the midst of it all, still found time to pray and seek guidance from his Boss.

Through the eighties, as his popularity soared and his reach expanded, Jimmy increasingly sensed that he was uniquely positioned to deliver the message of hope and deliverance to the world and that he was specially called by God to accomplish great things of which others were incapable. More and more, the voice Jimmy heard exhorted him to preach the message of the gospel on every television station in the world, and to do so quickly. It became an obsession.

"I must do it," Jimmy said, "God has called me to do it. If I do not do it, it will not be done. I know that to be the truth."

He made urgent pleas to supporters to help him accomplish this task, to support efforts of the ministry to reach the millions and tens of millions waiting to hear the message.

As the purview and reach of the ministry expanded, an ever-expanding physical complex, continued international outreach, and most significantly, the escalating cost of television expansion produced a growing animal that needed to be fed continually. Significant amounts of television time were devoted to fund-raising and the constant mention of looming financial difficulty was so frequent that Jimmy was quoted by the *New York Times* as saying, "Sometimes I think that I sound like a broken record."

With this constant focus on raising money it was easy to lose the message being delivered. Because the ministry operated as a church—changing its status from a tax-exempt organization in the early eighties—it was difficult for the outside world to follow the financial workings of the organization, leading to further questions and pressures.

As the ministry loomed larger it attracted more attention from the media. Over time a strained relationship evolved with the press. In 1983, investigative journalist John Camp produced *Give Me That Big-Time Religion*, a documentary about the ministry that aired on WBRZ in Baton Rouge and later won the reporter a prestigious Peabody Award. It was the first significant investigative piece into the ministry, a learning experience for the world and for the Swaggarts.

After being contacted by both a current and former employee of the ministry about their misgivings, Camp gathered information about the operational and financial dealings of the ministry. After extensive research and discussions with many close to the ministry, John developed a direct relationship with Jimmy.

"After I had built up an accumulation of material that I thought might be worth following through on, I called Jimmy and he came on the line. 'John, I've been waiting for your call. I've heard that you've talked to several people and that you're gathering information. I welcome you to come into our ministry. I think you can get your best insight of what's going on here if you travel with me to a crusade.' So I went with him to Hampton, Virginia, and that was my first exposure to Jimmy. I was blown away. He was one of the great preachers. Dan Rather called him a great orator of the twentieth century. Fantastic."

Camp's area of primary focus was financial, especially questions surrounding whether funds were used for the causes for which they were initially raised. Inconsistencies were found and concerns were raised over misrepresentations in the fund-raising practices of the ministry.

Camp remembered the trepidation with which he developed and presented his information. "I had my own spiritual concerns before that piece ran. Thousands and thousands of people out here were getting their spiritual sustenance from this guy. I'm not exactly a Holy Roller, but I have a great deal of gratitude to God for what's occurred in my life and the last thing I wanted to do is undercut the faith of people."

Many questions arose from the lack of financial accountability required of television ministries in general. Kenneth Woodward of *Newsweek* commented, "in the unregulated market of televangelism, only God and the IRS really know a preacher's personal income. Even the IRS can't always keep up with the homes, cars, and other courtesies that followers bestow on celebrity preachers."

In moving from a tax-exempt organization to church status, the ministry exacerbated the scrutiny because they became even less accountable for providing information to the public.

The press had a field day with the lifestyle of the Swaggarts. The lavish homes built on Highland Road property in Baton Rouge—one for Jimmy and Frances and another for Donnie and his family—were seen by many as extravagant. While Jimmy's talent and success would have rendered these amenities reasonable and well earned in the eyes of most people, his status as a preacher combined with fund-raising techniques that regularly presented dire circumstances—along with his own tendency to hide or downplay the truth about where he lived and what kind of car he drove—only made the situation worse than it needed to be.

With the number of issues raised over time in the news media—some valid and some not—the Swaggarts developed a negative and distrusting view of reporters in general. Frances in particular became more guarded and less available to news gatherers. Employees of the ministry were encouraged to keep a distance from anyone on the outside seeking information. Jimmy was bothered by the outside perception, telling the Associated Press, "If it was just a money-making racket or gimmick, you wouldn't have to go into the huge effort we go into to prove a point. If it were just a rip-off, I wouldn't have to try and feed tens of thousands of starving kids each day. You could do it with just a few hundred and get by."

Jimmy felt the attacks on televangelists emanated largely from the media's dislike of preachers who had the ear of the public and a forum to disseminate their views without a secular filter. "The news media as a whole thinks we're out for the money or trying to gain power or trying to take over the country," Jimmy said. "None of it is true. Yes, we're misunderstood by the press, but I don't care. Most of the accusations about finances are smears. They do not understand the Gospel and they think we're a bunch of crooks and thieves. A lot of the media are plain wicked. If I refuse to do an interview, they go ahead and write it anyway."

Jimmy's style of preaching didn't help to endear him to people outside the ministry, whether in the media or not. Reminiscent of the "voice crying in the wilderness" style of John the Baptist, it was direct, and it ruffled feathers. Through television and extensive writing he had a broad forum for communicating his ideas and some of his comments drew headlines and produced anger over time. He unashamedly spoke out against rock 'n' roll, pornography, homosexuality, ban on school prayer, abortion, and a variety of sensitive topics. He spoke out against beliefs and practices of other groups, Christians and non-Christians alike. Many of his comments were taken out of context. But there was a variety of sensitive topics upon which he touched that gave offense to those with differing opinions. He was called the Farrakhan of the Religious Right. The *Washington Post* quoted the president of the People for the American Way, saying, "Actually, that's an insult to Louis Farrakhan. Farrakhan only hates some people. Swaggart at various times has said similar kinds of hateful things about Catholics, Jews, Baptists. . . . He's an equal-opportunity bigot."

Jimmy addressed Jews and Catholics in his sermons, pointing out areas where he saw their teachings as false or perceived their doctrine as being in error. Of the Jews he wrote, "Because of their rejection of Christ . . . they have known sorrow and heartache like have no other people on the face of the Earth." In trying to illustrate the Jews' loss of protection from God, he even displayed Holocaust images during a televised sermon.

He addressed teachings in the Catholic Church which he found unscriptural. He referred to Roman Catholicism as a false religion, asserting that those who followed its teaching would be lost. When he said that all of Mother Teresa's works would not help her achieve a place in heaven, he further angered Catholics.

"I admire what Mother Teresa does," he said, "I, too, am building schools all over the world and we ought to do it. But none of the things that Mother Teresa does will add one thing toward her salvation."

While many appreciated Jimmy's willingness to boldly proclaim what they supported and what they believed, others were put off by his air of authority, including his cousin Mickey. "One thing I didn't like about Jimmy was how he used to get on the Catholics. I asked my mama one time, 'Who gives him the authority to be the one who is always right?' I didn't like that about Jimmy or him preaching that hellfire and brimstone."

Jimmy didn't hold back his honest opinions on fellow Christian preachers and televangelists either. At different points he took issue with a lengthy list of other ministers on a variety of topics. Particularly offensive to him was the ideology of "health and wealth" espoused by many preachers, whereby financial giving was encouraged with the promise of receiving worldly financial gain and wealth back from God in return. "Television preachers have a tremendous amount of power," he commented. "God told me, 'If you ever exploit the people, I'll destroy you.' Some ministers, I think, do not develop the people, they exploit them."

Even his friend Oral Roberts was not off-limits. In January 1987 Roberts claimed God was going to "call him home" if he did not receive eight million dollars by the end of March, creating scrutiny and criticism from the church and secular worlds. "I love Oral Roberts," Jimmy told *Nightline's* Ted Koppel, "but I think this is bringing terrible reproach on the Kingdom of God. I'm embarrassed by it and I'm ashamed of it."

In early 1987, the PTL network, the 130-million-dollar evangelistic undertaking of Jim and Tammy Bakker, fell into disgrace as stories emerged about a 1980 liaison between Jim Bakker and a former employee, Jessica Hahn, and the $265,000 paid to keep her quiet.

As other serious charges of sexual misconduct about Jim were circulating, PTL also faced heavy scrutiny from the IRS and others about financial questions. The Bakkers were under constant criticism for their opulent lifestyle and Tammy entered a drug rehabilitation facility.

In March 1987, this information became available to the public, leading to shock, embarrassment, and a flurry of activity. Shortly thereafter, the Bakkers resigned from PTL, leading to temporary oversight of the prestigious ministry by Jerry Falwell and ultimately an end to it.

Once again, Jimmy was drawn into a scandal. No two televangelists were more successful in the eighties than Jimmy and Jim Bakker. No two men could have been more different in their personalities and their methods. While Swaggart was an old-school, fire-and-brimstone, Bible-waving bear of a man bounding back and forth across the podium, Bakker was a gentle, soft-spoken man who some considered effeminate and who was constantly smiling and asserting a loving, friendly, all-inclusive message in a talk-show style format.

While Jimmy often felt like an outsider within the denomination, Bakker was more esteemed by many of the higher-ups in the Assemblies of God. The two had never been close and didn't care for each other's styles. While at a California crusade that March, Jimmy was reported by the Associated Press to have told his audience, "God deliver us from these pompadour boys, hair done, nails done, fresh from the beauty shop, preaching the gospel."

As Bakker's downfall took place, Jimmy was accused by Bakker and his attorney of plotting a takeover of PTL. He was blasted by most of the big names in Christian television. Even Oral Roberts chastised him, accusing Jimmy of being "holier than thou" and suggesting "Satan has put something in your heart."

Jimmy fought back, telling the world, "I don't appreciate preachers that get mixed up in adultery and every other type of sin that one can imagine and then blame Jimmy Swaggart for it."

He went on CNN with Larry King and Pat Robertson's *The 700 Club.* He told Ted Koppel on *Nightline,* referring to the PTL scandal and Bakker's ouster, "I felt that entire debacle was a cancer that needed to be excised from the body of Christ. It's a very painful experience but it was something that needed to be done." As to the rumored hostile takeover of the ministry and the Christian-themed amusement park that was part of the Bakker empire, Jimmy flatly asked, "What am I going to do with a water slide?"

USA Today reported his denial of any such attempt. "It's totally anathema to my philosophy in every shape, form, or fashion. It's like trying to incorporate day and night. For one thing, I don't have any spare time. Secondly, the philosophy of PTL is totally different from what we do. That is more of an entertainment concept. We are world evangelization, trying to get the Gospel to the whole world. To take over somebody else's work or ministry is wrong."

Jimmy gained significant credibility with men like Ted Koppel, who saw him as open, direct, and able to communicate in clear, effective terms. Ultimately, the claims of an attempted takeover were fully discredited and Jimmy emerged as the leading voice of reason and credibility within the Christian television world, if only for a short time.

– 42 –

CALM BEFORE THE STORM

In October 1987, Jimmy parked his Cadillac outside a cheap motel on Airline Highway near New Orleans. Glancing around, he stepped out of the car and swiftly proceeded to Room 7 where a woman waited for him. Across the street, a man watched him closely. The man was Randy Gorman, the son of Marvin Gorman, a local pastor whose ministry had fallen apart when his sexual indiscretions were revealed.

In the early 1980s, Gorman was a New Orleans Assembly of God pastor with a congregation of 5,000 and a growing presence in television. Then in 1986 his brief involvement with a woman eight years earlier came to light. He was confronted and ousted from his post by several men, including Jimmy. Gorman, who was honest when confronted about the infidelity, ended up as the victim of additional accusations. He was forced to resign as pastor from the First Assembly of God of New Orleans in July 1986 and was dismissed from the Assemblies of God denomination.

As the biggest fish in the Louisiana Assemblies of God pond, Jimmy had been key to Gorman's fate and many felt he had been overly harsh. Some said he expanded the charges against Gorman without appropriate substantiation and was motivated by jealousy of Gorman's growing popularity and fear of the negative impact it would have on his own ministry. Jimmy's supporters suggested that Jimmy was brought into the matter by others and simply tried to be as honest as possible in providing information and helping to reach an appropriate outcome. But Gorman didn't see it that way.

Gorman was convinced that Jimmy had a hand in making his bad situation much worse.

Now aware of what Jimmy was doing at the motel, Randy Gorman let the air out of one of Jimmy's tires, called his father, and urged him to come quickly.

Shortly afterward, Jimmy left the motel room, having been, for a brief time, with a woman who plied her trade just as other women in the area did in motel rooms up and down Airline Highway. As he approached his car he noticed that he had a flat tire. Visibly nervous, he attempted to change the tire, but put the spare on backwards. As he worked feverishly to correct the problem, Marvin Gorman pulled up in his car and approached him. At that moment, on that otherwise inauspicious afternoon, at what seemed the most unlikely of locations, the humbling of Jimmy Swaggart began.

For months Jimmy had been disappearing from Baton Rouge, driving to New Orleans to visit Debra Murphree, the same woman he visited that October day in Room 7. Turning twenty-seven years old that year, Debra's face showed the effects of a difficult life that began in Indiana and included marriage at sixteen and the birth of three children over the next five years. It was a life that had led her to that fateful day in a rundown section of New Orleans where she made her living and survived as best she was able.

By her later accounts she met and saw this visitor—who always referred to himself as Billy—around twenty times or so. She knew who he was, as rumors had circulated quietly in the area that Jimmy Swaggart would show up from time to time, but she didn't force the issue. He wasn't her only customer who preferred to hide his identity.

Marvin Gorman's son, Randy, became aware of the rumors. Randy had a police background and staked out the area, waiting for an event like the one that finally transpired.

After Marvin Gorman confronted Jimmy, they talked for a while in Marvin's car. According to Gorman, Jimmy was upset, admitting that he had struggled with sexual sin for decades and that he wanted to do what he could to make the situation right.

The next day Gorman and a man who was an attorney and friend met in a Baton Rouge hotel with the Swaggarts. While a flood of emotions must have flowed through Frances—hurt, embarrassment, anguish, fear—she was, as always, stoic, strong, and unwilling to show weakness or disappointment to anyone outside of her family.

Gorman was looking for two things. First, he wanted Jimmy to come forward with his mistake, face the consequences, and work towards reconciliation and restoration. Second, he wanted help in restoring the viability and reputation of his own ministry. Gorman was sympathetic and understanding, not rushing to church authorities or the public with his newfound information.

Jimmy agreed to do what Gorman asked.

Through the remainder of the year and into early 1988, Marvin Gorman waited for Jimmy to take steps to address his misdeeds and carry through on his plan as discussed with Marvin. But nothing happened. As time went by it appeared that Swaggart was going to renege on his commitment. Perhaps he didn't believe that Randy Gorman had taken pictures of that eventful day. If he thought he was calling Gorman's bluff, it was a dangerous hand to play.

During this time however, some noticed that Jimmy's sermons and remarks became more self-critical, as he referred to himself in a sermon as a "pitiful, flawed preacher." The possibility of an impending reckoning lurking over the horizon was making him shudder.

In February 1988, feeling that Jimmy would fail to take any action unless his hand was forced, Gorman set the wheels in motion for Jimmy's exposure, disclosing his findings to key leaders within the Assemblies of God. Two days later, Jimmy and Frances Swaggart flew to denomination headquarters in Springfield, Missouri, where Jimmy spent ten hours with the thirteen-member Executive Presbytery of the General Council describing the situation and answering questions. The *Washington Post*, based on the reports of an unnamed source, stated that Jimmy acknowledged the longstanding struggle he had waged against sexual addiction, a battle he had fought mightily but unsuccessfully, and admitted paying someone to perform pornographic acts that he watched.

The *New York Times*, quoting Glen Cole, a member of the thirteen-member group, commented, "He tried and tried and tried through prayer and fasting and everything he could do to lick it and it beat him."

Two days later the story was receiving broad coverage nationwide.

The following Sunday, February 21, 1988, Jimmy addressed the packed house at Family Worship Center, during which he delivered his famous apology sermon to 7,500 attendees and millions around the world on television. During the tearful apology, Jimmy was contrite and humble, addressing his failure head-on.

"I do not plan in any way to whitewash my sin. And I do not call it a mistake, a mendacity. I call it sin. I have no one but myself to blame. I do not lay the fault or the blame or the charge at anyone else but me. For no one is to blame but Jimmy Swaggart. I take the responsibility. I take the blame. I take the fault."

The list of people to whom he apologized was long. It included Frances, Donnie, the ministry, other preachers, and his followers. He apologized to the Assemblies of God, "which helped bring the gospel to my little beleaguered town, when my family was lost without Jesus, this movement and fellowship that girdles the globe, that has been more instrumental in bringing this gospel through the stygian night of darkness to the far-flung hundreds of millions than maybe any effort in the annals of history."

At that moment, in the midst of the enormous problems he faced, Jimmy very likely thought about his mother, Minnie Bell; his grandmother, Ada; his Aunt Irene; and the other women who had held him up, encouraged him, prayed for him, and pushed him forward to believe in himself and his message.

As he looked heavenward, he apologized and asked forgiveness from his God. "I have sinned against you, my Lord, and I would ask that your Precious Blood would wash and cleanse every stain until it is in the seas of God's forgetfulness, never to be remembered against me anymore."

He invoked the name of King David, the Israelite king, whose own moral failure occurred when he was captivated by a woman, Bathsheba. It was pure drama. *Time* called it "without question, the most dramatic sermon ever aired over TV."

The reaction to Jimmy's epic stumble and sermon varied. Many walking out of the service were stunned, dazed. Others had tears rolling down their cheeks. They were devastated but felt Jimmy had set the standard for accepting blame and showing a repentant heart. Others felt betrayed that a man who had pointed his fingers at others had been involved in similar behavior.

John Camp, who had been close to many in the ministry and had studied Jimmy, was caught by surprise. "I had talked with people who were with him on a day-to-day basis. I didn't get into *Big-Time Religion* for the purpose of exposing that kind of misconduct. I was more interested in the financial affairs of the ministry, which had pulled me into it, but there's a natural Elmer Gantry question. Is this guy vulnerable in the area of sexual misconduct? And every one of these people, they would swear that there couldn't have possibly been anything that he would be involved in. They were absolutely certain. He was able to conceal that."

Most family members and relatives couldn't believe what had occurred. Aunt Stella, wife of Jimmy's namesake Lee Calhoun, scolded him. "Jimmy Lee, if it had been Jerry, we wouldn't have thought much about it. But we were looking for something better than that from you."

Cousin Mickey was caught off guard. "Surprise wasn't the word for it. I thought he was set up, and I told everybody, 'I guarantee you he was walking probably down the hallway of a hotel or a motel that he was staying in and some gal enticed him to come into the room. And they took pictures of that.' When I found out what really happened, I was totally shocked."

Then he continued lightheartedly, "My mama probably rolled over in her grave. I don't want to have her exhumed because she's probably on her stomach now."

– 43 –

THE AFTERMATH

Days after the dramatic television event emanating from Blue-bonnet Road in Baton Rouge, the Assemblies of God turned its attention to the punishment of Jimmy. Within a week the Louisiana Council met and established the rehabilitation plan for the fallen minister. There were five key points to the plan but the most significant required Jimmy to step down from preaching for three months, an unusually short time for ministers committing an offense similar to his.

The reaction to the three-month ban on preaching was met with a wide disparity of opinions. For many vocal members of the denomination, it didn't sit well. *Christianity Today* reported, "Once Assemblies of God members heard news reports that Swaggart's silencing might last a mere three months, hundreds of church members from across the country swamped headquarters with calls, complaining of favoritism."

Ultimately the Executive Presbytery overrode the ruling of the Louisiana District Council, exacting a more stringent punishment on Swaggart on several fronts—most notably requiring a one-year ban on preaching and television appearances by Jimmy.

While many supporters of Jimmy felt the punishment was too harsh, others—both supporters of Jimmy and many inside and outside the denomination—felt the punishment was like that applied in similar cases and was therefore more appropriate.

From the perspective of Jimmy and those around him, a primary concern was the damage a one-year absence would exact upon the ministry. In the few weeks following the February apology sermon the ministry was already suffering. Viewership dropped immediately as did financial contributions. While the ministry was built on the efforts of many, it was the personality of one man that kept it running. In his absence it was felt everything would crumble quickly. Jimmy, Frances, and others hoped to survive three months without doing irreparable harm. A year seemed like eternity.

Frances told viewers on the ministry's weekly television broadcast, "I've heard him up walking the floor, crying and praying in the wee hours of the morning, praying for you, praying for your lost loved ones, you who are sick, you who are lonely . . . if there's a failure among the people that work around him, it's that we've depended on him too much."

In response to the harsher punishment handed down by the Executive Presbytery, Jimmy decided to leave the Assemblies of God denomination, an organization he had been saved in at eight years of age and in which he had spent his entire life and preaching career.

On May 22, 1988, just three months after his exit from preaching and in accordance with the preliminary guidance provided by the Louisiana District Council, he returned to the pulpit and podium of Family Worship Center. In a matter of months, his life had changed amazingly. In his return sermon, he commented, "I've preached to some of the largest crowds in the world, but I guess that I stand today with more fear and more trembling than I ever stood before in all my life."

The immediate aftermath of Jimmy's mistake was devastating. The ministry lost 40 percent of its television viewership, 50 percent of the college students, 300 ministry staff positions, and 33 percent of its church attendees. Some of these figures would worsen over time. Contributions dropped precipitously and the weekly telecast was removed from hundreds of stations. Construction projects stopped almost immediately as employees were released from the payroll. Viewership of the ministry's syndicated weekly show fell from 1.9 million in February 1988 to 836,000 by July.

Employees, faculty, and churchgoers were forced to make a decision between their loyalties to the ministry and the denomination. Steve Badger, a former teacher at the college, related to Jimmy's biographer Anne Seaman, "All the people who had credentials in the Assemblies of God had to choose between Jimmy and the Assemblies of God. The Swaggarts had what some of us said was a misplaced sense of loyalty. They wished the loyalty to them was stronger than to the Assemblies of God."

Overnight, Jimmy Swaggart had become an outcast, both inside and outside the church world. He was used to being disliked by many in the secular media and public. But now at every turn he was shunned by Assembly of God and other Pentecostal supporters. People affiliated with the ministry were ostracized as well. Larry Thomas, who worked for Jimmy Swaggart Ministries during the 1980s, related to Seaman the impact on those involved with the Bible college. "Graduates are now ashamed to hang their degrees on the wall . . . For professors there, it's like three years are gone out of their lives; when they apply for jobs they don't want to say they taught there. Some of the younger ones who started out teaching there can't even say on their résumés they've taught at college level, because it was at JSBC. So the prospective employer asks, 'What about 1985–88? What were you doing? There's a big blank there.' They say, 'Well, I wasn't going to mention it, but I was at Jimmy Swaggart Bible College.' It's like his name is poison, you can't even say you got anything out of the experience."

In a bizarre twist of fate, Jimmy Swaggart now faced from those in the religious community the same ostracism that his cousin Jerry Lee Lewis had faced some thirty years earlier in the music community. For both men, the downfall had occurred when they were at the peak of their powers, influence, and fame.

In the wake of this storm, those who relied on the ministry for spiritual sustenance were left reeling. Donnie, painfully aware of this, commented to his father, "Dad, this is not about us. This is about all of the people who have found Jesus. What's this going to do to them?"

God, how we are going to get through this?"

Thirty-four-year-old Donnie Swaggart was lying on the floor, face down, feeling alone in a room of many.

Here on the second floor of the administration office building of Jimmy Swaggart Ministries, a small group would gather regularly to pray about the dire situation the ministry faced and gain some measure of comfort from each other's shared agony over circumstances.

The Airline Highway scandal had rocked the ministry's operations and outreach. Overnight, many employees of the ministry had been let go. Pay-as-you-go construction projects, funded by cash coming in the door and mail, had come to a grinding halt, evidenced by the huge, twenty-story, unfinished structure on Bluebonnet that would serve as a constant reminder for years to come of the upheaval created within the ministry. Donnie had always believed in his father, been his closest friend, his biggest supporter. He had never questioned the call of God on Jimmy's life, had seen too many miracles to doubt it, and had instinctively forgiven his father the moment he found out about his stumble.

"God, we are at the end of our rope," Donnie prayed. "We have no way to fix this situation."

The words expressed the hopelessness, the utter discouragement he felt at that moment. Stations were sending cancellation notices in droves—some because of severe delinquency in payment, others because of pressure exerted by outsiders who were offended by the sight of the shamed evangelist continuing to present the message of Christ over the airwaves.

Donnie, a key cog in the operational wheels of the ministry, had no idea whether the organization would even be able to meet next week's payroll for the dramatically reduced workforce. As the tears streamed down Donnie's face, he was at a loss to understand how things could go so quickly from the top of the mountain to the depth of the valley. His entire life, as well as his mother's and father's, were wrapped up in Jimmy Swaggart Ministries. An organization that had increasingly stretched itself to the end of—and even beyond—its means was sure to crumble under the enormous bills and debts that were accruing.

"God, how will I take care of my family? I have a wife and three children and no other job prospects, no other training. How will we ever get out from under this situation?"

The words continued to spill forth from the man who looked much younger than his nearly three and a half decades would suggest. His cries, partly prayer, partly a personal plea, and partly a litany of questions for which there seemed to be no answer, spilled forth without attempts at eloquence or shows of civilized restraint.

At that moment, in the deepest recess of discouragement, a strange peace flowed over Donnie Swaggart. In his heart and mind, God reached out to him. An overwhelming feeling impressed upon him, "Everything will be OK. Everything will be OK."

Perhaps that reassurance came from God. Maybe it was a product of the longing need for hope that comes whenever a desperate man cries out shamelessly and without pride. Maybe it was simply an instinctive coping mechanism that keeps life bearable when it seems not to be. Whatever it was, Donnie sensed it in a palpable way. He had felt it before but never as strongly as now, even in the face of other difficult times.

"How?" was all he could ask, like a child who wants to believe a parent's soothing explanation but cannot understand the logic.

No audible response came, but an overwhelming feeling continued to wash over Donnie. In his heart, he had the clear—although unexplainable—impression that the great things he had witnessed, the worldwide outreach, the people touched, were not over. He would see them again.

At that particular moment, the likelihood seemed so remote, so far away. Still, Donnie held tightly to that small kernel of hope, of encouragement. He would reach back and find it through other bouts of disappointment. Sometimes he didn't know why, but he found continual comfort in that faint but undying light in the distance that told him another mountaintop would be climbed. As far as the eye could see, there was nothing but flat plain, flat desert. Yet Donnie Swaggart plodded forward methodically, for he had no other direction in which to turn.

Jerry was stopping over in Las Vegas on the way back from the West Coast to Memphis. Coincidentally, this visit to Sin City happened to collide with performances Mickey was giving at the Golden Nugget downtown.

Jerry decided to head over to see his country-music-singing cousin with Al Embry, his agent and friend, who in later years would function as Mickey's agent.

When they arrived at Mickey's show they were directed to two prime seats about ten rows from the front. With capacity for only 300 to 400 people, this room at the Golden Nugget allowed attendees a chance to see a performance in an intimate gathering.

While Jerry's focus was on playing his music, his way, Mickey often sang without playing the piano and bantered with members of his band and even members of the audience. Fun-loving and irreverent, he was often the butt of jokes delivered during the performance and wasn't shy about poking fun at his cousins, balanced by frequent compliments of them as well, particularly of Jerry. A few minutes into his performance, he warmly greeted Jerry from the stage, letting everyone know that his iconic cousin was in the house.

Recently, Jimmy's public humiliation had drawn renewed attention due to the July 1988 issue of *Penthouse*, in which Debra

Murphree posed for raunchy photos and related her version of interactions with the shamed evangelist. A half an hour or so into his show, Mickey launched into a joke that involved a fictitious conversation with his preaching cousin. Having heard the joke earlier that day from a well-known entertainer, he was hesitant to use it but his band had found it humorous, giving him confidence that it would be funny but not offensive.

"Reverend Swaggart called me today. He said, 'You've been talking about me during your performances, haven't you?'

"I told him, 'Jimmy, I haven't been talking about anything people haven't already read about in the newspaper or seen on TV. I love you like a brother.'

"So Jimmy asks me, 'Mickey, I want your opinion on something. Do you think hookers and prostitutes can be saved?'

"And I told him, 'Well, we grew up in the Assembly of God church and we were taught everybody could be saved.'

Mickey paused as he looked at the audience and turned to his left to glance back at the knowing band.

"'Well,' Jimmy asks me, 'Do you think you could save a couple of 'em for me?'"

The joke drew hearty laughs from the crowd, with the key exception of one man seated ten rows back. Jerry jutted his head forward in surprise, irritation flaring in his eyes as he glared ahead at Mickey on the stage. He turned to talk to Al, his voice raised so that many nearby could overhear.

"What's he doing?!? That's our cousin he's talking about up there."

"It's just a joke, Jerry. He's being funny."

Jerry bristled, his irritation turning to anger.

"Man, that's bullshit! I don't like it one bit. He's talking about family."

Jerry stood, ready to walk out of the performance. From the stage, Mickey couldn't hear the exchange but he could tell a commotion had occurred. It wasn't difficult for him to guess that his attempted humor at the expense of Jimmy had not gone over well with Jerry.

Meanwhile, Al managed to calm down his companion. "Jerry, come on now. Let's stay cool here. We came to see the show. So let's see the show."

Jerry sat back down but the more he thought about it, the more he boiled. He barely noticed the rest of the performance as he sat in his seat, stewing. By the time the show ended he made a beeline to Mickey's dressing room.

"Boy, I don't like the way you cut down Jimmy," he told Mickey. "He's our cousin. What in the hell were you thinking?"

Mickey had seen his cousin hot under the collar many times before. While not apologetic, he was interested in calming Jerry down and putting the situation into perspective.

"It was just a joke, Jerry. I didn't mean any harm by it."

"That ain't no joke, man. It ain't right and it ain't funny. That's our family." The redness was slowly ebbing from Jerry's face as he vented his frustration and began to regain his composure.

"Everybody cracked up, Jerry. I wouldn't do anything to hurt Jimmy. You know I love Jimmy. I mean, we're men, you know, and I ain't lived a pristine life myself."

As high-running emotions subsided, the two visited backstage. But on the limousine ride back the hotel, Jerry couldn't let the matter go.

"You don't talk about family like that. Maybe other people will, but we shouldn't be treating Jimmy like that."

Jerry had defended Jimmy on other occasions in the midst of his double-cousin's public shame. He had also defended Mickey on occasions when Jerry's fans had ridiculed Gilley for seemingly trying to imitate him. He was quick to come to the defense of the two when others would attack. Never mind that he himself had criticized them both on many occasions. But there was hell to pay for anyone else who said anything critical about either of them. Thus was the world of a man who lived in constant contradiction with himself and whose impulses determined and changed his mood, literally from moment to moment.

– 44 –

THE RECKONING

What happened to Jimmy? As a complicated man in a complicated situation, a variety of factors came into play. As his fame and power grew, the trappings of success were also there. The changes—and their impact—didn't exact their full force overnight. They happened in small, subtle ways over an extended period of time. Dr. William Martin, a longtime Rice University sociologist and expert on preachers, made a poignant and widely reported observation, "I think what happens to this kind of person is that he begins to think, 'I couldn't have come this far if not for God.' Then he begins to say, 'Well, if I have this idea to build a Bible college or a mission, it must have come from God.' Next he starts to say, 'God told me this. God told me that.' And the next step from there is that he says, 'I think what God meant to say was . . .'"

Mickey offered his own opinion on the effects of Jimmy's success. "Yeah, I think it changed him. You can get so big until you feel like, 'Hey, I'm entitled to what I want.' You can get too big sometimes and it'll knock you down."

As Jimmy's star rose there were not enough people around him with a clear focus on keeping him accountable and humble, questioning him regularly, without a vested interested in him or his ministry. The list of high-profile preachers who had taken a wrong turn was a lengthy one. At one time or another, in one area of their life or another, almost all stumbled, owing to a variety of factors that all fall under the broad umbrella of being human.

Martin compared Jimmy to another man about whom he was highly knowledgeable in an article in the *Houston Chronicle*. "Everybody needs somebody to check them. Billy Graham was probably the first and most successful at that. He's avoided such problems because from the very beginning, he planted a lot of hedges around himself. He chose a board comprised of independent, strong, successful business people and religious leaders who could and would call his hand if he went too far . . . things like [what happened to Jimmy] are less likely to arise in a congregation where the pastor is answerable to a board."

Compounding the intoxication of tremendous power and influence, Jimmy was under enormous pressure. Never a laid-back, easygoing man, the numerous pressures of handling the myriad aspects of running the ministry, fulfilling his God-appointed destiny, and raising funds had resulted in a high degree of isolation that impacted his ability to develop close, trusting friendships. During his March 1987 appearance on *Nightline with Ted Koppel*, the strain and exhaustion were readily apparent in his face and eyes. With the energy and stamina of a horse, he had pounded forward for thirty years as the responsibilities and obligations continually mounted. It was more than he could ultimately sustain and, in retrospect, a breaking point was inevitable.

Psychologist Jim Dolan offered his opinion about how Jimmy's failing came to pass, an observation based on years of counseling successful businessmen and leaders who experienced similar travails. "So we have a growing separation between the preacher personality and the other side, the shadow side, that he apparently was struggling with, probably for some time. He achieved significant fame in the eighties and we've all seen how dangerous that is to people, to anyone, not just Jimmy Swaggart. A unique thing happens with certain people when their level of fame becomes unbearable.

"I think, on some level, he wanted to get out from underneath that onus of fame. That's a backbreaking load and I think that all of those people who achieve that level of fame start looking for ways to come out from underneath it and to return to themselves and be normal in some capacity, to be everyday human beings that can walk around in the world and be treated like everybody else. I think, on some level, he wanted to destroy Jimmy Swaggart, the image, the character, so he could go back to being himself."

The issue of sexual struggle was pervasive among preachers and was a by-product of conservative upbringings where natural impulses of teenage and early-adult maturation were labeled as evil, taboo, and a clear route to hell. For sincere, well-meaning men, many of whom ended up genuinely driven to become preachers, sex was not looked upon or understood in a healthy fashion. Many aspects of it were even considered shameful.

Working against Jimmy—and other preachers—was a reluctance to come forward with any admitted weaknesses because churches, particularly evangelical denominations like the Pentecostals, were historically poor at providing assistance and were likely to promote harsh punishment, even ostracism.

One does not have to reach far to imagine Jimmy Swaggart crying out to God, trying to will himself to overcome a personal struggle for which he felt ashamed and which posed an increasingly ominous threat as his ministry and outreach expanded.

Author Barbara Nauer commented on the church's self-defeating means of dealing with its ministers: "It seems to be only in churches that notables who fail in this particular way, sexually, find their careers and reputations destroyed totally and permanently. 'They're ministers, so they ought to know better.' That is shallow and hollow. All men 'know better.'"

The fear of how he would be received in conjunction with the typical pride that will deter men from asking for help contributed to a painful outcome for Jimmy. In his apology sermon of February 1988, he briefly addressed the question of why he failed. "I have asked myself that question ten thousand times through ten thousand tears. Maybe Jimmy Swaggart has tried to live his entire life as though he is not human. I think this is the reason I did not find the victory I sought, because I did not seek the help of my brothers and sisters in the Lord."

Compounding the problem was the strong aversion Jimmy felt toward counseling and psychological assistance in general, something he no doubt picked up from his strong traditional, Pentecostal roots. After railing against psychiatrists and psychologists from the pulpit, reaching out to find help from well-meaning therapists, even Christian-based counselors, was anathema to him, contrary in his mind to the Bible-based solutions he had been taught to rely on exclusively for his shelter and escape from trial and tribulations.

Other, more peripheral, considerations compounded Jimmy's problems when his trips to Airline Highway became public knowledge. Most dramatic were the charges of hypocrisy that rang out when his indiscretions found the light of day. Jimmy's direct, in-your-face method of communication hurt him considerably when he needed forgiveness from his supporters and the public.

Many of his public comments against Jim Bakker and others proved to be the most indicting remarks about his own behavior and unwillingness to subject to Assembly of God punishment. Before his scandal, he had said, "To allow a preacher of the Gospel, when he is caught beyond the shadow of a doubt committing an immoral act . . . to remain in his position as pastor, would be the most gross stupidity."

He had stood by the one-year exclusionary rule for ministers when writing in *The Evangelist* prior to his own difficulties. In response to Jim Bakker's confession, he was quoted in the *Dallas Morning News*, "The church cannot hide sin. When a preacher has been found out and it is fact—not hearsay—that he has performed an act of adultery, a hearing is convened and he has then to step down." Another quote gathered by the Associated Press was telling: "When a preacher of the Gospel falls, and he is known quite well, then it's naturally a scandal and it really ought to be because the minister of God is a moral yardstick."

Why he took these public stances is not a mystery. Dolan has seen similar behavior many times. "I think it was done in an unconscious attempt to direct guilt away from himself and to transcend what he thought was his own sin. If I can preach hard enough against it then maybe I can also conquer it in myself, and also, I can build an edifice behind which I can hide, that no one can see behind, while at the same time paradoxically giving every clue that I could possibly give for the intelligent observer to understand this is my problem. In psychotherapy, there are certain truisms that get kicked around and one is that we treat what we need to heal in ourselves. We teach what we need to learn."

Assembly of God pastor Tom McMahan echoed similar thoughts: "It's a venting of your own problem. Finding the heat in somebody else's kitchen is supposed to take care of your own kitchen temperature. If I can attack him and find the fly in his ointment, my fly doesn't look so bad. I can often listen to preaching and hear where a man is personally, based on how he's posturing. If he's taking a hard-nosed, condemning position, there's generally a real problem lurking somewhere. I've seen it over and over."

In sounding the alarm against important issues in the church and society—a role Jimmy assumed and felt was the responsibility of a conscientious evangelist—he alienated many who would not step out to defend or support him in his own hour of need. Barbara Nauer, a Catholic by background, offered this telling observation in her writing: "Swaggart's constitutional self-righteousness, in which he invariably included Frances and the clan, caused Jimmy, who is by nature a humble and fairly easygoing fellow, to act some of the time like a flaming egotist and cranky, monomaniacal tyrant."

In the course of his extensive operations, writing, preaching, and editorializing—which sometimes lacked extensive, airtight research and documentation—he had at one time or another upset almost every segment of the secular world, as well as Jews, Catholics, other Protestant denominations, and many within the Assemblies of God. Someone who might have agreed with 99 percent of what he said might also have been infuriated with the other 1 percent, based on his tendency to pull no punches and address sensitive topics aggressively.

Moreover, countless numbers of people who supported Jimmy, agreed with most if not all of his views, loved his music, and admired his charisma and convictions were turned off by the frequency and techniques of fund-raising he employed. Regardless of the rationale for devoting more time during the telecast to advertising products, emphasizing with regularity the dire circumstances of the ministry, and hyping each offer as the greatest ever presented by the ministry, it was ringing hollow with tens of thousands of potential viewers and supporters who would not tolerate the appearance of hucksterism from a preacher.

As much as Mickey cared for his cousin, fund-raising and monetary discussions drew a raised eyebrow. "He sent me a letter asking for $15,000 to name a school in Africa for my dad. He said we'd name the school after Arthur Gilley if I'd send him the money. It's his uncle. If he wanted to name the school after him, why didn't he do it? Don't send me a bill for $15,000 to put a name on a school. I threw it in the trash."

The appreciation for Jimmy's musical talent was almost universal. However, for all those who found his preaching style second to none, others were turned off by the theatrics and emotionalism. To the more buttoned-down churchgoers and those unfamiliar with Pentecostal tendencies, his delivery style was a mixture of manufactured emotions and manipulation.

Others felt he took liberties with the truth in his sermons in a manner that crossed a line of acceptability. Mickey observed a tendency to do this: "I love Jimmy. But he takes a story and embellishes it. If you're writing a movie script, I understand that. But in his case, he didn't need to tell the story and get it all out of whack.

Because I grew up with him, I know what really happened in some of those stories."

Author Barbara Nauer, whose writings clearly showed her devotion to Jimmy, was also uncomfortable with his tendency to embellish. "There is a serious problem with Swaggart's playing loose with facts, if only because, to date at least, churchgoing people have not entirely abandoned their allegiance to what we might call factuality, namely the correspondence between realities and what we perceive and say about them."

For all the difficulty it created, the infamous incident provided Jimmy the opportunity to come clean, to be more real to those around him and those who watched him. Just like the undefeated fighter who is knocked down and loses for the first time, defeat often allows the pugilist to become more beloved, as his fans are able to better relate to him and cheer for him as he climbs the mountain again. His cousin Frankie Jean, Jerry's sister, remembered her reaction to his dilemma. "He made a mistake. I was so glad that he wasn't an angel. I just didn't think he was real. I was glad to realize he was like me, human."

Jimmy was humble and accepting of blame in his apology sermon, putting the responsibility on no one but himself. He would have other moments of openness and frank honesty, recognizing and understanding people's reactions to his failures. At the time of his return from the three-month layoff, he asked for money on his telecast. "We have suffered a terrible blow. And to be frank and plain and honest with you I would not blame you, I do not blame you, for not sending us one dime or one dollar. And I want that to sink in because I mean it from my heart. I don't blame you for not sending anything. But I'm praying that somehow we can get past the human emotions and all the problems that I have."

Perhaps Jimmy would have been well advised to continue accepting responsibility for his actions, as he did early on, and rely on the ideas of repentance and forgiveness to be restored. Humility could have endeared him to supporters, appealed to the general public, and allowed him to seek real help. But the urge to muddy the waters, deflect blame, and confuse understanding of the issue—rooted in pride and the natural desire to hold on to what he had—alienated others and ultimately led to further difficulty and embarrassment.

As difficult as it would have been, the question looms: what if he had subjected himself to the authority and punishment of the Assemblies of God denomination? It is hard to say what would have been left of his ministry after a long year of enforced sabbatical. On the other hand, subjecting himself to it would have created additional opportunity to garner the support and return of many.

Cousin and Church of God preacher David Beatty commented, "I still believe to this day Jimmy should have had an attitude of 'The Assemblies of God has been good to me and I want to retain my integrity. I'm submitting myself to whatever y'all think that I need to do. I have brought great embarrassment to every preacher in the Assembly of God and Church of God. I'm sorry and I want to do whatever I have to do to try to make up for that terrible error.' I believe those people in his church would have mortgaged their homes to keep him. If he'd have carried it through and had that humility, I believe his people would have stayed with him."

Tom McMahan concurred, "Jimmy could have taken the punishment, stayed off of the air, and let his singers sing. That's why many watched the program anyway. They loved the music. There could have been a five-minute window during his broadcast to deal with what God was doing in his life to address this situation, to help us see a man work through a process, help all of us nationwide, worldwide, see the climb back to acceptance, to repentance, to restoration, to give all of us a path."

Because of pride, an aversion to ask for help, the pressure to maintain his ministry and fulfill his commitments, or because he truly felt God directing him to do otherwise, Jimmy did not choose that path.

The reaction of Billy Graham to the news of Jimmy's downfall was one of sadness and concern. Graham had little or no contact with the large majority of Pentecostal preachers, including Jimmy. He had a long friendship with Oral Roberts, but there was a clear distance in his own ideals about ministry and what he observed from Roberts's headquarters in Tulsa. He told his biographer William Martin, "I love Oral. I believe at times he is a real man of God. At times, though he talks about things that are just foreign to me. Among all those people I like Oral best, but when he does things like that people outside of Christ get very skeptical and cynical."

When it came to Jimmy's downfall and that of Jim Bakker, Graham was saddened for the cause of Christ, stating sincerely that he "prayed for them a lot."

When reporters and members of the media pressed him for a reaction to their mishaps, he attempted to distance himself and not be critical in any way. "Forty years ago, we took steps to avoid this," he told Martin, "but if I say that, I'll come off sounding self-righteous, and I don't want to do that. I may still make some bad mistakes." Graham did, however, find the bright spot in a difficult circumstances: "Things like this have happened down through church history—Protestant and Catholic—but the work goes on . . . The work of the Lord continues. In its own backhanded way, I think it may help the church . . . It's making everybody look to their financial integrity and responsibility and to their personal lifestyles. Public evangelists must watch themselves very carefully."

In an odd twist of fate, Billy Graham had become the Elvis of evangelism while Jimmy had become its Jerry Lee Lewis. Graham was smoother, better managed, less threatening, and more acceptable to the masses than Jimmy—or Jerry—could ever expect to become. While some would recognize Jimmy as more talented than Graham—just as rock 'n' roll purists would claim about Jerry in relation to his Memphis counterpart—he would never have the wide respect in the court of public opinion. Whether or not he quietly craved it is known only to him.

Jimmy was the Outsider to Billy Graham the Insider. Jimmy was the Holy Roller to Billy Graham the respectful Baptist who gave the invocation at presidential inaugurations.

But perhaps the key difference between Jimmy Swaggart and Billy Graham was that Graham was more adept at looking forward and understanding the crucial component of accountability and humility in every aspect of his life and Christian walk. This distinction may have been a reflection of upbringing, formal religious training, personal temperament, or pure foresight, but the impact in the eye of the public was, to the casual observer, a matter of day and night.

– 45 –

BURNOUT

Mickey heard it more and more, growing over the years to a point where it had become a significant problem. When he was out on the road he heard the comments from fans and from other performers. Many of them came to him secondhand through friends and acquaintances because those making the comments didn't want to upset him. The comments were about Gilley's. Little by little, the place had become run-down and the words "dump" and "dive" were used with increased regularity. Gilley's just wasn't the same.

Mickey's list of frustrations with the club became lengthy over time. It started with the parking lot, with potholes so big that a good rainstorm would allow it to be mistaken for part of the Houston Ship Channel.

Mickey approached Sherwood. "Look," he said, "let's take some of the money that I'm making on the road, buy a grader, and at least fix the parking lot so we can get rid of the ruts in it."

Sherwood said, "Let me think about it."

"If he said to let him think about it," Mickey recalled, "it was over. It would never happen."

Mickey wanted to improve the sound system, renovate the dressing rooms that marquee performers utilized, make general improvements to the décor of the club, and improve the men's and women's restrooms sorely in need of attention.

"Why don't we at least put an attendant in the ladies room," Mickey asked Sherwood, "like most places you go into where they have someone to hand you a towel when you wash your hands."

"Nah, we don't need that," said Sherwood, who was convinced that the rough ambiance of Gilley's was what drew people to the club.

Mickey was also upset about the prices customers were charged and the way they were treated in general. "I accused him of taking Gilley's and ruining it. I told him, 'You have a Wal-Mart operation and you are charging fancy department-store prices. Why do we need to charge these people so much? Why do we have to rob them when they come in? You may as well just bring them in and hold them upside down by their boots, take all their money, and kick them out.' That's the way he treated the public. Early on, it wasn't like that, but it slowly turned into that."

He had seen Sherwood knowingly advertise an upcoming performance by Loretta Lynn even though he knew Loretta was ill and had already canceled. He had used questionable practices and twisted interpretations of contract language on several occasions to underpay stellar performers like Waylon Jennings and George Strait.

Sherwood, why don't you take my name off that sign out there?"

The two men stood alone, in the rodeo arena area. With Mickey's touring schedule, he was at Gilley's infrequently. But he was irked by the comments about the increasing lack of care given to the honky-tonk that bore his name. Responsibility for running the club had always been Sherwood's but Mickey was truly concerned about the dilapidated state into which the storied nightclub was falling over time.

"When you don't take care of the place, Sherwood, it reflects on me. It makes me look bad when people come here and have a bad experience, are overcharged for tickets, and are told someone will be performing that canceled two weeks earlier."

By 1985, the relationship between Sherwood and Mickey was steadily worsening. Most of the *Urban Cowboy* craze had worn off by then. Mickey suspected that the quality of the interaction between them was only as strong as Sherwood's perception of Mickey's usefulness. He was sure that the relationship had soured partially because of his decreased popularity as a recording artist. "I think Sherwood thought I was done. He had used me up. I was someone no good to him anymore. Up until that time, I was making a lot of money. Once he thought that was in jeopardy, he didn't value me or my ideas anymore."

The crowds at Gilley's weren't as large as they had been in earlier years. There was more rumbling about Sherwood not taking care of his customers. He seemed impervious to it all, watching everything from a distance. Sherwood listened to and heeded the advice of his singing star in the decade of the seventies and following the *Urban Cowboy* excitement that had raised everything to a fevered pitch. But in recent years Mickey's feedback had fallen largely on deaf ears. Sherwood's "let me think about it" signified that little or nothing would happen.

For his part, Sherwood felt that Mickey's superstardom and worldly travels had blinded his sense of what made Gilley's unique. Hell, this wasn't a Las Vegas lounge. It was a south Texas honky-tonk. Those damn potholes and ragged edges to the club were key aspects to the place's appeal. His eyes narrowed, becoming fiery slits fixated on Mickey.

"Boy, I think you've gotten above your raisin'. This place ain't never gonna be no damn glitzy performance hall."

"I want my name off this dump. If you won't fix it up, take that sign down and call it Sherwood's or whatever the hell you want to call it."

Sherwood stepped forward to get closer to Mickey, his barrel chest protruding. His intense stare and intimidating presence, usually sufficient to bring most situations to a satisfying conclusion, grew more focused as his anger rose. His upper body tensed and his hands reflexively closed into fists as he became more frustrated with Mickey's complaints and insubordination.

Mickey had seen Sherwood's temper on rare occasions. The hard-raised, tough-as-nails nightclub and beer joint proprietor had a toughness and grittiness that drove him to use his fists whenever he thought the situation required it.

Having seen that violent nature before, Mickey took a proactive step. "Let me tell you something. If you want to hit me, think about this: If you ever do it, man, you better bury me. You better be prepared to finish the job if you start it. I'm a backwoods Louisiana boy and I'll kill you. No second thoughts."

A momentary silence ensued as the two men glared at each other. After a few seconds, the heightened tension of the moment slipped away. "I don't intend to hit you," Sherwood mumbled as he walked away.

Both men saw the relationship ending. "When" and "how" were unanswered questions and neither was willing to give in to the other.

As Mickey made suggestions to Sherwood and found little receptivity he realized that Sherwood didn't appreciate or care about the impact the negative perception of Gilley's was having on Mickey's personal reputation. On more than one occasion Sherwood reminded Mickey that he didn't tell the performer how to handle matters on the road and that Mickey should not tell him how to run a club.

The strain on the relationship escalated Mickey's concerns about the financial arrangement between the two men. "He came to me back in the early seventies and offered me half of Gilley's, but I never got half of Gilley's. I never got half of anything. The bottom line was I made more with him than I'd ever made in my life and I was satisfied with that. But I told him one time, 'I know that I'm not getting my appropriate cut of the club.' He said, 'Well, I don't even know what the club's making, Gilley,' and he probably didn't. But the problem was he hardly ever shared.

"The club made a lot of money. He was taking the money and putting it into other entities that he had. There was millions of dollars coming in from the product line at Gilley's, and he was going through it as fast as he could and I didn't see much of it."

Mickey thought back to the early seventies when Gilley's had just opened and the exciting, early days as crowds poured into the honky-tonk on Spencer Highway. He was so thrilled with the drastic improvements in his financial and performance situations that he never seriously confronted Sherwood about the money issue.

The beginning of the end of Mickey's relationship with Sherwood occurred in 1987. Vivian was in charge of replenishing the stock of products for sale, most notably the bevy of souvenirs and items emblazoned with the world-famous Gilley's logo. Costs for these orders were paid from a joint account where proceeds from sales were deposited and which Mickey and Sherwood shared.

One day Vivian told her husband, "Mickey, we have a significant payment due and our account does not have the funds to cover the cost. Tell Sherwood to move money into the account because the suppliers have been asking repeatedly for payment."

Mickey felt a sharp pain in his gut. He knew Sherwood had been making serious outlays of capital to establish and maintain the rodeo adjoining the nightclub. He also knew fewer people were coming to the increasingly run-down club. Sherwood was a savvy money man and a lack of funds in the aforementioned account was not an oversight.

Mickey took Vivian's issue to Sherwood. "Mrs. G has all this product and we've got to pay for it, Sherwood. They're about to send authorities out to confiscate it if we don't make payment." Sherwood's reluctance to pay for inventory replenishments created strain and suspicion of what other uses he had for the money being generated.

The event prompted Mickey to hire an auditor who uncovered significant financial irregularities. It was another big step toward the disintegration of Mickey's relationship with Sherwood.

Some months later the increasing discord culminated in a discussion between Mickey and Sherwood, as the two men stood in the club. Mickey was no longer willing to tolerate the suspicions and lack of trust that existed between them.

"Just give me fifty percent of what we have, and we'll go our separate ways."

Sherwood gauged his seriousness.

"So how do you want to split it?"

Mickey's response was instantaneous. He had anticipated this conversation for some time.

"Why don't we do this—you give me the two buses, the eighteen-wheeler, the airplane, which we still owe money on, and the property in Nashville. I assume you want everything in Pasadena, which you can have. That includes the club and the property it sits on here, the rodeo arena, the recording facility, and the property we have by the San Jacinto Monument. So I'll give you everything in Pasadena."

Sherwood's eyes narrowed. "I reckon you would," he retorted.

"Well, we can have everything appraised," said Mickey. "If what I take is more valuable than yours, I'll borrow the difference, and give it to you."

Sherwood looked away. Finally, Mickey spoke again.

"What do you want, Sherwood?"

Sherwood turned back to face him. "I tell you what . . . I'll keep all the property. You can have the two buses, the eighteen-wheeler, and the airplane. I'll let you out of your contract with me."

Mickey shook his head and responded calmly, "That agreement between us is already null and void."

A hint of surprise registered on Sherwood's poker face.

"What are you talking about?"

"Sherwood, that was a ten-year contract and you let it expire without renewing it."

Sherwood glared at him. "Are you sure?" he asked.

This contract had given Sherwood the right to represent Mickey in his music career. Sherwood had expected to hold it in order to exert control over the relationship. Now, as Mickey calmly pointed out that Sherwood had allowed the contract to expire, it tipped the balance of power in his own direction.

Shortly thereafter, a copy of a new contract was sent to Mickey—via registered mail—that appeared to extend the contract an additional year, an agreement Mickey claimed he never made and a contract he never signed. When the disagreement between the two men ultimately reached the courthouse, Mickey's attorneys demanded to see the original copy of the contract to establish its authenticity. The judge gave Sherwood and his attorneys forty-eight hours to produce the document.

Ultimately, the assertion of a renewed agreement between Mickey and Sherwood was rejected by the court, and Sherwood's attempts to maintain a grasp on the business relationship were severely hampered.

Mickey lamented the unraveling of the relationship. "He was like a father to me and I actually really loved the guy. When I first ran into him, I knew what he was and I was afraid of him. As I got to know him and be a part of his family, so to speak, I couldn't conceive that he would do some of the things he did to me since I was so close to him. But he wanted to own people."

Unable to reach agreement on an amenable splitting of the assets, Mickey finally filed a lawsuit against Sherwood. He demanded some of the profits which he believed had been withheld from him, and he wanted his name taken off the marquee and dissociated from the rapidly deteriorating and decidedly less popular and less profitable nightclub.

A plethora of court motions and legal machinations followed. A litany of verbal assaults was launched from both sides: in the newspaper, in the courtroom, and on the courthouse steps. Mickey and his attorneys cited the deterioration in the club, the money that Sherwood had cheated him out of, and the damage being incurred because of the public perception that he was responsible for the honky-tonk's shortcomings. Sherwood felt that he had been responsible for Gilley's success and that Mickey's behavior was inappropriate.

Vivian remarked on the difficulty of the trial for her and Mickey to the *Houston Chronicle*: "It was awful. Mickey actually would cry over it. He couldn't sleep at night. I couldn't sleep, either. I cried myself, lost fifteen pounds."

Ultimately, a Houston jury decided in Mickey's favor. The *Houston Chronicle* summarized the verdict on July 13, 1988: "A Harris County jury sang Mickey Gilley's tune loud and clear Tuesday, awarding the country and western singer $17 million damages in his lawsuit against his former business manager. The state district court jury also forbid the name Gilley's from being used for the famed Pasadena nightclub now run by the singer's seventeen-year partner, manager, and courtroom foe, Sherwood Cryer.

"The bulk of that money, $5.3 million, was in unreported profits on Gilley's souvenirs, the jury ruled, while Cryer also failed to account for $1.1 million in other unreported profits, payments to other companies and loans. The jury also awarded Gilley $8 million in punitive damages against Cryer."

Nine months later, at the end of March 1989, Gilley's was closed, shuttered, and padlocked. It was the end to an amazing run for Gilley's.

In its final days, a passerby happening along Spencer Highway would have seen a handful of cars in the parking lot of the former mecca of fun. Individuals with fond memories of time spent there over the years were melancholy upon hearing about the closing of the club. Many who had visited in recent years saw it as a logical conclusion to the club's inexorable descent. Few performers who had played there were sad to see the official closing, remembering the grueling double shows, the rough-and-tumble crowds, and the low-quality facilities. Legendary country-western crooner Hank Thompson commented to the *Houston Chronicle*, "It's a good idea to close it down; it looked like it was going to fall down. It was just a dump."

In July 1990, the club was victimized by arson. Many immediately suspected Sherwood's involvement but an investigation pinned blame on a sixteen-year-old local youth. Two months later, in September, bulldozers razed the last standing portions of the structure from the lot on which Gilley's had stood for nearly twenty years.

Occasional fans and prior patrons drove through the parking lot to get a last glimpse of the place where many had met spouses, learned to two-step, conquered their fear of riding that damn bull, drowned sorrows of their personal struggles of the seventies and eighties, and spent a sizable percentage of their Friday paychecks. A few older pickup trucks still had faded, barely recognizable Gilley's bumper stickers plastered on their rear fenders. Shortly following the judgment, Mickey filed another suit alleging Sherwood was hiding assets to avoid paying the final penalty assessed against him. Sherwood followed suit by seeking Chapter 11 bankruptcy protection. Ultimately, the two settled when Mickey gave up collecting any money—much less many millions—in exchange for most of the property and the few hard assets remaining from the venture together.

Many expected that Sherwood had done a nice job of tucking plenty of money away in safe places, but he claimed he was left with little or nothing due to the treatment from his former partner and the wheels of the justice system. He spent the rest of his life hanging on to a couple of his stores and liquor businesses. He was Sherwood Cryer until the end, the shrewd, hard-nosed, take-matters-into-your-own-hands businessman from the backwoods of East Texas, marching to his own drum and letting his opinions flow freely. In reference to the downturn his prospects had taken after 1988, he told a Houston journalist in 2007, as he stood and urinated on the exact spot where Gilley's once stood, "Don't do no good to cry about it."

The aftermath of the split with Sherwood was a difficult time for Mickey. The deterioration and ultimate demise of their relationship had been painful, and the legal proceedings and their consequences exacted another sort of pain. "I had a low point at the time of the lawsuit surrounding Gilley's. It broke me. I gave the last hundred thousand dollars I had to an attorney. The only thing that I had going for me was the roadwork I was doing. I was literally down to the bottom of the barrel, so to speak."

Little financial remuneration from the judgment and ensuing settlement remained, but Mickey gained back his freedom and name. "The only thing I got was property in Nashville and property there in Pasadena, which ultimately burnt. The reason why I settled it is because I wanted to keep the logo. Ultimately, my name meant more to me than the money."

Mickey's music career was heading into a winter of discontent also. In October 1988, "She Reminded Me of You" peaked outside the top twenty. It would be the last time any of Mickey's songs would make an appearance in the top forty. That same year Mickey's road dates declined significantly. His recording contract had not been renewed and country music abandoned many significant acts of the seventies and eighties in favor of younger, slicker performers with potential crossover appeal. Mickey told a reporter from the *San Francisco Chronicle*, "Yeah, the record companies are looking for younger acts. I think that's what's happened to everybody—that's what happened to Charley Pride and to Mel Tillis, and that's what's gonna happen to Mickey Gilley if I don't come up with some records. The only one who's hanging in there is Willie Nelson."

When Mickey looked back at his amazing climb over the prior fifteen years, he was stunned by the unexpected success he enjoyed after having his first hit at thirty-eight. At the same time, he recognized how much money he had burned through during those successful years.

"We were just on a perpetual party at the time. I finally burned myself out. My recording suffered."

By the late 1980s, with each year tumbling along faster than the one before, each of the three middle-aged cousins faced a unique set of challenges. Jerry simply tried to survive the effects of two decades of tragedy, self-destruction, and bad habits. Jimmy struggled mightily to overcome a near-fatal mistake for a Bible-thumping preacher. Mickey, while not encountering the grueling public struggle and dramatic ups and downs of the other two, faced the challenges of dwindling popularity and a volatile, confrontational business partnership. Each of them would spend a time in their own personal wilderness, trying to find his way to a happier, more satisfied place.

What all three men had in common was an instinctive, untaught ability to persevere, to survive. Just as their relatives and other inhabitants of Concordia Parish had stubbornly navigated the basic challenges that faced them each day a half century earlier, Jerry Lee Lewis, Jimmy Lee Swaggart, and Mickey Leroy Gilley would find the strength to just keep going. It never dawned on them to do anything else.

– 46 –

DEFIANCE

Jerry and Kerrie had a stormy relationship. There were frequent dust-ups, break-ups, separations, other partners, and significant discord. There were happy moments, to be sure, but as time went by they came fewer and further between.

Kerrie exerted control over Jerry, which startled everyone who knew how little propensity he'd shown for being controlled by anyone. But Kerrie had a bargaining chip, for she was the mother of Lee, born in January 1987, a child who filled a significant void in Jerry's life and was a balm on the wounds left by the loss of his sons Steve Allen in 1962 and Junior in 1973. Kerrie was nothing if not wily. Jerry adored his young son and she easily perceived that controlling access to her child enabled her to assert control over her husband. Even when credible information seriously questioned his paternity of Lee, this father-son relationship continued to be vitally important to him.

Kerrie also was effective in pushing many of the people who remained loyal to Jerry out of his life. When Kay Martin, Jerry's longtime fan club president, visited with them, she was upset by what she heard and saw. "During the course of the conversation," says Kay, "Kerrie trashed Lottie, who had been Jerry's maid and had lived in the house for years. Lottie was no good. Linda Gail was no good. Frankie Jean was no good. Phoebe, Jerry's daughter, was no good either. She trashed everybody who loved him and who tried to have his best interest at heart."

As Kerrie continued her quest to limit access to her husband, Linda Gail, who was close to Jerry and had been a backup singer for her brother during the sixties and seventies, was summarily pushed aside and for a prolonged period had little contact with her brother.

"Around 1986, I decided I wanted to get back in the music business after my marriage fell apart. I wanted to go back on the road. I went to see Jerry, and of course, he took me back because he's my brother and he loves me, and I guess he liked having me on the show as well. I was only there about a year. Kerrie really did not want me to be around Jerry and did not want me to be on the show. I thought, well, you know, Jerry has a little boy and he has a wife and I should bow out gracefully and let him have his life. So that's what I did.

"I could have fought for my relationship with Jerry stronger than I did and I could have maintained it. Phoebe did. His guitar player Kenny Lovelace did. Kerrie really wanted to get rid of everybody but she was never able to come between Jerry and Phoebe and she was never able to come between Jerry and Kenny, although she tried. It's just hard for me to understand why anybody would want to just totally take everybody out of somebody's life."

Kerrie also took over as Jerry's manager. She frustrated promoters and missed opportunities to market Jerry. His career went into a tailspin from which it seemed he would never recover. Many concert and tour promoters and other industry personnel were unwilling to deal with the demands and difficulty that Kerrie imposed. By the late nineties most had decided Jerry had given up, resigned to while away his final days holed up in his house, making fewer and fewer appearances.

Accordingly, Jerry's finances took a nosedive and he filed for bankruptcy on multiple occasions in the late eighties and early nineties. The IRS repeatedly raided his home, seizing property and personal possessions, and dispatched agents to linger around his concerts to garnish his fees, all in attempts to settle the sizable amount he owed to Uncle Sam in unpaid taxes, penalties, and interest. Finally a deal was negotiated, and several years later, Jerry paid off the full amount owed.

Kerrie had her own ideas about how to raise cash. She opened up the Lewis home for tours. For a fee, fans could pass through and view the furnishings of Jerry's home while the object of their affection was shut off in the back bedroom.

"Linda Gail, would you look at this?" an outraged Jerry said to his sister. "Kerrie is turning my house into some sort of tourist trap, another Graceland. Only I ain't even dead yet!"

His sixty-fourth birthday party occasioned another fund-raising gimmick, when Kerrie charged 500 guests $250 each to attend the festivities. In addition to touring the Lewis home, these guests got to meet Jerry and his band members. This tacky event appeared to signal the beginning of a sad end for one of rock's original superstars.

Throughout the late eighties and nineties, Jerry's performances became increasingly unpredictable, as did the man himself. After struggling with several small labels following his departure from Elektra, he was unable to land a deal with a major label. Word of his unreliability, obstinacy, and use of drugs had traveled through the industry for so long that no one wanted to take a chance on the aging performer.

Several live performance reviews skewered Jerry for his lack of commitment and professionalism. A June 1996 review in the *New York Times* declared, "Here's one working definition of a pop legend: a musician of a certain age who makes rare appearances, charges top prices, and performs for just under forty-five minutes . . . (and begins) a two-night stand with cranky arrogance."

During his regular tours to Europe where he continued to be highly popular, he might be at the top of his game or he might cancel shows, miss appearances, anger promoters, alienate fans, chastise or abandon his band, and be generally impossible.

Mickey, talking to a reporter from Omaha, discussed his cousin's unpredictability: "He reminds me of a great baseball pitcher. He either bombs at the park or pitches a no-hitter. I love him to death and I admire him and he's a legend, but it's a shame he doesn't have better control of his life."

The first two thirds or so of Jerry's normal fifty-minute show had gone pretty well. For thirty-five minutes or so, an enthusiastic crowd had enjoyed a typical performance from the rock 'n' roller.

Jerry seemed a little surly but not to a degree considered unusual by many of his fans. Sure, he had shot a couple of hard stares at the band when they didn't keep the beat or missed a key change, but nothing dramatic seemed to be brewing.

He acknowledged the crowd's applause following each song. He even avoided any nasty retorts to the dumbasses who started hollering ten minutes into the show to request "Whole Lotta Shakin'" and "Great Balls of Fire," his two closing numbers.

But then, a couple of minutes into a fast-charging tune, Jerry stopped playing, quickly bringing the song to a halt. He fixed his cold, hard eyes on the drummer in a familiar stare.

"You gonna play those drums or not?"

Knowing how to respond was always tricky in these situations. The drummer decided silence was the best approach. On this evening, it didn't suit Jerry. After several seconds of delivering an icy stare toward the percussionist, Jerry delivered a follow-up.

"Get away from those drums and get outta here!"

Several seconds elapsed without movement as the drummer waited to see if the moment would pass, as they sometimes did. When his boss's stare remained on him, the drummer swung his stool around, exited behind the drum set, and left the stage. The crowd roared its approval, feeling as though they had been treated to an authentic appearance from the Killer.

Jerry continued with the show. He was clearly frustrated about something as he became more stone-faced with each passing moment. At the end of the next number, he unleashed his venom toward the bass player standing at the right of the stage and in the direct line of sight of Jerry from his piano stool.

"What are you looking at? You ain't playin' any better than him. Why don't you take that damn instrument of yours and follow him?"

The crowd's reaction was more subdued, with a handful of laughs scattered throughout the audience, slightly outnumbering the visible headshakes of disapproval.

Before launching into the next song, with only Kenny left on stage, he turned a stubborn, hard glare on his sidekick of twenty-plus years, daring him for a reaction. Kenny, a natural peacekeeper, tended to keep a healthy distance from Jerry's bad moods. But having seen two of his fellow band members already exit stage left and the crumbling of an earlier good concert, he met Jerry's stern look with one of his own. Jerry was on a roll and Kenny's return look didn't sit well with him.

"You're fired too! Follow 'em!"

Now several in the crowd turned on Jerry. It was one thing to fire a couple of lesser-known backup musicians. But firing Kenny Lovelace and leaving them to enjoy a piano soloist for the remainder of the show didn't sit well. Some began heading for the doors. A few even sought out the promoter and ticket sellers for a refund.

A few minutes later Jerry Lee Lewis left the stage, head raised, defiant. A couple of nights later, at his next performance, he was back on stage, backed up by the same three musicians he had fired two nights before.

Such was the life of working for a volatile, unpredictable Jerry Lee Lewis in the 1980s.

The filming of a 1989 movie, *Great Balls of Fire*, was expected to provide a boost to Jerry's career and fostered great excitement and anticipation. Based on the 1982 book of the same name by Myra and Murray Silver, the film encountered numerous difficulties during the production phase. There was significant inconsistency between details of the events of his life as portrayed in the book and remembered by Jerry, Sam Phillips, and others. The entire movie focused on the year and half from Jerry's first trip to Memphis in 1956 up to the aftermath of his failed 1958 tour in England, leaving out important events and important characters in his life.

When Jerry read the first draft of the screenplay he sent it back with "Lies! Lies! Lies!" scrawled across it.

The movie's release was met with immediate disappointment. It performed very poorly at the box office. Dennis Quaid's portrayal of Jerry was that of a goofy, cartoonish character, a far cry from the complicated, serious individual he truly was. While the soundtrack was well received, it was not an exaggeration to call the movie a flop.

In the words of one reviewer, "*Great Balls of Fire* is synthetic hooey, a one-dimensional non-profile that recalls the worst made-for-television docudramas."

Jerry referred to the movie on more than one occasion as "Great Balls of Shit."

Jerry's struggles had reached a woefully sad state. His drug use continued and took the form of a dangerous concoction that he was given just to keep going on a day-to-day basis. According to biographer Charles White, in one month during 1988 he received seventy-one doses of methadone, eighty-six doses of Halcion (a sedative used to treat insomnia), forty Didrex (an amphetamine), and seventeen injections of Demerol or Demerol–methadone mixture for painkilling purposes.

In 1997, Jerry's former road manager, Tim Culbertson, testified during a court case—triggered by Culbertson's contention that he was owed compensation by Jerry—that his former boss was consuming Xanax, Ritalin, methadone, chloral hydrate, Pamelor, and heavy quantities of Scotch, and that Kerrie doled out the drugs daily in small packets in various combinations, one in the morning, one before show time, and another before going to sleep. The picture he painted of Jerry and Kerrie's relationship, and of Jerry's life as a whole, was a decidedly bleak portrait of an addict on the skids. His bouts of lethargy, disorientation, and weak mental state led many to fear the worst for the man who appeared to be in a never-ending downward spiral. A common word used in describing him was "tragic"—a tragic figure, tragic circumstances, a tragic life.

To his credit and everlasting discomfort, Jerry took the blame for his life on himself. That he assumed others took the same view became apparent during a concert in 1992 when he stopped in the middle of a song, looked at his audience, and declared with a stoic expression, "I see the way you're looking at me. You think I'm a sinnin' man."

Even those closest to him, the ones who had always been his biggest fans and his biggest defenders, saw the change. Kay Martin had loved Jerry from the first day she met him back in 1957, when she was just sixteen years old. He was always sweet to her, but now, to her sorrow, she was told by those close to him, "Kay, you think you know him, but you really don't know him anymore. He's changed so much."

By the early nineties, Jerry was taking a steady supply of methadone, which he'd begun taking years earlier in an effort to get off other substances. In the early years of his methadone consumption, he relied on six-month prescriptions from one of the country's primary methadone clinics located in California. One of Jerry's handlers would often accompany him to California for the obligatory office visit that yielded the half-year prescription. On one of these visits, Jerry walked into the office of his regular physician, one of the few men willing to take Jerry head-on.

"Well, Doctor, if you don't mind I would like to get my prescription," Jerry commented after the preliminary niceties had been performed. He was visibly frail, having aged a seeming twenty years in the last decade. The prolonged drug use, the poor care he took of himself, a difficult marriage to Kerrie, and a path to obscurity as a musician were taking a noticeable toll on the aging superstar. The eyes were increasingly hollowed, the face was gaunt, his complexion seemed unhealthily pale.

"Jerry, let's not call it a prescription. Do you mean you want your dope?" the doctor stared directly into his eyes as he posed the question.

Jerry was taken aback. "You don't need to talk to me like this. I have a medical condition that requires this."

"Jerry, you're a dope addict. Let's call the situation for what it is."

Jerry stormed out of the office, heading straight to the waiting area, his trademark angry glare intact. He explained the exchange to his loyal agent, Al Embry, who had also been a close friend and fan for nearly thirty years.

Al, with a well-earned life-experience degree in keeping the peace from all his years with the volatile, unpredictable star, calmed Jerry down and urged him to go back into the doctor's office. "Jerry, we came all the way out here for your medicine. Go back in there and smooth things over so you can get what you came here for."

Once back in the doctor's office, the physician posed a question to his patient, "Jerry, let's assume you were standing on a cliff that was about to collapse and on that cliff was your son, a brand-new Corvette, and the only supply of your 'prescription' you could get your hands on. You only have time to save one of the three before they plunge hundreds of feet down. Which one would you save?"

Jerry hesitated for an instant as he considered the scenario. Before he could answer, the doctor interjected. "See, you're an addict, Jerry!"

Jerry retorted, "That's not fair. I didn't have time to react. I was about to."

The doctor shook his head. "Your response to save your son should have been instantaneous," he said. "The fact that you even

362

needed time to think about it confirms what I am telling you. You're an addict, Jerry. There's no way to deny it."

In the midst of this dreary scenario, Jerry would still muster his faculties on rare occasions, turn back the clock, and produce a mind-boggling performance. His true grit, his open defiance, would not allow himself or others to count him out, even when everyone assumed he was finished. The scene played out, time after time, throughout his career. In 1995, a new album was released. While *Young Blood* was not a commercial success, critics and hardcore fans loved it, stunned to see that Jerry could still produce a quality album.

His public performances were even more astounding to those who caught him on the rare occasions when he was feeling well and in a good mood, for it was then that he would pour his soul into his music and demonstrate that he could still outplay and outsing anyone, of any age or skill set, in any genre.

At a 1992 concert in Houston, he showed that fire when he interrupted the slow, melodious "Over the Rainbow," declared "That ain't rock 'n' roll," and sent fans screaming with delight and amazement as he kicked over the piano bench and played a wild, vehement rock 'n' roll medley, pounding the keyboard with his fists, his feet, and his backside.

Throughout the years he had risen from the proverbial ashes time after time, as he did at his sixty-sixth birthday party when he played for three hours straight, rocking out with the unfettered heart and vigor and pure, exultant talent that made him who he was and proved once again the boundless enormity of his talent.

THE STEP TOO FAR

A s the eighties merged into the nineties, Jimmy Swaggart was in the fight of his life. At stake were his career and his calling, decades of commitment, perseverance, and grueling work.

In a March 7, 1988 article, *US News and World Report* disclosed that 57 percent of Americans believed that religion could answer most or all of the problems of the day. Approximately a third of those polled claimed to born-again Christians. A 1991 Gallup poll revealed that two out of every five Americans attended church regularly and at least ninety percent of Americans professed to pray at least weekly and believed in God's existence. Christian influence and its belief system remained vital in the United States, which meant Jimmy Swaggart Ministries still had a fertile field from which to harvest supporters if Jimmy could somehow battle his way back and overcome the stigma that had crippled his ministry and still threatened its existence.

Battle back he did. Many loyalists within the ministry and others outside stuck with him through the difficulties. He began to rebuild his flock of faithful, person by person, viewer by viewer, household by household. It was slow going, but each week and month brought renewed hope of reconciliation and renewal.

"We're still fighting for our lives," Jimmy's friend and attorney Bill Treeby told the *Baton Rouge Advocate* in early 1989, "but we're feeling good about that fight."

There were important—but rarely reported—developments on the international front. In 1989, the ministry was able to get Jimmy on Chinese television with exposure to a potential audience of 330 million viewers. There was no preaching; the program was comprised entirely of music from Jimmy, his singers, and musicians. After the first fifteen shows, they phased in a teaching portion on the show, similar to his weekday program *A Study in the Word.*

Jimmy was excited about this dramatic opportunity and described his feelings to a reporter at a Baton Rouge newspaper. "It's hard for western Christians, who can hear the gospel any time of the day or night, to understand that there are many people in other parts of the world who cannot. It is difficult for us to comprehend that the vast majority of Chinese people have never even heard of the name of Jesus. But now it's their turn to hear."

A year later he was able to get the weekly telecast on television in Russia with an estimated potential viewership of 350 million people. Jimmy's fierce defenders held their breath, wondering if it really was possible for him to rebound from his debilitating situation.

After two years of fighting to regain his good name, it appeared that Jimmy and the ministry had weathered the worst of the storm and, slowly but surely, were on their way back to being regarded as respectable and credible.

But Jimmy had enormous challenges to overcome, among them the indelible image of his tearful apology on nationwide television.

In July 1991, Marvin Gorman's ninety-million-dollar lawsuit went to trial. Gorman and his lawyer accused a long list of people in the suit, but the prime target was Reverend Jimmy Swaggart, who was accused of writing and speaking untruthfully against Gorman out of jealousy and malicious intent to ruin his career and eliminate the competitive threat that Gorman posed.

Gorman also asserted that lies had been spread by Jimmy and others which had unfairly resulted in his dismissal from the Assemblies of God and the ruination of his ministry. The situation was awkward for everyone involved as Gorman faced many women who testified about his alleged sexual misbehavior toward them.

There were articles comparing the two men, the two wives, recapping all that had transpired—both accurately and inaccurately—and much of the information did not reflect well on the Swaggarts, their relationship, or their ministry.

Marvin Gorman was awarded $10 million in damages. The case would be appealed and ultimately the two parties would settle out of court for an undisclosed amount, later reported at one and a half to two million dollars.

But then, on October 11, 1991, one day after his thirty-ninth wedding anniversary, Jimmy was stopped by police in Indio, California—twenty miles southeast of Palm Springs—driving a white Jaguar which he had just swerved into the lane of oncoming traffic. Inside the car was a stash of pornography and a prostitute he had picked up minutes earlier. Within hours the news was out that Jimmy Swaggart had been caught with pornography and a prostitute.

In that small California town, on the western edge of the Mojave desert, Jimmy stepped into his own barren wilderness in which he would travel for the next decade and well beyond.

He steeled himself to face Frances, Donnie, and those still associated with the ministry. To avoid attention on a commercial flight, he drove the 1,700 miles back to Baton Rouge. As day turned to night and night to day and the desert gave way to the flat, open stretches of Texas and Louisiana, he was swamped in shame, humiliation, fear, sorrow, and hopelessness, brought on by the lapse in judgment, the indulgence in human weakness, and the crushing effect it would have on his ministry and outreach.

This, he knew, could be the step too far. Now several men close to him who'd urged that he confide in them when temptation struck would walk away. Many who'd stayed with him through the Airline Highway debacle now questioned the sincerity of the ministry and the man who led it.

Many who had cautiously given him a second chance would not give him a third. Those who had invested so much of themselves in the hope that the ministry could reclaim its place were devastated. Many who had stuck with Jimmy through the painful Airline Highway incident couldn't bear another episode.

How could this happen again?" the aging yet still powerful man asked himself.

Jim Rentz was a copastor of Family Worship Center throughout the heyday of Jimmy Swaggart Ministries. A longtime Assembly of God preacher and staunch supporter of Jimmy's outreach to the world, Rentz had been a regular face in the ministry, seen often on the panel of preachers and educators that joined *A Study in the Word*. Lacking the natural charisma of Jimmy, Rentz was nevertheless considered a good minister and a strong administrator who had faithfully carried out any deed—easy or difficult—on behalf of Jimmy, Frances, and Donnie.

Despite pressure to leave after the Airline Highway event, Jim and his wife Esther had remained with the Swaggarts and the ministry through the darkest days, fighting valiantly through the hard times with their close friends, struggling toward a brighter day as the ministry slowly and agonizingly regained its momentum. Their decision to stay with the Swaggarts had not been a popular one in many circles of the Assembly of God denomination in which the couple largely existed.

But Jim understood the pressure that Jimmy faced and believed that the intense strain could push him to a grave misdeed. If Jimmy didn't understand how—or was simply unable—to reach out for help, Rentz could see how a wrong fork in the road could lead to the calamitous event that occurred. It was unfortunate but the Bible which Rentz relied on and trusted was full of godly men who had fallen under the weight of sin.

In the aftermath of the first occurrence, Jim had spoken directly with Jimmy, urging him to accept his own weakness and to seek the counsel of others close to him if he faced temptation.

He thought his message had been heard. He assumed that such a staggering and public humiliation would teach Jimmy a valuable lesson. It would be difficult to recover from such a trying episode but Jimmy would learn a lasting lesson about his own vulnerability and take on a new cloak of humility that would allow him to reach out for help in moments of personal trial.

When Jim heard about the Indio incident, he was shocked—and pained. The pain was visible around his squinted eyes.

As he walked into Jimmy's spacious office and the evangelist turned to look him, he saw on Jimmy's face a mixture of embarrassment and strained composure.

Jim wasted no time with pleasantries.

"Jimmy, what happened?"

After a momentary pause, Jimmy responded, "Jim, you have no idea what kind of pressure I am under. That pressure produces a huge battle and struggle that others can't appreciate." Jim had little patience for where this conversation was going. This was exactly what he had warned against three years before: the making of excuses, the attempt to explain away behavior that was personally destructive and threatened the ministry. He spoke firmly to Jimmy, avoiding judgment but making clear he was not heading down this path of special dispensation.

"That's not good enough. Not this time. I told you before to reach out to me or others if you are facing struggle. These struggles are what men face and must deal with."

Rentz looked at his friend, this man he had seen God use so mightily around the world to help reach millions with the gospel of Jesus Christ, attracting them to repentance and hope for a better life. He loved Jimmy but he knew good old-fashioned pride was part of the problem here. As he continued to speak, the profundity of what they had been through together bubbled to the surface.

"I can't stay here and condone this. And I can't watch this lack of accountability and the reflection it makes upon the cause of Christ."

Jim Rentz loved Jimmy Swaggart but the time had come to part ways.

The relapse highlighted anew Jimmy's recurring struggles against temptation. His endless prayers and supplications had not yielded the formula or the strength for success and once again he had been shamed.

The people who remained within the ministry were disheartened on many fronts as the situation became more desperate and the focus on survival supplanted the focus on missions and outreach. Years of what many felt were questionable tactics employed against workers, tight constraints kept on what employees said and did, and a controlling environment where decisions that affected many were held in the hands of a very few had become frequent topics of increasing frustration and consternation.

At the center of both the ministry's functional success and the existing frustrations was Frances Anderson Swaggart. Everyone who knew her acknowledged she was strong, focused, organized, and intense when it came to identifying and getting what she wanted for the operation of the ministry. Jimmy constantly praised her as a wife, mother, teacher, cheerleader, and assistant in his efforts. She was looked upon largely as a chief operations officer, with Jimmy bragging that she had the skills necessary to manage General Motors.

Jimmy and Donnie frequently used the word "backbone" in describing her role in the Swaggart family. In a rare 1991 interview with the *Baton Rouge State Times*, she spoke of her bulldog mentality. "I've never been afraid to tackle anything. If it has to be done, I can get it done. And if I don't know how, I'll find someone who does and get them to teach me." Women in the congregation who watched her from afar admired the assertive, self-assured Frances, the way she radiated power and the manner in which she had stuck with her husband, her head held high through enormous difficulty and embarrassment.

On the other hand, there was much consternation among many within the ministry about Frances's management style. Author Barbara Nauer, who worked for the ministry for a time and gained an inside perspective on its key personalities and workings, wrote extensively of her frustrations with Jimmy Swaggart Ministries, and specifically Frances. She, along with others, detailed an environment where Frances and a few close members of her inner circle, largely Anderson family members, insisted on a degree of control that was astonishing. At various times, employees were put on strict weight-control programs, forced to submit to lie detector tests to root out individuals who had spoken to the news media, and generally treated with suspicion. Employees were quick to be ostracized and even terminated if they voiced opinions that differed from those of Frances and the people she empowered.

Employees resented that they were expected to make huge sacrifices for the ministry, keep their mouths shut, and be happy in their roles. A "walking on eggshells" culture developed as employees surreptitiously whispered to one another, eyes darting around them, for fear that any thought or opinion would find its way through the mysterious grapevine back to the office of Frances and her confidants. Nauer chastised Frances for her tendencies to control and manipulate through intimidation, humiliation, and deceit.

In large measure, the atmosphere described by many that worked in the ministry suggested a company that had operated very effectively at a small and medium-size level but had not adapted to work well as a larger organization. The small, family-dominated board with operational decision making driven by two or three people worked well early on, but as the workforce grew to hundreds of people and the annual revenue grew to tens of millions of dollars, that centralized, concentrated control-and-command structure stunted growth, overlooked good ideas, and inevitably created higher dissatisfaction.

John Camp took a harsh view of the situation. "You had a couple of high school dropouts," he said, "and suddenly they were administering millions and millions of dollars. One came from a no-stoplight town up the road from Ferriday. The other came from a little town whose great stars were Jerry Lee Lewis and Howard K. Smith. So here was their chance to make a name for themselves."

Many were befuddled about Jimmy's role in, and knowledge of, the functioning of the ministry. He was kept largely off-limits to most workers within the ministry by Frances and his secretary, Frances's sister, Linda Westbrook. He oftentimes seemed to condone the culture of intimidation and frequent terminations with questionable cause, didn't responsibly counter the suspicions engendered by the family-dominated board and culture of nepotism, and appeared to have little knowledge of many of the important details of the ministry.

Many people within the organization were there because of their care for and loyalty to Jimmy, and they were frustrated that he didn't seem to be mindful—and even ignored—many aspects of the ministry's functions that were compromising its overall impact and driving away valuable, dedicated partners. All of this added up to more reasons for people in the ministry to be embittered and disappointed with the man they had supported and trusted.

Alone he wandered the grounds of his property, deep in prayer. Reflecting on the mountain he had climbed to establish his ministry and the bruising tumble down the other side, he thought many times of Israel's King David described in the Bible as a man after God's own heart. David was a sinner too, having gazed upon the lovely Bathsheba knowing all the reasons why he shouldn't.

Jimmy was familiar with the power of grace, yet every day he faced humiliation.

But he knew nothing but preaching, playing, singing, and serving God in the only way he had learned. His entire life and identity revolved around the God he sought and the ministry he had built. He had no choice but to push on. Once he had preached to tens of thousands. Now he sermonized before the few dozen stalwarts scattered around Family Worship Center, where thousands of seats were curtained off. He drew further inspiration from the Book of Job: "Though He slay me, yet will I trust Him."

– 48 –

HOLDING COURT

Gilley's Texas Café was located right off Highway 76, the main drag through Branson, Missouri, across a parking lot from the Mickey Gilley Theatre. At lunchtime on a bright, warm—almost hot—day, a handful of cars already dotted the parking lot as the lunch crowd migrated into the dining area.

There, families looked over the menu, deciding between ribs, fajitas, burgers, or a variety of other options. An elderly couple sat twenty feet from the front door, having lunch together for seemingly the millionth time in their fifty years of marriage. They communicated without talking, by the subtle movements of their eyes, their body language, even the way they stirred artificial sweetener into their iced tea. Nearby a young mother tried to appease a youngster who had just discovered the amazing fun of dropping anything in sight on the floor.

The bar was separated from the rest of the restaurant by an open doorway six feet wide. A television played sports highlights and the walls displayed a variety of framed pictures forming a who's who of music stars.

On most days, Mickey Gilley sat at his favorite table near the bar, talking and laughing with others.

Employees from his theater and restaurant came by to say hello or to ask questions. He was always gracious and able to provide knowing input and guidance. As friends came in—some he'd known for a short time and others he'd known for decades—he was friendly to all. When strangers arrived they were surprised that the feature attraction was nestled in the back of his restaurant, wearing shorts and a baseball cap from the local Thousand Hills Golf Club. Initially bashful, they soon realized that Mickey was accessible. They were from places like North Carolina, Texas, and Iowa and never counted on meeting and visiting with Mickey Gilley.

As a few guests at his table departed, others joined him to hang out and chat. He held court on a variety of topics, ranging from how his several-night-per-week shows were going, to moments of his career that fans asked about, to the current Houston Astros baseball season and their prospects in the National League Central division.

His words poured out a mile per minute. His mind was sharp, his wit in top form. A smile rarely left his face and a twinkle never left his eye as he told stories from thirty years ago or two hours earlier. His loud, boisterous laugh was infectious, suggesting a hint of friendly mischief.

Another pair of strangers headed through the door and straight to the bar. After a few minutes, they whispered to each other as they realized the namesake of the restaurant and the theater next door was seated in their midst. He was having iced tea and shooting the breeze, sharing a hamburger with the quiet-but-friendly general manager of the theater who joined the group for lunch following her earlier meeting.

Mickey Gilley was in his element—just one of "the guys." Everyone who knew him well talked about how kind, friendly, and down-to-earth he was even before the discussion turned to his numerous accomplishments. He didn't crave the recognition that Jerry expected nor the love and acceptance of God for which Jimmy so seriously toiled. His interest was his fans, the folks who showed up year after year to see him put on a good show. They were the people he wanted to please, and when they were pleased, he was fulfilled.

Fifty years ago, Branson was a tiny town in the hills of the southern part of Missouri. When Roy Clark built a theater there in the early 1980s and began performing, the town became a preeminent location attracting other top names. By 1992, the town attracted over four million visitors each year, injecting $1.5 billion into the local economy. Names like Glen Campbell, Mel Tillis, Moe Bandy, and the Gatlin Brothers appeared on the digital signs in front of theaters up and down the main drag of Highway 76.

In 1987, Mickey made his first appearance as a guest act in Branson, at the Roy Clark Theater. Slated for two shows the same day, he was skeptical.

"What idiot would book me at a theater to do a two o'clock in the afternoon," he said, "and an eight o'clock at night?"

Then his agent called and said, "Hey, Gilley, you've got six sold-out shows."

Mickey was astonished. "Something's happening in this little town," he said, "that I don't know about."

Three years later, in the spring of 1990, Mickey opened up the 900-seat Mickey Gilley Theatre, spending on it every dime he had. The venture had a slow start. A few months later the outlook was grim. "We're broke," he told his friend Jim Thomas, "but if you'll loan me the money to pay the taxes owed on the place, I promise you that I can make the theater work."

Thomas thought about it a few minutes and said, "OK, let's go down there and pay these things up."

"I signed a note with him to pay him back," Mickey recalls, "for about $80,000. It wasn't a whole lot but it was more than I had."

"I'd figured up the lights and the help and the band and I'd factored in what the notes were on the theater and everything else. Within six months, I had repaid him, had money in the bank, and we never looked back. People have asked, 'How have you been able to stay in Branson over two decades?' Simple. Leave the money in the theater and let it operate."

The nineties were a booming time for Branson and Mickey Gilley. Longtime employee Tracy Dalton remembered those years fondly. "During those days, we sold out shows for ninety days straight. The parking lot guys had to tell people, 'I'm sorry, we're full.' Those were the best of times here. He was at the top in Branson, reaping so many benefits that he had worked so hard for."

Mickey had come to Branson to make a buck and continue his career. What he found in Branson was a town, a people, and a way of life that he loved.

Mickey was surprised to receive an invitation to Jerry's birthday party. He didn't see much of his aging cousin anymore yet he thought it might be nice to fly to Memphis and head south to Jerry's place in Nesbit, Mississippi. Maybe they would have a chance to visit and talk about old times.

In their earlier days, Jerry had been a lot of fun to be around, the life of the party, constantly laughing and cutting up. Mickey had seen little of that Jerry in the last couple of decades. On the infrequent occasions when they did see each other, their interactions were dominated by Jerry's mood swings and unpredictability. Maybe with time—and age—Jerry had settled down a bit.

When Mickey arrived at Jerry's, a sizable crowd was milling around in the backyard, the scene of the party. He recognized very few people, as he and Jerry had long since stopped traveling in the same circles. At that point, most would have been strangers to Jerry, as he had become increasingly reclusive. David Beatty, Jerry's cousin, also happened to be there, surprised to have been invited. David, too, had little to do with Jerry lately, aside from an infrequent phone conversation.

After some time, Jerry finally emerged from the house. He was wearing what appeared to Mickey to be an expensive-looking bathrobe. What quickly became of more interest to Mickey was the fact that in each hand Jerry carried a gun.

Mickey hoped he was just playing around, given his longtime affinity for firearms. But he wasn't about to hang around to find out. He had heard enough of the legend of Jerry Lee Lewis and none of it concurred with Mickey's desire to keep things simple and safe. He climbed into his vehicle and left without ever speaking to the birthday boy.

– 49 –

STYGIAN NIGHT

Around the time of the controversy involving Jim Bakker, the preacher Jerry Falwell told Ted Koppel, "As long as we are dealing with human beings, there will be human errors and human frailty."

That poignant statement applied as well to Jimmy Swaggart, who was first and foremost just a human. Author Barbara Nauer summed it up well, "Perhaps more than any churchman of recent memory, Jimmy Swaggart has been a most powerfully anointed soul-winner. But Jimmy is also rather miserably one of us . . . which means confused and even foolish some of the time, sinful, and despite extraordinary lovableness, not always level-headed and discerning and judicious and wise."

Depending on your viewpoint, Jimmy Swaggart was the lion of the gospel, spreading a message of hope and deliverance that the world needed to hear, or a self-righteous, arrogant man imposing his ideas on others without the intention of subscribing to them himself. Millions gave it thought and reached their own conclusions.

It is arguable that Jimmy Swaggart reached more people with the message of Christian salvation than anyone in human history. Most who knew him well believed in his talent and sincerity. Scores of others believed his actions and ministry were inspired by God.

An article written by Randall Balmer for *Christianity Today* published in 1998 captured Jimmy as he was then. "For more than a decade," it reads, "Jimmy Swaggart has been struggling against the current. But when he responds to his critics by saying that 'as many scars as I have, another one doesn't really matter,' I suspect he's talking about something more than scorn and ridicule and declining revenues. When Swaggart refers to the 'stygian night of darkness,' the reference is internal as well . . . When, in the course of a sermon he segues into 'Amazing grace, how sweet the sound that saved a wretch like me,' some would dismiss that as contrived and disingenuous, just another part of his act. I think he knows whereof he speaks."

Jimmy Swaggart was a master at seeing the correlation between Biblical illustration and modern man. When Jimmy considered his ministry in the 1990s in Biblical terms, it would likely have seemed analogous to the years Moses spent in isolation before fulfilling God's call to lead the children of Israel from Egyptian bonds. He might have recalled the decades the freed children of Israel spent wandering in the wilderness, unable to enter God's Promised Land because of their sin and lack of obedience. He may have thought again of Job, who lost everything as God tested his faith and allowed Satan to heap all manner of disappointment, loss, and tragedy on his life.

Jimmy spent time alone in prayer and study. He reflected on the mountain he had climbed and his painful tumble down the other side. He believed in God's forgiveness.

Yet each day he was faced anew with the difficulty he had brought upon himself. It was there as the lack of funds forced the cancellation of programs whose payments were months in arrears; it was there as scores of ministry employees were forced to find other means of livelihood and outreach; it was there as the heavy flow of letters and testimonies slowed to a trickle; and it was there as he became increasingly irrelevant in the world of ministers spreading the Christian message.

In the boom of the 1980s, construction projects for the ministry were a constant up and down Bluebonnet Road. In early 1988 a second tower was being erected to house students in Jimmy's growing college facility when the Airline Highway debacle became public knowledge. The large building was left unfinished, and remained for many years a concrete skeleton towering into the sky, a massive snapshot in time and a glowing reminder of Jimmy's fall from the heights of success, prosperity, and public acclaim. Yet the lowered status in the eyes of the Christian community, while a disappointment, didn't cripple Jimmy. He had grown up as an outsider to most Christians from the time his mother and father found a home, and a hope, in the small Assembly of God church in Ferriday. He had always been a loner, never feeling entirely comfortable around the other boys his age. His seriousness, his contemplation of matters that many children didn't fathom, his forced need to grow up quickly had always created emotional distance from others. His battles weren't fought living up to the opinions of others. As a man who believed that his calling as an evangelist was to make people uncomfortable, he could live with the shame thrust upon him, as painful and unpleasant as it might be.

No, the real struggle, the real difficulty, was reconciling the lowly place to which he had fallen with the great commission to which he felt called by God. Despite his best efforts to understand his weakness and accept his humbled status, there had to be periods of remembrance and agony. There had to be moments when he could picture the small child who benefited from the ministry's outreach, or the face of the alcoholic who happened upon his televised ministry and discovered an answer he'd lost hope of finding, or the tear-stained cheeks of the barefoot, impoverished South American who sprinted across the stadium when the thousands came forward for prayer. Jimmy had been God's vessel for those needy people. But now, who would find them? Who would help them? Who would share that message that he believed was their only hope? Never mind that other ministers—some credible and many not—

still had active and successful ministries. Jimmy could only speak for his own calling from God to preach. And now he was stranded in his own wilderness.

− 50 −

LAST MAN STANDING

One afternoon, Jerry's wife Kerrie called his daughter. "I'm leaving your daddy," she told Phoebe. "I've filed for divorce and I'm not coming back. He will be here in a few hours, flying in from somewhere."

Phoebe had always believed that her daddy would need her someday. "I'm going to be the one that's there," she'd say, "when everybody else is gone."

Within a half hour of Kerrie's call, Phoebe left Nashville, where she had been sharing an apartment with a friend, singing backup, and putting a career together for herself. She got to Memphis ahead of Jerry, picked him up at the airport, and moved in with him.

"Phoebe is a devoted little character," her mother, Myra, said. "She runs a real tight ship. She takes care of her daddy. She believes that's what she was meant to do and that girl has turned his life around."

Part of Jerry's turnaround was his desire—and Phoebe's faithful watchfulness—to overcome nearly half a century of drug use in a variety and a quantity that would be fatal to most people.

During the nineties, Jerry developed an allergic reaction to alcohol that produced a severe rash on his body when he drank. He was able to leave the bottle behind. "I can't handle it," he said, "I didn't think anything could ever make me stop drinking."

Leaving behind drugs was the next step in the process to sobriety and a painfully difficult one. Kerrie, according to many accounts, had kept him drugged. "Often when you'd talk to him," Myra recalls, "he couldn't even make a sentence."

When Phoebe went to live with him, he was taking methadone as well as a variety of pills. She called his doctor and told him, "I want my daddy to stop taking this methadone."

The doctor laughed at her and said, "Phoebe, your daddy will die taking methadone. He can't get off of it at this point."

"Well," said Phoebe, "we'll see."

"She withdrew it drop by drop," Myra recalled. "Phoebe told me, 'Mother, I didn't do it. My daddy said it was OK. He wanted to get off it, too.' But he would have never gotten off it without her. She helped him more than six wives and several managers were ever able to do."

For the aging Jerry Lee Lewis, life became quieter and more peaceful. Much of his time was spent at home in Nesbit, Mississippi, away from the public eye. He played with his Chihuahuas. A sign posted at the front of the property declared, "God made the animals—love them, don't hurt them."

When his longtime pet, a chihuahua named Topaz, died at an advanced age, he was depressed for days.

He spent a lot of time watching reruns of *Gunsmoke*, loved westerns and horror movies, and roamed around the house in pajamas. Even with his newfound sobriety, Jerry was noticeably weathered. His hard life had taken its toll. He was sometimes difficult to hear when he spoke, a result of his scratchy Southern dialect, and he had a tendency to mumble, not caring if people understood him. He had put on weight and was no longer the slender man from the seventies and eighties whose diet had consisted largely of drugs and alcohol. His full head of wavy hair was now gray, but it was still as thick as it had been fifty years ago. Those near him commented on his improved appearance.

Relatives who didn't see him frequently were struck by how

much he had slowed physically and mentally when they saw him. His cousin Jerry Beatty, who had seen him backstage before and after a concert in Louisiana, said, "When he came walking backstage, I didn't see how he had played that piano. He tore it up, but he couldn't hardly walk when he got back there."

Cousin Sherry Calhoun Jacobs had a similar encounter when visiting with him at a concert. "I went backstage and sat with him and talked, and I really did most of the talking. I'm used to Jerry popping and snapping. I can't imagine him being an old man. Every now and then he'll have little spurts of energy but I think he has abused himself so long with the drugs and the alcohol. Your body can only take so much, you know."

Jerry continued to be a private man. To those outside of his inner circle, he was typically aloof. Myra saw him occasionally when spending time with Phoebe.

"He still has his love of music," Myra said, "but he's just tired, I think. He's done this for so long and it's old hat to him now."

He recognized the necessity of promoting new albums and maintaining a connection with the public but regarded those practices as nothing more than the price he had to pay to continue to play and sing and connect with his music—the one constant, and the great love, in his life. With sobriety and the wisdom that generally comes with advancing years, Jerry changed.

Kenny Lovelace remarked about the increasingly relaxed nature of his friend and leader. "I see a change from year after year . . . Jerry's just real humble. He smiles and he talks more. Some of the rough edges have rubbed off, he's mellowed out, and he's good to be around. He's always been good to be around for me. I've always respected Jerry and he always has been nice to me and helped me over the years. But I can see he is generally nicer to everyone now."

With the departure of Kerrie from his life and a general improvement in his own mental and physical state, his relationship with his sisters and friends from the past improved over time. Linda Gail became more a part of his life, performing more frequently in his shows. He forged a closer relationship with Frankie Jean and even snuck into Ferriday on regular occasions to see her, unbeknownst to the locals.

Many were surprised by Jerry's kindness and generosity, as he was sometimes a victim of the legend surrounding his persona as the Killer. "I get crazy sometimes, upside down," Jerry once said. "But . . . if everything they say I've done is true, I'd have been put in the penitentiary long ago. A lot of times people make up things, and I just go along with 'em."

Jerry's most enduring challenge was living with the sorrows of life itself. "It wasn't the marriages that brought me down," he once said, "it was just the passin' of the caskets."

Throughout these losses and the grief and rage they engendered, Jerry sought to reconcile his worldly ways with the God and religion that were introduced to him in Ferriday. Despite his hell-raising behavior, he was never far away from the faith of his youth. His comments to his audiences often sounded like sermons, and he was known to break into a gospel song in the most unlikely performance venues. With time, Jerry made peace with the seemingly wide gulf between playing rock 'n' roll music and living the narrow-gait life of the devoted Christian. As Linda Gail said recently, "I don't know if he really believes all that stuff about the Devil's music anymore."

By 2002, the more peaceable Jerry had been relegated to obscurity and was becoming ever more reclusive. Then, after a concert he gave in Mississippi he was approached by music personality Jimmy Rip and Steve Bing, a successful businessman in the entertainment field, who told him that they were interested in reviving his career. Jerry was suspicious. "What do you want, anyway?" he said. What they wanted was to make an album with Jerry.

Jerry wasn't interested but Jimmy and Steve were not discouraged. They understood that he had reasons for his attitude. "He'd been burned so many times," Jimmy would say later, "He was just very sad at the time, which happens a lot to older musicians. Just a reaction to getting treated like shit."

Over time, bit by bit, Jimmy and Steve got through to Jerry. "Jerry's an incredibly intuitive guy, a human lie detector," Jimmy said. "He can tell when someone's fibbing a mile away. It took him a while to realize we were for real and wanted to get his talent front and center. He'd kind of given up a little bit. He was absolutely languishing."

Finally, Jerry committed to the project. He came to the early sessions in red pajamas and flip-flops, but he showed up prepared and on time and open to anything. "Not to bust any myths," says Jimmy, "but he was never a problem. We never had cross words."

As he watched Jerry record, Jimmy repeatedly witnessed the transformation of a tired, aging man. As he later recounted to *Rolling Stone*, he would look at Jerry and think, *This guy isn't going to reach the piano bench*, but "when his hands hit the keys, something metaphysical happens."

The 2006 release of *Last Man Standing* was a rousing success. A who's who roster of music greats—including Bruce Springsteen, George Jones, Willie Nelson, Mick Jagger, and Little Richard—jumped at the opportunity to perform with Jerry, yet gave him room to dominate the music. From the first-track duet with Jimmy Page to the twenty-first and final number with Kris Kristofferson, Jerry was as good as ever. Fans and critics loved the album and it surprised everyone who thought Jerry Lee Lewis was finished. Once more his indomitable spirit and talent had lifted him from the ashes.

"The whole thing has been such a boost," said Phoebe. "He's happier. He's got this reputation. He can be a wild, mean, crazy hell-raiser, but the person inside is a good, loving man."

In 2010, Jerry built on the success of *Last Man Standing* by recording and releasing another duet album, *Mean Old Man*. He was a step slower by then and the album emphasized older, grass-roots-type songs that were closely connected to the earlier, simpler style of music he knew in his youth. As he introduced the song "Railway to Heaven," he boomed into the microphone, "You know, I used to do this song back when I was a kid, in a little, small Assembly of God church there in Ferriday, with all my kin people looking right down my throat. It was good then and it's good now."

When he sang that song, the listener could feel Jerry's soul and could sense how profoundly the life he lived and the people he loved resonated in his consciousness and in his identity.

The list of honors for Jerry Lee Lewis is long and will only grow longer with time. His impact on music and American culture is still undervalued, but time offers clarity and his legend will continue to burgeon after he is gone.

His greatness has often been publicly acknowledged, as it was in January 1986 when he was part of the initial class of inductees into the Rock 'n' Roll Hall of Fame. Two of his hits—"Great Balls of Fire" and "Whole Lotta Shakin' Going On"—remain among the most recognizable and best-loved songs of all time. In 2005, he was given a Grammy Lifetime Achievement Award. "He likes recognition," commented J. W. Whitten. "He likes to be honored in the proper way. It was a big deal when he got the Lifetime Grammy. Led Zeppelin was honored at the same time. They got up and said it was an honor to be recognized alongside Jerry Lee Lewis. That touched him because he knew how big those guys were."

In 2008, Jerry performed for 300,000 people in front of the Capitol in Washington, DC, as part of the nation's Independence Day celebration. In 2009, the Tennessee Legislature named a section of thoroughfare the Jerry Lee Lewis Highway. In 2010, HBO's Twenty-Fifth Anniversary Rock 'n' Roll Hall of Fame concert opened with Jerry playing an instrumental version of "Great Balls of Fire." When he finished and kicked the piano stool over, he was given a standing ovation.

Perhaps there is no truer testimony to Jerry's greatness than the fact that whenever he performs on a bill with other stars, they invariably stand in the wings to watch one of the few performers who piques their interest and even excites them.

One of the greatest tributes came from John Lennon, who said in 1971, "I like rock 'n' roll, man, I don't like much else. That's the music that inspired me to play music. There is nothing conceptually better than rock 'n' roll. No group, be it the Beatles, Dylan, or Stones, have ever improved on "Whole Lot of Shakin' Going On" for my money."

Two years later, Lennon and Yoko Ono attended one of Jerry's shows in California and afterward came backstage. Lennon got down on his knees, crawled across the room, and literally kissed Jerry's feet. He thanked him for being such an inspiration. Jerry, who had been displeased when the British Invasion rocked America in the sixties, was visibly moved and honored.

Jerry's musical talent was nothing short of genius. "You talk about a talent," Sam Phillips once said. "Good God Almighty! I'm not talking about voice, piano, any one thing. He is one of the great talents of all time, in any category."

Roland Janes, the guitarist for some of the Jerry's key musical recordings, told the author Colin Escott, "People are always trying to compare musicians, but I can't find anyone to compare to Jerry. What you hear him doing on records is only a small percentage of what he's capable of doing. I don't think even he knows how great he is. He can take a solo with either hand and sing a song five different ways, every one of them great. I remember when we worked the package shows—Jerry would sit backstage after the show at the piano and all the big stars would gather around him and watch. Chuck Berry, Buddy Holly, the Everly Brothers, and so on. Jerry would be leading the chorus and everyone would be having a ball."

His own sister, Linda Gail, may be his biggest fan. "Jerry's different from everybody in the whole world because of his genius as far as singing and playing the piano is concerned. When you listen to the vocals that he did on his country stuff and if you listen to the piano he played on those albums, he played classical-style music on country songs and it worked simply because he's a genius. If anybody else had tried to do that it would have sounded awful. Jerry's always going to be different—not just from his two cousins—but from everybody. I mean, that's just the way it is."

Jerry's music and style supersede genre. As the writer Joe Bonomo declared, "The category in which Jerry Lee Lewis belongs is Jerry Lee Lewis."

His iconic status is largely owed to his one-of-a-kind, flamboyant, charismatic, dangerous, and—yes, even self-destructive—personality. Robert Palmer characterized it well when he wrote, "There has never been another American pop musician with Lewis's particular mixture of egotistical self-confidence, innate taste and sensitivity, eclecticism, formidable and entirely idiosyncratic technique, and sheer bravura."

Charles White's introductory paragraph in his authorized biography of Jerry reads beautifully: "Jerry Lee Lewis is the last American wildman. The tapestry of his life is founded on his musical genius, which is supreme; his repertoire is a storehouse of vital twentieth-century American music with which even the Smithsonian Institute would find it hard to compete. On stage he can sing literally thousands of songs redefining and reinterpreting them every time he plays. This is not a show, it is real life. The most fundamental conventions of show business fall by the wayside as he acts out his life through his music. It is a life that reads like a mixture of Shakespeare and Tennessee Williams—murder stories—death—insanity—bigamy—drug abuse—violence—bankruptcy—vandalism—racism—arrogance—egotism—genius. All these are part of Jerry Lee's incredible life and style."

Beyond his musical talent, Jerry Lee Lewis will be ultimately defined by his ability to survive. Based on everything he did and everything he endured, it was nothing short of miraculous that in his seventies he was still playing music, and still rousing and moving his exultant audiences.

– 51 –

GOING HOME

As one heads onto Highway 84 West and drives into Ferriday, the sign greeting him points out the famous people who came from this small town, including three dirt-poor cousins who grew up together and then went different directions to affect the world.

A visitor can readily see lingering traces of the town in which these three lived many decades ago: the empty lot where Haney's Big House once stood proudly, the little white building at the corner of Eighth Street and Texas Avenue that once housed the Assembly of God church, and the Arcade Theater in the heart of downtown, recently renovated.

The town of Ferriday has always taken pride in its famous—and sometimes wayward—cousins. In the 1990s the Ferriday Chamber of Commerce authorized the development of a local Ferriday Museum, funded on its own nickel. Concordia Parish librarian Amanda Taylor was given the challenging task of gathering and organizing—from scratch—sufficient materials and information for a museum on Jerry, Jimmy, and Mickey, as well as other famous Ferriday citizens: journalist Howard K. Smith, Hollywood personality Anne Boyer Warner, and trombonist Peewee Whitaker. With the help of several key relatives and local citizens, as well as a persistent letter-writing and phone-calling campaign, the initial Ferriday Museum was established.

With the later ability to secure use of the historic former post office in Ferriday and the interest of the Louisiana Secretary of State in Louisiana's music heritage, state funding was secured and the establishment migrated into the state-run and funded Delta Music Museum, directed by local citizen Judith Bingham.

With great anticipation and planning, public excitement built toward the opening of the new museum and induction of its first class of honorees into its halls. On March 2, 2002, despite rainy weather, cars lined up and down Louisiana Avenue to the east and west, up and down Highway 84 to the north and south, and in all manner of directions. People came from as far away as Europe and Australia to see Jerry, Jimmy, and Mickey as they made a rare public appearance together. With people everywhere—estimates ranged as high as 6,000—little Ferriday found itself facing its largest crowd in its boisterous but private-nook-of-the-world history.

The favorite son, Mickey, had been in town—as he frequently was—to play in a local golf tournament to raise money for yet another local cause. While the golf tournament was canceled due to weather, he had been out and about among the people, at a local party, and performing in nearby Natchez—ten miles away and just across the bridge where, sixty years earlier, with eyes as big as saucers, he had watched his larger-than-life cousin walk the railing in a successful attempt to prove himself the most daring. Mickey's warm smile and giddy demeanor suggested the pride and thrill he felt by being honored in his hometown, in front of so many he knew so well and whose acclaim and applause he enjoyed receiving.

Jimmy made the hundred-mile trip up from Baton Rouge the morning of the induction ceremony. Having told Louisiana Secretary of State Fox McKeithen a few days earlier that getting the three cousins together "would be a miracle," he seemed to grasp and understand the historical significance of the moment. Jimmy was happy and cheerful as he made the trip back to the town of his youth, where memories of childhood prophecies and teenage burglaries lingered in his heart and mind. He remembered

Pentecostal gospel and Haney's Big House blues, Son's heavy-handedness and Minnie Bell's constant encouragement. With him came a sizable caravan of Family Worship Center faithful, there to make sure that Jimmy would be loudly supported and honored in the unfamiliar surroundings.

Perhaps the most anticipation was reserved for the wildest of Ferriday's sons—the man who had led the way out of Ferriday, into music acclaim. He had most captured the imagination of its citizens while earning the most curiosity. He was the son who had been most absent from Ferriday in recent years, likely to be here in recent decades only to bury another parent, or son, or spouse.

To the disappointment of everyone—but somehow fitting for the man who had become the epitome of unpredictability and going against the flow—Jerry never made it to Ferriday that rainy Saturday afternoon. Stories abounded concerning the reason for his absence. The most frequently invoked—and most likely—involved the plane sent by the Louisiana Secretary of State's Office to retrieve him at the Memphis airport. Knowing Jerry's preferences, his handlers had been clear about the type of aircraft to be sent to fetch him for the flight to Ferriday. For some unexplained reason, a smaller aircraft was sent for him. Always a nervous flyer—and the previous owner of the plane in which Ricky Nelson later died—he was superstitious about small planes and refused to board the one that came to retrieve him.

Despite dampened spirits, dampened women's hairdos, and dampened men's coats and slacks, Mickey and Jimmy admirably carried the show. Jimmy sang a moving rendition of "Amazing Grace" that stirred the crowd. In his familiar deflecting style, Mickey mixed his "The Girls All Get Prettier at Closing Time" with Jerry's "Great Balls of Fire," always sensitive to make sure the fans were pleased.

No one was more disappointed about Jerry's absence than his two cousins who, despite the distant direction their lives had taken, always maintained admiration for Jerry. They had both struggled at various points in their lives to escape his overshadowing presence. They had both enjoyed periods in their life where their own accomplishments and popularity had exceeded his. Yet somewhere—from a place and pecking order established long ago—they still felt the shadow that came from a musical genius to which they would never lay claim.

In the town of Ferriday, Jerry was recognized as the most talented musician of the cousins and the wildest character of the three. Music lovers there still love him—as do those Louisiana natives who take a certain pride in fostering someone who grew to be such a stubborn, independent man.

Still, Jerry had little to do with his hometown. The reasons varied: strained relations with family members, lingering warrants and judgments (most of which have long since expired), and the many funerals that brought him back there in the last fifty years. "There's really nothing [in Ferriday] for me anymore," Jerry once told a reporter. "It's just bad memories. I'll be buried there someday, if God's willing."

In Ferriday, Jimmy had the most loyal supporters and the most vocal detractors of the three cousins. Some of the town's many poor folks disapproved of his affluent lifestyle which they heard and read about during his heyday. Others were disturbed by his public stumbles. Others were quick to paint a picture of respect, admiration, and forgiveness for the hometown evangelist. Judith Bingham, director of the Delta Music Museum, says, "We have had many people question whether Jimmy belongs in the museum," she says. "I tell them, 'Jimmy said that he sinned. He asked God to forgive him. If God forgives him, who are we not to?' That is exactly how I feel about it. All of us have sinned and come short of the glory of God. He was in the limelight with his career and his ministry and I know his mistake was painful and detrimental to him, his family, and his ministry."

Bingham had a chance to see Jimmy up close and personally during his rare, unexpected visits to the local museum. "He came by the museum twice when nothing was going on—totally unannounced. He and Donnie walked in and it was a very pleasurable meeting. He's somebody you feel like you can talk to, and we conversed for probably an hour or so. He was a great guy to be around. He really was."

But for those individuals in Ferriday who aren't personally close to one of the cousins, Mickey was most beloved of the three.

"Mickey's been here for the opening of the hotel over in Vidalia," says Bobby Marks, Mickey's close friend, schoolmate of the three cousins and a legendary, retired high school football coach in the area. "He's been here for the opening of the Delta Music Museum. He's been there for the reopening of the Arcade Theater. He's been here for every little thing they've asked him to be here for. He came to so many golf tournaments. If he's made Ferriday a hundred thousand dollars in the last several years, the other two haven't made the town a dime."

"Mickey has been such a proponent of our museum," says Bingham. "For several years, the Chamber of Commerce would have a golf tournament in his honor, and he'd fly in here at his own expense and participate and then go back to Branson to perform that night. As for the museum, every time we've asked him to do something for us, he's been more than willing."

For Jerry, Jimmy, and Mickey, music has been a force that flows within them, their lifeblood, a power source from which they have found direction, inner strength, and a source of regeneration.

Perhaps the power of music has been strongest for Jerry, for whom music was the vehicle to rouse himself—over and over—from the depths to new heights.

His loyal fans have always waited patiently for flashes of brilliance and genius that have resided within this man. Never adept or comfortable expressing his emotions in conversation, his singing and playing have communicated a deep emotion, feelings that bundle tightly the pain, struggle, love, and elation of his amazing life, as becomes apparent to anyone who has seen the tears roll down his cheeks on rare occasion as he belted out the sorrowful, longing ballads.

Asked how her rock 'n' roll cousin could still play so well at the later stages of his hard-lived life, Sherrie Calhoun Jacobs replied, "Music is just in his damn soul . . . in his blood. When his fingers kiss those keys, the relationship between the two is indescribable. He comes alive then."

In describing how he captures his audience, Teresa Pullon, a Ferriday native who knew him growing up, says, "Jerry just gives his all when he performs, his whole human voice, body, everything. He just gives it all out there. He holds nothing back, whether you like it or not. That's his attitude. You came here to see me. You're going to see all of me."

As Jerry has said often, "I don't regret any of the years that God's let me live on this earth. I've had a wonderful life, a great career. I just want to be remembered for my music."

There are a myriad of things for which Jerry could be remembered, but his music will outlive the rest by a wide distance.

Jimmy Lee Swaggart has often described music as the purest form of worship man can offer to God. Although Jimmy has relied on his musical talent to generate appeal, help build his ministry, and express a God-given ability, he hasn't relied on music for pure survival the way Jerry seemed to over the years. He didn't throw himself into music as a child as obsessively as Jerry, didn't rush away from performances early in his career to follow up with two-hour encore jam sessions backstage or at the hotel, and didn't rely on the piano to drag himself through the most painful days of his life.

Nonetheless, like his volatile cousin, Jimmy has been able to communicate more honestly and openly through music. What Jimmy has found too difficult to express when he preaches—his humanity, his struggles, and his weaknesses—he has expressed clearly when sitting at the piano and playing. That is why Jimmy's lasting contribution—his legacy—will also be his music.

While Jimmy's hands never moved over the keys as quickly as Jerry's and he always struggled to keep up with his more musically talented cousin, Jimmy can rival Jerry in touching human emotions through his soulful style of gospel music.

In October 2007, Jerry was honored by the Rock 'n' Roll Hall of Fame as an American Music Master, the first living recipient of the award. After a week of festivities, the final event was a star-packed tribute concert in which Jimmy surprisingly agreed to perform given that it was a wholly secular event.

"If there was one truly anticipated appearance," wrote Bob Mehr of the *Commercial Appeal* out of Memphis, "it was that of Lewis's first cousin, Reverend Jimmy Swaggart. As he took his place at the piano, the wings of the stage suddenly filled with a phalanx of fellow performers curious to see what the famed televangelist would do. Swaggart spoke in booming tones of his deep bond with Lewis: 'To say I love my cousin would be an understatement,' he said, noting that they'd literally grown up together learning to play on the same piano. While his oratory was moving, Swaggart's performance was the real revelation; he sang a gorgeous version of 'Precious Lord, Take My Hand' that was deeply soulful and downright bluesy, pitched perfectly between the church house and the roadhouse."

Donnie would describe the scene later in a sermon, speaking of the hushed impact on the crowd, the tears that flowed from many in the audience, and afterward the speechlessness of the evening's master of ceremonies, Kris Kristofferson.

Only Jimmy rivaled Jerry on this night full of stars. Everyone assumed Jerry would perform "Great Balls of Fire"—if he decided to play at all—so none of the other entertainers had been allowed to do it. But Jerry would never do just what was expected of him. He didn't perform "Great Balls of Fire." "Typical Jerry," said his sister Linda Gail, "he comes up there, and he does 'Over the Rainbow.'"

It is a song of great yearning. He did not choose it by chance. He played and sang it in a way that was excruciatingly sweet and true and sad. He was doing what he'd heard Hank Williams do some sixty years before: he was imbuing his music with his own hopes, shattered and not, and his own suffering. And that night, his fingers caressed the keys as he sang the last words of the song, punctuating it, as usual, with some lyrics of his own: "Somewhere over the rainbow, bluebirds fly. Flying high over that ol' rainbow, I just wonder why can't I?"

Had he looked out at the people in the audience, he would have seen that many of them had tears in their eyes.

– 52 –

MICKEY'S SPIRIT

In the early nineties, Mickey had cosmetic surgery. He was in his midfifties and beginning to look tired. Wrinkles had begun to accumulate in his face and the skin around his neck sagged, the normal indicators of age. A successful $15,000 procedure helped Mickey address his concerns.

"I did it because I wanted to look decent onstage," he says, "I didn't do it because I was concerned about showing my age. I didn't do it for anyone else but me and it came off great. When I started recovering from the surgery, my face really looked like I wanted it to look."

In 2004, Mickey decided he needed a follow-up procedure to tighten up the sagging in his neck again. He found a highly recommended, reputable doctor in Clear Lake, just outside of Houston, who performed the hour-long, $7,500 procedure in his office, after which Mickey headed home.

Al Embry had been in Houston that day and stopped by to visit Mickey in the early afternoon, just in time to drive him back over to the doctor's office to correct some minor swelling due to a blood vessel that was nicked during the surgery. Shortly after their return to Mickey's home, the drama stepped up a few notches.

"Al, come up here! Something is wrong with Mickey!"

Vivian's voice erupted over the banister in Mickey's Pasadena home. Al was in their living room getting ready to head for the airport and his flight back to Nashville.

The swelling had not subsided. It had worsened. Mickey's neck and face took on a bluish color and he was sitting in his walk-in closet, shaking uncontrollably. Within moments, he passed out.

Vivian called 911 and an ambulance was dispatched to get him. She then called the plastic surgeon and listened to him for a moment.

"Al, take the phone," she said. "I can't handle this."

The doctor's words to Al were delivered as calmly as possibly, but with maximum urgency.

"There's no time for the ambulance to get there. He'll be dead before they arrive. You have to cut that stitch and release the blood that has accumulated inside his face and neck!"

Vivian found suitable scissors. She held the phone to Al's ear as he followed the doctor's directive step-by-step, cutting through two layers of stitches until he found the vein from which the internal bleeding was occurring.

Moments later the ambulance arrived. On the way to the hospital, Mickey stopped breathing. The medical team on board used a defibrillator to revive him.

At the hospital, the plastic surgeon rushed through the door. After getting a quick update from the medical staff, he went to Mickey's bedside and saw that, although he was still in serious condition, his eyes were open. The doctor made a beeline for Al and planted a kiss on his cheek.

The next day, while still in intensive care, Al took a break from updating the media—with a careful blend of accurate and inaccurate information—to visit his friend and client. Mickey was still in bed but the swelling had already subsided significantly. He smiled weakly.

"Al," he said, "you saved my life."

What's the matter with Mickey Gilley? Is he drunk out there?"

Employees at the theater and friends of Mickey were fielding these questions with increasing frequency and growing alarm.

Beginning in 2006, Mickey experienced a gradual decline in his physical and mental health.

"I lost my strength," he recalls. "I lost my balance. I got to where I could barely walk. I could tell when I was driving my car that things weren't coming into focus. In 2007 I ran my airplane off the end of the runway because my brain wasn't working properly."

After an initial visit to a neurologist in Houston, the condition was diagnosed as hydrocephalus, characterized by a buildup of fluid on the brain. A series of exercises and therapeutic steps meant to help him cope with the condition had no positive impact. Meanwhile, his strength continued to fade.

The hydrocephalus affected every aspect of his life, including his onstage performances. The loss of balance and lapses in judgment produced an impact that was clearly visible to those who came to see the show. Employees at the theater received frequent questions from fans about Mickey's eroding performance on stage. The whispers and questions about whether he had been drinking excessively, based on his awkward balance and lack of clarity, continued to mount. The worries of Mickey's band, production group, and theater staff continued to grow.

After two years during which his health continued to deteriorate, in 2008, Mickey reached out for further help in hopes of addressing the downward spiral in which he found himself. A neurologist in Springfield, Missouri, provided a blunt evaluation after performing a CAT scan and other tests.

"Mickey, you look like you have a swimming pool in your head. There's only one way to correct it—you're going to have to have a shunt."

"When they told me they had to put a hole in my skull," recalls Mickey, "and pull this drain down through my neck to feed the fluid into my perineum, it scared the hell out of me. But I knew it was either do that or die."

The surgical procedure was a resounding success. It produced an immediate restoration of Mickey's physical and mental faculties.

The slow path the now seventy-two-year-old was trekking to his demise was reversed overnight.

"When I woke up after having that shunt put in, I was a new person. It was like I'd been reborn. Almost immediately, I stood up and asked, 'Where's my cape? I'm ready to fly.'"

The biggest health challenge of Mickey's life would occur as a result of an incident on July 5, 2009. "I was helping a friend of mine move furniture," he recalls, "I stepped the wrong way, and I fell eighteen or twenty inches, right on the back of my neck. I damaged several vertebrae—C4, C5, and C6—my spinal cord swelled up, and it left me paralyzed from the neck down. The only things I could move were my eyes.

"I thought, *God, please just let me die. If I have to live like this, I'm ready to go now. Please don't make me live like this.*"

Looking at the unfamiliar surroundings of the hospital room, Mickey's eyes shifted from side to side. They were the only part of his body that would move. For a man who had always been on the go, lying here in a neck brace—totally paralyzed—put Mickey into a state of panic. Those around him had to calm him down and explain what had happened after he was rushed to Cox South Hospital in Springfield, Missouri. Mickey had spent the next two days disconnected entirely from his surroundings. Medical staff and a few trusted friends and family members heard him mumbling incoherently from time to time, but Mickey was just barely hanging on, his life in the balance.

It was at his first moments of consciousness, two days later, that he made his plea for his Maker to take his life.

His son Michael stepped forward and stood over his father. Mickey would hear Michael's reassuring voice throughout the next nine months of intense therapy—and beyond—through days in which his gains were so small they were unrecognizable.

"It's OK, Dad. It's going to be OK."

The long, uphill climb back began. Mickey was in intensive care for two weeks, followed by an additional three-week stay in the hospital. Besides the physical threat of permanent paralysis, which doctors believed would slowly improve—up to a point—there was the mental and emotional nightmare with which to contend.

Mickey was forced to rely on nurses and medical staff for help with everything. All bodily functions and basic tasks required the assistance of others. He was helpless to do anything for himself and it mortified him.

"I lost all dignity after the accident," he says.

After five weeks, the piano player with immobile hands and fingers was transferred to TIRR Memorial Hermann Hospital in Houston to continue his rehabilitation. Over the ensuing months, he would achieve tiny, microscopic improvements which provided some hope, some confirmation that he was getting better. He migrated slowly from a full-time hospital stay to outpatient treatment to finally being sent home to Pasadena to continue rehabilitation there.

Doctors thought he would remain permanently paralyzed on his left side. But Mickey's positive outlook and dogged determination returned quickly. There were days when the fight seemed fruitless, depression set in, and Mickey wondered how he could have gone so quickly from the life he enjoyed so much to this existence, one which felt like a living hell. On rare occasions, the despondence seemed too much to overcome. His weight dropped from 190 to 140 pounds. But over time his sense of humor and inherent sense of hope would return to buoy him.

"I'm on my eighth life," he said, recounting all the close calls he encountered.

Mickey was forced to take out a line of credit of $300,000 to keep the theater in operation while he recuperated. But his commitment to the theater, his key employees, and his band members never waned. As the rehabilitation process extended, his expected return to the theater was postponed again and again. A planned return in October 2009 was pushed forward to November, November was pushed to January, and so on. Employees and band members worried that he would never make it back and Mickey was frustrated by his inability to improve more quickly.

"The fall just turned his life completely upside down," commented Michelle Nilges, the general manager of the Mickey Gilley Theatre and longtime employee. "It was tragic for him. I think he was angry with himself that he had the accident and he felt like he let us down. That's just him."

Michael observed the impact the fall had on his dad on those days when the struggle took its toll mentally: "The only time that Dad ever changed was after he fell. There's been a dramatic mental change in him. Up until then, his quality of life was great. He enjoyed playing golf, enjoyed the people around him, and liked to entertain people—not just onstage, but one-on-one. With the accident, it was just so difficult for him, he sometimes wanted to give up. I told him, 'Dad, you've come so far in a short period of time. When I went to Branson and brought you back to Houston, you couldn't move anything but your head. Look at you now. You're starting to walk again.'

"But he had those days where he said, 'I should have died. I shouldn't be here.' He got in a mood where he felt like he wasn't getting any better. I told him, 'Dad, you're making progress every day. You can't see it because it's such a small amount, but it is progress. Don't give up.' He hasn't. He's been strong."

On April 12, 2010—nine months after his accident—Mickey returned to the stage of the Mickey Gilley Theatre, walking carefully—and with help—to a chair in the center of the stage. The packed house that night included other local stars, dignitaries, friends, and fans of the legendary country performer. It was an emotional evening for everyone as they saw the physical toll the accident had taken on him yet heard the strong voice that magically emanated from the still-weak body.

The accident has had a spiritual impact on the Ferriday boy who grew up resenting the fear-based Pentecostal upbringing that left him frightened in bed each night, fearful of dying and going to hell. The boy—and man—who never underestimated the miracle-working power of his mother's fervent prayers sees a miracle in his own case. "I should have died," he says. "I don't know. Maybe my heart wasn't with God at the time and he said, 'You need to stick around and repent.'"

The key to Mickey's popularity is his ability to connect on a personal level, within a group or individually. Sandy Brokaw, Mickey's longtime publicist and close friend, once related to author Elaine Dundy, "He just likes playing his music, going around the country playing his music. As long as he can make a buck playing his music and play some golf and watch TV and have a beer, he's happy. He's a real 'people' person. That's his strength, but it's also his weakness. He's so easy with people. I've seen him talk to anybody, and that's great, but sometimes I wish that instead of spending time with those people, he could put that energy into meeting the people who can benefit him more. I'll be trying to get him to meet somebody and he'll be off talking to some drunk at a Howard Johnson's."

Essentially, Mickey likes being one of the folks, which separates him from his two famous cousins.

It was 7:20 backstage at the Mickey Gilley Theatre, a little over half an hour until show time.

A steady bustle and flow of people went in and out of Mickey's dressing area backstage. Fifty or sixty feet away, the band was onstage behind a closed curtain, moving and setting up equipment.

In Mickey's dressing room, bandleader Norman Carlson talked to a visitor about how he spent his day before heading over for work. A golfing buddy sat in a chair next to a big-screen television, telling jokes as Mickey listened to the friendly commotion.

He wore shorts, drank coffee, and thoroughly enjoyed being surrounded by people, making sure everyone was comfortable and had a full cup.

His eyes sparkled and he looked fresh, having taken his now-regular afternoon nap so he could be ready for the show and the ensuing interaction with his fans in the theater or across the parking lot in the restaurant and cantina, where show attendees were invited—even encouraged—to drop by for autographs, pictures, and a chance to visit with him.

Various band members moseyed in and out of the room. They got themselves a cup of Gilley's coffee, to which they were always welcome, and asked how he was feeling. Gary Cornelius, the drummer, talked to Mickey about how his tomato plants were coming along. Guitarist Gary Myers eased in to talk about last night's turnout and what the ticket sales looked like for that evening. The fiddler, steel guitarist, and the show's comic relief, Joey Riley, came in briefly and without even trying had everyone laughing within minutes.

Mickey's friendliness is another thing that distinguished him from his cousins. Jerry became intensely private, and access to him before a show was a rarity, as he preferred to stay alone, away from the band and other performers. After a show, if he felt well, he could be cordial, even friendly, but he had no need or desire to be with crowds of people. His inner circle became small and he avoided making himself available to well-wishers and others hoping for a chance to meet him.

Similarly, Jimmy was guarded, seemingly uncomfortable around those he did not know well. Many longtime churchgoers to his Family Worship Center knew little or nothing of his real personality. He too was courteous to those he encountered but it was clear when watching him closely that he did not enjoy engaging with strangers around him.

Following most church services, Jimmy looked to his wife or the assigned usher who, for lack of a better term, "guarded" the platform area of the auditorium to control the flow of people who might have wished to move toward him. He may have talked to one or two people momentarily but quickly made his way through the door behind the stage and, having passed through it, found solitude and sanctuary.

But Mickey always loved to meet strangers and make sure to accommodate every fan who wanted his or her picture taken with him.

Jerry was set to perform in southeast Texas, a few miles from Beaumont, at a sizable venue that handled everything from concerts to semi-pro basketball games. Mickey and friends made arrangements to attend the show and to visit Jerry. It had been more than three years since Mickey had last seen his rock 'n' roll cousin.

Driving eastward down the fifty-mile stretch of Interstate 10 from Houston, Mickey thought about all the miles he had driven on this road fifty years earlier, traveling along the Interstate between here and New Orleans, spending many nights in clubs and lounges in places like Lake Charles and Lafayette, trying to gain a toehold in the music business in which Jerry was already a superstar.

As they drove along, he wondered quietly how many more chances he would have to see Jerry. The continuing physical struggles from the paralyzing fall eighteen months earlier had cast his life in a new perspective. He now saw it for what life is: fleeting and fragile, a vapor that can vanish in an instant.

Mickey and his entourage reached the venue and headed backstage before Jerry and his handlers drove over from a hotel nearby. Reclining in a chair, adorned in a jacket to keep out the chill, wearing gloves to warm the hands now constantly cold from poor circulation, and donning a baseball cap as usual, Mickey visited with Jerry's band. Kenny Lovelace, Buck Hutcheson, B. B. Cunningham, and drummer Robert Hall were glad to see him, and he fit right in just like one of the guys, as always. As they and others passed through the room, everyone showed a genuine interest in his accident and recuperation, most not having seen him since his perilous fall.

"You playin' the piano yet, Mickey?" inquired Kenny, always a gentleman in the eyes of those who knew him.

"Not yet, Kenny," Mickey said, "but I hope to be back by the end of the year. I hope to be back swinging a golf club even sooner."

It was not lost on Mickey that decades earlier his conversations with fellow musicians had been about wild parties and wild shows and wild women, but now they were mostly about recent health issues and long-forgotten or dead musicians they knew in common.

Percy Sledge was out onstage leading up to the evening's final act when Jerry entered the room through a side door. His road manager and another close friend helped him remove his heavy black coat, worn to shield him from the biting cold on the walk from the car into the building. Most of those in the room were hustled out to allow time for Jerry and Mickey to visit with a minimum of interruptions. Jerry was excited that his cousin had come to see him.

They talked about the old days in Ferriday, about growing up together, walking bridge railings, playing piano, and getting into trouble. They talked about how each was feeling and taking care of himself. They spoke of common friends and relatives.

"Jerry, I just wanted to come tonight and see you because I don't know how long it will be before one of us is called home," Mickey said.

"Well, we're not gettin' any younger," said Jerry, "but hopefully we still have a few more miles to go." He did not want to think or talk too much about serious matters that might produce an uncomfortable feeling he preferred to avoid.

Mickey had only planned to visit Jerry prior to the performance and return to Houston at showtime, but Jerry asked him to stay. The more Mickey sat and visited, the better he felt, and he decided to hang around for a while.

Mickey listened to Jerry's band perform the first three or four songs. As always, Jerry stayed back in the room alone, away from the crowds, seeking a few minutes of solitude before emerging and heading up on the stage.

The band played, anticipation grew, and the audience prepared to see a living rock 'n' roll legend.

When Jerry neared the stage he was energized thanks to increased exercise and an improved diet. Though he moved slowly onstage, a small spring still crept into his step as he made his way to the piano. While not overly talkative by any means, he engaged the crowd between songs more than was customary, with the audience hanging on every word he spoke in his hard-to-understand, gravelly voice. As he finished singing "Drinkin' Wine Spo-dee-o-dee," he chuckled.

"A bottle of wine is just what I need," he said. "In fact, it would probably finish me right off. Nowadays, I like a cold Sprite . . . or maybe a Diet Coke." The audience laughed in appreciation, happy to see him in a mood that made him reachable. These days, his fans were willing to extend him great latitude as performer—what choice did they have?—latching on as they would treasured family heirlooms to shows that went a few minutes longer than normal or included a song they hadn't heard him perform live in years.

From the side of the stage, Mickey sat between two friends. He marveled at the show his seventy-five-year-old cousin could still put on. He noted the charisma and the way Jerry held the rapt attention of the audience. Still, he shook his head at Jerry's approach to doing things—*his* way.

Why doesn't he play more of his hits? he thought. *Where's "Another Place, Another Time"? How about "What Made Milwaukee Famous Made a Loser Out of Me"?*

Outside the occasional number one like "She Even Woke Me Up to Say Good-Bye," the wildly popular "You Win Again" by Hank Williams, and the standard closers of "Whole Lotta Shakin' Going On" and "Great Balls of Fire," Mickey was surprised and underwhelmed at many of the songs to which Jerry gravitated.

To Mickey, who wanted to make sure he did everything possible to please audiences, including focusing on his collection of chart-toppers, Jerry's approach made no sense, focusing as it did on playing what he preferred and expecting everyone to love it, no matter what it was.

Jerry played close to an hour, longer than the forty or fifty minutes he often gave his audiences at this point in his career. His fans were delighted and the crowd was having a great time, evidenced by their fervent cheers and applause. Mickey wondered how much Jerry still cared and how much he might just be going through the motions. He thought about his own shows, which lasted two hours. He thought about a recent occasion when he'd seen Elton John play for nearly three hours. "What a shame," he said to himself. "Jerry could still draw even bigger crowds if he would perform with more commitment, more dedication, and even more drive to please his fans."

Near the end of the performance, Jerry stopped in between songs and said, "Everyone, I want to introduce my cousin from Ferriday, Louisiana—Mickey Gilley."

As Mickey stood up, the crowd rose to its feet, giving him a standing ovation. They had come to see Jerry, but they also knew how special it was to have these two men in the same place. Mickey was emotional, visibly moved to receive this appreciation, acknowledging with a raised hand and nod of his head the kindness of his cousin, a man known for rarely doling out recognition to others.

"God bless you, Mickey," Jerry added, before launching into his finale for the evening, "Whole Lotta Shakin' Going On." As he finished and stood to leave the stage, the crowd erupted, jumping to its collective feet with a rousing ovation. When Jerry neared the edge of the stage, he slowly turned and sauntered back in front of the rowdy crowd, acknowledging their heartfelt appreciation.

Backstage after the show, there were no long discussions or parties like past days. Jerry put his coat on, exchanged a few pleasantries and embraces, and made a quick exit.

Jerry and his entourage proceeded to their car on the cold, blustery evening, with Mickey and his small group of friends following closely behind toward their vehicle parked nearby. As the two cars left the crowded parking lot, the two cousins thought about their encounter and wondered when—or if—the next one might occur.

Backstage, upstairs, a small crowd milled about. Several people stood in a serving line, stabbing chicken fried steaks and spooning mashed potatoes, green beans, and creamed corn on their plates. Downstairs was a 1,000-seat venue in downtown Arlington, Texas, fifteen minutes west of Dallas and fifteen minutes east of Fort Worth. While it sweltered outside, the restaurant adjoining the performance hall was packed, primarily with an over-fifty crowd here to see the evening's performer.

Band members and back-up singers sat at two small, round tables, eating dinner. The promoter's mother made the rounds, offering to get everyone a bottle of water or their favorite soft drink, a refill of tea, or a cold beer. An employee of the music hall spooned banana pudding onto his plate.

On a couch a few feet away Mickey Gilley sat surrounded by friends. He commented on how good the catered dinner was, discussed the meet-and-greet session to start at 7:15, and watched Fox News out of the corner of his eye on the big-screen TV in front of him.

A little later, he lounged on his bus behind the venue. He listened to a demo of a recent song he cut with his band back in his theater in Branson, petted his aging dog, and chatted with Ron Crooks, his keyboard player, and Troy Payne, a fan who had driven up from Houston for the show. He occasionally launched into a humorous verbal sparring session with Al Embry, staged to elicit laughs and smiles from anyone who was listening.

Forty-five minutes before the 8 p.m. opening of the show in the theater, he was back upstairs, taking pictures with a steady stream of admirers filing through, being given a chance to meet, shake hands, and have their picture taken with a country western star. He was friendly to everyone, talking at length as organizers tried to keep the line moving.

An hour later, the show was in full force. Mickey sang many of his number one hits from years gone by and a few lesser-known tunes, told the crowd stories from his career, and produced roaring laughter from his banter with comedian and steel guitarist, Joey Riley.

After the show and a quick change of clothes, Mickey was out among the people. As the band and crew considered the drive tomorrow to another show 200 miles east of here and the performance to follow, they thought about retiring to the bus or hotel. At the suggestion of a long-known songwriter friend of Mickey's that they meet at the hotel bar for additional conversation, the lone voice to sing a ringing endorsement was Mickey himself.

"If you're up for it, so am I!"

– 53 –

JIMMY'S REDEMPTION

There's a light in the window the table's spread in splendor
Someone's standing by the open door
I can see a crystal river I must be near forever
Lord, I've never been this homesick before

Jimmy sat at the Baldwin piano to the left of the stage and
began to sing the Dottie Rambo gospel classic "I've Never Been
This Homesick Before." As the words flowed, the emotion of his
long walk as a preacher, and a man, along this narrow path overtook him.

See the bright light shine, it's just about home time
I can see my Father standing at the door
This world's been a wilderness, I'm ready for deliverance
Lord, I've never been this homesick before

Never shy about showing emotion, the tears ran freely down
his cheeks. He thought about his family, spurring a new stream of
tears.

I can see the family gather sweet faces all familiar
No one's old or feeble anymore
This lonesome heart is crying; think I'll spread my wings for flying
Lord, I've never been this homesick before

Jimmy brought the music to a temporary halt, lips quivering, as he addressed the congregation. Most were seated, either watching him closely, or with eyes closed, lost in their own thoughts and memories.

"I can see all my family at that table." His eyes roamed from the audience, turning upward, looking heavenward toward a picture that only his mind could see. "My mother is there. My grandmother is there. My sister is there. My father and my grandfather are there."

He thought first and foremost about the two key women in the formative years of his life, before the third key woman in his life, sitting across the stage from him now, came along. Both women have now been dead for over half a century, but their loving faces and staunch encouragement never left him.

See the bright light shine, it's just about home time
I can see my Father standing at the door
This world's been a wilderness, I'm ready for deliverance
Lord, I've never been this homesick before

For thirty minutes the music continued. When the emotion came, Jimmy did what always came naturally. His fingers glided over the piano keys and the song began anew.

More than three quarters of a century after first drawing breath, well over half a century after entering the ministry, and a quarter of a decade after his great stumble, Reverend Jimmy Swaggart still pushed forward, tirelessly, relentlessly, doing the things he believed he was destined to do—preaching, playing, singing, and sharing with those who will still listen to the message that changed the lives of his family and himself in that small, white wooden church in Ferriday many decades ago.

Always able to bear an enormous workload, he maintained an amazing pace for a man in his seventies, a pace that would have challenged a man half his age. He still conducted his daily teaching program, preached regularly, was active in ministry activities, and continued to devote considerable time to his own personal walk. Those that supported him marveled at his stamina and strength. Jerry would easily pass for a man ten years older; Jimmy would just as easily convince an observer he was ten years younger than he was.

At the piano, his voice was still rich and full. His fingers didn't move quite as quickly, but his piano playing never was driven by speed. His fingers still glided over the keys expertly and softly, and his right hand runs were unchanged from those of two decades ago. He was noticeably more tired after a two-hour service—which included a fifty- to sixty-minute sermon—but he delivered it with vigor and enthusiasm. Over time, he came to rely more on Donnie and other ministers to assist with the preaching.

He never lost sight of his beginnings. "I still see myself sitting on the floor," he wrote, "leaning on the couch with my back up against it. There was an utterance in tongues given. I don't remember who gave it . . . but it said something that had been dealing with my little nine-year-old heart for months. 'You will preach my gospel all over the world. You will take it even to Africa'—I remember that distinctly. I knew the Holy Spirit was talking about this poor, pitiful, now preacher, then child. I knew it. I had no doubt about it."

As would any man raised by Son and Minnie Bell Swaggart, Jimmy still held to his fierce personal convictions. Despite all the criticisms of his uncompromising remarks, he remained fearless in the sermons he preached. On regular occasions, he would look out beyond the church crowd to one of the television cameras scattered throughout the sanctuary, peer into the camera with a finger pointing, and declare, "I want you sitting in this church and listening by radio or watching by TV or the Internet to know that this church still preaches the Cross, and the power of Jesus, and that Greater is He that is within me than he that is in the world!"

He had long been accustomed to raising eyebrows. He grew up seeing them when his family walked down Louisiana Avenue on their way to church; he saw them when he didn't follow other boys into the Arcade Theater Saturday matinee. He learned that the Pentecostals were a mysterious bunch, a group with whom he felt increasingly comfortable. As he once told a reporter from *Mother Jones,* "This is what's fun about being a Pentecostal. The world already thinks you're crazy. The people on the block think you're dealing with half a deck, so you have nothing to lose."

Just as Jerry faced the challenge of reconciling his worldly self with his spiritual being, Jimmy faced the challenge of reconciling his own spiritual being with the human who lived and breathed in this world. At various moments in his sermons, one could hear the never-ending reconciliation process at work, and these snippets gave the sense that Jimmy had learned much in his own personal struggle.

"I did not understand how to live victoriously in the 1980s," he told his congregation.

The core central message of the ministry became the message of the cross of Christ and the power it has to produce not only salvation but sanctification—clean living, if you will—in the life of the believer. Key in Jimmy's words was the message that self-reliance promotes lack of reliance on God, that it produces pride and, ultimately, failure.

When Jimmy preached a soft-voiced sermon about the power of sin and the gospel message of redemption for that sin, an objective listener could feel the honesty with which he delivered the message—honesty built upon decades of fighting a tireless human struggle.

It was a struggle built on failure and forgiveness, repeated time and time again, as imperfection and weakness yielded harmful results that led, over and over again, to conviction and repentance.

As everyone must, Jimmy was forced to come to grips with his humanity, but in a much more public way than others. He was forced to face the disappointment he felt in himself. For the thoughtful observer, the aftermath of his mishaps are more instructive and helpful than all the great works and great sermons that came before. Author Lawrence Wright wrote, "Many people try to hide human frailty behind the mask of holiness and spiritual certitude. Their faith is a portrayal of the life they would lead if they were something other than the all-too-human they actually are."

In Randall Balmer's article about Jimmy for *Christianity Today*, he wrote about the public's response to Jimmy's failings: "All of us wrestle with demons, whether we use that terminology or not. They may or may not be sexual, as with Swaggart, but from time to time we feel ourselves slipping into dark waters, and the undertow seems all too overwhelming. Swaggart, with his tears and his sweat and his tortured confession, seems all too human, and let's face it, we evangelicals prefer our heroes to be anodyne and in control, tidy and triumphant. Swaggart makes us uncomfortable by reminding us of ourselves, but rather than facing our faults, our humanity, it's easier to change the subject and dismiss Swaggart with ridicule. More the pity, for it is only by gazing into the mirror of our own wretchedness that we begin to comprehend the magnificence of grace."

It is clear, over time, that many forgave Jimmy. By 2010, their faith, in the form of contributions, made it possible for the Swaggarts to establish the SonLife Broadcasting Network, a worldwide television ministry broadcast to tens of millions of homes in the United States within a year of its inception, with no end in sight to its continued growth, both domestic and international. Jimmy's ministry always flew under the radar of many in the mainstream media, but the next meteoric rise of his expansive television presence was quite remarkable.

On the air seven days a week, twenty-four hours per day with programming that emanated solely from the ministry were shows hosted by Jimmy, Frances, and other ministers, taped services and sermons featuring Jimmy and Donnie, hours of music by Jimmy and other musicians and singers, and live church services from Family Worship Center broadcasted on Sunday morning and Wednesday and Sunday evenings.

The ministry's twice-annual "camp meetings"—four to five days around Easter and Thanksgiving with, typically, four services per day—brought in large crowds of supporters from around the country and the world. The crowds did not reach the levels of the ministry's heyday over two decades ago, but a sense of optimism and momentum within the Bluebonnet Road headquarters existed, especially in the heart and mind of a man who still believed, as he did some fifty years ago, that he was a notable traveler on a great and noble journey.

These weren't the $150-million-per-year days, but they were a cause for great excitement for Jimmy's long suffering sympathizers and a reconfirmation to everyone of the power of perseverance.

In the short time following its inception, the new network had reached a new generation of potential viewers and prior supporters, producing a significant increase in outreach. Through radio, television, and Internet distribution to the masses, the pews of the Family Worship Center began to refill and the spigots of financial support began to flow more freely.

Jimmy acknowledged the oddity of establishing and operating a successful around-the-clock television network at this stage of life, but he drew strength from Old Testament figures whose greatest accomplishments came at advanced ages.

While the enterprise will face a monumental task to thrive when its leader is no longer there to guide it, there are concerted efforts to establish a replacement-by-committee solution to the enemy of time. Jimmy's son, Donnie, has become an improved preacher and is an effective public speaker who can weave a fascinating story nearly as well as his dad. To his credit, Donnie has been better in toning down much of the anger and inflammatory tone of his messages from his earlier years of preaching. Jimmy's grandson, Gabriel, has also become a minister at Family Worship Center and on the road. Several other preachers in the ministry fill key niches, though none offer Jimmy's combination of talent, appeal, and charisma. And none of the younger Swaggart men have the musical talent of their patriarch.

Conclusive history is written long after the ink has dried on the final page of the book that tells a person's life. Just as the talent and persona of Jerry Lee Lewis point to an increasingly favorable view of him in rock 'n' roll history, so will the impact of Reverend Jimmy Swaggart likely shine brighter as the weight of his human frailties recedes with time, and the impact of his accomplishments is seen with greater clarity.

His extensive reach into Central and South America produced a Pentecostal toehold that has impacted tens of millions today and for generations to come. In his short-lived but historic televised appearances in China and the Soviet Union, his message was heard by tens of millions.

As a gospel musician, he reached countless people directly and, according to ministry statistics, sold more than eighteen million albums in the over fifty years he recorded, sang, and played his "golden gospel piano."

Ultimately, Jimmy's story—like Jerry's and Mickey's—is one of perseverance. "I don't know how to overcome the world," Jimmy once said, "but by the grace of God, I'm going to find out."

The man who often called himself "an old-fashioned, Holy Ghost-filled, shouting, weeping, soul-winning, gospel-preaching preacher" couldn't avoid being knocked down in shocking fashion, but he plowed ahead, determined, unbending, even in the face of his own internal fear and trembling.

"God told me to preach," he once said, "and I'm going to preach this Book . . . Even if Frances and I have to go back to pulling that little old U-Haul, and this Book is all I have left in the whole wide world, I'm gonna preach it. So write it down, church. When they get it all but the clothes on my back, I'm just gonna take this Book an' find me an oak tree somewhere—and preach the Gospel!"

When they were counted out, Jerry, Jimmy, and Mickey hung in, facing adversity. It will be interesting to see if the man his cousin Linda Gail Lewis described as being "as close to a living saint as I have ever physically known" will have the last laugh in the final evaluation of his life and his ministry.

How will the world remember him? As is the case with his rock 'n' roll and country western cousins, it is difficult to determine how much he cares—if at all.

– 54 –

SURVIVAL

It was a cool evening, the first weekend of October in Memphis, self-proclaimed home of rock 'n' roll. A few minutes before 7 p.m.—the start time designated in the official invitation—it was still light outside, but the day was fading fast.

The venue was the Warehouse, converted from a historic place of business into a frequent locale for parties, events, and fund-raisers and situated only seven blocks south and three blocks east of the heart of storied Beale Street, where the Blues was born. As guests entered they saw a giant sign that read *Happy 75th Birthday, Jerry Lee Lewis.*

A huge screen in one corner of the room was emblazoned with an image of the cover of his 2006 album, *Last Man Standing*, and pictured him in a bright yellow jacket and black slacks hovering over a grand piano that had flames blazing from it. Videos were projected onto an overhead screen. One was made in England in 1964 and depicts Jerry pounding mercilessly on the piano, displaying an enormous energy contrasted with a deadness in his eyes betraying utter exhaustion.

Hanging to the right of the stage on which a number of musical instruments were arranged was a replica of Sun Records album 267 that measured six feet in diameter and featured an outsized replica of the famous yellow Sun label, and the name of the record "Whole Lotta Shakin' Going On." The wooden beams throughout

420

the building were adorned with streamers and rock 'n' roll memorabilia. Tables and chairs dotted the large room. Some 300 people milled about as they awaited the guest of honor. They bought drinks at the cash bar and ate chicken fingers, meatballs, and cookies. Many of them were Memphis locals who knew each other well. Others had come from as far away as New York and California. They roamed about, taking pictures and greeting old friends, while the hardcore music fans sought out many of the older gentlemen whom they recognized as notable performers of yesteryear. Two security guards observed the evening's activities, ready to prevent any surprise behavior, although this crowd was a lot more docile than it might have been twenty-five years earlier—which could also be said of the evening's man of honor.

There were many here from Jerry's past. J. M. Van Eaton, the drummer who had to be picked up after high school back in 1957 and taken to the recording sessions at Sun, mingled with the crowd. There was Cowboy Jack Clement, the first man to ever record Jerry at Sun Records, who made the trek down from his home in Nashville to be here on this special occasion.

Milling through the crowd was Jerry's bandleader and friend of nearly half a century, Kenny Lovelace. Jerry's guitar players, Buck Hutcheson and B. B. Cunningham, were here; so was his drummer, Robert Hall. A local television reporter interviewed George Klein, one of rock 'n' roll's most famous disc jockeys and a close friend of Elvis.

With the room filled to near capacity, a door in one corner of the Warehouse opened and a small entourage emerged. In its midst was the seventy-five-year-old center of attention, adorned in dark jeans, white shirt, black vest, and jacket. He walked slowly and with a noticeable stoop. He was led to a group of booths in the center, roped off from the rest of the room, where he sat down, facing the stage.

The crowd began to circle the roped-off area, clamoring to see him, snapping endless pictures, changing angles, snapping more pictures. Slowly, a few individuals—disproportionately attractive women and aging music personalities—were allowed within the roped area to offer him personal birthday wishes. A few old-timers leaned in to have a chuckle with the Killer and most of the good-looking women had their picture taken as they nestled up close to him.

Jerry was keenly aware of what was occurring. The excitement, the bustle to catch a glimpse or get that perfect snapshot were familiar reactions. He became engaged every so often by some greeting or comment but was largely detached from the scene, one that he had experienced so many times since he was barely twenty years old that he had come to expect it.

He appreciated the adoration of his fans as a referendum on his talent and ability but suffered through occasions like this one, when it appeared he would rather be at home in his pajamas watching *Gunsmoke* or an old black-and-white movie. He knew the game and he played it but did so on his own terms, and by now everyone had come to accept that about him. No one here had any idea whether he would stay fifteen minutes or three hours but accepted that from him.

During a brief ceremony, the Chamber of Commerce gave an award to Jerry and announced a commemoration of Jerry Lee Lewis Day, local personalities and politicians spoke a few words, and George Klein offered kind remarks and a couple of interesting stories from times past. Afterward, Jerry smoked a large cigar and, never moving from his seat, smiled occasionally and shook hands with those that entered the "circle" formed by the ropes.

After an hour, Jerry slowly rose from his seat and made his way through the crowd. As he did so, a young man stepped out to shake his hand and offered him birthday congratulations. Jerry stopped, turned his head, and looked at the stranger. His fiery eyes looked into those of the man standing before him. In that instant, it was unclear whether this was a moment of a warm handshake or an ice-cold glare. Ever since Jerry has entered the public eye, his nature has been a matter of debate. Is Jerry Lee Lewis a warm, caring, God-fearing man or an icy, standoffish hellion? Or is he somehow both?

In either case, he left the room and the revelers, and headed off into the night.

It was late spring. In Las Vegas, 12,000 people came from all over the world for a rockabilly festival that featured a variety of music acts and vintage car shows. Many in attendance, young and old, were dressed as though preparing for an audition of *Grease*, with leather jackets, slicked back hair, crinolines, and bobby sox. They spent the afternoon looking at endless rows of classic automobiles, buying all manner of old rock 'n' roll souvenirs and memorabilia, and applying gallons of sun screen and consuming large reservoirs of beverages—alcoholic and nonalcoholic—to fight off the effects of the Nevada sun. The men ranged from young motorcycle gang members to mellowed old-timers. The women varied from twenty-something hotties with a variety of cosmetic enhancements to sweet little old ladies who still enjoyed the music of their youth.

They steadily congregated in front of the main stage, listening to music and readying themselves for the headlining music act, the "Last Man Standing" from Sun Records glory days of the fifties— Jerry Lee Lewis.

Inside the green room, away from the outdoor venue where the crowd was building, were the members of Jerry's entourage. Kenny, Buck, and Robert sat quietly and chatted about the Betty Page lookalike contest Robert happened upon earlier in the day. Buck wandered toward the back of the room, his eyes wandering over the iced water and soft drinks provided for the group. J. W. Whitten was in and out of the room, coordinating details—significant and insignificant—with event staff and other notables in attendance.

In a separate room across the hall, Linda Gail sat and chatted with Jerry and his friend Judith. The three were discussing a long-ago performance where the mixture of hot sun, a long afternoon of music, and free-flowing liquor had produced a rowdy, disagreeable audience.

Jerry watched the interaction. With his increased focus on taking care of himself physically and the increased presence of Linda Gail, Frankie Jean, and other family members in his life, Jerry seemed happier than he had in decades. His popularity had resurged, and many of those close to him who were largely absent during his years with Kerrie were back. As showtime neared, the opening-act duo of Linda Gail and her daughter Annie Marie Dolan and each of the Memphis Beats, Jerry's band, filed out slowly toward the stage. With the hint of music from the stage dissipating when the door closed behind Kenny, the last musician out the door, this backstage area became strangely quiet. The hum of the air conditioner was a steady sound filling the air. The only other sounds were the faint discussion between Jerry and Judith, like two people sitting in an empty waiting room at the doctor's office, voices hushed as they speak about "normal" kinds of things—the longtime friend from Los Angeles who had been allowed backstage briefly to say hello, a missed button on the sleeve of Jerry's shirt, the first Cadillac Jerry ever bought, a remembrance sparked by his having seen the same model when driving by the car show on the way to the venue. Someone knocked softly and poked his head in the door.

"Sorry to bother you. The limo should pull up in the arena in about ten minutes to take you out to the stage."

"Will you let us know when it's here?" inquired Judith, receiving an expected nod and affirmative remark.

"Are they pickin' and grinnin' out there?" Jerry asked in his rough, Southern voice.

"They're warming them up for you, Mr. Lewis."

"That's what I figured," responded Jerry, a warm smile on his face.

A quarter hour later, Jerry Lee Lewis climbed the steps to the stage, a few feet from the backseat of his limousine. Thousands of cheering, clapping fans, flashing cameras, security personnel, and fans leaning over railings greeted him as he took his seat at the piano.

He looked out over the crowd, a size of which he would never have expected ten years ago as he sat feeling abandoned in his home just south of Memphis "waiting to die." He adjusted the microphone and turned to his right from the piano stool to face this Vegas crowd.

"That sunshine sure is bright. But it looks like we're gonna have us a crowd today."

His performance was customarily short but his piano solos were strong; he engaged with the audience and was in a visibly good mood. These were the moments his die-hard fans waited for, when Jerry was in good spirits. After several songs, he yelled an emphatic "Mercy!" and on one occasion leaned back on his stool and gave a spirited karate chop over the top of the piano. On a piano solo during "Headstone on My Grave," his right hand ran up the keys playfully and continued a dozen inches beyond the rightmost end of the piano; at another point he extended his left hand over his right as both worked on dual magic tricks at the high end of the keyboard, signs that he was pushing himself to give a little extra today.

His discourse with the audience covered a wide variety of topics that flowed through his head.

"This is a good piano but it's outta tune. I thought I'd let you know in case some of you were wonderin'. But sometimes that's the way it goes."

"That's rock 'n' roll! Not bad for a Louisiana boy, huh?"

"I want a play a little Gene Autry for ya. My daddy loved this song. I like it. So I think you oughta like it too," he asserted before launching into "Mexicali Rose."

He closed with "Whole Lotta Shakin' Going On," after which he knocked the piano stool over and across the stage; he spent a longer-than-normal time playing the piano standing up, thrilling his fans. His hands were amazingly crisp and still lightning-quick on the keys. He had long since stopped jumping on top of the piano and playing the instrument with his feet, but this was still an impressive display of daunting speed and talent.

Dancing a little for the audience on his way off stage, Jerry enjoyed the crowd. Watching the intimate gatherings backstage and the public interactions in front of this crowd, it seemed that this man, who had made so many people happy yet had been so swamped in misery, had reached a good place in his life.

Jerry Lee Lewis and Jimmy Lee Swaggart become more intriguing when considered together. Linked through the DNA of being double-cousins and similar, close childhoods, they have been called alter egos and opposite sides of the same coin. Both have wondered about the "what ifs" had each chosen the path of the other. Psychologist Jim Dolan observed an unusual connection in the two men: "Jerry's public identity is Jimmy's repressed identity, while Jimmy's public identity has been Jerry's repressed identity. The two men were amazingly connected to one another psychologically."

They were similar in other ways, too. Both had musical gifts and charisma that overwhelmed them at various junctures. Both were unprepared by their backgrounds to deal with the issues that come with world-class talent and superstardom. Both had a dual sense of grandiosity and inferiority, though they coped with it differently. As opposed to the down-to-earth Mickey, both Jerry and Jimmy seem larger than life. Yet neither man has Mickey's sense of comfort when dealing with everyday life and everyday people.

All three men have grappled with the human condition, with the weakness and fears and fallibility that inevitably accompany it. Yet their music seems to emanate from a different place and has the power to inspire, excite, produce tears or laughter, and above all, give hope.

Their story is not about good and bad or right and wrong. It is a story that suggests that hope should never be lost. It is not the story of man overcoming who he is—it is the story of man's accepting who he is, and who he is not, so that he can become something better.

Their story is about finding the good within the bad, accepting the bad within the good, and recognizing all men are a mixture of both.

Jerry Lee Lewis, Jimmy Lee Swaggart, and Mickey Leroy Gilley are ultimately defined by their music and their perseverance. Their music will last; it will never cease to communicate to those who listen, ready to be amazed and waiting to be moved.

As children playing Conquered Unconquered on the bridge spanning over the mighty Mississippi River, Jerry had climbed up the railing and challenged Jimmy and Mickey to follow him. They had refused. Yet as men, all three would be forced to climb up on the railing and face challenges in their life more fearsome and threatening than the rushing waters on that day so long ago.

They faced those challenges—sometimes majestically, sometimes haltingly, and sometimes painfully. What is most remarkable about these three cousins from Ferriday, Louisiana, is that they have remained truly unconquered.

Appendix A
SUMMARIZED FAMILY TREE

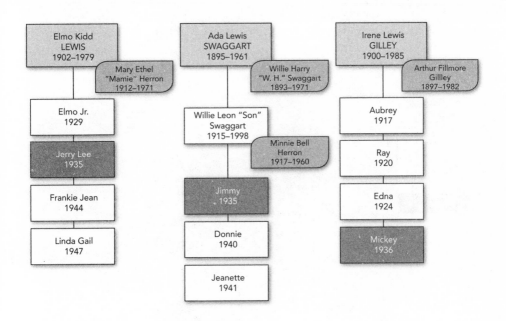

Comments:

- On the Lewis side:
  - » Jerry and Mickey are first cousins (Jerry's father and Mickey's mother are siblings)
  - » Jerry and Jimmy are first cousins once removed (Jerry's father and Jimmy's grandmother are siblings)
  - » Jimmy and Mickey are first cousins once removed (Jimmy's grandmother and Mickey's mother are siblings)
- On the Herron side, Jerry and Jimmy are first cousins (their mothers are sisters)
- The family of Elmo, Ada, and Irene Lewis included eleven siblings
- Another of the Lewis siblings, Jane, is the grandmother of Myra Brown Lewis (Jerry's third wife), making Jerry and Myra first cousins once removed
- The family of Mamie and Minnie Bell Herron included seven siblings

Appendix B

MAP 1

Downtown Ferriday
(and surrounding streets)

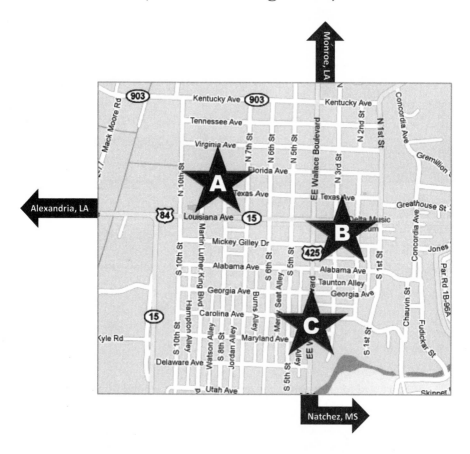

A   Assembly of God Church (NW corner Eighth and Texas)

B   Arcade Theater (Second and Louisiana)

C   Former Site of Haney's Big House
         (SW corner Carolina and Fourth; now EE Wallace Blvd)

MAP 2

Key Origins and Destinations

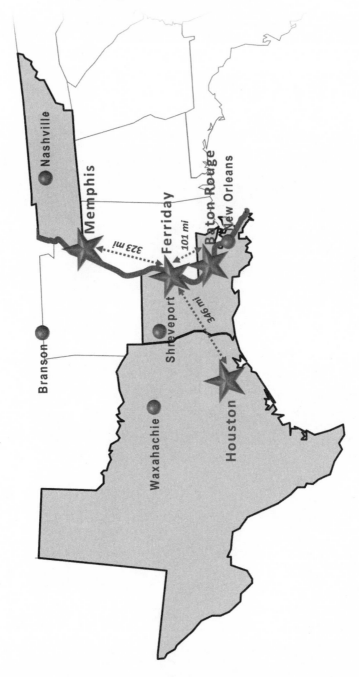

Appendix C

TIME LINE OF EVENTS

1856 Leroy Lewis born (Jerry and Mickey's grandfather, Jimmy's great-grandfather).

1874 Arilla Hampton Lewis born (Jerry and Mickey's grandmother, Jimmy's great-grandmother).

1888 Leroy Lewis marries Arilla Hampton.

1893 Willie Harry "W. H." Swaggart born (Jimmy's grandfather).

1895 Ada Lewis Swaggart born (Jimmy's grandmother).

1897 Arthur Fillmore Gilley born (Mickey's father).

1900 Modern Pentecostal revival begins in Topeka, Kansas, as Agnes Ozman prays in tongues. Irene Lewis Gilley born (Mickey's mother).

1902 Elmo Kidd Lewis born (Jerry's father).

1906 Ferriday, Louisiana, is officially incorporated.

1911 Robert Johnson born in Hazlehurst, Mississippi.

1912 Mary Ethel "Mamie" Herron Lewis born (Jerry's mother).

1914 Assembly of God denomination established in Hot Springs, Arkansas.

1915 W. H. "Son" Swaggart born (Jimmy's father).

1917 Minnie Bell Herron Swaggart born (Jimmy's mother).

1918 Billy Graham born near Charlotte, North Carolina.

1923 Sam Phillips born near Florence, Alabama. Hank Williams born near Georgiana, Alabama.

1924 Edna Gilley Mequet born (Mickey's sister).

1925 *The Grand Ole Opry* begins on WSM.

1926 Chuck Berry born in St. Louis, Missouri.

1927 Jimmie Rodgers, the "Singing Brakeman," makes his first recording. Sherwood Cryer born in Diboll, Texas.

1929 Elmo marries Mamie. Elmo Jr. born (Jerry's brother).

1932 Richard Penniman (a.k.a. Little Richard) born in Macon, Georgia.

1934 Son marries Minnie Bell.

1935 Elvis Presley born. Huey Long is assassinated. Lee, Elmo, and Son caught moonshining. Jerry Lee Lewis and Jimmy Lee Swaggart born.

1936 Leona and Mother Sumrall come to Ferriday to begin an Assembly of God church. Mickey Leroy Gilley born.

1937 Leroy Lewis dies.

1938 Robert Johnson dies after being poisoned three days earlier. Elmo Jr. is killed by a drunk driver.

1940 Donnie Swaggart born (Jimmy's brother).

1941 The Assembly of God church building is constructed in Ferriday. Donnie dies. Jeannette born (Jimmy's sister).

1942 Son and Minnie Bell get saved at the Assembly of God church.

1943 Irene Gilley, Minnie Bell Swaggart, and Mamie Lewis, and later Jimmy, are filled with the Holy Ghost in Assembly of God church in Ferriday.

1944 National Religious Broadcasters (NRB) is formed. Ferriday has a massive flood. Jimmy speaks in tongues and prophetically in English, some believe about the "bomb." Myra Gale Brown Lewis and Frankie Jean Lewis Terrell (Jerry's sister) born.

1945 Atomic bombs are dropped on Hiroshima and later Nagasaki. Soon afterward, the Japanese formally surrender aboard the USS Missouri on V-J Day.

1947 Jimmy "backslides" and begins to take part in burglary and petty crime around Ferriday. Linda Gail Lewis Braddock born (Jerry's sister).

1949 Hank Williams's "Lovesick Blues" reaches the top of the charts, becoming his first number one hit; he later debuts on *The Grand Ole Opry* in a memorable performance. Jerry plays at the Ford dealership in Ferriday, considered by many his first public performance. Son Swaggart becomes a full-time preacher, and Billy Graham arrives in Los Angeles for the revival that will give him notoriety throughout the country.

1950 Sam Phillips opens his Memphis Recording Service (later Sun Records) at 706 Union Avenue. Jimmy and Jerry participate in a talent show; Jimmy feels "the anointing of the devil." Oral Roberts bursts on the scene as a tent revivalist.

1952 Hank Williams plays his final performance at the Skyline Club in Austin, Texas. Jerry marries Dorothy Barton and attends Southwestern Bible College in Waxahachie, Texas. Jimmy marries Frances Orelia Anderson.

1953 Hank Williams dies in the middle of the night in the backseat of a car on the way to a performance in Canton, Ohio. Jerry marries Jane Mitcham, and Mickey marries Geraldine Garrett. Jimmy recommits his life to God. Dorothy is granted a divorce from Jerry.

1954 Elvis Presley records "That's All Right" at Sun Records in Memphis. Jerry goes to Shreveport to audition for *Louisiana Hayride*, and later travels to Nashville to attempt to break into the music industry. Jerry Lee Lewis Jr., Donnie Swaggart, and Michael Gilley born.

1955 Chuck Berry records "Maybellene" at Chess Records in Chicago; Little Richard records "Tutti Frutti" at J&M Recording Service in New Orleans. Sam Phillips sells Elvis's recording contract to RCA, Hill & Range, and Colonel Tom Parker.

1956 Jerry makes two visits to Sun Records in Memphis, where "Crazy Arms" is recorded. He later participates in the Million-Dollar Quartet session at Sun Records.

1957 Sun Records releases "Whole Lotta Shakin' Going On"; Mickey sees Jerry perform when he comes to Dement Stadium outside Houston and decides to try the music business. Jerry gives his first performance on *The Steve Allen Show*. "Great Balls of Fire" is recorded; Jerry and Sam have their famous "hell" argument. Jerry marries Myra Gale Brown.

1958 "Down the Line–Breathless," Jerry's fourth record for Sun, is released; Alan Freed's 68-concert, 42-day, 37-city Big Beat Tour begins in New York. Jane is granted a divorce from Jerry, and there is confusion whether the marriage was ever legal in the first place. Ferriday celebrates Jerry Lee Lewis Day. Jerry arrives in London for his first England tour, which is later cancelled. Jimmy enters the ministry full-time; he later contracts pneumonia and questions his decision to go into ministry. Jimmy also turns down offer from Sun Records to record gospel music. Kathy Kay and Keith Ray Gilley born.

1959   Buddy Holly, Ritchie Valens, and J. P. "The Big Bopper" Richardson die in a plane crash. Jimmy is refused ordination into the Assemblies of God. Mickey's song "Is It Wrong" becomes a local hit in Houston. Stevie Allen Lewis born.

1960   Minnie Bell Herron Swaggart dies. Mickey moves from the Ranch House to the Nesadel as the nightly entertainer, where he will stay for ten years.

1961   Ada Lewis Swaggart dies. Mickey and Geraldine divorce.

1962   Steve Allen Lewis drowns; Jerry arrives in London for his second England tour, a resounding success in the midst of his own mourning. Elmo and Mamie Lewis divorce. Jimmy records his second album, *God Took Away My Yesterdays*, and begins to become established as a musician. Mickey marries Vivian McDonald.

1963   Beatles release "I Want to Hold Your Hand"; Beatlemania begins. Jerry's contract with Sun Records ends, and he signs a new one with Smash, a division of Mercury. Phoebe Allen Lewis is born.

1964   Jerry gives a famous performance at the Star Club in Hamburg, Germany, followed by his "Greatest Live Show on Earth" in Birmingham, Alabama. "Lonely Wine" becomes Mickey's biggest hit so far, but still mostly regional.

1965   Alan Freed dies, broke and suffering from alcoholism. Jerry's band members are busted with drugs in Grand Prairie, Texas.

1966   Haney's Big House burns down. Gregory Gilley born.

1967   Norman Carlson joins Mickey's band; Kenny Lovelace meets Jerry and joins his band. Jimmy and Frances build their first home, in Baton Rouge.

1968   Jerry records "Another Place, Another Time," which will produce his return to the charts, this time in country music. Later, "To Make Love Sweeter for You" is recorded and becomes his first number one hit since "Great Balls of Fire."

1969   Will Haney and Lee Calhoun die. Billboard names Jerry "Country Music Artist of the Year." The *Camp Meeting Hour* radio program begins and Jimmy becomes the youngest keynote speaker at the General Assembly of the Assemblies of God.

1970   Janis Joplin dies of a heroin overdose in Los Angeles. Mickey leaves the Nesadel and joins the Bellaire Ballroom. Myra files for divorce from Jerry. *CBS Evening News with Walter Cronkite* reports that Jerry is giving up rock 'n' roll for gospel.

1971   Mamie Lewis and W. H. "Pa" Swaggart die. Myra's divorce from Jerry is finalized and Jerry marries Jaren Gunn Pate. Jimmy has the best-selling gospel album in the country. Gilley's opens in Pasadena, Texas.

1973   Jimmy begins to air a program on television. Mickey records "She Called Me Baby" for local jukeboxes at the request of Minnie Elerick and records "Room Full of Roses" as a B side. Jerry makes his debut at *The Grand Ole Opry*; he is nominated for his first Grammy with "Chantilly Lace," and John Lennon kisses Jerry's feet backstage at the Roxy in California. Jerry Lee Jr. is killed in a car accident.

1974   "Room Full of Roses" is released and becomes Mickey's first number one hit. He makes his first appearance at *The Grand Ole Opry* and is recognized by the Country Music Association as the "Most Promising Male Artist" after three number one hits in 1974.

1975   Authorities meet Jerry's plane in Denver and find drugs onboard.

1976   Jerry shoots guitarist Butch Owens in the chest; Jimmy makes a televised plea for the salvation of Jerry's soul, and Mickey and Jerry perform together at Gilley's. Later, less than twenty-four hours after overturning a Rolls Royce, Jerry is arrested trying to break through the gates of Graceland.

1977   Elvis Presley dies. Jerry's gallbladder is removed and a litany of health issues are addressed in a Memphis hospital. Mickey wins six awards at the Academy of Country Music Awards, including Entertainer of the Year. Mickey Gilley Day is proclaimed in the state of Texas.

1978   Aaron Latham's article, "Ballad of the Urban Cowboy," is published in *Esquire* magazine.

1979   Filming of *Urban Cowboy* at Gilley's begins. IRS seizes property from the Lewis Ranch in Nesbit, Mississippi. Elmo Lewis dies.

1980   Jim Bakker has a sexual liason with Jessica Hahn. *Urban Cowboy* premieres in the Houston area. "True Love Ways" and "Stand by Me" are released simultaneously and both go to number one on the country charts.

1981   Zoe Vance dies and leaves her estate to Jimmy Swaggart Ministries; the will is contested in court by the family. Jerry undergoes 4.5-hour emergency operation in Memphis to repair a two-inch perforation in his stomach, and is near death.

1982 Jaren Lewis drowns. Jimmy rescues Jerry off the stage in Ohio. Arthur Gilley dies. Later, Mickey and Jerry play six sellout shows together.

1983 Jerry marries Shawn Stephens; the same year, Shawn dies of a methadone overdose. Jimmy's Family Worship Center receives a dedication, and John Camp and WBRZ in Baton Rouge air *Give Me That Big Time Religion*, a profile of Jimmy and his ministry.

1984 Mickey goes on *Hour Magazine* with Irene and gets a star on the Hollywood Walk of Fame. The Jimmy Swaggart Bible College begins. Jerry marries Kerrie McCarver. He is acquitted of income tax evasion, but still owes approximately $650,000 to the IRS.

1985 Jerry nearly dies from a bleeding ulcer. In a four-hour operation, doctors remove one third of Jerry's stomach, but his survival is questionable. Mickey performs on the White House lawn for President Reagan at his Congressional BBQ. Irene Gilley dies.

1986 Marvin Gorman steps down as pastor of New Orleans First Assembly of God. Jerry is part of the inaugural class of inductees in the Rock 'n' Roll Hall of Fame. Jerry enrolls in the Betty Ford Clinic for forty days, but only stays two.

1987 Jerry Lee Lewis III born. Oral Roberts announces on his program that God will "take him home" if he doesn't raise $8 million by March 31. Jim Bakker resigns from PTL Ministry after financial and moral mishaps are uncovered. Marvin Gorman sues Jimmy for $90 million. Later, Jimmy is caught outside a New Orleans hotel with Debra Murphree. Mickey files suit against Sherwood Cryer for business improprieties and gives his first performance in Branson, Missouri, at the Roy Clark Theatre. Jerry wins his first Grammy for "Class of '55."

1988 Roy Orbison dies. Mickey is awarded $17 million in his lawsuit against Sherwood Cryer; Mickey charts, for the last time, with "She Reminded Me of You" at number twenty-two. Jimmy is called to meet with the Executive Presbytery of the Assemblies of God in Springfield, Missouri to discuss his mishap. Jimmy delivers his tearful "I Have Sinned" apology on television; the Executive Presbytery of Assembly of God overrules the Louisiana Council's three-month ban on Swaggart and instead issues one-year ban. Jimmy resigns from Assemblies of God and is dismissed. Jimmy then returns to the pulpit after three months, despite the harsher punishment from Assemblies of God. Debra Murphree appears in *Penthouse*.

1989 *Great Balls of Fire* the film is released by Orion to poor reviews and lackluster box office performance. Jimmy's telecast goes on in China largely unreported. The doors of Gilley's close permanently.

1990 Jimmy's telecast goes on in Russia, also largely unreported. Gilley's Family Theatre opens in Branson, Missouri, and Gilley's in Pasadena, Texas, burns down. Mickey and Sherwood settle.

1991 Marvin Gorman is awarded $10 million from Jimmy; the decision is later appealed and settled out of court. Jimmy is stopped by police in Indio, California, with a prostitute and pornography in the car.

1993 Conway Twitty, a country-music legend and a regular performer at Mickey's theatre, dies. Jerry and the family move to Ireland to escape IRS problems. A fire closes Mickey Gilley's theater in Branson for eleven months.

1994 Jerry reaches a settlement agreement with the IRS.

1995 Charlie Rich dies.

1996 Stella Calhoun dies. Jimmy Swaggart Ministries sells 175 acres of land, later to become the Mall of Louisiana.

1997 The infamous Travel Inn on Airline Highway is torn down to make way for new construction. *CNN Impact* does a story on Jimmy, questioning the financial practices of the ministry.

1998 Carl Perkins and Son Swaggart die.

2002 The three cousins are inducted into the Delta Music Museum in Ferriday; Jimmy and Mickey attend, Jerry does not.

2003 Sam Phillips and Johnny Cash die. Mickey avoids disaster as his appendix bursts just before he boards his airplane for a flight.

2005 Jerry receives a Grammy Lifetime Achievement Award and finalizes his divorce from Kerrie.

2006 *Last Man Standing,* Jerry's improbable comeback album, is released.

2007 Jerry is recognized as the first living American Music Master; Jimmy makes a rare appearance at a secular event to perform for the ceremony. Jerry closes the show with "Over the Rainbow."

2008 Mickey undergoes surgery in Springfield to drain fluid off his brain and address related effects.

2009 Mickey suffers a fall and is temporarily paralyzed from the neck down. Sherwood Cryer dies.

2010   Mickey makes his return to his theatre, nine months after his fall. Jimmy oversees the beginning of the twenty-four-hour, seven-days-a-week SonLife Broadcasting Network.

Appendix D

AUTHOR'S FAVORITE SONGS

	Jerry Lee Lewis	Jimmy Swaggart	Mickey Gilley
1	Great Balls Of Fire	Precious Lord Take My Hand	Room Full of Roses
2	Rockin' My Life Away	It's Beginning To Rain	Stand By Me
3	Why You Been Gone So Long	I Don't Need To Understand	A Headache Tomorrow
4	Another Place Another Time	His Voice Makes The Difference	Tears Of The Lonely
5	Middle Aged Crazy	There Is A River	That's All That Matters To Me
6	What I'd Say	Mercy Rewrote My Life	She Called Me Baby
7	Whole Lotta Shakin' Going On	Thank You Again	True Love Ways
8	You Can Have Her	His Blood Still Sets Men Free	You Don't Know Me
9	I Am What I Am	I'll Never Be Lonely Again	Couldn't Love Have Picked A Better Place To Die
10	I Don't Want To Be Lonely Tonight	Let Your Living Water Flow	Here Comes The Hurt Again

11	Chantilly Lace	Joy Comes In The Morning	What Am I Living For
12	Please Release Me	He Whispers Sweet Peace	Fool For Your Love
13	Mexicali Rose	Looking For A City	Put Your Dreams Away
14	Before The Night Is Over	Jesus Just The Mention Of Your Name	She's Pulling Me Back Again
15	Hi Heel Sneakers	My God Is Real	Your Love Shines Through
16	Mona Lisa	When I See The Blood	Talk To Me
17	Roll Over Beethoven	It Matters To Him About You	The Girls All Get Prettier At Closing Time
18	Headstone On My Grave	I've Never Been This Homesick Before	Giving up on Getting over You
19	You Win Again	Royal Telephone	Welcome To My World
20	Sweet Little Sixteen	He Just Put Himself In My Place	Lonely Nights
21	Trouble In Mind	What A Healing Jesus	Window Up Above
22	The Pilgrim	I'll Fly Away	You've Really Got A Hold On Me

23	Me And Bobby McGee	No One Ever Cared For Me Like Jesus	The Most Beautiful Girl In The World
24	Wild One	Higher Ground	There Goes My Everything
25	Thirty-Nine And Holding	The Best Of The Trade	Bring It On Home To Me
26	Breathless	He's Coming Back	I Overlooked An Orchid
27	Rita May	If God Is Dead	For The Good Times
28	What Made Milwaukee Famous (Made a Loser Out of Me)	In The Garden	Lonely Wine
29	I'm On Fire	Farther Along	Make The World Go Away
30	I Can't Stop Loving You	Glory To His Name	You Look So Good in Love
31	You Are My Sunshine	Finally Home	She Reminded Me of You
32	Sunday Morning Coming Down	We Shall See Jesus	City Lights
33	She Even Woke Me Up To Say Good-Bye	The Lord Accepted Me	There! I've Said It Again

This list reflects the listening preferences of the author only. Although some songs have been recorded by more than one of the three men, for purposes of this list, no song appears for more than one of the three.

ACKNOWLEDGMENTS

This book has truly been a labor of love—with vast quantities of labor and vast quantities of love. Hundreds of individuals have played various roles, each important. I would like to take the opportunity to recognize many of them here and express my gratitude for their contribution and assistance.

Several individuals deserve special thanks for key roles and above-and-beyond contributions. They include Mickey Gilley, Al Embry, Linda Gail Lewis Braddock, Frankie Jean Lewis Terrell, J. W. Whitten, Michelle Nilges, Sherrie Calhoun Jacobs, Hyram Copeland, Edna Gilley Mequet, Judith Bingham, Troy Payne, Michael Gilley, and Joey Martin. Without each of them, the project would have never taken the specific path on which it ultimately journeyed.

Thanks to the team assembled to help with the vision, research, and preparation of the book as well as others who provided valuable input and support. Key contributors include Elizabeth Kaye, Rayven Williams, Pat Davis, Cathy Williams, Cindy Birne, Joyce Byrd, Lisa Durham, Michael Cramer, Leigh Donahue, Austin Talbert, Mike Farris, and Milli Brown.

Hundreds of sources—books, articles, video, and more—were utilized. Many of the key authors whose writings have proven most valuable include Jimmy Swaggart, Anne Seaman, Nick Tosches, Elaine Dundy, Bob Claypool, Myra Lewis Williams, Paul MacPhail,

Jimmy Guterman, Charles White, Robert Cain, Linda Gail Lewis, Robert Palmer, Colin Escott, J. W. Brown, Lawrence Wright, and Barbara Nauer. I would like to thank each of them for their notable contributions to the body of knowledge on these three fascinating men.

Additional thanks go out to Bobby Marks, Sandy Brokaw, David Beatty, Myra Lewis Williams, Kenny Lovelace, Kay Martin, Cecil Harrelson, Rae Beatty, Jerry Beatty, John Camp, Norman Carlson, Marion Terrell, B. D. Taylor, Matt Miles, Tim Vance, Gary Skala, Clyde Webber, Glen McGlothin, Rose Watkins, Amanda Taylor, Maudine Calhoun Jacobs, Jim Dolan, Jack Clement, Tom McMahon, and Annie Marie Dolan. For the many others that participated in interviews, answered questions, or participated in discussion relating to this book, thank you. While not named specifically, you are truly appreciated.

Finally, I would like to thank the three primary subjects of this book and their family. I am honored that the countless hours of discussion and interactions with Mickey have evolved into a profound friendship. While Jerry and Jimmy were both reluctant to participate directly in this effort—each for reasons of his own—both men were cordial and friendly to me on the occasions that we interacted. To the numerous family members with whom I have spent time, I want to thank you all for your kindness. What an amazing family!

BIBLIOGRAPHY

Books, Articles, and Reviews

Ackerman, Todd. "1927 Sherwood Cryer 2009." *Houston Chronicle*. August 18, 2009.

Aguilar, Melissa Ward, Marty Racine, Bruce Westbrook, and Bill DiSessa. "Gilley's: The Decline of Country-Western Civilization." *Houston Chronicle*. April 1, 1989.

Aikman, Davis. *Billy Graham: His Life and Influence*. Nashville: Thomas Nelson, 2007.

Applebome, Peter. "Scandal Spurs Interest in Swaggart Finances." *New York Times*. February 25, 1988.

———. "Swaggart's Troubles Show Tension of Passion and Power in TV Evangelism." *New York Times*. February 28, 1988.

Associated Press. "Christian Rock Group Disputes Claims by Evangelist Swaggart." *Omaha World-Herald*. June 27, 1987.

———. "Gilley Music Theater to Reopen." *Tulsa World*. May 12, 1993.

———. "Gilley's Falls to Wreckers." *Tulsa World*. September 22, 1990.

Associated Press. "Country-Western Singer Files Suit against Business Partner." April 15, 1987.

———. "Fire Consumes Part of Landmark Gilley's Bar." July 5, 1990.

———. "Fire-Gutted Remains of Honky-Tonk Headed for Wrecking Ball." September 7, 1990.

———. "Gilley's Club Owner Files for Protection, Owes Singer $16 Million." August 20, 1988.

———. "Gilley's Owner, Featured in Film *Urban Cowboy*, Dead at 83." August 17, 2009.

———. "Investigators: Nightclub Fire Was Arson." July 10, 1990.

———. "People in the News." September 17, 1988.

―――. "Rock 'n' Roller Comments on Cousin Evangelist." March 26, 1987.

―――. "Site of Old Gilley's Honky-Tonk to Be a School." February 28, 2005.

Auchmutey, Jim. "Gone with the Kin: Small Town in Louisiana Gamely Carries on in the Shadow of Larger-Than-Life Native Sons." *Atlanta Journal-Constitution.* October 30, 1988.

Austin American-Statesman. "Judge Shutters Gilley's Club, Billy Bob's Reopens; Owner Goes Bankrupt, Ordered to Reimburse Nightclub's Namesake." April 1, 1989.

Babineck, Mark. "A Kinder, Gentler Gilley's Takes Root in Pasadena." *Associated Press.* January 26, 2003.

―――. "It's Still a Bull Market for Former Gilley's Owner." *Associated Press.* September 10, 1999.

―――. "*Urban Cowboy* Spirit Lives on 20 Years after Filming." *Associated Press.* September 10, 1999.

Balmer, Randall. "Still Wrestling with the Devil." *Christianity Today.* March 2, 1998.

Bartleman, Frank. *Azusa Street.* New Kensington, PA: Whitaker House, 1982.

Baton Rouge Advocate. "Motel Tied to Swaggart Scandal Sold to Developers to Be Razed." January 13, 1997.

Baton Rouge Morning Advocate. "Singer's Mother Dies." August 16, 1985.

―――. "Swaggart Is Son of Evangelists." October 16, 1991.

Baton Rouge State-Times. "Frances Swaggart and Virginia Gorman Appear to Be More Dissimilar Than Alike." August 12, 1991.

―――. "Swaggart Reported Focus of Church Probe." February 20, 1988.

Beck, Aaron. "Gilley Still Enjoys Hitting the Road with Music New and Old." *Columbus Dispatch.* July 20, 2002.

Bernstein, Alan. "Gilley Sues Partner, Wants Name Removed from Famous Nightclub." *Houston Chronicle.* April 15, 1987.

Berry, Chuck. *Chuck Berry: The Autobiography.* New York: Harmony Books, 1987.

Bevan, Nathan. "Tom Jones Recalls Jerry Lee Lewis Concert." Wales Online. Accessed July 25, 2010. http://www.walesonline.co.uk/news/wales-news/2010/07/24/.

Blinn, Johna. "A Good Ear for Country Cooking." *New Jersey Record*. July 25, 1984.

Blow, Steve. "Famed Names Don't Faze the Folks in Ferriday." *Dallas Morning News*. August 17, 1986.

Bonomo, Joe. *Jerry Lee Lewis: Lost and Found*. New York: Continuum, 2009.

Bordsen, John. "Goodness, Gracious, Those Lewises!" *Charlotte Observer*. August 7, 2005.

Brandt, Lisa. *Celebrity Tantrums!: The Official Dirt*. Chicago: ECW Press, 2003.

Brown, J. W., with Rusty Brown. *Whole Lotta Shakin': 50 Years of Memories: A Tribute to Jerry Lee Lewis*. Savannah, GA: Continental Shelf, 2010.

Bruce, Tracey. "Ferriday's Day in the Sun." *Concordia Sentinel*. March 6, 2002.

Brunt, Stephen. "Swaggart Is the King of Showbiz Gospel." *Globe and Mail*. June 17, 1985.

Burke, Ken. *Country Music Changed My Life: The Tales of Tough Times and Triumph from Country's Legends*. Chicago: A Cappela Books, 2004.

Cain, Robert. *Whole Lotta Shakin' Goin' On*. New York: Dial Press, 1981.

Camp, John B. *Odyssey of a Derelict Gunslinger*. BookSurge, 2008.

Chapple, Steve. "The Gospel According to Jimmy Lee Swaggart: Whole Lotta Savin' Goin' On." *Mother Jones*. July/August 1986.

Chicago Sun-Times. "Gilley's Honky-Tonk Fades into the Sunset." April 1, 1989.

Christianity Today. "Why the Assemblies Dismissed Swaggart." May 13, 1988.

Claypool, Robert. *Saturday Night at Gilley's*. New York: Random House, 1980.

Coates, Guy. "Mayor-Barber Keeps 'Em Rockin' in Ferriday." *Baton Rouge Morning Advocate*. May 5, 1989.

Conconi, Chuck. Personalities. *Washington Post*. April 16, 1987.

Concordia Sentinel. "Gilley Carries Day with Swaggart's Help for Ferriday Event."

Congdon, Tim. "The House and the Lewis Family." The Italian Jerry Lee Lewis Fansite. Accessed January 4, 2010. http://www.jerrylee.it/Lewis_house.html.

Cox, Cathi. "Gilley, Lewis and Swaggart Join Delta Music Hall of Fame." CMT News. March 4, 2002. http://www.cmt.com/news/country-music/1452735/gilley-lewis-and-swaggart-join-delta-music-hall-of-fame.jhtml.

Cramer, Richard Ben. "The Strange and Mysterious Death of Mrs. Jerry Lee Lewis." *Rolling Stone*. March 1, 1984.

Crowe, Robert. "If You Are Looking for Bulls . . . You Still Will Find Them in All the 'Right' Places, Even after the Demise of Gilley's." *Houston Chronicle*. July 4, 2002.

Crowell, Rodney. *Chinaberry Sidewalks*. New York: Knopf, 2011.

Culpepper, Steve. "JSM Founder Just Normal, Relatives Say." *Baton Rouge Morning Advocate*. October 16, 1991.

Curry, Bill. "A Honky-Tonk Paradise in Texas's 'Other Houston.'" *Washington Post*. August 31, 1978.

D'Antonio, Michael. "Flamboyant TV Minister Preached and Performed." *Newsday*. February 21, 1988.

Dawson, Walter. "The Killer on the Rocks." *Country Music Magazine*. June 1977.

Deslatte, Melinda. "Jerry Lee Lewis, Swaggart, Gilley Reunite in Ferriday." *Baton Rouge Advocate*. March 2, 2002.

DiSessa, Bill. "Arson Fire Guts Studio by Gilley's Club." *Houston Chronicle*. September 14, 1990.

———. "Fire Labeled 'Suspicious' Guts Gilley's Club." *Houston Chronicle*. July 6, 1990.

———. "Gilley's Faithful Converge on Ruins; Hallowed Honky-Tonk Draws Crowd." *Houston Chronicle*. July 16, 1990.

———. "Pasadena Boy Reportedly Admits He Set Gilley's Fire." Houston Chronicle. July 14, 1990.

Dixon, Lydia. "Mickey Gilley: Looking Back, Looking Ahead." *Music City News*. March 1982.

Donahue, Kathleen. "Jerry Lee Lewis Has Minor Surgery in OLOL." Baton Rouge Morning Advocate. August 12, 1987.

Dundy, Elaine. *Ferriday, Louisiana*. New York: Donald I. Fine, 1991.

Dunne, Mike, and Katheryn Flournoy. "Swaggart's Spiritual Empire Soaring." Baton Rouge Morning Advocate. May 1, 1987.

Dyer, R. A., and Bill DiSessa. "Judge Closes Gilley's; Cryer Says It's Finished." Houston Chronicle. March 31, 1989.

Ellis, Iain. *Rebels with Attitude: Subversive Rock Humorists*. New York: Soft Skull Press, 2008.

Edwards, Joe. "Nashville Sound: Mickey Gilley Reflects on *Urban Cowboy*." *Associated Press*. June 12, 1988.

Erlewine, Stephen Thomas. Review of *Live at the Star-Club, Hamburg*. Allmusic. Accessed January 22, 2010. http://www.allmusic.com/ album/live-at-the-star-club-hamburg-rhino-r78332.

Escott, Colin, and Martin Hawkins. *Good Rockin' Tonight: Sun Records and the Birth of Rock 'n' Roll*. New York: St. Martin's Press, 1991.

Falkenberg, Lisa. "Urban Cowboy Gets a New Home: Remake of Immortalized Gilley's Honky-Tonk Opens in Dallas." *Houston Chronicle*. October 12, 2003.

Flippo, Chet. "Don't Fuck with the Lewises!" Nashville Skyline. *CMT*. April 25, 2005.

Fontaine, Charles R., and Lynda K. Fontaine. *Jimmy Swaggart: To Obey God Rather Than Men*. N.p.: Kerusso, 1989.

Formanek, Ray. "Jimmy Swaggart, King of TV Preachers." Associated Press. March 1, 1985.

Fossum, Merle A., and Marilyn J. Mason. *Facing Shame: Families in Recovery*. New York: Norton, 1986.

Friedman, Steve. "'I May Have to Retire,' Gilley Says after Court's Ruling Favors Cryer." *Houston Chronicle*. June 5, 1987.

Friskics-Warren, Bill. "Shelby Singleton, Nashville Producer, Dies at 77." *New York Times*. October 11, 2009.

Gallagher, Pat. "Mickey Gilley Recovering from Life-Threatening Accident." The Boot. Accessed June 15, 2010. http://www.theboot. com/2009/11/02/mickey-gilley-recovering-from-life-threatening-accident/.

———. "Mickey Gilley Returning to Branson after Long Recovery." The Boot. Accessed June 15, 2010. http://www.theboot. com/2010/04/07/mickey-gilley-concert-2010/.

Gillespie, Elgy. "The Holy Rock 'n' Roller." *Sydney Morning Herald*. January 9, 1988.

Giuliano, Michael J. *Thrice-Born: The Rhetorical Comeback of Jimmy Swaggart*. Macon, GA: Mercer University Press, 1999.

Goddard, Peter. "Fats and Jerry Lee among Key Heroes of Rock." *Toronto Star*. July 6, 1986.

————. "Give Me That Prime-Time Religion." *Toronto Star*. April 12, 1987.

Goldman, Stuart. "Jerry Lee Lewis, White Wild Man of Rock." *OUI*. May 1981.

Goldsmith, Sarah Sue. "Finding God's Jewels among Ferriday's Sinners." Write at Home. *Baton Rouge Sunday Advocate*. July 7, 1991.

Goldstein, Patrick. "Moral Right Vs. Rockers: Swaggart Calls the Tune." *San Francisco Chronicle*. August 17, 1986.

Gordon, Robert. "Natural Born Killer." *Playboy*. February 2005.

Graves, Rachel. "Looking Back on a Wild Ride." *Houston Chronicle*. May 15, 2005.

Grizzard, Lewis. "Say 'Hallelujah,' Swaggart's King of TV Pleaders." *Atlanta Constitution*. February 22, 1988.

Grove, Lloyd. "Jimmy Swaggart: Wonders of the Lord and TV." *Washington Post*. September 29, 1986.

Gundersen, Edna. "Lewis Is 'Last Man Standing.'" *USA Today*. September 29, 2006.

Guralnick, Peter. *Lost Highway: Journeys and Arrivals of American Musicians*. Boston: David R. Godine, 1979.

————. "Perfect Imperfection." *Oxford American* 63 (2008): 20–30.

Guterman, Jimmy. *Rockin' My Life Away: Listening to Jerry Lee Lewis*. Nashville: Rutledge Hill Press, 1991.

Gyan Jr., Joe. "Gorman Cites Swaggart Call." *Baton Rouge State-Times*. August 12, 1991.

Halbfinger, David. "Memphis Shaken as Rock 'n' Roll Heart Is Stilled." *New York Times*. August 1, 2003.

Harrell Jr., David Edwin. *All Things Are Possible: The Healing and Charismatic Revivals in Modern America*. Bloomington: Indiana University Press, 1975.

Harrington, Richard. "Mickey Gilley's Honky-Tonk Winnin'." *Washington Post*. January 24, 1981.

————. "Wal-Mart Halts Sale of Rock Magazines." *Washington Post*. July 17, 1986.

Harris, Art. "Jerry Lee Lewis, Rock, Stock, and Barrel." *Washington Post*. June 28, 1989.

————. "Jimmy Swaggart's Other Woman." *Penthouse*. March 1989.

Harris, Art, and Jason Berry. "Jimmy Swaggart's Secret Sex Life." *Penthouse*. July 1988.

Hawkins, Robert J. "Great Balls of Fire! What If They Gave a Jerry Lee Lewis Concert and He Almost Didn't Show Up?" *San Diego Union-Tribune*. June 21, 1989.

Hemphill, Paul. *Lovesick Blue: The Life of Hank Williams*. New York: Penguin, 2005.

Henican, Ellis. "Inside Two Kingdoms Swaggart: Fire and Brimstone in Big Doses." *Newsday*. March 29, 1987.

Herbers, John. "Burning of a Negro Arouses Louisiana." *New York Times*. December 24, 1964.

Higginbotham, Adam. "Dear Superstar: Jerry Lee Lewis." *Blender* Online. December 12, 2006. Accessed June 7, 2010. www.blender.com/guide/68535/dear-superstar-jerry-lee-lewis 12/12/2006.

Hilburn, Robert. "Cousins of Sin and Salvation." *Chicago Sun-Times*. March 29, 1987.

Houston Chronicle. "Cryer Files for Bankruptcy." August 20, 1988.

———. "Goodbye to a Cuss: Sherwood Cryer, the Honky-Tonk King." August 22, 2009.

———. "Mickey Gilley Takes Battle with Longtime Partner to Courtroom." June 17, 1988.

———. "Newsmakers." May 11, 1993.

———. "Personal Mention." March 10, 1986.

———. "Singer Gilley Faces Tax Suit." May 21, 1985.

Hurst, Jack. "Mickey Gilley Defends Country Music's Era of the Urban Cowboy." *Kitchener-Waterloo Record*. July 29, 1993.

Jackson, Jerma. "Sister Rosetta Tharpe and the Evolution of Gospel Music." *Religion in the American South*. Chapel Hill, NC: University of North Carolina Press, 2004.

Jordan, Mark. "Gilley's Career Still Riding high—No Bull." *Commercial Appeal*. August 26, 2005.

Kaufman, Bill. "The Top of the Week Cowboy Mickey Gilley's Traveling in Style Now." *Newsday*. May 18, 1986.

Kaufman, Joanne. "The Fall of Jimmy Swaggart." *People Magazine*. March 7, 1988.

Kaye, Elizabeth. "Billy Graham Rises." *George*. December 1996.

———. "The Memphis Blues Again." *Rolling Stone*. November 21, 1985.

Kelley, Jack. "Topic: TV Evangelism; This 'Spiritual Regression' Has Broken My Heart." *USA Today*. April 23, 1987.

Kelly, Joan. "Coliseum Crusade from Swaggart, Prayer with a Punch." *Newsday*. August 30, 1987.

Kent, Nick. *The Dark Stuff: Selected Writings on Rock Music*. New York: De Capo Press, 1994.

King, Wayne. "Church Orders Two-Year Rehabilitation for Swaggart: Nature of Incident Unclear." *New York Times*. February 23, 1988.

Kirby, David. *Little Richard: The Birth of Rock 'n' Roll*. New York: Continuum, 2009.

Korones, Susan. "Jerry Lee Lewis Can Still Stir Things Up." *New York Times*. January 15, 1989.

Lamont, Kristi. "Remembering Jerry." Natchez Democrat. July 16, 1989.

Latham, Aaron. "The Ballad of the Urban Cowboy: America's Search for True Grit." *Esquire*. September 12, 1978.

Leblanc, Doug. "7,000-plus Pack New Church for Easter Dedication." *Baton Rouge Morning Advocate*. April 8, 1985.

Lewis, Linda Gail. *The Devil, Me, and Jerry Lee*. Atlanta: Longstreet Press, 1998.

Lewis, Myra, and Murray Silver. *Great Balls of Fire*. New York: William Morrow, 1982.

Lord, Lewis J. "An Unholy War in the TV Pulpits." *US News and World Report*. April 6, 1987.

Lundy, Hunter. *Let Us Prey: The Public Trial of Jimmy Swaggart*. Columbus, MS: Genesis Press, 1999.

MacPhail, Paul. *The Ferriday Fireball: Jerry Lee Lewis*. Rev. ed. N.p.: printed by author, 2008.

———. *The World of Mickey Gilley*. N.p.: printed by author, 2007.

Martin, Joey. "Copeland Remembers Childhood with the Cousins." Concordia Sentinel. February 27, 2001.

Martin, William. *A Prophet without Honor*. New York: William Morrow, 1991.

Mason, Julie. "Gilley's Finally Bucks Its Legal Hassles." Houston Chronicle. September 13, 1990.

Maynard, Steve. "Bakker and Swaggart Clashed in Style Long Before 'Unholy War.'" *Houston Chronicle*. March 29, 1987.

McCartney, Scott. "Swaggart Sees Bright Future Despite Drop in Revenues." *Dallas Morning News*. April 27, 1987.

McDaniel, Cindy. "Mickey Gilley: He's Not Dreaming Alone." *Arthritis Today*. March 1, 1988.

McGill, Kevin. "Swaggart Didn't Spare the Fire and Brimstone for Bakker, Gorman." *Associated Press*. February 21, 1988.

Mehr, Bob. "Jerry Lee Lewis Honored as 'American Music Master.'" *Memphis Commercial Appeal*. November 11, 2007.

Mesinger, Maxine. "Big City Beat." *Houston Chronicle*. September 15, 1985.

———. "Magazine Revives Gilley's Legend." *Houston Chronicle*. August 4, 2000.

Miller, Brett. *Divine Apology: The Discourse of Religious Image Restoration*. Santa Barbara, CA: Praeger, 2002.

Miller, Jim, and David T. Friendly. "Country Goes Mellow." *Newsweek*. March 30, 1981.

Mitchell, Rick. "Jerry Lee Lewis Still Breathing Fire." *Houston Chronicle*. March 24, 1992.

———. "Nashville Agent Tells Country Secrets: Book Sheds New Light on Gilley Legend." *Houston Chronicle*. January 17, 1993.

Mojo. "Big Bangs: 100 Records That Changed the World." June 2007. 60–95.

Montreal Gazette. "Singer Recovering from Burst Appendix." July 11, 2003.

Morin, Richard. "Unconventional Wisdom." *Washington Post*. January 15, 1996.

Myers, Marc. "Killer Poised to Strike Again." *Wall Street Journal*. September 8, 2010.

Nauer, Barbara. "Catholic Calls Swaggart 'Holy Scourge.'" *Baton Rouge Advocate*. February 16, 1985.

———. *Jimmy Swaggart: Dead Man Rising*. Baton Rouge: Glory Arts, 1998.

Neff, Jim. "Interview: Jerry Lee Lewis." *Genesis*. July 1979.

Nelson, Pennye. "Country, Rock, Gospel Are All in Gilley's Family." *San Francisco Chronicle*. April 12, 1987.

Nelson, Stanley. "Haney's Big House." Under the Hill Saloon. Accessed February 10, 2010. http://www.underthehillsaloon.com/custom/webpage.cfm?content=News&id=56.

New York Times. "Pasadena Journal; Beneath Rubble, a Legend of Sorts." September 27, 1990.

Nichols, Bruce. "Honky-Tonk Blues Singer, Business Associate Hit Sour Note over Future of Renowned Gilley's Club." *Dallas Morning News.* April 27, 1987.

Notable Names Database. "Jerry Lee Lewis." Accessed January 4, 2010. http://www.nndb.com/people/867/000023798/.

Palmer, Robert. *Blues & Chaos: The Music Writing of Robert Palmer.* Edited by Anthony DeCurtis. New York: Scribner, 2009.

———. *Jerry Lee Lewis Rocks!* New York: Delilah Books, 1981.

———. "Pop Piano: Mickey Gilley." *New York Times.* December 8, 1980.

———. "The Pop Life." *New York Times.* March 20, 1985.

———. "When Is It Rock and When Rock 'n' Roll? A Critic Ventures an Answer." *New York Times.* August 6, 1978.

Palmer, Robert (II). "Wammack Teams up with Sun Records Legend for Tour." TimesDaily. July 18, 2010. Accessed July 28, 2010. www.timesdaily.com/article/20100728/NEWS/100729826/1011/NEWS.

Papard, Tony. "Jerry Lee Lewis (a.k.a the Killer) and Family." Accessed January 22, 2010. www.btinternet.com/~tony.papard/JERRYLEELEWIS.HTM.

Pareles, Jon. "Weathered But Scrappy, Jerry Lee Lewis Rocks On." *New York Times.* September 28, 2006.

Parmley, Helen. "Swaggart Confesses to 'Moral Problem.'" *Dallas Morning News.* February 21, 1988.

Patterson, Jim. "No Nostalgia for *Urban Cowboy* Days: Mickey Gilley Puts Attention on Clubs, Music." *Houston Chronicle.* June 23, 1993.

Patterson, Randall. "Sherwood's Rules." *Houston Press.* May 15, 1997.

People Magazine. "Ferriday's Gift to Gospel and Rock." October 27, 1986.

Perry, Andrew. "Hellbound!" *Mojo.* December 2006.

Peterson, John. "Schools Likely to Spawn Stars." *San Francisco Chronicle.* August 14, 1987.

Peterson, Karla. "It's Not an Act?/ Pie in the Sky/All in the Family/At Home with Jimmy." *San Diego Union-Tribune.* February 29, 1988.

Porterfield, Bill. "Honky-Tonk Dreams Outlast Travolta's Urban Two-Step." *Austin American-Statesman.* September 17, 1990.

———. *The Greatest Honky-Tonks in Texas.* Dallas: Taylor, 1983.

Pratt, Edward. "Swaggart Followers Express Sympathy." *Baton Rouge State-Times.* February 22, 1988.

Puhala, Bob. "Branson: Country Boom Where Glitz Meets Grits." *Chicago Sun-Times*. May 24, 1992.

Raab, Scott. "Jerry Lee Lewis." *Esquire*. January 2010.

Racine, Marty. "Life after Gilley's: He Still Calls Pasadena Home, but on Weekends Mickey Gilley Really Owns the Stage in Branson." *Houston Chronicle*. May 12, 1996.

Radcliffe, Donnie. "South Lawn Roundup: The President Sets a Mexican Table for His Pardners from Congress." *Washington Post*. September 19, 1985.

Ratliff, Ben. "Rock Review: No Piano-Slamming but Still Intimidating." *New York Times*. October 21, 1997.

Rector, Lee. "Mickey Gilley: America Looked for the 'Urban Cowboy'— He Banked on It." *Music City News*. January 1983.

Rendon, Ruth. "Gilley's Rodeo Arena Blaze Is Ruled Arson." *Houston Chronicle*. September 4, 1991.

Reuters. "Gilley Wants Name Removed from Nightclub." *Dallas Morning News*. April 15, 1987.

Roberts, Frank. "Mickey Gilley's Country: Along the Way, He's Turned Tragedies into Triumphs." *Virginian-Pilot and Ledger-Star*. July 16, 1993.

Rogers, John. "A New Life Without Any (Mechanical) Bull: Singer Gilley Establishes Post–*Urban Cowboy* Success." *Austin American-Statesman*, 7/20/1998. E2.

Rosellini, Lynn. "Of Rolexes and Repentance." *US News and World Report*. March 7, 1988.

Saperstein, Saundra. "Swaggart Ministry Spreads a $600,000-a-Day Message." *Washington Post*. June 7, 1987.

Sasfy, Joe. "Good Ol' Country Businessmen." *Washington Post*. August 26, 1982.

Sayre, Alan. "Swaggart Stepping Down Pending Investigation." *Associated Press*. February 21, 1988.

Schwartz, John, Frank Gibney Jr., and James Gill. "Jimmy Swaggart: Breaking Away." *Newsweek*. April 11, 1988.

Seaman, Anne Rowe. *Swaggart: The Unauthorized Biography of an American Evangelist*. New York: Continuum, 1999.

Simoneaux, Angela. "One Year Later, Swaggart Still Alive and Preaching." *Baton Rouge Advocate*. February 19, 1989.

———. "Swaggart Begins China Venture." *Baton Rouge Advocate*. February 9, 1989.

———. "Swaggart Warns 'Rag Magazines.'" *Baton Rouge Advocate.* January 31, 1989.

Slover, Pete. "Gilley, Cryer Trade Bitter Words; Jury Deliberates Lawsuit." *Houston Chronicle.* July 12, 1988.

———. "Jury Awards Gilley $17 million in Suit." *Houston Chronicle.* July 13, 1988.

Smith, Russell. "Rock On, Believe On: Christian Message Rolls through Petra." *Dallas Morning News.* July 3, 1985.

Stambler, Irwin, and Grelun Landon. *Country Music: The Encyclopedia.* 3rd ed. New York: St. Martin's Press, 1997.

Stewart, Richard. "Swaggart Calls Himself 'Holy Ghost Preacher.'" Houston Chronicle. August 17, 1987.

St. Petersburg Times. "Swaggart's Miracle Car." November 11, 1986.

Sumrall, Harry. "Mickey Gilley Down Home at the Kennedy Center." Washington Post. January 23, 1981.

Swaggart, Jimmy. *The Cup Which My Father Hath Given Me.* Baton Rouge: World Evangelism Press, 1991.

Swaggart, Jimmy, and Robert Paul Lamb. *To Cross A River.* Baton Rouge: Jimmy Swaggart Ministries, 1984.

Synan, Vinson. *The Holiness-Pentecostal Movement in the United States.* Grand Rapids: Eerdmans, 1971.

Tabor, Terri. "Jerry Lee Lewis Returns Home for Mardi Gras Celebration." *Natchez Democrat.* date unknown.

Taggart, Patrick. "Great ball of Fluff! Movie Neglects Depth of Jerry Lee Lewis's Intriguing Character." *Austin American-Statesman.* June 30, 1989.

Times Wire Services. "Swaggart Barred from TV, Pulpit; 2-Year Rehabilitation." *Los Angeles Times.* March 29, 1988.

Tisserand, Michael. "Great Balls of Fire!" *Times-Picayune.* January 30, 1994.

———. "Jerry Lee's Legacy." *Offbeat.* August 1993.

Tosches, Nick. *Country: The Twisted Roots of Rock 'n' Roll.* New York: De Capo Press, 1977.

———. *Hellfire.* New York: Grove Press, 1982.

Turner, Steve. *Hungry for Heaven: Rock 'n' Roll and the Search for Redemption.* Rev. ed. Downers Grove, IL: InterVarsity Press, 1995.

Under the Hill Saloon. "Jerry Lee Lewis: An American Original." Accessed February 10, 2010. http://www.underthehillsaloon.com/custom/webpage.cfm?content=News&id=55.

United Press International. "Joint Owner Mickey Gilley Tries Fitness." *San Francisco Chronicle*. March 28, 1995.

———. "Swaggart Up for Dove Award." *Baton Rouge Morning Advocate*. April 3, 1985.

Waddell, Ray. "Gilley Taking Branson Concept to Music City." *Amusement Business*. May 10, 1993.

Wald, Elijah. *How the Beatles Destroyed Rock 'n' Roll*. New York: Oxford University Press, 2009.

Ward, Matt. "Gilley's Plans Good-Bye." *Las Vegas Business Press*. June 11, 2007.

Westbrook, Bruce. "The Killer's Tale: Rock 'n' Roll's Jerry Lee Lewis Singing Praises of Film Biography." *Houston Chronicle*. June 25, 1989.

White, Cecile Holmes. "The Paradox of a Pastor's Slide into Sin." *Houston Chronicle*. February 28, 1988.

White, Charles, and Jerry Lee Lewis. *Killer*. London: Century, 1995.

Wilcox, Lauren. "Big Time in Tune Town." *Washington Post*. March 25, 2007.

Wilson, Charles Reagan. "Just a Little Talk with Jesus: Elvis Presley, Religious Music, and Southern Spirituality." *Southern Crossroads*. Louisville: University of Kentucky Press, 2008.

Winfrey, Lee. "Mickey Gilley Picks up Pieces of Broken Dream." *Houston Chronicle*. May 10, 1990.

Woodward, Kenneth, and Mark Miller. "What Profits a Preacher?" *Newsweek*. May 4, 1987.

Woodward, Kenneth, and Vincent Coppola. "King of Honky-Tonk Heaven." *Newsweek*. May 30, 1983.

Wooley, John. "Country Music in the 80s: Life after *Urban Cowboy*." *Tulsa World*. December 31, 1989.

Woulfe, Molly. "Singer Gilley Gains Reputation in Business." *Omaha World-Herald*. December 8, 1992.

Wright, Lawrence. "False Messiah: Little Church Left Big Mark." *Houston Chronicle*. July 18, 1988.

———. "False Messiah: Swaggart, Lewis Were Like Brothers." *Houston Chronicle*. July 19, 1988.

———. *Saints and Sinners*. New York: Vintage Books, 1993.

Wright, William. "Local Pastor Chose Ministry over Music: Cousin to Singers Jerry Lee Lewis, Jimmy Swaggart, and Mickey Gilley Tells Why." *Cleveland Daily Banner*. September 21, 2010.

Wuntch, Phillip. "Goodness, Gracious! Jerry Lee Lewis Is 'The Killer' of Rock 'n' Roll." *Dallas Morning News*. June 25, 1989.

Young, Charles. "The Killer Reloaded." *Rolling Stone*. October 19, 2006.

Zak, Dan. "Honky Tonkin': Where the Two-Stepping Crowd Heads to Get Its Country-and-Western Fix." *Washington Post*. September 7, 2007.

Film and Video

Camp, John, producer. *CNN Impact*. Aired September 28, 1997.

———. *Give Me That Big-Time Religion*. Aired February 13, 1984.

Can't You Hear the Wind Howl?: The Life and Music of Robert Johnson. Directed by Peter Mayer. Sweet Home Pictures. 1997.

"Episode 1.509." *The Porter Wagoner Show*. Aired 1974.

I Am What I Am. Directed by Gary Hall. 1987.

Klein, George, host. *George Klein's Memphis Sounds*. Aired June 2011.

Koppel, Ted, host. *Nightline*. Aired February 19, 1988.

———. *Nightline*. Aired February 22, 1988.

———. *Nightline*. Aired March 23, 1987.

———. *Nightline*. Aired March 24, 1987.

"Mickey Gilley, Gary Stewart, and Ronnie Milsap." *10th Annual Country Music Association Awards*. Aired October 11, 1976.

"Opening Video Footage." *The Mickey Gilley Show*. Mickey Gilley Theatre. Branson, MO. Aired July 3, 2010.

Pop! Goes the Country. Aired December 17, 1977.

The Mickey Gilley Show. Branson, MO. Performed June 27, 2010.

Urban Cowboy. Directed by James Bridges. Paramount Pictures. 1980.

*Various other resources were utilized in the research of this book, including museum information, sermons, miscellaneous notes, and personal interviews.

INDEX

Jerry Lee Lewis, Mickey Gilley, and Jimmy Swaggart are denoted by JLL, MG, and JS respectively. Photograph page numbers are in **bold**.

ABOUT THE AUTHOR

J. D. Davis has been a fan of the music of Jerry Lee Lewis, Jimmy Swaggart, and Mickey Gilley much of his life. He spent several years researching the lives of these men for this book.

Davis was raised in Quitman, Texas, a quiet community in the piney woods of East Texas. He earned a bachelor's degree with highest honors in economics from the University of Texas and later received a master's degree from Southern Methodist University. A successful businessman and entrepreneur, he achieved the rare distinction of partnership in his twenties at a major actuarial consulting firm, where he continues to manage a large practice. He has three daughters and lives near Dallas.